A Political Theory of Territory

OXFORD POLITICAL PHILOSOPHY

SERIES EDITOR: SAMUEL FREEMAN,
UNIVERSITY OF PENNSYLVANIA

Oxford Political Philosophy publishes books on theoretical and applied political philosophy within the Anglo-American tradition. The series welcomes submissions on social, political, and global justice, individual rights, democracy, liberalism, socialism, and constitutionalism.

N. Scott Arnold
Imposing Values: An Essay on Liberalism and Regulation

Peter de Marneffe
Liberalism and Prostitution

William J. Talbott
Human Rights and Human Well-being

Iris Marion Young
Responsibility for Justice

Paul Weithman
Why Political Liberalism? On John Rawls's Political Turn

Aaron James
Fairness in Practice: A Social Contract for a Global Economy

Margaret Moore
A Political Theory of Territory

A Political Theory of Territory

MARGARET MOORE

OXFORD
UNIVERSITY PRESS

OXFORD
UNIVERSITY PRESS

Oxford University Press is a department of the University of
Oxford. It furthers the University's objective of excellence in research,
scholarship, and education by publishing worldwide.

Oxford   New York
Auckland   Cape Town   Dar es Salaam   Hong Kong   Karachi
Kuala Lumpur   Madrid   Melbourne   Mexico City   Nairobi
New Delhi   Shanghai   Taipei   Toronto

With offices in
Argentina   Austria   Brazil   Chile   Czech Republic   France   Greece
Guatemala   Hungary   Italy   Japan   Poland   Portugal   Singapore
South Korea   Switzerland   Thailand   Turkey   Ukraine   Vietnam

Oxford is a registered trademark of Oxford University Press
in the UK and certain other countries.

Published in the United States of America by
Oxford University Press
198 Madison Avenue, New York, NY 10016

© Oxford University Press 2015

First issued as an Oxford University Press paperback, 2017

Library of Congress Cataloging-in-Publication Data
Moore, Margaret (Professor in Political Theory)
A political theory of territory / Margaret Moore.
pages cm — (Oxford political philosophy)
ISBN 978–0–19–022224–6 (hardback); 978–0–19–084579-7 (paperback)
1. Territory, National—Philosophy.   2. Jurisdiction, Territorial—Philosophy.   3. State,
The—Philosophy.   I. Title.
JZ3675.M66 2015
320.1'201—dc23
2014032096

... calm seas, auspicious gales
And sail so expeditious that shall catch
Your royal fleet far off.
—William Shakespeare, *The Tempest*
(also inspired by the founding
of Bermuda) (1610–11)

In modern political thought, the connection between a political society and its territory is so close that the two notions almost blend.
—Henry Sidgwick, *The Elements of Politics* (1891)

Farewell my Country a Long farewell
My tale of anguish no tongue can tell
For I'm forced to fly o'er the ocean wide
from the home I love by Lough Sheelin side.
—Irish ballad 'The Lough Sheelin Eviction', based on
early nineteenth-century evictions in Ireland

Almost all the governments, which exist at present, or of which there remains any record in story, have been founded originally, either on usurpation or conquest, or both.
—David Hume, 'Of the Original Contract' (1742)

CONTENTS

ACKNOWLEDGEMENTS

On the whole, I have enjoyed writing this book, although I must confess that I am happy to be finished. I have been interested in territory and political theory for a very long time: indeed, I first argued that territory was seriously under-theorized in a chapter in my volume *National Self-Determination and Secession* (Oxford: Oxford University Press, 1998). Although I recognized the deficiency, I was unable to correct it: I did not at that time have a *theory* about territory.

I began to focus in a more systematic way on issues of territory and territorial rights in political theory when I was first included in 2009 in Chris Bertram's and Cara Nine's wonderful Territory and Justice network. One of the reasons why working on this topic has been rewarding is that it has been a cooperative endeavour in many ways. Indeed, there are some parts of this book where it was very hard to disentangle my own original arguments from the reactions of various people to my arguments and my reactions to these. Much of this was facilitated by their initial network. On more occasions than I can recount, I received emails from my friends, alerting me to recent work on territory or case studies related to it or thoughts on some part of my argument. It was, however, less gratifying when I was asked how my book is coming along (the answer was: slowly).

I am pleased to be able to acknowledge at least some of the debts I incurred while working on this book. I have learned much not only from classical political theorists but from contemporary theorists on territory, who have thought analytically and systematically about these subjects and have defined the contemporary field: Allen Buchanan, David Miller, and John Simmons. I could not possibly have developed my own theory without the benefit of their work on the subject. In terms of interactions with people about this project and the ideas contained therein, I have incurred numerous debts (in addition to the debt I owe to the above three). My gratitude extends to Andrew Altman,

George Anderson, Chris Armstrong, Mira Bachvarova, Ayelet Banai, Ludvig Beckman, Chris Bertram, Colin Bird, Daniel Butt, Simon Caney, Joe Carens, Amandine Catala, Simone Chambers, John Charvet, Andrew I. Cohen, Richard Dagger, Monique Deveaux, Avigail Eisenberg, Chikako Endo, Paulina Ochoa Espejo, Cécile Fabre, Colin Farrelly, Kerah Gordon-Solman, Burke Hendrix, Michael Ignatieff, Loren King, George Klosko, Michael Kocsis, Daniel Kofman, Peggy Kohn, Avery Kolers, Rahul Kumar, Will Kymlicka, Seth Lazar, Daniel Lee, David Lefkowitz, Jacob Levy, Catharine Lu, Alistair Macleod, Andrei Marmor, John McGarry, Tamar Meisels, Ulf Morkenstam, Cara Nine, Zoran Oklopcic, Gianfranco Pellegrino, Nahshon Perez, Ryan Pevnick, Jouni Reinikainen, Clara Sandelind, Alex Schwartz, Jonathan Seglow, Michel Seymour, Andrew Shorten, Sarah Song, Jeff Spinner-Halev, Anna Stilz, Christine Straehle, Christine Sypnowich, Patrick Tomlin, Kathy Walker, Daniel Weinstock, Kit Wellman, Greg Whitfield, Melissa Williams, Caleb Yong, and Lea Ypi. In a couple of cases, this took the form of very good questions at conference presentations, which led me to respond to the concern or objection in writing; more typically, the people listed above supplied me with good written comments on a paper or chapter of the book, which helped to improve it, or a wonderfully helpful conversation on some part of the book. I received extremely detailed and helpful comments from two referees from Oxford University Press, which have made it a much better book than it would otherwise be. And finally, I have to single out Allen Buchanan, Patti Tamara Lenard, Andrew Lister, David Miller, and John Simmons for special thanks. They read and gave me extensive written comments on large parts of this book, and it is very humbling to be a recipient of their intellectual generosity.

Earlier versions of parts of this book have been previously published and I am grateful to the publishers for permission to adapt the material for this book. I have adapted some parts of the organizational structure for parts of chapters 2 and 5 from 'Justice et théories contestées du territoire', *Philosophiques*, vol. 39, no. 2 (2012), 339–351. Some sentences in chapters 3 and 5 have been adapted from a chapter co-written with Mira Bachvarova and published as 'A Conceptual and Normative Analysis of Territorial Pluralism', in Karlo Bastia, John McGarry, and Richard Simeon, eds, *Territorial Pluralism: Managing Difference in Multinational States* (Vancouver: University of British Columbia Press, 2015); I owe a special thanks to Mira Bachvarova, who gave me permission to use ideas initially developed in our article. Some parts of chapter 4 and 5 appear in 'Which People and What Land? Territorial Right-Holders and Attachment to Territory', *International Theory*, vol. 6, no. 1 (2014), 121–140. An earlier version of chapter 8 appears as 'Natural Resources, Territorial Right, and Global Distributive Justice', *Political Theory*, vol. 40, no. 1 (2012), 84–107. An earlier version of part of chapter 7 is published as 'On Rights to

Land, Expulsions, and Corrective Justice', *Ethics & International Affairs*, vol. 27, no. 4 (2013), 429–447. Some arguments in chapter 10 received an early expression in my chapter 'Collective Self-Determination, Institutions of Justice, and Wars of National Defence', in Cécile Fabre and Seth Lazar, eds, *The Morality of Defensive War*, 185–202 (Oxford: Oxford University Press, 2014).

I have given versions of parts of this book (in some cases before I even knew I was going to write a book) at a number of venues, and have learned much from participants and audiences at two *Territories and Justice* workshops in London 2009 and Dublin 2010; during visits to Keio University, Tokyo, 2010; at a conference on global justice and territory at Concordia University, Montreal, 2011; a workshop of the Queen's University / Université du Québec à Montréal / University of Toronto EDG (Ethnicity and Democratic Governance) / Universidad de Guadalajara project in Guadalajara, Mexico, June 2011; at the University of Southern California in Los Angeles, 2011; a conference on self-determination at Hartwell House, Aylesbury, United Kingdom, jointly organized by Christ Church, Oxford, St Andrews, and the London School of Economics, and a presentation at Nuffield College, Oxford, both February 2012; presentations at the University of Frankfurt, October 2012, University of Virginia, February 2013, University of Helsinki, May 2013; the annual meeting of the Society of Applied Philosophy, University of Zurich, June 2013; seminar presentations at the University of North Carolina at Chapel Hill, October 2013, Carleton University, November 2013, and Université du Québec à Montréal, December 2013; London School of Economics Department of Government, Nuffield College, Oxford, and University College Dublin, in February 2014, and University College Cork in March 2014; the Centre for Social Justice at Oxford University in May 2014; and three meetings of the American Political Science Association, Toronto 2009, Washington 2011, Chicago 2013. I have benefited enormously from two manuscript workshops, at the University of Ottawa and University of Toronto Centre of Ethics, both held in November 2013, which provided extremely helpful and diverse comments, and helped me in the final stages of revising this book; and also from my colleagues in Philosophy and Political Studies in the Queen's political philosophy reading group on more than one occasion.

I must also thank Emily Sacharin, the editor at Oxford University Press, for her encouragement and efficiency. I am grateful too to the Social Sciences and Humanities Research Council of Canada for a research grant to facilitate this work, and to my employer, Queen's University, Canada, for awarding me a time-limited Peacock Professorship, which helped reduce my teaching load at a crucial juncture. It is over now and I am back to being an ordinary faculty member, but it was great while it lasted.

I did the revisions for the book in Oxford, UK, affiliated with the Centre for the Study of Social Justice and Nuffield College. I am grateful to Simon Caney and David Miller for arranging these affiliations. Nuffield College, where my office was located, was an ideal environment to complete the book and I am grateful to the Warden, Sir Andrew Dilnot, and the College for this opportunity. I am particularly grateful to David for his support and rapid feedback during the final stages of revising (and for suggesting the cover picture). This is especially true since he expressed an 'allergic' reaction to parts of the argument of the book, especially the term 'peoples'.

It would be remiss not to acknowledge more personal debts. I would like to thank Mira Bachvarova, Patti Tamara Lenard, and Anthea Morgan for their friendship and moral support; and my family for their patience during the finishing stages of this book. I think many academics who are engaged in a book-length project face the question: why bother? There are many other things one can do with one's life. I would particularly like to thank my daughter Ciara McGarry. She did more than anyone else to pull me away from my work, but also the fact that she did so, and that I missed her when I was somewhere presenting this or that piece of the book or working on it, reinforced my sense of how important our place-related attachments and relationships are. This book is dedicated to her.

Margaret Moore, June 2014

Why Do We Need a Political Theory of Territory?

On 10 April 1606, James I of England established by royal charter a joint-stock company, the London Company, for the purpose of establishing colonial settlements in North America and claiming land for the English crown to the exclusion of other European powers. Under this charter, territory was granted to the company from the thirty-fourth parallel north to the forty-first parallel, and included a large portion of Atlantic and inland Canada. Although the land was 'claimed' in the charter, there was an expectation that these claims needed to be consolidated with long-term English settlement and military defence of the settlements. Under the auspices of the London Company, Sir George Somers, an admiral of the company's Third Supply relief fleet, set sail from Plymouth, England, on 2 June 1609, destined for Jamestown, Virginia, carrying 500–600 people, including crew and settlers. On 25 July, the fleet ran into a hurricane and one of the ships eventually ran aground on the rocks just off the shores of an uninhabited island, and the passengers and crew (and a dog) were able to make it to the shores of what we now know as Bermuda. The crew and passengers set to work building a settlement there, including a church and some houses, and this original settlement is now thought to constitute the founding of Bermuda.[1]

The assumption that a royal charter accompanied by colonization with an aim to affect control would legitimately 'claim' land for England is now thought to be antiquated, deeply rooted in an imperial mentality that ignored the claims and agency of indigenous people. But what exactly is the appropriate relationship between people and territory? If we no longer accept the basic assumptions underlying the London Company, which founded settlements and claimed land on behalf of the English Crown regardless of the wishes and aspirations of the people living on the land, what theory of territory do we now hold, consonant with democratic values? And what do we think of claims in places like Bermuda, which, at the time that Sir George Somers landed, was completely uninhabited? Is land that is uninhabited simply 'up for grabs'? Can any state or people settle on such land and claim rights to it?

If the idea of Sir George Somers claiming land in Bermuda seems defensible, that may be because there were no other people in the picture. It was uninhabited; islands are clearly demarcated spaces, surrounded on all sides by water; and there were no other human beings present to make rival claims. It is, however, not at all obvious that the idea of particular peoples having control over, or special entitlement to, particular pieces of land can be justified at all. This is particularly so when we reflect on the image that all of us have internalized, that of a fragile blue planet, hurtling through space, which we share with one another. From this perspective, it seems natural to think not only that we all have an obligation to work together to preserve this blue planet but that we are all equally entitled to its fruits, as Locke initially suggested at the beginning of the *Second Treatise*.[2] The division of the world into separate territories seems deeply problematic from a normative perspective as cosmopolitan theorists in particular have argued.

Territorial rights seem even more troubling when we reflect on some of their practical implications. Consider the right to control the flow of people and goods across borders, which we normally associate with rights over territory. Keeping people out of territory is deeply, normatively problematic: many people have argued that it violates people's fundamental rights (to freedom of association, freedom of movement) and that it prevents deprived people from improving their situation and so perpetuates poverty. There is a similar concern about resource rights—namely that control over resources within a territory allows rich political communities to 'hog' the resources for themselves. As with immigration, territorial rights over resources seem to privilege people in particular territories (especially rich ones) and keep people from poor geographical zones from participating in and benefitting from these riches. Beyond the question of the appropriate scope of territorial rights (whether this should extend to control over immigration and resources), the very idea of territorial zones may suggest that the world can be neatly divided into homogeneous, sharply bounded communities. State boundaries do not and cannot match the variegated nature of the political communities that they govern; and there are many people who have relationships of various kinds with people across territories, across zones, and seek to deepen them. Perhaps what is needed is not a political theory of territory, but a theory beyond territory, a sketch of a normatively attractive, institutionally feasible de-territorialized world.

I find this vision of a de-territorialized world, a world held in common by all, attractive at some levels, but nevertheless I resist it. In this book, I advance a theory of territory which defends the idea of having rights over territory, and I argue that a philosophical account of territorial rights is necessary to address many issues facing us today, including: territory that is disputed between states; secessionist conflicts; conflicts over stolen land; unoccupied islands, and frozen lands in the Arctic or territory under the sea; control over resources; control over boundaries; and the right to use force in defence of territory, to name a few.

One might think that defending the idea of rights over territory requires mainly an excavation into the standard operating assumptions of our world. After all, the idea of states having control over, indeed rights to, territory is a standard background assumption, in political science and international relations, and in law. It is also assumed by citizens, whose rights, duties, and entitlements are defined by their territorially organized communities. Despite much academic and popular talk of globalization and de-territorialization,[3] we live on a planet that is completely divided into distinct, mutually exclusive territorial units. Indeed, the entire usable landmass is divided into political units; and this process is not yet complete, as states seek to extend their control to the area under the seabed, to the frozen Arctic, and perhaps eventually beyond the Earth. Yet, while the territorial imperative is in full force, and territorial disputes are at the centre of some of the most intractable controversies facing us today, it is also one of the most undertheorized concepts that we rely on. We do not have a clear consensus either about what territory is, or how disputes about territory should be resolved, or the appropriate justice limits of territorial rights.

This is true of work in both international relations and political science more generally, and most normative analysis by political philosophers. Political scientists operating within the general field of international relations typically begin by noting that it is inherent in state sovereignty that it involves political authority over a territory (a geographical domain), and while they theorize extensively the relations between such sovereign units, the territorial dimension of sovereignty is rarely questioned, or theorized. This reflects the general assumption that having rights over territory is part of what it means to be 'sovereign', and sovereignty, especially state sovereignty, is assumed to range across a geographic domain. Indeed, having control over territory, or territorial rights, is often thought in international law (as well as international relations) to be *definitional* of what it is to be a state.[4] For example, under the 1933 Montevideo Convention on the Rights and Duties of States (Art. 1), states are defined as 'entities *with fixed territories* (and permanent populations) under government control and with the capacity to enter into relations with other states'.[5]

Territory is also one of the most undertheorized elements in political theory. This is because we often think, unreflectively, that state sovereignty involves control over territory; and this is a natural thought, since there are good reasons (connected to efficiency, solving collective-action problems, dispute resolution, and realizing equality) why states are territorial entities. However, there is relatively little further normative analysis of the specific issues raised by territorial control or how these territorial rights are interrelated. Consider for example John Rawls's work, which is typical of much political theory, in its focus on the appropriate relations between citizen and state, the limits of state power, and principles of distributive justice, but which fails to address the territorial or geographical domain of 'sovereignty' or the 'state'. In *A Theory of Justice* Rawls begins with the convenient simplifying assumption that the just society is closed: that it is a 'self-sufficient association of persons',[6] thereby abstracting from the issue of the territory to which 'the just society' is entitled and the relationship of that territory to other territories. Rawls's conception that justice is concerned with the principles that ought to govern the basic institutional structure of the society, which, for simplifying purposes, he conceptualizes as a self-sufficient entity, sparked a considerable debate amongst people interested in global justice. Global-justice theorists disagreed with Rawls about limiting the scope of justice to the state, and pointed out that the global realm is not an arena where simply strictures of morality apply, but rules of justice too,[7] and they have developed distinct justificatory arguments for this move.[8] However, little attention was drawn to the fact that Rawls also assumed that justice operated within a *territorially* delimited political community (a state) and the territorial dimension of the state was not addressed in anything like adequate terms. Although of course global-justice theorists tend to be sceptical of statist arguments, they rarely advocate *political* cosmopolitanism, so they also need to address issues of territory and the various justice issues that are thereby raised. Indeed, the dominant view—that state sovereignty necessarily involves control over territory and that whatever justifies the state also justifies the territory of the state—is the basis of virtually all our contemporary thinking about states and their territories.

This dominant view is wrong, in two main ways. First, even if we accept the central claim of the Westphalian order that the modern state must be or should be territorial, it is not clear that this requires the full range of territorial rights that we normally associate with state sovereignty.[9] In the discussion about international relations and political theory treatments of territory, I was using the term 'territory' as if it were synonymous with the right of jurisdictional authority over a territorial or geographical domain, and while I think that is the most fundamental right, it is too simplistic. Territorial rights are typically assumed to include rights of jurisdiction, rights to control borders, rights to control resources; and it is not at all clear that the justificatory argument for one dimension of territorial right will also apply straightforwardly to other things.

Second, the statist view of territory—where whatever justifies states will necessarily justify the state's territory—is limited in its response to a number of questions or controversies raised by the claim to territory. It is not obvious how that view can respond to contested territory, as when two states claim rights over the same bit of territory. It is also not clear how the statist view responds to territory claimed but not yet part of a state, such as in the oceans or uninhabited lands. The statist argument is retrospective, in the sense that it justifies the state in exerting authority across a geographical domain but tends to do so once the state has exerted its authority, but not to do so in advance, when there might be rival claims to the same territory. This is another way of saying that this argument doesn't address a fairly fundamental element of any theory of territory, namely, it doesn't have a theory about which group, which right-holder, gets rights to which bits of territory. And if it can't do those two things, it doesn't seem well equipped to answer some of the central questions that arise in political life, connected to the idea of rights over territory. It tells us that states should have control, but doesn't tell us which state should have control nor where it should do so. And it does not explain the principles on which territory is acquired in the first place, nor how we should think about corrective justice in cases that involve territory. Indeed, because it lacks a philosophical and normative account of territory specifically, this statist view ironically ends up endorsing a key element of a realist view of international relations, where might, or in this case actual control, over territory is what justifies it. It does not, in short, sit easily with the liberal democratic norms which animate other aspects of our thinking about the state and its relationship to people.

We need therefore to pay close attention to territory itself. We live in a world of territorial states and treat territorial boundaries and territorial rights as, more or less, sacrosanct, as something that just follows from the idea of a state-governed order. This is problematic, as I noted above, because it fails to address many issues that arise in relation to territory, but also because, at the most fundamental level, it seems that territory could be described as a universal good, to which all people are entitled, and so should not be parcelled out between different states. Many people attuned to justice considerations lament the complete territorial division of the world, adopting instead the attractive view from space of a single blue planet, to which we all have equal entitlements and equal responsibilities. The idea of territory, and of distinct territories, requires a *defence*.

1.1. The General Approach of this Book

My theory of territory rests on two fundamental insights. The first is that there are morally important particular relations among people, which can generate moral reasons and obligations, in addition to the general duties that we owe to people as such. It is morally important—both important to individuals and morally valuable in an objective sense—that individuals have control over the collective conditions of their lives, and control in the relationships that give meaning to their lives, including their relationships with each other and with place. This book explains the importance of jurisdictional authority and other kinds of control that people aspire to over the world that they share with others through appeal to the value of collective self-determination.

Second, I argue that an intuitively plausible, attractive account of justice in territory has to acknowledge that there are important, normatively significant relationships between peoples and places. I argue that an important point of departure for theorizing about land and justice is the idea that land is both a universal good and a highly particular good. Land is a universal good, in the sense that everyone has an interest in the benefits that having it brings, and this general interest is important to grounding rights to it. People have an interest in land as a place to graze cattle, grow crops, and build factories. The interest that people have in land, however, is also highly particularized—people have an interest in particular territories, geographical locations, and property—and the particularized aspect of the good makes rights to land especially problematic. This may be true even of the banana-farming peasant who, in some sense, is treating land as a commodity similar to a large land-owning multinational corporation that produces bananas for export. However, that peasant farmer may also have an attachment to his particular plot of land, which he inherited from his father and which could not be matched by another (perhaps equally fertile) patch of land somewhere else in the world. This is typically true of gardeners who labour on their creations, and of burial sites where people pay respect to their ancestors. The particularistic aspect of the good explains why territorial rights cannot be theorized in exactly the same way as those human rights that are based on general and substitutable interests, such as a right to food or a right to shelter.

These two insights, taken together, lead me to reject the dominant ways of thinking about territory: territory as an artefact of state control; territory as property; territory as a distributable good. I do not think of territory as like property, to which either individuals or the state have an ownership relationship, as I will explain in the next chapter. There are different problems with the two different (individual and collective) property theories, as I will explain, but the central problem that infects both versions of the conception of territory as property is that it fails to capture the non-instrumental relationship of individuals and groups to land and the kinds of entitlements that develop from there.

I also reject the view of territory as an artefact of states. This is the dominant view, which I complained above fails to explain many things that we expect a theory of territory to answer. But at a more fundamental level, it ignores the diverse ways in which individuals and groups are related to place, and the relationships between people and place which are not necessarily confined within the state or even state institutions.

I also reject the idea of territory as a distributable good, in the sense in which we think goods ought to be distributed in accordance with our favoured theory of distributive justice. I do not deny that there are significant justice issues connected to who has territory, how much territory that group has, and what kind of territory it is. These are the topics discussed in chapters 5 and 6. Nevertheless, I argue that this impartial global-justice focus fails to capture the complexity of our moral relationship to land. If we arrived via a spaceship on an uninhabited planet, the central question confronting us would be a question of distributive justice: how should the resources of the planet, including the land, be distributed? It would make sense to argue, in this case, that the land or resources should either be held in common, or distributed equally. However, given that people are already attached to land, are already related to it and to each other in complex and normatively significant ways, this (egalitarian) distributive principle cannot be realized without doing violence to people's motivational commitments and psychological proclivities. But the central idea here is not that of the relative costs of realizing the just distribution: it is that this this idea of land as a pure distributive good would ignore the normatively significant relations that people have developed with each other and to place, from which I think moral reasoning should begin.

In developing a political self-determination theory of territory, this book examines the kinds of attachments that people have to place and the rights that might be generated by this. It also examines the kinds of relations that people develop with one another and why these are morally important, and the rights that are necessary to protect these morally important human interests. In various ways throughout the book, I limit these rights principally by considering cases where they come into conflict with other values and other rights.

1.2. What Should a Theory of Territory Do?

If we are to defend the very idea of territory, and address in a coherent manner many issues that are central to our political and international order, we require a philosophical theory of territory. These issues include the justifiability of secession and the boundaries of the seceding entity, immigration control, control over resources, and territorial disputes of various kinds. If we are to develop a coherent philosophy of the international order, we need an overarching, background theory of territory. We need a conceptual analysis of what territory is, what kind of a good territory is, what territory is for, and the extent to which the normative argument that grounds rights to territory can justify the different dimensions of territorial right that we commonly associate with it.

How should we measure better or worse accounts of territory? What are the *desiderata* for a theory of territory?

(1) First, it should offer a *theory* of territory. It should offer a justificatory and explanatory argument, which links together the various elements that are commonly associated with rights over territory. There are a number of different components of a theory of territory. As David Miller has argued, to almost universal acceptance, when we think of territory, we tend to think of it as involving a triangular relationship between three key elements: (1) a piece of land, (2) a group of people residing on the land, and (3) a set of political institutions that govern the people within the geographical domain (the territory).[10] There are many different possible relationships between people, land, and the state, and correspondingly different ideas of what territory is for, which suggest different conceptions of the appropriate territorial right-holder and territorial attachment, and so on, with the main division between non-statist and statist theories of the territorial right-holder.

Moreover, to count as a *theory*, it is necessary to have a normative and explanatory account of the various different elements that we commonly associate with rights over territory.[11] There are a number of distinct dimensions or elements clustered together under the idea of territorial rights, and the unreflective view of territory as automatically related to the functions of the state, and thereby naturally associated with state sovereignty, tends to cluster together these elements, and assume that having a territory or territorial rights over domain T automatically encompasses all these elements. This is not obvious. When we say that a state S has territorial rights in a certain area, we can distinguish between three elements embedded in that claim. First, it involves right to jurisdictional authority, that is, a right to make and enforce laws in the geographical domain. Second, there is a right to tax, regulate, and control natural resources within the territory of the state. Third, there are rights to control or prohibit movement across the borders of the territory.[12] Once these are disaggregated in this way, it is clear that justificatory arguments for jurisdictional authority over territory (to solve collective action problems, say) will not necessarily involve the whole range of rights, liberties, powers, and immunities that we normally associate with territorial control (which is termed in the literature 'territorial right') and will not necessarily encompass rights to control the flow of goods or people across borders, for example, or a right to defend the territory of the state, when attacked. These need to be argued for and the relations between these different elements explained.[13] An important aspect of the theory advanced here is that it offers an explanation of the different elements that we associate with territorial right: it treats jurisdictional authority as fundamental but rejects the view that the justificatory argument for that right automatically translates into the other elements that we associate with control over territory. It examines the extent to which the argument justifying authority over territory can justify (or not) rights to control resources under the ground, for example, or the right to control borders.

(2) Second, the theory should be primarily about *territory*—about land understood as a political and jurisdictional concept. The theory of territory has to be rooted in a plausible and coherent account of the kind of thing that territory is.

(3) Third, it should have a coherent and persuasive account of the territorial right-holder, or collective agent. The theories considered in chapters 3, 4, and 5 of this book give different answers to the question of the appropriate territorial right-holder. Some argue that it is the state (chapter 5). Some argue that it is the cultural nation or ethnogeographic community (chapter 4). I argue (chapter 3) that it is the people, defined in non-cultural terms. While there is an important distinction to be drawn between statist and non-statist theories of the appropriate right-holder, it is I think significant that no one writing on territory denies that politically organized entities are the kind that can apply laws and exercise rights of jurisdiction. So this means that even if the fundamental holder of territorial right is a cultural group or an ethnogeographic community or a 'people' defined politically, as Miller and Kolers and I respectively argue, they need a political entity, like a state, to exercise these rights within the domain. The state or some state-like entity does not disappear from view but it is in a kind of fiduciary relationship to the community on whose behalf it exercises the rights. This makes a difference, as I will argue in chapter 4, to such things as obligations in the case of a failed state or obligations regarding the conquest of an unjust state.

(4) The fourth *desideratum* of the account is that it should offer a plausible theory of how to attach particular groups to particular bits of land. The theory has to be able to explain the relationship or link between territorial right-holder and the geographical domain (or territory) in which these rights are exercised. This is an important challenge, since it is not sufficient to show that people, however defined, require territory in order to realize justice or protect culture or be self-determining: one must present an argument which is able to link particular territorial right-holders with particular territories. Everyone has an interest in land, and this general interest is important to grounding rights to it. However, the interest that people have in land is also highly particularized, which is why rights to land and/or territory cannot simply be conceived of as a good that should be equalized or

prioritized, depending on our preferred theory of (global) justice. In this book, I argue that people have an important interest in access to land that supports the way of life that is fundamental to their projects and identities, the place where they live and have relationships, the geographical domain of their self-determination, and the property that they hold, and that these interests are sufficiently important to be protected by right and hold others under obligations to protect or promote those rights.

(5) Finally, this book adopts a particular methodological approach to the issue of rights over territory. Since there is no consensus on who has rights to territory, nor on what kind of agent is or ought to be the appropriate right-holder, the justificatory arguments advanced have to be generalizable at least in the sense that the justifications on which they rely are accessible to the different groups that might conceivably lay claim to a particular territory. This does not mean that all groups must agree with the argument or the principle, but that the method of *justification* is comprehensible to and accessible to the various groups. This rules out certain kinds of justifications for territory— ones that rely on religious truth or the authoritativeness of some doctrinal text to justify a group's right to a particular land.

(6) More generally this book adopts as a central methodological commitment to something like Rawlsian reflective equilibrium to define better and worse account. Rawls argued that, if the principles or theories have counter-intuitive consequences when applied to a specific context, we can either modify our fundamental principles (in Rawls's terms, our account of the initial situation) or we can revise our existing judgments. In this book, I test the kind of account I offer by examining concrete cases, either imaginative twists on real cases or cases from the relatively recent past or the news. I apply the principles I have developed to ensure, in a somewhat Rawlsian fashion, that they (the principles) generate intuitively plausible, defensible commitments.

I argue that the theory proffered in this book meets these 'tests'. It provides the conceptual resources so that we can address all of these issues from a common understanding of what territory is, why it is important, and why (and the extent to which) we have rights over territory. For example, the account of legitimate residency or occupancy developed in chapter 3, when applied to Sir George Somers and the settlers and crew washed up on the shores of Bermuda, makes it clear that they were indeed at liberty to settle there and subsequently establish forms of jurisdictional authority to govern their collective lives. It also considers many other pressing contemporary issues relevant to territory: secession, boundary drawing, immigration, rights over natural resources, and corrective justice as applied to territory, such as forcible expulsion and settlement, and the rights that attach to these.

1.3. Structure of the Book

The structure of the book is straightforward. Chapter 2 is a conceptual chapter, which explains in detail what territory is, what rights are included in territorial rights, and what is the relationship between territory and cognate notions, such as property. Chapter 3 is a foundational chapter, which sets out my basic theory of territory. It aims to achieve three things: (1) it defends the moral right of residency or occupancy (and what it means to 'legitimately occupy' a land); (2) it explains the conditions under which individuals form a people with claims to self-determination; and (3) it explains why collective self-determination is valuable. Chapters 4 and 5 examine the principal rival theories of territory, which are mainly distinguished by their different views of the fundamental holder of territorial rights: culturalist theories and statist theories. Chapter 4 examines culturalist theories, with a focus on David Miller's and Avery Kolers's theories respectively. Chapter 5 examines statist-functionalist theories of territory, beginning with Hobbes and Kant, but also including Sidgwick, and encompassing contemporary accounts, such as the accounts of Lea Ypi, Allen Buchanan, Jeremy Waldron, Anna Stilz, and Cara Nine. These two chapters (4 and 5) are important because they are designed to show that the principal rivals have problems that are avoided in my theory.

I then move from the questions 'what is territory?' and 'who has territory?' (chapters 3, 4, 5) to the question: 'how much territory?' (chapter 6). To approach this question, I examine the limits of the occupancy principle, and especially the question of how we can tell whether territory is or is not occupied. This chapter addresses questions about the physical extent of territory and applies this analysis to cases which are of pressing contemporary importance, such as those involving boundary disputes between neighbouring states and the territorial claims of secessionists. In that context, I deal with standard cases of boundary drawing, as well as cases of contested land—Northern Ireland, Kashmir, and Kurdistan—and the implications of my theory of territory for a theory of secession.

Chapter 7 addresses the problem of territorial injustice. The discussion of legitimate residency in the case of Sir George Somers's landing on Bermuda has an idealizing component: it begins with a case where a group can establish legitimate occupancy of the land on which they live merely by going to live there. This, however, is rarely the case, and a full theory of territory must have an account of when a group is not in legitimate occupancy. There is an important question of what to do and how we should think about cases in which people have been expelled from their land and another group has settled there. The dispossessed people feel that an injustice has been done

and that the land should be returned to their control. The people in possession of the land, over time, and especially over generations, come to feel that
the territory is theirs and organize their lives around the assumption that they
control the land. A theory of territory has to be able to address many issues
relating to territory that arise in non-ideal circumstances such as this.

Chapter 8 considers whether the theory of territory can be extended to
include a right to control resources within the territory. There are two aspects
to this chapter. First, I am concerned to address a potential criticism of my
theory: that a theory of territory such as the one advanced here—where legitimate occupancy is an important component—cannot address territorial disputes over unoccupied land. There is currently intense competition around the
world for control of the oceans, with countries staking rival claims to parts of
the seabed, a competition which is fuelled by the desire to control the rich natural resources thought to be on the ocean floor. There are also many particular
disputes over maritime borders, the frozen Arctic, and uninhabited rocks and
islands dotted around the oceans of the world. In this chapter, I reconceptual-
ize these as property disputes and suggest institutions and principles appropriate to their just resolution. I also discuss the justice limitations of control over
resources within the territory, in cases where the collective self-determination
of the political community is directly relevant, but outsiders to the political
and territorial project also make claims to the resources within the territory,
usually based on fairness considerations.

Chapter 9 considers the implications of the argument advanced above for
control over the flow of people and goods across borders (which is commonly
associated with having sovereignty over a territory). I discuss the extent to
which the self-determination argument can justify border control and the
implications of this for a theory of immigration.

These more applied chapters—on boundary drawing, immigration,
and control over resources—to some extent define the limits of the self-
determination argument. They are partly limits of what can be justified by
appeal to self-determination and partly limits of justice. I discuss the constraints on collective self-determination that are set by the rights of people
within the self-determining communities and especially people outside it,
who are affected by its decisions and actions.

Finally, in chapter 10, I focus on the idea of territorial integrity, and the
use of force either to defend or breach it. I begin with the implications of my
argument in a relatively uncontroversial case, which is the right of the state
to defend itself, and particularly to defend its territory. I suggest that, even in
this standard case, the argument developed here yields different and illuminating results. I then move on to more contentious cases and consider what
my theory says about: (1) military force used to regain territory that has been

taken unjustly at some point in the past; (2) annexing territory that contains a majority of people who identify with the state; (3) force used by secessionists to break up an existing territorial state; (4) force used by a majority against the secessionists; and (5) finally, what does my self-determination argument for the territorial rights of people imply for outside intervention in a state that arguably contains two or more disparate communities, resulting in break-up of the state, e.g. the invasion. This chapter is the most direct practical application of the theory of territory defended in this book.

By the time the book ends, I will have considered many of the dilemmas surrounding control over territory that are not considered in the relatively simple case of Sir George Somers landing on an unoccupied and uninhabited island. Throughout this book I complicate the simple picture of Sir George Somers in various ways. I consider cases in which the island on which they landed on was not in fact completely uninhabited. For example, the settlers find the remains of some deserted buildings but no people. Some years later, however, a fleet of canoes is sighted out to sea: the natives are attempting to return. Must the settlers allow them to? Or imagine that some years later a Spanish ship arrives and wants to settle another part of the island. What is the scope of the occupancy right of the original Somers group? Can they claim the whole island even if they only live on a part of it? Or imagine that some of Somers's women and men want to strike out on their own and found a new settlement in a different part of the island and take some of the territory with them. Are they entitled to do this? Are they entitled to some portion of the territory, and, if so, how ought this to be decided? In this book, I aim to set out a theory that provides normative guidance, which we desperately need in a world which we assume is territorially divided but where we have no clear idea of what territory is for, or what justifies it.

Notes

1. For a history of the founding of Bermuda, see Owen H. Darrell, *Sir George Somers Links Bermuda with Lyme Regis*, 2nd edn (Hamilton, Bermuda: O. H. Darrell, [1997] 2005). I tweak this example in a number of ways, but the factual story is that only two people from the original group of Sir George Somers remained on the island. Somers, crew, and settlers repaired their ship and went on to the original destination, which badly needed resupplying. However, the discovery of Bermuda did lead to a publication advertising its attractive qualities and the colonization of the island began shortly thereafter. The said publication advertises itself as one that 'truly sets forth the commodities and profits of that rich, pleasant, and healthfull countrie'. Silvester Jourdan, *Discovery of the Barmudas, otherwise called the Isle of Divels by Sir Thomas Gates, Sir George Sommers and Captayne Newpont, with divers others* (London: John Windet, 1610; Early English Books Online).
2. However, Locke then went on to justify unequal appropriation of the earth.
3. Nikos Papastergiardis, *The Turbulence of Migration: Globalization, Deterroritorialization and Hybridity* (Cambridge, UK: Polity, 2000); John Tomlinson, *Globalization and Culture* (Chicago: University of Chicago Press, 1999).

4. A. John Simmons, 'On the Territorial Rights of States', in Ernest Sosa and Enrique Villanueva, eds, *Social, Political and Legal Philosophy: Philosophical Issues*, vol. 11, 300–326 (Malden, MA, and Oxford: Blackwell, 2003), at 321.

5. Simmons, 'On the Territorial Rights of States', 321, n. 5. Italics are mine.

6. John Rawls, *A Theory of Justice* (Cambridge, MA: Harvard University Press, 1971), 4.

7. Gerry Cohen and Liam Murphy both reject the division between justice and morality, social institutions and personal morality. Liam B. Murphy, 'Institutions and the Demands of Justice', *Philosophy & Public Affairs*, vol. 27, no. 4 (1999), 251–291, at 280; and G. A. Cohen, 'Where the Action Is: On the Site of Distributive Justice', *Philosophy & Public Affairs*, vol. 26, no. 1 (1997), 3–30, at 22–23.

8. Both Thomas Pogge, in *World Poverty and Human Rights* (Cambridge, UK: Polity, 2002), and Charles Beitz, in *Political Theory and International Relations* (Princeton: Princeton University Press, 1979), put forward a form of institutionalism, in the sense that they accept Rawls's view that justice applies to a set of institutions, but then argue that, in this increasingly globalized world, the global order constitutes a set of institutions, and membership in institutional systems is of moral relevance.

9. David Miller, 'Territorial Rights: Concept and Justification', *Political Studies*, vol. 60, no. 1 (2012), 252–268.

10. Miller, 'Territorial Rights'.

11. The demand is not to justify this or that particular territorial right, but to justify a system of holdings, which would then justify tokens in the system. In this way, territorial rights are analogous to private property rights: the justification is for the *system* of private property holdings, not each *particular* private property holding. This point is also made by Cara Nine, *Global Justice and Territory* (Oxford: Oxford University Press, 2012), chapter 4.

12. This taxonomy is partly based on that of Simmons, 'On the Territorial Rights of States'.

13. On the concept of rights relied on here, it is an important feature that when rights are violated, we say that the right-bearer has been wronged. Jeremy Waldron, ed., *Theories of Rights* (Oxford: Clarendon Press, 1984), 8. See also David Rodin, *War and Self-Defense* (Oxford: Clarendon Press, 2002), for an excellent analysis. While the interest can be identified as an interest that individuals have, this interest is inextricably linked to their participation in collectives, and in groups. The right-holder in the case of territory is that of a collective agent.

2

What Is Territory? Conceptual Analysis and Justificatory Burdens

The origin and meaning of the term 'territory' are contested, but it is generally acknowledged that it comes from the Latin notion of 'territorium', from *terra*, meaning 'earth', and the suffix *-torium*, indicating 'place of occurrence'. Some people have argued that the etymological root is not the Latin *terra* meaning 'earth', but *terror*, 'to frighten', which would mean that the concepts of 'territory' and 'terrorist' share the same root derivation.[1] Although I do not examine this debate here, the reference to earth is the more plausible underlying root of the concept. I argue in this chapter that the development of the modern notion of 'territory' is inextricably linked to the rights of jurisdictional authority over a territorial or geographical domain, and so is a profoundly political notion.[2]

In this book, when I discuss territorial rights, I am not referring to a single right: the diverse rights associated with territory are typically understood to be configured in ways analogous to property rights—that is, a complex mixture of claim rights, powers, liberties, and immunities—and operating in different ways across different domains (resources, control over borders, corrective justice, jurisdiction).[3] Each of these has to be examined separately; liberty claims are different from moral powers and these are different from claim rights. I have already emphasized that the interrelationship between the different rights (jurisdiction, immigration, resources) needs to be explained, but, in addition, this has to be situated within a wider context of the justice limits of rights, which are explored primarily in the later chapters of the book.

Although the rights associated with the idea of territorial rights might be configured in ways similar to property rights, this does not mean that territory itself is related to people or to the state in ways analogous to property. Here, it is helpful to distinguish between land, territory, and property. 'Land' refers to the portion of the earth's surface that is not covered by water; 'territory' is a political concept, referring to the geographical domain of a political entity, typically the state; and 'property' refers to a complex collection of rights, moral powers, immunities, and duties, which generally gives the right-holder the moral and legal rights to access and control objects and to exclude others from them. The distinction above—between land, territory, and property—assumes that territory and property are distinct concepts, and indeed that the political or jurisdictional order creates the rules of acquisition, transfer, bequest, and the like, which we generally associate with property rights. This makes an account of territory conceptually prior to that of property. This is not uncontroversial. There is a strong current or tradition in political theory which conceives of territory as a kind of property, either as an amalgam of individual property holdings or as a kind of property held by the state.

What do I mean by a property account of territory? On a property theory of territory, when we say that state S has territorial rights in land L, what we mean is that the relationship between the state and the land is analogous to the relationship between an individual property-owner and his or her property, and encompasses rights to make decisions about the land, to exclude people from it (control over immigration), and to exploit the resources on the land for the property-owner's instrumental benefit (right to resources). The central relationship is between the state and the land: the relationship of people to both these (the state and territory) is purely contingent. Although a particular property theory of territory could include the requirement that the state (analogous to the property-owner) must relate to the people in the territory in a certain way (e.g., stipulate that they treat them justly), this further requirement sits uneasily with the conception that state territory is analogous to property, since we don't normally require that property-owners treat the property in a particular way in order to remain an owner.

Before we can make progress examining rights to territory, it is important to elaborate what the concept of territory refers to, why I don't adopt a property account of territory, what rights or entitlements are included in the concept of territory, and more generally, what the relationship is between territory and these other elements, and between the concept of territory and the various rights that we associate with territory, which are included in the idea of 'territorial right'.

To make this argument, I begin in this chapter by distinguishing between two different kinds of property accounts: a Lockean version, where the state is made up of individual property-holders; and a neo-Lockean version, where the state is the collective agent, and territory is conceptualized as the property of the state. The Lockean version views territory primarily in individualist terms, as denoting an aggregate of individual properties; the neo-Lockean version views territory as something like property held by a collective. With respect to both kinds of property accounts, I argue that the view that territory is a kind of property is problematic because it does not properly conceptualize the relationship of people to either the land or the state. It was a dominant way to conceive of territory historically, prior to the democratic era, when the relationship of the people to the state was mainly that of subjects, but today we tend to think that the relevant relationships are not simply between state and territory but between these two and the people who are living on the territory. Consistent with this diagnosis, I will go on to argue in this book that although I reject the property conception of territory as a *general* approach to territorial rights, there are residual effects of the property conception of territory in international law and politics, which partly explain why we are so confused about territory. I also argue that the property conception is relevant in cases of disputes over unoccupied areas, which are conceived of almost entirely in instrumental terms, as a valuable possession. This has implications for how we think of some territorial disputes, such as disputes over the seabed or over uninhabited islands.

2.1. Individualist Property Theories of Territory

One of the most developed accounts of territory has its origins in Locke's theory, where territory is viewed as derived from a collection of individual private property holdings. Most theoretically sophisticated versions of the individualist territory-as-property account acknowledge their origins in Locke. They typically begin from an account of property as an individual (natural) right and then conceive of territory as arrived at by the consent of many individual property owners who agree to establish a government (legislative, executive, and judiciary) to rule over them.[4] In his 'Second Treatise', Locke argues that there is a natural right to private property, stemming from the idea that all people have a right to the fruits of the earth:

> Whether we consider natural *Reason*, which tells us, that Men, being once born, have a right to their Preservation, and consequently to Meat and Drink, and such other things, as Nature affords for their Subsistence: Or *Revelation*, which gives us an account of those Grants God made of the World to *Adam*, . . . 'tis very clear, that God . . . *has given the Earth* . . . to Mankind in common.[5]

This fundamental right (to subsistence) is combined, in Locke's thought, with the idea that labour is the mediating device by which individuals can transform external objects in the state of nature into private property. Natural rights to property can be seen as rooted in the fundamental importance of private holdings to the exercise of liberty, that is, to the ability of persons to engage in individual or collective projects. Locke writes: 'Whatsoever then he removes out of the State that Nature hath provided, and left it in, he hath mixed his *Labour* with, and joined to it something that is his own, and thereby makes it his *Property*'.[6] The right to private property is limited by the right to subsistence (to preservation and consequently the fruits of the earth). The limits of the right are defined by 'the Lockean proviso', which requires that individuals may only legitimately appropriate un-owned land where there is 'enough, and as good left' in common with others, although this rather strong statement of the proviso is subsequently significantly weakened.[7] A crucial point, for our purposes, is that this account rests on the acceptance of natural property rights.

Locke then asks us to imagine persons, either individuals or loosely associated persons (e.g., families), many of whom have property in land, combining together to create a state. The crucial passage in Locke linking the creation of authority over persons and authority over territory is the following:

> By the same Act therefore, whereby any one unites his Person, which was before free, to any Commonwealth; by the same he unites his Possessions, which were before free, to it also; and they become, both of them, Person and Possession, subject to the Government and Dominion of the Commonwealth, as long as it hath a being.[8]

Consent here is important to the creation of political authority. As Simmons writes: 'When people consent to make or join a political society, their consent should normally be understood as consent to whatever arrangements are necessary for a peaceful, stable society'.[9] Locke argues that people would consent to majority rule, to obedience and support for law (within the limits of natural law), and, importantly for this account of territory, consent to incorporate their rightful landholdings into that territory over which the society will have jurisdiction.[10] In this way, territory is created as a result of the consent of individual property holders, and the natural right to property is conceptually prior to the state, and defines the domain of state jurisdiction. Legitimate territorial right is established, on this account, through the subjection, by free consent, of persons and their land to state authority.

There are a number of advantages of this conception of territory which I'll rehearse quickly here (but return to in specific chapters later). The most important one is that it explains both the creation of authority over persons and authority over territory. It does not focus just on the first and assume that this gets us the second. They are treated as conceptually distinct.

It also offers a strong basis for historical rights. Unlike conventional accounts, where property rights are conceived of as created by the state—as a bundle

of rights that are the creation of the exercise of jurisdictional authorities—
the idea of a natural right to property may be able to justify historically persist-
ing claims to land that are no longer occupied by the group. Claims by groups
or persons lacking legal entitlement can be explained in terms of a natural right
to property. This has strategic advantages for the plight of colonized and dispossessed groups, such as indigenous peoples, where natural property right
claims may be the most straightforward way to regain control over sacred
ancestral lands.

Moreover, this type of account easily explains the link between the three
elements that are normally thought to be part of 'territorial right'. As Simmons
has noted, territorial right typically encompasses rights to control borders
(immigration as well as the flow of goods across borders) and right to control resources. If we think of territory as like property we might think that
we have little difficulty arguing that it should include border control: just as a
property-owner can decide who can enter and stay in his or her house, so individual members of the state can collectively exercise their capacity to permit
entry and exclude certain individuals and goods from the state. The same is
true for control over and benefit from resources within the territory: if territory is a kind of property, it is natural to assume that the owners will seek to use
territory and benefit from it.

Although in many ways this is an attractive theory of territory, it is also
subject to a number of problems. First, there is the issue of the plausibility of
a natural right to private property. It is not hard to defend the bare idea of a
natural (moral) right, but much more difficult to argue for the specific right
of property, if we include all the different liberties, powers, and immunities
that we typically associate with property-holding regimes. If we think of the
right to private property as grounded in natural liberty, this would give us
some kind of natural or moral right, but it is hard to see how this extends
easily to other rights that we associate with property rights, such as the specific rules around bequest or concerning transfer of property. For this reason,
most political theorists conceive of property rights as conventions to regulate
the relations between people and things. Since conventions are set by political authorities, this makes political or jurisdictional authorities conceptually prior: the political authority defines the rules under which people have
entitlements (to wealth or objects). Of course, conventional (institutional)
approaches and natural law (or moral rights) approaches to property can be
rendered compatible.[11] We could, for example, think of property rights as primarily legal rights, but we might still draw on moral theory to explain why
the institution should be structured in certain ways, typically emphasizing
principles of desert and responsibility and a universal basic right to subsistence, to justify (or not) particular institutional forms.[12] This though would

justify the bare idea of a moral right to property, rather than show that the specific features—the liberties, claims, and powers typically associated with property—can be justified in natural rights terms. This makes the argument somewhat limited, because many of the features that we associate with property rights—including zoning laws and many other regulations in the common interest, rights of bequest and transfer—are the creation of the exercise of jurisdictional authority, even if the specific institutional forms can (and should) be subject to moral assessment.

There is also a problem with the transition between individual private property holdings as the fundamental building block of this account and territorial jurisdiction, which it is supposed to explain. On the most sophisticated versions of this account (Simmons, Steiner), individuals who rightfully hold property in land agree to the establishment of government to preserve peace and enforce natural law. The individualist Lockean account is able to explain how there might be legitimate jurisdictional authority over various chunks of land, but it also seems likely that these would be punctuated by land held by dissenters, or at the least non-continuous boundaries.[13] It has difficulty justifying the contiguous jurisdictional authority of territorial states, where the writ of law applies to all those contained within the external boundaries but there is no unowned or unconsented interior land. In other words, this argument does not justify territorial right *as we know it*, where territorial rights and especially jurisdictional authority are consistently or evenly applied across the territory. Although this is not a flaw in itself—we shouldn't think of normative theory as intent on justifying contemporary practices—I think it is a problem that the account does not explain territorial right in a way that is related to the performance of functions relating to the exercise of jurisdictional authority.[14] Hillel Steiner, who develops an otherwise persuasive version of the individualist Lockean theory of territorial rights, is aware that if territorial rights are established on the basis of voluntary consent of individual property holders, it cannot justify the conventional view of territory. But, he argues, so much the worse for the conventional view. Steiner writes: 'precisely because a nation's territory is legitimately composed of the real estate of its members, the decision of any of them to resign that membership and, as it were, to take their real estate with them is a decision that must be respected'.[15]

Simmons avoids this problem by emphasizing that the consent of individual private property owners to the creation of a common authority leads to a collective (common authority) with jurisdictional rights, which is itself distinct from property rights, and intended to regulate property disputes. Property rights only serve to define the location of the jurisdictional authority. The crucial move then is *consent to political authority*. Simmons interprets

Locke's theory as able to address two sources of non-contiguity (secession and sale or bequest to people outside the territory) because he argues that the authority can be created in such a way that it limits the ability of property owners to exit or sell their land to people who do not accept the sovereign's jurisdictional authority. He argues that property owners, in creating a political community, implicitly agree or consent to the 'following arrangement: subjects will not bequeath, sell or otherwise alienate land incorporated into that state's territories except on the condition that subsequent holders of that land will also be bound by the obligations of membership, including subjection of the land to state jurisdiction.'[16] This interpretation of the consent requirement helps to address the criticism that the territory would be perforated by seceders, dissenters, or alien presences, and so promises to give us a more functional account of state territory than Steiner's similar view.[17]

However, this solution highlights the importance of consent in Locke's argument, and thus is suggestive of an even more serious problem with the individualist Lockean account. This is the problem that no states are actually legitimated through individual consent of private property holders and this seems to condemn all existing territorial states to illegitimacy. Simmons, who is a philosophical anarchist, is happy enough to accept this conclusion: he thinks that all states *are* to some extent illegitimate, because they are not really based on the consent of free individuals to state jurisdiction.[18] This does not seem persuasive to the non-anarchists among us who think that states can be legitimate and that there might be something like territorial right.[19] It also is insufficiently nuanced. The standard for state legitimacy is set so high that no state can meet it. The problem with this is that it tends to fail our ordinary-language use of the term 'legitimacy', which we tend to think of as either a threshold concept, which some states can meet and others can't, or a scalar concept, where we can identify some states as more legitimate than others. The emphasis on free consent seems to be an all-or-nothing matter and to be at odds with how the concept of state legitimacy functions.

Simmons's interpretation of Locke makes sense of the distinction between property and jurisdiction, but it also suggests that the important element is consent to the creation of a collective authority, empowered to secure property claims, legislate and enforce rules surrounding bequest, purchase, alienation, and so on, define their limits, and arbitrate amongst conflicting claims. If this is so, perhaps we should move directly to a collectivist account, which has the conceptual resources to distinguish between (individual) property rights and (state) territorial rights, and which identifies territorial rights specifically with the state, which is the collective right-holder.[20]

2.2. Collectivist Property Accounts of Territory

This brings us to the collectivist version of the conception of territory-as-property, mainly associated with Cara Nine. Her theory is neo-Lockean because, although indebted to Locke, she does not view territory as *derived from* the consent of individual property holders in the exercise of their natural right to property. Rather, the state is conceived of as a collective that can hold property: the territory of the state is analogous to the property of the state. Like Locke, Nine takes the view that territorial rights are established by certain kinds of value-creating activities on the part of the state in relation to land. Nine writes, 'According to [my] collectivist Lockean theory, *the state* acquires territorial rights in much the same way that individuals acquire property rights'.[21] She argues:

> States change the land in the same way as individuals, via labour. Laws and customs governing land use directly create unique systems of agriculture and other forms of resource usage in several ways. (1) Market systems established and maintained by political institutions determine and create value in land and all of the products coming from the land. Market systems also influence the way that the land's resources are developed. (2) Individuals organised by political institutions will develop land and its resources in certain ways encouraged by the political order. (3) States are responsible for interpreting and enforcing personal property rights, and property rights are an integral component in determining how land is developed and by whom. Through the creation, adjudication and enforcement of laws, states have world-altering abilities that may be the source of rights claims to land.[22]

On Nine's argument in this article, where a state has engaged in value-creating activities—it has transformed the land through its institutional activities, its laws and regulations, shaping the landscape through zoning, private property rules, and so on—it is entitled to enjoy those rights, it would seem, in perpetuity. Her view has since changed—as I will note in chapter 5—particularly in locating the holder of territorial right in the society, rather than the state. But let me focus here on this argument as an exemplar of a kind of neo-Lockean position, where territory is conceived of as property held by the state.

This view—of the state as a collective agent and the territory of the state as its property—is subject to two serious, but quite different, lines of criticism. One criticism presses on the profoundly conservative thrust of the idea of territory as a kind of right that states possess through their activities as the bearers of collective rights. Nine does not consider directly the possibility that states themselves might be the creation of force or conquest, nor that there are other potential right-holders that could also have performed these right-conferring activities. Her view considers only *existing* states, however they were created, but seems unable to envision such rights as flowing from other agents. It is conservative because it seems to entail always supporting the existing regime for its increased value-creating activities (vis-à-vis a baseline of no state), while ignoring the fact that the state excludes other potential claimants by coercion, even if they could and would also have engaged in value-creating legislation, zoning, and so on. It is a conservative argument, transferring territorial right to all existing states, but not really explaining the original basis of the state's legitimacy or how it comes initially to exercise authority over the area.

Moreover, although this theory seems to confer rights over territory on the grounds that states are themselves valuable as instruments of justice—valuable because an important means by which people create justice together—the theory of political legitimacy implicit in that move is not explained nor are its implications spelled out. The implications (of the reliance on the idea of justice) are quite different from the conception of political legitimacy that is forefronted by the Lockean or territory argument. To see that they are different, consider the (likely) scenario where states are engaged in value-creating activities—zoning, regulating, and thereby transforming the land—but at the same time they are engaging in human rights violations against (some of) their citizens. Although the state is justified in implementing rules of justice, the basis of state authority over territory is in terms of value-creating and value-enhancing activities, as people try to fulfil their needs, and it's not entirely clear how these two elements are related. At the very least, the response that Nine gives to the attachment problem—about the value-creating basis of attachment over particular territory—does not sit easily or coherently with a focus on the state as a site of justice in any stronger sense.

2.3. Collectivist Property Theories of Territory in Historical Perspective

The view of territory as the property of the state was the dominant view of territory historically and, I argue, well suited to an age prior to the advent of democracy. In the past, the king or sovereign was related to the jurisdictional unit that s/he reigned over in a way roughly analogous to the relationship between a property owner and his/her land: it was something s/he (largely) controlled and was transferred by inheritance, just as individual property holdings were. The jurisdictional territory of the sovereign was carried with the sovereign into marriage, just as property might be. Many dynastic marriages were designed to gain or secure territory for the realm, just as aristocratic marriages were often decided on the basis of the lands that the marriage partners brought with them. Many European states are the product of territorial acquisition through well-designed dynastic marriages: most famously the marriage of Ferdinand of Aragon to Isabella of Castile was crucial to the creation of the territory of modern-day Spain, and the inheritance of the English throne by James VI, King of Scotland, was a crucial step in facilitating the union of England and Scotland.

Of course, in many cases, the sovereign king was not an absolute monarch, but one whose power was limited in various ways, most notably by the historic privileges of certain nobles and regions of the country, just as property rights are often limited in various ways. This meant, in the Scottish case, that Scotland remained institutionally distinct from England in a dual-monarchy arrangement until the Act of Union in 1707, when the Scottish nobles voted in favour of legislative union with England. This is still partly analogous to the relationship of a property owner to his/her property, for, in many cases, alliances between property owners did not result in the full incorporation of the various properties. Imagine, for example, a case where a daughter inherits an estate and then marries; under the sexist rules of the time, the estate becomes part of her husband's properties, along with any other estates he might have. But it would often be the case that the different estates would be run somewhat separately and were often subject to distinct kinds of limitations; each estate might have certain tenants enjoying historic rights and privileges.

If we think of territory as the property of the state or the sovereign, there are no conceptual resources to consider the wishes and well-being of the people who live on the territory. There were, of course, conceptions of good governance and, relatedly, numerous guides to how a prince should behave, but these are analogous to conceptions of how a lord should treat his vassals and rule over his own property. The main link was between the sovereign and his/her territory, conceived of as a kind of property, and no integral relationship was established between the people and political authority or people and territory.

Not only were territorial jurisdictions subject to dynastic alliances and marriages, they were also considered part of the 'spoils' of war. For example, the European powers sometimes exchanged North American lands as part of peace settlements for wars fought in Europe, without regard for the wishes of the people living on the land. This conception was mirrored also in an older understanding of just-war theory. While modern just- (or justified-) war theory emphasizes that warfare can enforce entitlements, it also specifies that there can be no new rights through war.[23] Grotius's account, however, is typical of the older way in which war was understood, which is consistent with the idea of land as a kind of property. Grotius argued that 'any one whatever, engaged in regular and formal war, becomes absolute proprietor of every thing which he takes from the enemy: so that all nations respect his title'.[24] If you can secure the land with permanent fortifications or hold the captured vessels in dock for twenty-four hours, you are entitled to keep whatever territory you can seize.[25] Grotius's conception did not have the same view of the rights of the people living on the land: Grotius wrote, 'by conquest, a prince succeeds to all the rights of the conquered sovereign or state, and if it be a commonwealth, he acquires all the rights and privileges, which the people possessed'.[26] Although in many ways Grotius was prescient in asking modern questions about what justifies war and its limits, he also seemed to hold to the older idea that territorial control was akin to property, something to be acquired, and was largely indifferent to the entitlements of the people living on the territory.

It is difficult to pinpoint exactly when territory became associated primarily with the idea of a geographical domain of self-government, rather than understood simply as property. We can trace the beginnings of the self-determination idea of territory at least from 1791. In article II.2 of the 1791 Constitution of France, the sovereign is described in a way that relates him primarily to the people, rather than to the territory: he is referred to as the king of the French rather than the king of France, with the attendant implication that the main legitimating relationship is with the people, and that the geographical domain is determined by the area occupied by the people. This is reinforced by the abolition of the nobility, the affirmation of the ultimate sovereignty of the nation, the constitutional permanence of the National Assembly, the representative body, in creating and ratifying legislation, and the abolition of previous feudal geographical divisions, which had local and historical kinds of legitimacy, in favour of a view where the territory of the kingdom of the French was divided into mere administrative units, or *départements*.[27]

There was no clear transition from a property view to the jurisdictional authority view: the older idea persisted and still persists in various forms, both in our thinking about international relations and in specific elements of international law. I have already hinted at one—in the attitude that states and state officials take to unoccupied land or the seabed, which is typically viewed in instrumental terms, as a means of enrichment, or as a kind of property.

It also follows from the view of territorial jurisdictions as analogous to property, held by the sovereign authority, that territory can be purchased. This was unusual, since territorial expansion was almost always regarded as a benefit to the state, and a measure of its power and importance. Nevertheless, it did occur, most notably, when the United States bought Alaska from Russia in 1867. Even as late as 1916, the United States purchased territories in the

West Indies from Denmark. Territory is also viewed in property-like terms, as a possession of the state, but lacking tight normative connection to the people living on the land, in the principle of *uti posseditis*, which is typically applied to boundaries and boundary disputes.[28] *Uti posseditis* is the principle that at the end of a conflict the territory remains with the possessor; and is related to the idea of territory as a possession, and is often justified instrumentally, as a principle of peace and stability. It is, I argue in this book, at odds with the central presuppositions of both justice theory, understood broadly, and democratic theory. It is therefore important to think through what kind of theory of territory would be appropriate to an international order that accepts the idea of fundamental human rights and especially the democratic principle that the ruled ought to have a say in who rules them, and in how they are governed.

2.4. Territory as the Domain of Jurisdictional Authority

The current international order contains principles and rules that reflect both property and jurisdictional domain views of territory: it does not, in other words, articulate or rely on a coherent overall conception of territory. Uncertainty about these two ways of conceiving of territory is reflected in confusion about the principles we should apply in cases of conquest, and obligations regarding failed states, which I discuss in chapter 5, and contradictory intuitions in disputes over oil-rich seabeds and uninhabited rocks in the Pacific Ocean, discussed in chapter 6.

The dominant view in the political theory literature is not the property or possession view, but the view that territory is the geographical domain of jurisdictional authority. On the jurisdictional domain view, when we say that state S has territorial rights in land L, what we mean is that the state (or state-like entity) has rights to jurisdiction over the land; that this jurisdictional authority is justified by appeal to a particular moral value V; and that the land is the domain in which the jurisdictional authority is exercised. This account leaves open, or underdetermined, the relationship of jurisdictional authority (the power to make and enforce laws in the domain) to other elements that we normally associate with territorial rights, such as a right to control borders and exclude others from the territory, and the right to tax, extract, and make rules about resources within the territory. On this view, territory is not owned or a thing merely *possessed* by the state or other collective agents. It is the geographical domain in which people exercise jurisdiction over their collective lives.

I do not think it is an accident that the jurisdictional domain conception of territory emerged with the demise of an older, feudal order and the first stirrings of mobilization towards the new democratic order. This is not because applying democratic procedures to the issue can determine directly the territorial dimensions of the state, or the boundaries of the *demos*—a point which I explore in chapter 6, and which is frequently commented on as a limitation of democratic theory.[29] Nor is it because having territorial right depends on the territorial right-holder (the state or the people or the nation) being democratically organized. Rather, democracy and the jurisdictional authority conception of territory are linked at a fundamental, conceptual level, because they share some of the same underlying values or norms. This is most clearly seen through exploring one of the core concepts in democratic theory—that of 'popular sovereignty'.

The ideal of popular sovereignty is based on the fundamental norm of the equal moral and political status of citizens, and especially the view that no one is naturally entitled to have authority over anybody else. One (democratic) implication of this view is that the institutions of government, the institutions of the state, have to be designed in such a way that they are ultimately accountable to the people. This has led to the view that this norm is best realized by giving equal voice, equal political input into the institutions of government, and so organizing the institutions of government in ways that we recognize as democratic, that is, characterized by competitive elections, equal political rights, and representative government—all of which are intended to give effect roughly to the people's will or, less metaphorically, to represent ways of making social choices that are consistent with the fundamental ideal that government ought to be in the interests of, and authorized by, the people who are governed by it.

Territory, on the jurisdictional authority view, is the geographical domain in which (ideally) the people express their will through institutions. The term also invokes the idea of a collective people to whom the sovereign authority (the government) is ultimately accountable. It shares the same broad picture of the relationship between the people, who are the source of legitimacy, the state, and its territory, as is implied in the popular sovereignty ideal of democratic theory. However, the jurisdictional domain view is not a single view, but encompasses at least three distinct justificatory arguments for territory and relatedly, three distinct conceptions of the holder of territorial rights. There is a self-determination view, which I advance in chapter 3, which justifies rights over territory in terms of the exercise of collective self-determination of the people. There is a cultural nationalist view, which similarly associates territory with the exercise of jurisdictional authority but justifies this in terms of the role of the state (having jurisdiction) in protecting cultures and cultural values—this is the subject of chapter 4. There is the statist view, which identifies territory as a necessary precondition for the state to fulfil its functions, and therefore argues that whatever justifies the state (typically, in Hobbesian fashion, the maintenance of order and stability) also justifies its possession of territory, and a more moralized version, associated with the works of Kant, among others, which justifies the state and its entitlements over territory if it achieves a certain standard of justice or legitimacy, externally defined. These statist views are the subject of chapter 5. Although these rival accounts of the holders of territorial right all view territory as a domain of jurisdictional authority, and in ways closely related to the democratic ideal, their practical implications are different. For example, on my view of territory, there is a contingent relationship between the people and the state in the sense that the people, as a collective agent, can preexist the state and they can survive the state (if it collapses). This is relevant when we consider military occupation, state failure, and secession. The statist view, by contrast, conceives of the state as organized to achieve justice for the people, and the people as coming into existence *as a people*, as a collective entity, through the state. This means that the basis of territorial right cannot preexist the state (nor, arguably, endure after the collapse or failure of a state).

There is another value that is implicit in the idea of territory as jurisdiction, which is appealed to (implicitly or explicitly) by the three rival jurisdictional authority views. This is the value inherent in having a uniform system of law in a geographical domain rather than a patchwork of local regimes. This is necessary to solve collective action problems, to distribute responsibilities, adjudicate disputes and to enable people to have some control over the life that they share together.

The basic elements in a theory of territory are the people, land, and the state. If we view the people as the locus of popular sovereignty, the state as the instrument through which they realize some value (e.g., self-determination, justice, or protection of cultural value), and territory as the geographic domain in which they express that value, then territory L is defined by the institutional structures of the state. However, since the justification for the institutional structure is in terms of the realization of a particular moral value, it is possible that the moral value cannot be realized by any and all institutional structures and by any territorial configuration. Indeed, depending on the moral value in question, it might require that the people have a particular relationship to land in order to claim moral rights to it. The precise relationship will be discussed in chapters 3, 6 and 10.

2.5. Territorial Rights, Moral Reasoning, and Institutional Design

In order to consider in greater depth the relationship between a normative theory of rights over territory and a descriptive theory of territory— by which I mean territory understood as attaching to recognized states in the international order—it is necessary to say something about the complex

relationship between claims in moral theory, especially moral rights to
territory (which are the main focus of this book), and the institutional
mechanisms for realizing what the principles of the moral theory require or
recommend.[30]

In the course of the book I often appeal to the idea of rights. Some rights are
held by individuals, some by groups, and some by institutions. I argue in the
next chapter for three sorts of place-related rights: rights of residency, which
are held by individuals; rights of occupancy, which are held by groups; and
territorial rights, which are held by (political) institutions. In all three cases,
I justify these rights in terms of a deeper appeal to the fundamental interests
of persons, who, I argue, have important relational and associative interests,
which ought to be protected by both individual and collective rights.[31] In all
cases, however, I regard these rights not as absolute claims, but as subject to
certain limitations: that the rights are feasible (to be explained below) and that
the rights as a set are compatible.[32]

Let us consider these two in reverse order. What do I mean by the compatibility requirement? I mean that the right should be defined in such a way
that it does not come into necessary conflict with other fundamental rights,
which also identify and protect fundamental human interests.[33] Consider as
an example a strong right to free speech. The right is justified by an appeal
to interests (in free speech), but its limits are justified by rights to privacy
and by other legitimate interests that people have which warrant protection,
with which it will conflict unless it is defined in a way that recognizes these
justice limits. Similarly, a strong right to collective self-determination that
infringed the self-determination of some other people or group would fail the
compatibility requirement. An account of rights that imposed excessive costs
on those who are responsible for discharging the obligation generated by the
right would also fail the compatibility requirement. The compatibility requirement is meant to indicate the limits of the rights. In this book, I argue that
territorial rights that are justified as a set, as necessary to protect our interest in collective self-determination, must be conceived in a way that meets
the compatibility requirement. Where this is manifestly not the case, such as
Northern Ireland and Kashmir, which I examine in some detail in chapter 6,
I consider more imaginative institutional solutions that still respect the moral
relationships of the community and their aspirations to control the collective
conditions of their existence, but that recognize that the rights of collective
self-determination are constrained by the importance of other rights. I proceed similarly in the two applied chapters—on resources and immigration—
where I limit territorial rights when they conflict with other rights, such as the
right to a decent life (defined at least in part as a right to basic subsistence and
protection from severe harm).

If moral rights are to be action-guiding, as I think they must, they must be feasible, and the term 'feasible' is typically used in at least two different senses. One is a binary understanding: a principle is feasible if it is not *impossible*—that is, if the principle is logically consistent, not in violation of laws of nature, compatible with resource limits, and so on. But there is another sense of the word 'feasible' which means that it is quite likely to be agreed to or implemented. This sense of the term appeals to an assessment of the probability of bringing about a state of affairs or set of institutions or practices, and some proposals are described as infeasible if the probability of getting institutional recognition of these rights is very low. We often employ this scalar sense of the concept when we speak of policies or practices or institutions as more or less feasible. Some of the institutional proposals advanced in this book are feasible in the first sense but not in the second. For example, in various places, I argue that the certain kinds of resources ought to be under the jurisdictional control of an international governance agency. In other places, I suggest that the territory currently claimed by many states cannot be justified in terms of the self-determination of the people, but are more correctly theorized as an exercise of power, and ought to be internationally governed or, less ideally, jointly governed. These proposals might be dubbed infeasible in the sense that there is no direct, easy, and one-step route from the state of affairs we are at now to the state of affairs being proposed, but they pass the binary feasibility test. Here I think it's important that normative theory isn't too captive to feasibility in the crude sense of whether people are likely to agree. What we must be able to do, however, is map out a path from our current state A to desired state of affairs Z, transitional through Q. In that case, we can say that A is accessible to us in the sense that there is a path to Z, even though it is an indirect path which can be pursued only over time. Even when the moral rights to territory are not directly realizable, the normative theory of territorial rights put forward in this book enables us to consider the justifiability of our current institutions and practices, and gives us reason to work, through our political organizations, through social groups, or even directly in our actions, towards a better world order.[34]

Notes

1. See Lea Ypi, 'Territorial Rights and Exclusion', *Philosophy Compass*, 2013, vol. 8, no. 3 (2013), 241–253; and Stuart Elden, *Terror and Territory: The Spatial Extent of Sovereignty* (Minneapolis: University of Minnesota Press, 2009).
2. Thomas Baldwin, 'The Territorial State', in Hyman Gross and Ross Harrison, eds, *Jurisprudence: Cambridge Essays*, 207–230 (Oxford: Clarendon Press, 1992), at 209–210; Carl Watner, 'The Territorial Assumption: Rationale for Conquest', *Journal of Libertarian Studies*, vol. 22 (2010), 247–260, at 249.

3. This follows the typology developed by Wesley Newcomb Hohfeld, who distinguishes among different sorts of rights in terms of the normative relationships between right-holders and the bearers of obligations. See Wesley Newcomb Hohfeld, *Fundamental Legal Conceptions as Applied in Judicial Reasoning*, ed. Arthur Corbin (Westport, CT: Greenwood, [1920] 1978); and Carl Wellman, *A Theory of Rights: Persons under Laws, Institutions, and Morals* (Totowa, NJ: Rowman and Allanheld, 1985).

4. Simmons, 'On the Territorial Rights of States', 300–326.

5. John Locke, 'The Second Treatise of Government', bk II, chap. V, para. 25; in Peter Laslett, ed., *Two Treatises of Government* (Cambridge: Cambridge University Press, [1689] 1988), 285–286.

6. Locke, 'Second Treatise', bk II, chap. V, para. 27; in Laslett, ed., *Two Treatises*, 288.

7. Locke, 'Second Treatise', bk II, chap. V, para. 33; in Laslett, ed., *Two Treatises*, 291.

8. Locke, 'Second Treatise', bk II, chap. VIII, para. 120; in Laslett, ed., *Two Treatises*, 348.

9. Simmons, 'On the Territorial Rights of States', 313.

10. Simmons, 'On the Territorial Rights of States', 313.

11. See here Christopher Bertram, 'Property in the Moral Life of Human Beings', *Social Philosophy & Policy*, vol. 30, nos. 1–2 (2013), 404–424.

12. This seems to underlie Burke Hendrix's attempt to draw on Nozick's Lockean property argument to justify indigenous claims to land. Hendrix offers a very good detailed argument that moral rights themselves are not implausible—and he includes prohibitions against killing, maiming, or otherwise damaging someone's physical body as among the most obvious natural rights that people have—and then goes on to suggest that natural property rights can be similarly defended as a way of respecting persons fully and ensuring natural liberty. Burke Hendrix, *Ownership, Authority, and Self-Determination* (University Park: Pennsylvania State University Press, 2008), 42–59.

13. David Miller, 'Property and Territory: Locke, Kant, and Steiner', *Journal of Political Philosophy*, vol. 19, no. 1 (2011), 90–109.

14. Cara Nine has also argued, I think persuasively, that it is unclear how Lockean individuals give up metajurisdictional authority, namely the right to create or alter jurisdictions, including geographical jurisdictions. It is unclear how free individuals can bind other holders of land. See Cara Nine, 'A Lockean Theory of Territory', *Political Studies*, vol. 56, no. 1 (2008), 148–165.

15. Hillel Steiner, 'Territorial Justice', in Simon Caney, David George, and Peter Jones, eds, *National Rights, International Obligations*, 139–168 (Boulder, CO: Westview, 1996), 144.

16. Simmons, 'On the Territorial Rights of States', 313.

17. This more sophisticated reading of Locke—as having a two-part argument—is also suggested (though with some significant differences) by Bas van der Vossen, 'Locke on Territorial Rights', *Political Studies* [early view, 8 January 2014].

18. Simmons, 'On the Territorial Rights of States', 315.

19. Nevertheless, I have a grudging admiration for Hillel Steiner's and A. John Simmons's willingness to accept the full logic of their arguments.

20. Nine, 'Lockean Theory', 151.

21. Nine, 'Lockean Theory', 155, emphasis mine.

22. Nine, 'Lockean Theory', 155.

23. See especially Seth Lazar, 'Endings and Aftermath in the Ethics of War', CSSJ Working Papers Series, SJ016, November 2010. I owe to Seth Lazar's paper an interest in Grotius's ideas of territory and property and the transition from this to democratic or self-determination ideas.

24. Hugo Grotius, 'On the Acquisition of Territory and Property by Rights of Conquest', *The Rights of War and Peace, Including the Law of Nature and of Nations* (New York: Cosimo Classics, [1625] 2007), bk III, chap. VI, para. ii, 335.

25. Grotius, *Rights of War and Peace*, bk III, chap. VI, paras iii and iv, 336.

26. Grotius, *Rights of War and Peace*, bk III, chap. VIII, para. i, 348.

27. For excellent analyses of this period, see Christopher Hibbert, *The French Revolution* (London: Penguin, 1982), and Colin Jones, *The Great Nation: France from Louis XV to Napoleon* (New York: Columbia University Press, 2002).

28. Sebastian C. St. J. Anstis and Mark W. Zacher, 'The Normative Bases of the Global Territorial Order', *Diplomacy and Statecraft*, vol. 21, no. 2 (2010), 306–323.
29. See Arash Abizadeh, 'Democratic Theory and Border Coercion: No Right to Unilaterally Control Your Own Border', *Political Theory*, vol. 36, no. 1 (2008), 37–65; David Miller, 'Democracy's Domain', *Philosophy & Public Affairs*, vol. 37, no. 3 (2009), 201–228.
30. Allen Buchanan provides a precise discussion of this. He argues that institutional moral reasoning justifies policies and practices as a set, in terms of: (1) its function in the system; (2) its content; and (3) criteria for determining what counts as morally progressive. The first issue—function—concerns the purpose that a theory of territorial rights ought to serve and considers the role that the practice or right plays within the system, situating the rights in question within a framework of laws, practices, and principles, which determine the scope and limits of the right. Policies, practices, and rights should be judged functionally, in terms of the role that the practice or right plays within the system, and must be assessed in the context of the design of morally progressive institutions. The content of the right requires normative argument, as does the criteria for determining 'moral progress'. The reasoning employed is consequentialist in the sense that it is important to consider what the goals of the institution are and which institutional arrangement is likely to facilitate their achievement. More technically, the institution, Buchanan argues, should be minimally feasible, and avoid perverse consequences. I argue that the institutional rules that attach to jurisdictional authority over territory should contribute to a situation where people co-create rules to govern their lives within their political communities. They should aim, that is, at the overall achievement of the value of self-determination. This is adapted from Allen Buchanan's discussion in *Justice, Legitimacy, and Self-Determination: Moral Foundations for International Law* (Oxford: Oxford University Press, 2004).
31. I rely on a modified interest-theory of rights, which combines the idea of wrong or disrespect to the equal moral status of the right-holder with the idea of damage or harm to important interests of the right-holder. It is a *modified* interest theory, because I am persuaded that that an account rooted only in welfare fails to account for the trumping character of rights. After all, if rights are merely designed to protect welfare, so that all the work is done by the idea that the interest is very, very important, and not likely to be outweighed by another interest, we don't need the idea of rights to capture that balance of reasons. If that's the view, rights do not do any independent work. To understand the special status of rights we have to incorporate the idea of the special status of right-holders and see the violation of rights as a violation of this status and so as a wrong. See here Seth Lazar, 'The Nature and Disvalue of Injury', *Res Publica*, vol. 15, no. 3 (2009), 289–304; and Seth Lazar, 'Corrective Justice and the Possibility of Rectification', *Ethical Theory and Moral Practice*, vol. 11, no. 4 (2008), 355–368.
32. I treat rights as possessing moral stringency in the sense that they generally override competing moral (welfarist) considerations. This point is made by Dworkin's metaphor of rights as a 'trump card', where they are 'best understood as trumps over some background justification for political decisions that states a goal for the community as a whole'; Ronald Dworkin, 'Rights as Trumps', in Jeremy Waldron, ed., *Theories of Rights*, 153–167 (Oxford: Clarendon Press, 1984), 153. However, rights may conflict (or more precisely the duties generated by a right may conflict). This is hardly surprising: if the interest is sufficiently morally important to ground a right, it will give rise not to a single corresponding duty but to a number of duties. Consider as an example Jeremy Waldron's analysis of the right not to be tortured and the successive waves of duties that it generates: a duty to refrain from torturing people, a duty to punish people who have tortured people, duties to create institutions that make torture less likely, duties to educate people about the wrong of torturing, and so on; Jeremy Waldron, 'Rights in Conflict', *Ethics*, vol. 99, no. 3 (1989), 503–519.
33. One way to resolve conflicts amongst rights that themselves presuppose a wider theory of human interests is to advance a general theory of well-being and develop priority relations among rights in accordance with that. Although, occasionally, I do rely on intuitive understandings of which rights are more important (especially if they protect interests that are widely agreed to be amongst the most fundamental), I do not think that progress

in political theory requires a full account of human well-being which would enable us to assess trade-offs along a single metric. Just because a particular interest is morally more important than another interest does not mean that it has lexical priority in any particular rights conflict. There are other considerations at work, such as how close or direct the relationship is between the duty in question and the interest that underlies it and whether that interest can be protected in ways that also recognize other rights that conflict with it (for these other rights do not just drop out of the picture).

34. In many cases, the moral rights that I argue for can be instantiated, though not perfectly, in a number of different institutional arrangements. This is fine as long as they represent an improvement over the previous state of affairs, either in being a closer approximation of the ideally justified state of affairs or in being a temporary step towards the ideally justified state of affairs. In many cases there is a trade-off between probability of success (which can change over time, as some of the obstacles decrease) and the normative attractiveness of the institutional set aimed at.

3

Foundations of a Theory of Territory

Individual Moral Rights of Residency, Collective Moral Rights of Occupancy, and a People's Rights of Self-Determination

In chapter 1, I argued that too little attention has been paid to issues of territory and that we need a political theory of territory. I then set out a number of *desiderata* of a good political theory of territory. I argued (1) that it has to be a *theory*, not just a set of local judgments about the relative superiority of one policy or arrangement over another. (2) It has to be a theory of *territory*, which is land over which some agent has political authority, meaning authority to make and enforce laws governing the conduct of inhabitants on the land, including laws defining and delimiting property rights. (3) It has to explain what kind of collective agents are candidates for having territorial rights. (4) It must answer the attachment question by explaining why and how particular territorial right-holders are attached to particular pieces of land. (5) It must appeal to reasons that are in some appropriate sense 'accessible' to all; and (6) it has to confirm or sensibly revise our considered convictions about specific cases (reflective equilibrium).

This chapter focuses on addressing the two related questions that any theory of territory should have answers to—the question of the appropriate territorial right-holders and how they are attached to land. Two of the other *desiderata*—the accessibility of the argument and the consequences of the view—are relevant to justifying the account of territorial attachment. Forms of justification that rely on assumptions internal to a particular group's specific tradition or religion or culture or view of history to 'attach' specific peoples to specific lands are ruled out.[1]

Finally, the theory of attachment has to have plausible and morally acceptable implications in the real world. This follows from the methodological approach of the book as a whole, and the way that I define better and worse accounts. It is an important part of the defence of my view that it can be applied usefully and persuasively in actual contexts, which I do in later chapters.

This chapter, then, sets out a number of basic or foundational arguments which underpin my political self-determination theory of territory. It addresses the third and fourth *desiderata* of a theory of territory outlined above, especially in linking the holder of territorial rights with the land. The requirement that the theory must either confirm or revise our considered convictions about specific cases is pursued mainly in later chapters—4 and 5—where I compare my answers to the other two dominant types of theories and then, in chapters 6-9, apply the theory to difficult questions—resources, immigration, drawing boundaries, and secession.

3.1. Territorial Right-Holders and Attachment to Land

In this chapter, I argue that a 'people' (still to be defined) has jurisdictional rights (and the related liberties, claims, and entitlements that generally flow from this, subject of course to justice constraints) over land on which members of the group reside, if the group is in legitimate occupancy of the land. By 'legitimate' I mean something like 'morally legitimate': I am not referring to something conferred by the state. The right kind of relationship of the people to land is a necessary, not sufficient, condition for holding territorial rights.

There are three distinct elements embedded in my political self-determination theory of territory. I begin with two place-related moral rights: a moral right of residency, which attaches to individuals, and a moral right of occupancy, which attaches to groups. These are distinct but interconnected moral rights. They are philosophically basic, and they are necessary to address the problem, not of justifying territory in general (as necessary to the good functioning of states), but of justifying particular pieces of territory for particular groups.

Second, a theory of territory has to give a plausible and coherent account of the group, the collective agent, which is the appropriate holder of territorial rights. I offer, in sections 3.4–3.5 of this chapter, an account of how to identify a 'people'; how to distinguish 'a people' from other kinds of groups that are not appropriate territorial right-holders; and then, in section 3.7, I offer an account of how a 'people' jointly creates, through relationships between its members, a number of intrinsic and instrumental goods. I argue that a 'people' has rights to jurisdictional authority over the geographical area that the group legitimately occupies if and only if: (1) a large majority of people are in a relationship with one another that involves a shared political commitment to establish rules and practices of self-determination; (2) they have the political capacity to establish and sustain institutions of political self-determination; and (3) they possess an objective history of political cooperation together, through for example participating in state or substate institutions or in a resistance movement.

In section 3.7 of this chapter, I give an account of the moral value of the goods that a 'people' produces in the relationships between its members, and here I focus on the good of collective self-determination. There are many goods that are achieved through the exercise of jurisdictional authority, but I focus on goods that are relationship dependent. I also address some possible criticisms of this account.

This theory is distinct from both statist and nationalist theories of territory and in the two chapters that follow, I contrast it with its main rivals: non-statist accounts of the right-holder, such as Koler's ethnogeographic theory, and Meisels's and Miller's cultural nationalism; and statist accounts, identified with Hobbes and Kant, and, in the contemporary era, with contemporary Kantian-inspired theories such as developed by Buchanan, Waldron, Stilz, and Ypi, as well as hybrid theories, such as Nine's. I argue that my self-determination account is superior to these rival views. An important element in the defence of my account is that it offers a better (more intuitive and more coherent) account of territory, territorial rights, and the appropriate right-holding agent than the extant rival accounts. That comparative argument is pursued in chapters 4 and 5.

3.2. Place-Related Rights: Individual Rights of Residency and Group Rights of Occupancy

The first step in solving the attachment problem (explaining how particular groups can have rights to particular pieces of land) is to consider people's relations to land, and in this context I explore two kinds of place-related rights: an individual moral right of residency and a collective moral right of occupancy.

I understand a *moral right of residency* as a right that belongs to individuals and has two components: a liberty right to settle in an unoccupied area, and a right of non-dispossession, a right to remain, at liberty, in one's own home and community and not to be removed from the place of one's projects, aims, and relationships. I also think, as an extension of this right, that it involves a right of return, when an individual has been unjustly excluded from land on which s/he has a right to reside (I defend this thought more fully in chapter 7).

I also argue for a collective moral right of occupancy. This is a collective right which a group may have, over and above the individual residency rights of its members. Occupancy rights help to define the domain of residency rights, and include a right to control the land or geographical area on which the people live and in which they have a special interest. Although this right of control is limited in important ways, it is necessary to justify territorial rights (of self-determination). I argue that that a group can be self-determining through political institutions only in the area in which the group enjoys occupancy rights. Thus, the moral right of occupancy is important to justify territorial rights *over a particular place*. Rights to collective self-determination do not build straightforwardly on individual residency rights, but the individual members of the group must be in the right relationship to the land (legitimately resident there) for the group to be said to occupy it, and this latter place-related right is necessary for a claim to territorial control over a particular geographical domain.

In this section, I advance an argument for why we might think that individuals who live on a particular area of land have a moral entitlement to live there, and I discuss what is involved in the ideas of moral rights of residency and occupancy. This idea is so basic to our view that many theorists take this idea as the starting point for a justification of state control over territory (and so build derivative rights from this jurisdictional right—such as the right to exclude others, control natural resources, and so on).[2] First, though, I defend the basic right of individuals to live in a place, free from the threat of expulsion. Some arguments for this basic right seem to justify only the right to reside somewhere, but I argue in this section for a stronger version of a moral residency right, that is the right to reside in the place you are currently in, assuming for the moment that you have not displaced another person who had moral residency rights.

What do I mean by 'legitimate residency'? I began this book with the case of Sir George Somers and his accompanying settlers, landing in Bermuda, where the land was unoccupied and settlement did not involve any coercion or unjust act. He and his settlers would meet the test of legitimate residency. The condition (of legitimate residency) is also met by people who are born in a place, whose parents were also resident on the land, perhaps even settled over many generations, even though the land was acquired unjustly long ago, by their ancestors. This is because—as I argue in this chapter (and clarify its implications in chapter 7)—people acquire moral residency rights through living in a place and having relationships, commitments, and attachments which are connected to residing there. The condition is not so rigorous as to exclude land that was once transferred unjustly.

The idea of moral rights of residency has been put forward, with somewhat different emphasis and terminology, by a number of different political theorists. In *Spheres of Justice* Walzer argues that people have 'a locational right', which he describes as a right to a place, and argues that this place is typically where they and their families have lived and made a life. Walzer cites Hobbes's argument on this, in *Leviathan*, that people entering the social contract give up their right to all things, to live under the rule of a sovereign, but they retain some rights, and amongst the retained rights are the right of self-defence, as well as the basic necessities of life: 'the use of fire, water, free air, *and place to live in*, and . . . all things necessary to life'.[3] While the place is typically their own place, membership in the political community means that this right has to be respected somewhere within it, and Hobbes even suggests that it should be upheld by the sovereign.

Why might we think that individuals have moral rights of residency? The principal appeal, I think, is to the idea that people have a right to a place: as Hobbes and Walzer suggested, we are physical beings and so we occupy space; but also within that place we develop projects and relationships and pursue a general way of life to which we are typically attached. Some of these connections are *to* the place,[4] but some are to our projects and to the people who share the space with us, to our family and friends and the community which forms the background context in which we live our lives.

The particular place where we live is important, then, for two reasons. First, people form relations and attachments with others in a particular place; our individual plans and pursuits depend on a stable background framework, and this is provided by security of place. If we are to have any control over our lives, we have to have control over the most fundamental elements in the background conditions of our existence, and among these is the ability to stay in our communities, amongst people with whom we have a relationship, and not be expelled or forced to leave unless there is a compelling reason.[5] This is not an autonomy argument for a moral right of residency, at least not if autonomy is understood in the liberal sense, as requiring that a person should have reflected critically on the plan of life she has adopted. Residency rights matter for all people, autonomous and non-autonomous in the liberal sense; indeed, you might even argue that residency rights matter more for non-autonomous people, since being autonomous (in the liberal sense) might make one better able to cope with established patterns of life being disrupted.

Second, people's aims and activities often rely on background assumptions about the physical place that they live in. In many cases, the projects and aims that give meaning to one's life can be pursued only in a particular location, with a particular institutional structure and geography and so on. Individuals make choices and develop aims and activities on the assumption that they live in that place, and, often, that place is integral to their choices and projects. Focusing entirely on the relationships developed in the place would have the counter-intuitive implication that the wholesale expulsion of a community is less damaging than individual expulsion.[6] Here we note that there is also an important physical connection to the place, and not simply the relationships to people formed in the place. Both arguments support the idea of a moral right to remain in a place, not to be expelled or barred from our communities, at least not without very good reasons, such as that of safety or some compelling public interest, though the second gives us reason to think that there is often something particular about the place which makes expulsion of the whole community a more egregious violation of their rights. And the argument suggests that there are both individual and collective dimensions of these locational rights, which, for clarity, I have called 'individual rights of residency' and 'group rights of occupancy'. The group right of occupancy relies on the idea that its individual members reside there not unjustly, but the individual right of residency does not presuppose that the individual is a member of a group. A single individual who is expelled and who is not a member of the relevant group has had his or her (residency) rights violated. In cases where a whole group has been forcibly expelled, both individual and group rights are violated.

The moral right of residency does not rely on a right to property. People can have a right to residency even when they don't own real estate or immovable property in the community. People who rent an apartment and are not property owners but are forcibly expelled have had their moral rights of residency violated.[7] Moreover, the moral right of residency does not apply only to eviction from one's home: it refers to the disruption and dislocation involved in exile from the place one lives in, defined in an expansive way. If I had to leave my house today, but was given a comparable house nearby, I don't think I'd be much worse off, though there would still be dislocation and frustration, and some loss, because I do have some attachment to my particular home, as I will argue in chapter 7. Nevertheless, my life would not be materially different. People move around quite frequently. There is however a far more significant disruption when people are exiled from the area of their community, defined expansively to include the institutional and physical context in which they live their lives, for they may not easily be able to feel 'at home' in the world in some other community or location. One of the justificatory arguments behind an individual right of residency is that people form relationships to each other within a particular place, but that seems to suggest that it would be better to move the community wholesale. Yet we often think that, instead of being a mitigating factor, a complete expulsion of the group constitutes a more serious wrong. Why would this be? This might be partly because we are aggregating many individual wrongs, but I think it's also because we recognize that individuals think of themselves as members of groups, who share a place-related connection, who see themselves as located within a specific geographical area, which is properly theirs, and that the right in question is not simply a right held by individuals, but a right held by the collective, the group, which in turn is valuable because important to the individuals who are members of the group. This means that not only are individual moral rights of residency violated in the course of forcible expulsion, but so it the group right of occupancy, which, I'll argue below, is not merely an aggregation of residency rights.

While residency rights are individual rights, in the sense that they attach to individuals and protect individual interests, individuals are not isolated and atomistic, but operate within a structure of relationships which give meaning to their lives. This brings us to a discussion of the place-related rights that attach to groups that individuals are members of, and to the relationship between the individual right of residency and the group right of occupancy.

What justifies a *collective right of occupancy* and what does it involve? In addition to individual identities, individuals have collective identities—as members of this or that religion or people or ethnic group—and these are also integral to their sense of who they are, and their collective aspirations as members of these groups are an important part of their lives. In many cases, the connection that individuals have to a place is not simply a connection forged independently by individuals living in a place, but is a connection experienced by individuals as members of a collective, a group, whose members share a geographical location with one another. The idea here is that individuals see the land as not only important for them individually, as the locus of their relationship and plans and projects, but they also see themselves as members of groups which are attached to specific areas, specific bits of land, which form an important source of the group's identity.

Many of the collective identities that people have as members of groups are not free-floating identities but are located in a specific place. The group's way of life and identity and history are bound up with the specific geographical area, and the members of the group are attached to a specific area, which is the locus of their plans and projects. Occupancy rights, which attach to groups, give the group the same rights that attach to individuals—rights of non-dispossession and rights of return—but they are not merely an aggregative form of individual residency rights. In addition, occupancy rights serve the function of helping to define the location of these individual rights, and they also confer a (defeasible) right to control the land on which the group lives.

There is a complex interrelationship between individual residency rights and collective occupancy rights; indeed, we cannot articulate the domain of individual residency rights without reference to the collective context in which people live. To see this, consider the difficulty in figuring out what should count as the relevant location in which a people has moral residency rights. It would seem that this at least partly depends on the cultural and institutional context in which people live. Thus, specifying the location of residency rights depends on a further argument about group occupancy rights. For people living in remote or culturally or institutionally distinctive communities, the relevant community might not correspond to the political and institutional demarcations that we commonly think of as relevant in modern, industrialized societies (France, Britain, Canada). There is extensive empirical evidence of this, particularly in the case of isolated indigenous communities who were often relocated within these larger political communities, sometimes for benign reasons—connected to accessing services and opportunities, and, interestingly, many of these individuals were relocated together, where they could still retain relationships—but their way of life required them to live in a particular place. This relocation resulted in dislocation and social problems, as the people found it difficult to adjust to their new environment. This was true of the relocation of Inuit people from Labrador, mainly in 1968 and 1969, which left them unclear about how to get food in this new context, away from their traditional hunting grounds, and so initiated (or deepened) a culture of dependency and dislocation, and social ills. Adaptation was difficult, not because the policy involved the rupture of personal relationships, but because it was closely bound up with the way of life of the people in the community, and it was very difficult, culturally and personally, to adapt to a context in which caribou hunting was not possible; the migratory patterns which the people had been taught were no longer relevant; and people were left without their past cultural resources, unable to adapt to this new, quite different context.[8] Unfortunately, however, similar treatment has been meted out to many other indigenous groups at the hands of insensitive white governments, eager to centralize services, and without regard for the moral rights of the occupants of the communities that are destroyed.[9] A number of different indigenous people in Canada were moved as a community (so that they could retain their social relationships) and relocated to another place, mainly to facilitate the provision of services to these groups.[10] Indeed, the Canadian Royal Commission Study finds that all these relocations resulted in dislocation, increased dependence on government programmes, loss of economic self-sufficiency, social and health problems, and a breakdown of community leadership. The report cites more than twenty-five studies around the world which 'indicate without exception that the relocation, without informed consent, of low-income rural populations with strong ties to their land and homes is a traumatic experience. For the majority of those who have been moved, the profound shock of compulsory relocation is much like the bereavement caused by the death of a parent, spouse or child'.[11]

At this point, an objection might be raised that most people do not have a close, normatively significant relationship to land. The argument works in my example of the Labrador Inuit, who were forcibly displaced from their homes and hunting ground, and for other indigenous people, such as the Haida, whose identities and lives are inextricably linked to their place, and whose homeland (in the Queen's Charlotte Islands off the coast of British Columbia, Canada) is called 'land of the people'. In this case, the homeland defines the people (the

Haida) and the people define the land. Someone might complain, however, that this close connection between groups and land works for a few groups, such as indigenous people, but is not generalizable: it is not true for nomadic people, for example, or for urban dwellers in contemporary liberal democratic states.

I think this objection relies on a very narrow interpretation of what is meant by a relationship between people and land. Bedouin, for example, who, as nomads, might be thought not to have specific locational rights, are in fact nomadic *over a particular area*; they are familiar with the specific features of the landscape, the stars and the location of water-holes, in order to live that particular way of life. Rice farmers sometimes depend on particular rivers and the pattern of flooding and dry season which is integral to their way of life. Residency rights, in other words, are bound up in the projects and aims and way of life to which people are committed, which assume a particular location; and bound up too with the collective identities that people share, which often operate across a certain geographical area.

Even urban people in liberal democratic societies, who would not seem to have an intimate relationship with a particular landscape, do rely for their way of life on a particular cultural, economic, and institutional setting which is located where they live, which cannot be transferred to another institutional setting without loss or disruption. At the minimum, they think of themselves as British or French or Canadian, as the case may be; and there is a certain map-image of what that involves, and a corresponding institutional and political structure which relates to this identity and which defines the location of this collective identity. We should not, however, think of urban liberal democratic peoples as possessing only or even primarily national or statist territorial attachments. For many people, residency rights and occupancy rights apply to much more specific locations and more specific communities. Consider, for example, Africville, an area of Halifax, Nova Scotia, which was populated by freed slaves, by descendants of Black Loyalists, who were promised land in return for fighting on the British side in the American War of Independence, and by descendants of escaped black slaves, who came at a time when the (non-slave-owning) Northern states were required under the terms of the Fugitive Slave Act to return escaped black slaves. The people living in Africville had a deep historic connection to this area of Halifax, marked by relationships with one another which reached back into the past, and a distinct community identity. In 1961 the city of Halifax's Department of Development decided that the community had to be moved in the interests of economic development (expansion of the port and highway interchange serving the bridge). This was opposed by the people who lived in the community, in spite of the fact that they were promised social assistance, job training, employment assistance, and education services. Between 1964 and 1967, most of Africville was destroyed; people were expropriated from their property, forced to move from their homes, and dispersed throughout Halifax. The Africville church, which was at the heart of the community's life, was razed to the ground in the middle of the night in 1969 to avoid protests and rioting. The emotional significance of this neighbourhood and the role that it played in facilitating a community that made its members feel at home in the world was barely considered by the functional mind-set of the Halifax authorities, who dismissed the idea of being attached to a place and failed to recognize the importance of place in facilitating certain kinds of relationships. For the people who lived there, the destruction of their physical community was a real loss: they were dispersed throughout Halifax, where they found it difficult to maintain relationships. Since that time, former members of that community have sought a formal apology for the event and an inquiry into the reasons for the destruction of their community.[12]

This case and others like it illustrate the point that a group's forcible dislocation from the areas in which they live is an egregious wrong: it's not simply that individual rights of residency are violated, but expulsion can be profoundly disruptive to collective identities as people of a particular kind, which in turn is partly defined by the location of the group. Occupancy rights do not mean that people should not under any circumstance be moved, but their occupancy rights have to be taken seriously, and removal needs to be justified by compelling safety or public-good reasons. An account that took place-related attachments seriously would have a different attitude to place and people than the functional and bureaucratic attitude of many governments, interested only in economic development. Moreover, the loss that is experienced when whole groups are expelled from a particular location is not completely captured by the idea of a violation of a right to residency, held by individuals. In this book, I focus on rights of residency and occupancy as foundational to an account of territorial rights, but it's important to note that residency rights and occupancy rights have implications far beyond their role in fixing the geographical location of territorial rights. There are public policy and institutional implications of such rights, including for groups that do not have wide-ranging territorial rights (though they might have some more limited municipal or limited governance rights as a community of interest) or groups who do not meet the criteria of 'peoplehood' but who can nevertheless make a moral occupancy claim to a particular location within the broader political community.

This brings me to the second dimension of a collective occupancy right: this is the interest that members of a community have in controlling the place, the geographical location, which they live in and are attached to. Just as expulsion from a place is disruptive to people's plans and projects and relationships, including relationships to place, so transformation of the place in ways that the person, or the community, does not control, can also make the person insecure and feel not 'at home' in their own community.

Let me clarify the nature of the interest that individuals and groups have in ensuring some stability and security over the place that they live in, and the precise rights that are thereby entailed. First, the interest that people have in ensuring that the location of their community retains a certain character, or has a certain institutional structure, or is stable in some other way, is a defeasible one, and it can potentially clash with other individual and collective rights, such as the right to free movement. But first I want to claim that this interest in stability, in ensuring some element of control over place, can ground some public policies designed to resist non-coercive (market) change. Consider, for example, how an individual right of residency can ground public policy interests in resisting gentrification of neighbourhoods and communities. In many areas—such as London, England, which has experienced large increases in the market value of property—many poor people, who do not own their own homes, find that they face increased rents from landlords, which in turn reflects the increased value of the rented property. This often forces the tenants to move to cheaper locations, which has many undesirable effects: it increases the stress on individuals and families; children have to change schools frequently; the families do not enjoy security in the places that they live; and indeed find it hard to identify with neighbourhoods in which they have just arrived, and which they predict may be short term.[13] If we thought that there were morally significant relationships between people and places, we would be concerned about this dynamic. My analysis of residency rights gives us reason to enact public policies to resist involuntary, market-driven movement: this might mean placing limits on rental increases that landlords can charge to people who already have tenancy in particular location.[14] This doesn't stop gentrification of neighbourhoods entirely, because once long-standing tenants move, landlords are able to charge market-value rents. However, if we take seriously people's place-related interests, including their rights of residency, we have reason to try to limit market forces in ways that protect people's rights to remain in place (residency rights).

The group right of occupancy, and particularly the interest that communities have in retaining control over their physical environment, its character, and institutional structure, also has public policy implications that stretch beyond the rights that attach to individuals in these communities. It suggests for example that groups with occupancy rights in a particular area should have some ability to resist unwelcome change, such as gentrification of their neighbourhood, which can transform the places in which people live in ways that often fail to register. Here we can think of communities that cater to less well-off people, perhaps people without a car, and have local schools and local stores that are accessible by foot or bicycle. Of course, in a market society, which upholds various kinds of liberty rights and market exchanges, there are limits to what the state can do, but there is nevertheless surely a case for appropriate regulation and taxation policies to encourage certain kinds of shops (that is: shops other than ones that serve only luxury items, for well-heeled customers) and that encourages that place to remain one with a particular character, tied in important ways to the community who lives there. This does not mean that the state or the community can prevent certain people from leaving, nor does it generally generate a right to exclude people who do not 'belong' to the neighbourhood, because that would clash with other rights (e.g., rights to freedom of movement). Nevertheless, I argue that a community that has special ties to place—as do indigenous people in their communities, or as the residents of Africville did in Halifax—should be able to exercise some control over the character and shape and physical appearance and structure of the places that they live in, as long as that control is exercised in ways that do not violate rights.

On the argument I present below, one of the necessary conditions for the possession of territorial rights is that the group has occupancy rights over the land. However, occupancy rights can be held by groups that do not possess territorial rights (e.g., rights of jurisdiction, rights of exclusion, and so on): there are indigenous people and people who live in distinctive historical areas that have occupancy rights in a place—defined in terms of members legitimately residing there and the group having a special relationship to place—yet who are not the right kind of group to hold full territorial rights. In the next section, I discuss what kind of group is eligible as a holder of territorial rights. There, I develop an account of the collective agent, the people, which is composed of individuals who enjoy a moral right of residency on the land, and which forms a group that can be said to occupy the territory.

The general picture, then, is not that of a state controlling a homogeneous territory, but of different people, and different communities, having different kinds of interests in place, and different kinds of relations with each other, which the state should recognize and protect. While some groups may enjoy limited forms of occupancy rights without full territorial rights, territorial rights are held by a 'people' which is in the right relation to the land over which it claims jurisdiction: it has occupancy rights on it.[15] Indeed, in the argument that I'm going to develop in the rest of the chapter, occupancy rights are a necessary but not sufficient condition for full territorial rights. We cannot justify rights over place unless people are in the right kind of relation to place to justify jurisdiction over it. And the group has to be the right kind of group to exercise territorial rights. In the next section, I discuss what kind of group ought to hold territorial rights (which, at this stage of the argument, I define purely in terms of rights of jurisdiction).

3.3. Individual and Collective Agency

There are a number of approaches in political and moral philosophy that are sceptical of the idea of collective agency, arguing that collective agents are analytically reducible to the individual agents who comprise the collective. This is not my view. I recognize that individuals are the ones who ultimately live lives, experience value, happiness, and sorrow, and die, and so in the end I adopt a value-individualist position.[16] However, we are not atomistic or isolated individuals. An important part of our moral landscape is the matrix of relationships that we find ourselves in, identities that we share with others, and many of our interests are interests in collective projects and collective relationships. We are parents and children, friends and lovers; we work on common projects with others; and we try to exercise control over the collective conditions of our existence in a variety of ways. Indeed, people often define their lives and the moral conflicts that they face in terms of their relationships with others; and their entitlements, obligations, and dilemmas are often related to demands and values that arise in relationships with others. These represent much of the substance of our social lives. We are situated within identity-conferring groups; we have relationship-dependent interests, and obligations and entitlements not only as individuals but as members of groups. This section offers an account of collective agency that presupposes the importance of these social relationships.

The first step towards loosening the grip of the individualist position is to explain what a collective agent is, without assuming adherence to a problematic metaphysical thesis about group 'being'. I distinguish between arguments for treating a collection of persons as a group, and arguments that suggest that a particular group constitutes a collective agent. Then I examine why a particular collective agent—a people—ought to be the appropriate holder of territorial rights (such as rights of jurisdiction or rights to control boundaries).

There are many different groups that are not corporate or collective *agents*. We can distinguish, for example, between social groups and aggregates. Aggregates are any set of people who share a certain feature—all blue-eyed people, for example, or all people who drive a Volkswagen. These are not important to the argument in this book.

There are other kinds of social groups—such as ethnic groups or classes—which are not mere aggregates but are not collective agents either. Ethnic groups, for example, are social groups, characterized by myths of common descent, some common culture, and mutual recognition, and complex rituals regarding boundary maintenance. They are not aggregates because there is mutual recognition: people are viewed by others as a member of a particular ethnic group, based on such things as their accent or language, last name, or whatever other features are normally germane to the construction of the group and the maintenance of its social boundaries; and the individual partially shares that identity because he or she recognizes that it is ascribed to him/her by others. But an ethnic group is not normally a collective agent, because it lacks mechanisms for making collective decisions or acting jointly.[17] This is also true of other social groups, such as the proletariat or women. (Yet all of these groups *can* transform themselves into collective agents, as I argue below.)

In this book I rely on the idea of 'a people' which I conceive of as a collective agent that is the appropriate holder of territorial rights. The idea of collective agency has been widely discussed in the philosophical literature: most discussions focus on simple two-person examples to show that collective agency is not reducible to individual agency. Consider for example Margaret Gilbert's analysis of a plural subject, which is designed to show that we can think of collective entities as the subject of rights and duties. As she argues, two people who go for a walk together thereby create a collective will in the sense that this activity cannot be fully explicated in terms of person A's intention to walk with B, and B's intention to walk with A. Instead, we should think of it as involving a collective 'we', formed in the joint decision to walk together, which involves forms of cooperation (concerning where to walk, how far to walk, and the pace at which one walks). On this account, the collective is united by what we might call, following Searle, shared 'we' intentions. Like Gilbert, Searle argues that we can distinguish social activity from individual activity in virtue of the presence of 'we' intentions, which, in Searle's work, refers to collective, or shared, intentional states.[18] As an adaptation of Searle, and moving away from the language of 'intentions', we could say that action is collective when individuals conceive of themselves as participating in a plural subject, which may not have a formal group structure.[19] Similarly, Raimo Tuomela argues that groups consist of collections of persons with a shared conception of themselves as 'we' and that they act by way of a special kind of group intention.[20] The most important point, however, in all these accounts is that we can think of a collective 'we' as having collective agency at least in the sense that the actions of the collective are not reducible to the actions of any of the individuals in the group. We do not need to presuppose a metaphysically suspicious appeal to a collective mind over and above the minds of individuals: the 'we' here is created by the intentions and identification and projects of the individual people who are members, but is not reducible to them.

Following from the work of Gilbert, Tuomela, and Searle on collective agency, I use the term 'collective agent' to refer to an entity with two or more members that can perform joint actions. This means that two people dancing the tango can be a collective agent, as well as more conventional examples such as: a soccer team, a university, the board of directors of a company, or a country (state).[21]

The conceptual definition offered here is neutral between intentional accounts of collective agency and more action-orientated accounts, where joint commitment on behalf of a plural subject is at the core of the idea of collective agency. It is also neutral on the question of whether or what kind of responsibility follows from participation in or identity with a collective group, which seems at least partly to depend on the internal decision-making structure of the group in question. However, in order to be a collective agent, the group has to be able to act *as* a group. The decision-making dynamics of the individual members of the group, who are related in complex ways within the group, must be such that the group's decisions may not correspond to the choices the individual members would make when acting independently.[22]

The collective agent—the people—who are the concern of this book are defined in ways that are more demanding in a number of dimensions than Gilbert's account of two people going for a walk. First, the account of joint actions or Tuomela's focus on joint intentions can be episodic: I can engage in joint actions with a neighbour, as when I offer to help him carry a piece of furniture into his house. I can dance a tango with an acquaintance, whom I've never spoken to beyond the dance floor. None of this amounts to a *relationship*, it is only an interaction. The account of a 'people' that I develop in the next section requires more than just collective agency. It requires that the individual members are engaged in a relationship that is temporally extended—both with a history and with (in normal cases) the expectation of a future—and that realizes moral goods intrinsic to that relationship. Furthermore, it views the collective agent as both a holder of rights and a subject of duties.

Precisely because the concept of collective agent in the Gilbert or Tuomela and Searle accounts is defined minimally, it is not clear that their account can justify associative *duties*. Consider for example Gilbert's contention that rights and obligations follow from the very simple collective agency example of two people going for a walk together. Gilbert argues that joint actions, which are central to her account of collective agency, can give rise to rights and duties: she says that I could rightly complain if my walking companion refuses to adjust his pace to mine, or dashes off in his own direction.[23] It is, however, not at all clear that this is so: it is hard to see how this gives rise to a duty proper, which implies both relative stringency and enforceability, unless we presuppose that he and I have also engaged in some kind of duty-generating activity such as making a promise. If my walking partner decides that he no longer wishes to walk with me, it is not at all clear that I can require performance of the duty rather than something weaker, such as giving me an explanation if he changes his mind (and even then, it seems that this explanation is required if we have a relationship marked by respect, rather than a duty that specifically flows from our walking together).[24]

By contrast, families constitute collective agents, and parents and children are in a temporally extended *relationship* with each other in which children are dependent on parents, which gives rise to a number of duties and entitlements. And these duties and entitlements emerge from the relationship because they are central to realizing the moral value—the relationship goods—which is implicit in the relationship. Of course some of these goods are generic goods: children need to be looked after, clothed, housed, and so on. But in addition, they need this form of love and care *from significant others* in their lives: it advances their relationship with their parents, and parent's relationship with their children, if this particular kind of concern marks the relationship. Food and clothes are an important interest, to be sure, but the kind of intimacy that is typical of families can be enhanced by ensuring that it is the parents that meet these needs of the children, and especially their other relationship-specific needs, such as having someone who loves and cares in particular for them, and with whom they are in intimate relations.

Relying on the contrast just drawn between mere collective agency and a genuine relationship, I will argue later in this chapter that 'a people' is also more than just a collective agent; its members are in a temporally extended relationship with each other, which carries with it a number of important relationship-dependent goods.

3.4. Who Should Hold Territorial Rights?

This brings me to the question of what kind of collective agent can hold robust jurisdictional rights over territory.

Before I begin, an important caveat is in order: in the introduction, and throughout this book, I do not assume that there is one territorial right and one corresponding right-holder. That is a neat picture, and it does seem to be suggested by the argument of this chapter, which examines which entity, which collective agent, ought to hold territorial rights. However, it prompts an important question. I made clear earlier that I hold a 'bundle' account of territorial rights: like property, territory should not be thought of as a single right (with a corresponding single right-holder) but a complex bundle of claims, liberties, powers, and immunities. This means, potentially at least, that there might be more than one holder of territorial right in the same geographical area (which is certainly the case in any federal system, where jurisdictional competences are parcelled out to different levels), and different rights could have different right-holders; they could be held appropriately at different levels, by different collective agents. At this point of the argument, for the sake of simplicity, I focus on the right to robust forms of jurisdictional authority over territory, and when I ask what kind of entity or collective agent ought to hold territorial right, and compare it with rival accounts, I am assuming that the scope of discussion is confined to the jurisdictional authority. I will address the question later of the relationship between that right (and right-holder) and the other rights that we tend to associate with rights over territory. The focus of the argument here is on the appropriate collective agent for holding and exercising jurisdictional rights, which I argue is a 'people'.

I conceive of a 'people' as a collective agent that meets the following three conditions. First, they must share a conception of themselves as a group—they subjectively identify with co-members, in terms of either being engaged, or desiring to be engaged, *in a common political project* and they are mobilized in actions orientated towards that goal.[25] Second, they must have the capacity to establish and maintain political institutions, through which they can exercise self-determination. Third, the people have a history of political cooperation together; we can identify objective and historically rooted bonds of solidarity, forged by their relationships directed at political goals or within political practices.

Why are these necessary conditions? The first is a necessary condition for the kind of collective agent that can be the subject of duties and holder of rights. A group must be able to make decisions and act on the basis of a sense of themselves as a group. 'Peoplehood', as distinct from other social groups or types of collective agents, is defined not simply in terms of a shared 'we', but by a relationship marked by a shared aspiration to exercise collective self-government. There is an explicitly political dimension, then, to this first condition: the people are united by an aspiration for wide-ranging powers of jurisdictional authority or political control over the territory. They are not organized simply on behalf of a particular goal or particular practice, but to exercise a comprehensive set of territorial rights that we associate with collective self-government.[26]

Second, the group in question must have the *capacity* for political self-determination. There are, however, two ways in which we could think of the 'capacity' requirement. We could think of it as a blocking condition in cases where groups lack capacity, lack an essential precondition, and where this lack cannot be corrected except by unjust measures. Or we could think of failure to meet the capacity condition as giving rise to duties of assistance on the part of third parties. What do I mean by 'lacking capacity' in the first (blocking) sense? Think of the requirement that the group has to be territorially concentrated in an area that it legitimately occupies. I have discussed the idea of legitimate occupancy earlier but here I deploy it as a requirement that the group must meet, to make good its claim to political capacity. Territorial concentration is a necessary precondition for the exercise of territorial forms of collective self-determination. In the current world order, where all usable land is divided between territorial right-holders, that problem cannot be solved easily, except by aggressing on existing territorial right-holders, expelling them from land that is currently occupied. The capacity condition is meant to exclude such landless groups from the exercise of territorial rights.

However, we might think of 'capacity' more broadly: to refer to a predicted and/or demonstrated ability to exercise self-determination and maintain effective forms of governance. In cases where a group occupies land but it is not large enough or is in some way insufficient to be viable as an independent state, the group also lacks capacity, although they may have enough 'capacity' to support forms of collective self-determination within a larger state.

Other kinds of lack of capacity—perhaps lack of state infrastructure or dire poverty—could be corrected by third-party assistance to help the group exercise jurisdictional authority over the area. Lack of capacity in this sense does not necessarily represent a blocking condition; it suggests that we may have third-party duties to ensure that the group is provided with the means to exercise effective governance, if these duties could be discharged without perpetrating injustice.

Behind this discussion of 'capacity' or lack thereof is a worry that capacity could be used inappropriately as a blocking condition in cases where 'capacity' refers to a judgement about the possession of qualities or characteristics that the group ought to have. It would be deeply problematic if capacity were used as a blocking condition in such cases, in part for reasons emphasized by James Scott: even well-intentioned members of dominant groups have difficulty interpreting accurately groups over whom they wield power because there are situational barriers to gaining good information about such groups.[27] This is one of the reasons why interpreting 'capacity' in terms of the possession of particular characteristics or qualities that are purportedly relevant to good governance practices may give scope for problematic 'Orientalizing' or imperialist assumptions about the group in question.[28]

However, there may be some kinds of disadvantages from which a group suffers that impact on its ability to be collectively self-governing, without suggesting that the group is *incapable* of governing itself. Relative poverty or poor infrastructure are disadvantages in this category. (Rawls, in *The Law of Peoples*, describes these as 'burdens' suffered by non-aggressive societies who lack appropriate resources, infrastructure, technology, or traditions to be well ordered.[29]) On my view, if the group meets the other conditions for a people—that is, they seek to be collectively self-determining, they are territorially concentrated on land that they occupy legitimately, and they have a history of political action or relationships involving political cooperation or political mobilization—then the appropriate response to their being burdened is not to deny them the right of self-determination but to assist them in overcoming burdens so that they can realize their legitimate aspirations.

In some cases, however, the group's lack of capacity cannot be met through (just) assistance: in that case, the group cannot have territorial rights: and the reason for this is that they will be unable to realize the moral value associated with collective self-determination. This may mean that the group is entitled to internal forms of self-determination, within a local or regional entity or forms of power-sharing for groups that seek to exercise self-determination but cannot do so on their own, with a full set of territorial rights.

The third condition is that the members of the group have a history of joint action, of mobilization in terms of political goals or projects. A 'people' that is entitled to exercise collective self-determination (over a territory) is not a collection of individuals, but a group whose shared identity has been forged and maintained by actual historical relations—such as a history of sharing a substate unit or a history of political mobilization against an oppressive colonial state. The territorial right-holder should be characterized by group solidarities that spring from a valuable history of shared political association, which will be important not only in creating the moral bonds between group members but also in forging a shared collective world where people's interests and lives are intertwined such that it makes sense for members of that group to be collectively self-determining in shaping the collective conditions of their existence.[30] Many different forms of political cooperation can be important to creating a 'people'.[31]

There are two dimensions to this third condition. The first is the requirement that the identity should be rooted in a valuable history of shared practices and relations. Historically extended cooperation is important because the exercise of jurisdictional authority over a territory requires more than a will, more than the hope and sentiment that self-government could be exciting or interesting. A past history of cooperative practices provides evidence about the likelihood of productive future cooperation. It is also relevant because continuity is valuable: past cooperation provides an important basis from which future cooperation can proceed, in establishing processes that are deemed to be fair and have been worked out historically, from which political power can be exercised. Relationships of cooperation also help to reduce disagreement because they often involve working out an understanding of the priority relations among normative principles, and this might also be important in establishing good governance practices.

This historical dimension is important because it indicates that there is a morally important *relationship* in place, not just the presence of subjective aspirations. Through shared ties and cooperative practices, we develop moral bonds which structure our relationship. For example, in a cooperative practice characterized by reciprocity over time, we develop duties which we would not have had in the absence of that relationship, and some of these are the sort of duties that are important in embarking on and maintaining a political project. It requires that we think of people as engaged in a joint project with us, and this project as generating obligations, and the relationship with these people as also giving rise to entitlements and obligations.

The second element, in addition to the historical dimension, is that the group solidarities should spring from *political* associations, though not necessarily from governance in a shared political project. What is special about political associations, which is not found in other kinds of solidaristic communities? The answer is that political mobilization involves the aspiration to form a political community that creates and maintains rules to govern all people within the unit;[32] and this should involve not simply the institutionalization of one dimension of life (e.g., religion) on all aspects of life, but the kind of cooperation and compromise that is implicit in modes of political self-determination, where people from a wide range of backgrounds and with different conceptions of the good are nevertheless prepared to cooperate and compromise in the creation of and maintenance of rules to govern their lives.

While the first dimension emphasizes the need for ongoing solidarity, the second suggests that there is something special about *political* solidarity, that is, solidarity arising from a shared conception of the group as engaged in a common political project. It suggests that political relations are different from family and religious relationships because they involve a relation of coequals subject to and creating a common political power. This is appropriate to the kind of cooperation and especially compromise that is needed in territorial self-governance projects, where people are likely to disagree about values, projects and priorities. It is not necessary that everyone aim at the same end or have the same values, but it is important that they all share a common interest in making the political association and institutions work.

On this three-part definition (political aspirations, political capacity, political history), a number of social groups count as 'peoples'. It includes those living in an already existing state, who have institutions of government and who value these institutions, and want to maintain them. It includes those who for various (cultural or historical or geographic) reasons seek to exercise self-government amongst themselves (as indigenous peoples, or decolonized peoples), have the ability to do so, and have a history of shared relations and ties together forged by political cooperation. Indeed, in many cases—as with indigenous people in the Americas—the group has experienced a history of subjugation and marginalization at the hands of the demographically dominant group in the state, and the relationship of equality and intertwined interests that we might associate with co-citizenship is absent. In such cases we would expect the relevant (indigenous) people to mobilize on behalf of their own collective self-determination, and to be entitled to territorial rights if they are in the appropriate relationship to land and meet the three criteria.

3.5. The Concept of a 'People'

In this section, I argue that the concept of a 'people' can explain how one 'people' can be distinguished from another (call this the 'individuation condition'); how a people can be identified over time (call this the 'continuity condition'); and how a people can change over time while still remaining the same people (call this the 'change condition'). I also argue that this concept avoids essentializing assumptions and can explain why a people so defined would value jurisdictional authority.[33]

It is an important element of a theory of a collective agent that it contains a criterion of individuation: that it enables us to distinguish between different collective agents. The individuation condition in my account of a 'people' is identity-based: it examines who is a 'people' by looking at self-identification, and in particular whether people have *political identities* as people of a certain kind, identities as members of groups that aspire to create or continue to maintain shared rules and procedures together. This identity typically has both subjective and objective elements: individual members often have political identities—they think of themselves as French or Ojibway, Kurdish or Brazilian or Canadian, whatever the case may be, and they are recognized by others as having this identity. Even if you do not wish to be regarded as a Kurd, for example, others may regard you as one, by looking at various elements that are associated with that particular identity—language, last name, and so on. This is true of all sorts of identities—ethnic identities,[34] gender identities, and so on—but is I think also true of political identities, by which I mean group-based identities, the content of which is centred on an aspiration to be politically self-governing. Thus a Kurdish identity in Canada (as a Kurdish-Canadian) is different from a Kurdish identity in Iraq (which typically involves the idea that the group should be politically self-governing, either within a larger Iraq or in a separate political unit).

The relationship between subjective and objective dimensions of identity is exceedingly complex. It has been theorized by Iris Young in relation to the idea of *throwness* of identities: the idea is that identities are not purely subjective phenomena. If I walk into a room and do not identify as a woman but everyone looking at me thinks that I am a woman, I am still subject to the assumptions, discrimination, and objectification that is involved in belonging to that identity category, even if I do not think of that as a primary or important identity for me.[35] The idea of 'throwness' refers to the fact that most identities have to be ratified by others: there is a limit to the identities that are genuinely available to one, and some identities are difficult to escape. This is not simply the point that the identities that one comes to have are partly the product of involuntary socialization and education by others—I think all identities may be described this way—but in the much deeper sense that identities depend, to a large extent, on how others see one and identify one.

Are both subjective and objective identity conditions required? This is a difficult question. It is certainly true that subjective identification is a necessary condition for having an identity of a certain kind. Collective identities in particular are experienced by their bearers as relatively fixed and are clustered around quite predictable axes and in quite predictable groups: they are a stable sociological feature of particular communities. In the typical case, membership in the group can be generally recognized by outsiders, and is subjectively affirmed by the person him or herself. However, in some cases, and especially for groups seeking political self-determination as a group of a particular kind, the existence of the group is subject to contestation. Consider, for example, the persistent claim by members of the Turkish elite that the Kurdish population in their country, largely concentrated in the southeast, is not a separate 'people' but they are just 'mountain Turks', by which they meant Turkish people with some distinctive cultural elements because they lived in the mountains. This view was not shared by the Kurds themselves. This is meant to illustrate the point that requiring that an identity be generally recognized by others in order to count as an identity can, as in this case, serve to make people's own identities, and claims for recognition, hostage to other groups who have assimilationist impulses, or who seek to deny recognition to the identity. For this reason, I think that subjective identity is a necessary and sufficient condition for having an identity of a particular kind: individual subjective identity is required for individual identities and group subjective identities for group identities. In most cases, these identities will be confirmed by objective recognition, and people often find that this objective conferring of an identity makes the identity unavoidable for them, as Young noted.

Shared subjective identity serves to distinguish one group from another: it performs an individuation function. This does not mean that every group that sees itself as a people is a 'people', or can claim the rights of peoplehood. Rather, the idea is that when the identity condition is met, and people see themselves as people of a particular kind, we can then look backwards to see if the identity is supported by relationships of the right kind, and these are important to explaining both the continuity and the change condition.

3.5.1. Continuity, Change, and Relationships

Although the individuation condition is subjective self-identification, the explanation for why people are a people of a certain kind, both in the sense of how they came to possess a certain kind of identity, and in the sense of how that identity is maintained, centres on the relationships that exist between those who have a political identity as a particular people. These relationships are a necessary condition for peoplehood, and play a vital role in explaining two crucial elements that any concept of group agency should be able to explain: the group's continuity over time, and how the group can change over time while remaining the same group. I will argue below that they help to explain why people seek control of the group destiny, and connect the idea of a people to the aspiration for collective self-determination.

Once groups see themselves as a group of a particular kind—as a 'people' say, who aspire to collective self-government—the next step is to examine the relationships among the people who claim this identity. In many cases, these relationships have been mediated by shared subjection to common institutions, such as common political, religious, or other kinds of formative institutions. People are in many different (kinds of) relationships with different people, so relationships themselves do not help us to distinguish between different groups or different 'peoples'. Consider even a simple case, where all the people in an area have been subject to the rule of an imperial authority and so are all related together within this institutional structure. However, there have been diverse reactions to this shared subjection: some people who have been so subjected to the imperial order have identified with it, whereas others have resisted it. While all are enveloped within the institutional relationship (under the imperial order) there are two different political groups, based on two different sorts of political aspirations; one, acceptance of and assimilation to the subjecting order, the others, mobilization against it. The divergent response to their experience under imperialism has given rise to two distinct political identities. It is also a further condition that these political identities have to be supported by a network of shared political relationships. But here the important thing to note is that the relationships do not perform an individuating function, since in this example all the people were in the same overarching political relationship.

It is worth reflecting at some length on why relationships within an institutional context, such as subjection to common institutions, cannot be the mechanism by which we *individuate* groups. Someone might object to my argument above by noting that in fact a relationship account *can* distinguish between the two groups without recourse to identity, because presumably people in a resistance movement against imperialism will be related to each other in ways that are distinct from the supporters of the imperial order. Moreover, in many cases, in order to distinguish groups, we do look at institutional demarcations, common subjection, and the relationships that are so created, without examining identities, which seem somehow connected to a mental state. Consider the case of Scots, who see themselves as Scottish because they are in a relationship structured by Scottish institutions, which have been distinct from England prior to and even since the Act of Union in 1707. That would suggest an account of group continuity, focused not on the individual but on the common institutions to which people are subject.[36]

One serious problem that would face a pure relationship account (where relationships are used to satisfy the individuation condition) is tracking how many relationships (or institutionally mediated relationships within formative institutions) would have to be shared to count as being a distinct group or people, and, related to this, how important the relationship or the shared institution within which they are related would have to be to either group identity or resulting group behaviour. What if members of group A share three formative institutions and so have institutionally mediated relationships with members of group B, but there are three other formative institutions that they do not share with members of group B? Are they members of the same group in virtue of being related within three formative institutions? Or are they members of two distinct groups, group A and group B, which overlap to some extent? Does every non-shared formative institution yield a different group? There are two dimensions here, obviously. One is the number of relationships within formative institutions that have to be shared to count as belonging to the same group and the other is the importance (in 'formative influence' terms) of the institutionally mediated relationships in question. I cannot rule out the possibility of an empirical analysis of this problem, some kind of sliding scale which will give us a partially or completely determinate answer. However, I suspect that to answer this question plausibly we already have to have in mind an idea of a particular kind of group which shares an identity as As or Bs, and then we can trace backwards to see how many institutionally mediated relationships within formative institutions they shared (and which are explanatory of their identity as As). If this is so, then, the crucial element to individuate groups is identity, not the relationships developed within a shared institutional structure.

The focus on relationships and common subjection to institutions is an important element of the identity account in that it explains the factors underlying group mobilization and reinforcing group identity. We need to rely on an identity theory of individuation, but these identities are formed by and/or reinforced through people's relationships with others, and in particular, in the case of political identities, by relationships that are typically institutionally structured and institutionally mediated. On this view, a central or defining feature of a 'people' is the political identity that they share, but the relationship account offers a very good *explanation* of the relationship between group identity and of social relationships between people that underlie and reinforce those identities.

Moreover, the idea of people being in control of their relationships has an important role to play in explaining both group continuity and change. To see this, consider the example of Quebec, which changed rapidly during the 1960s Quiet Revolution, from a largely agrarian, Catholic society, characterized by largely conservative values, to a more urban, secular society, with values dominated by linguistic and political nationalism and a commitment to social justice.[37] How can we explain the continuity of the group while at the same time acknowledging the very rapid transformation of many of its defining characteristics? An identity-based criterion and the relationships that support that identity help to explain group continuity: the people, who are changing rapidly, are related together in ways that enable them to control change, to adapt to it, to negotiate different kinds of responses. They are able to change, often in significant ways, while remaining the same (identity) group. Once people are mobilized to think of themselves as people of a certain kind—in this case, being Québécois is the salient political identity—this identity can remain constant even while members of the group are subject to unremitting cultural, linguistic, or value change. We do not need to associate rapid social and cultural change with changes in identity, nor associate groups with essential features or characteristics that hold them together. People in a particular identity group will experience change as non-threatening if they have the mechanisms to negotiate the change.

We can see this point also by examining the opposite case, where groups (rightly) felt that they had no control over the processes of their socialization. In contrast to Quebec during the Quiet Revolution, many indigenous people in Canada were taken from their homes and subject to residential schooling, where they were prevented from speaking their language and practicing their religion and way of life. This attempt at assimilation was unsuccessful: they could not regard the new culture as theirs; they experienced this cultural transformation as cultural *loss*, but none of this changed their identity as indigenous people. The new (white) culture, which the residential schools were designed to teach, was not available to them, in part because of racism on the part of the dominant white society, but also because, as I've argued elsewhere, it is very difficult to adopt the identity of the group and embrace the way of life of a group that has stolen from you and dominated you.[38] Since indigenous people were not in control of any of the mechanisms by which they were able to transmit their way of life to new generations or to newcomers, they could regard these practices and institutions only as the imposition of an alien way of life, rather than as simple culture change. Moreover the cultural change or loss did not impact on the identity markers, since group distinctiveness was not defined in terms of the possession of cultural features x or y or z but by the possession of a particular identity. While of course all identities do have some markers to distinguish insiders from outsiders, these can change as the group itself changes. This example supports the argument above by suggesting the following: (1) group identity is the crucial individuating element; (2) relationships amongst people in an identity group are important supports for these identities; (3) identities can remain constant even in the face of striking cultural or other kinds of changes; and (4) the relationships between people should be structured in such a way that the people feel that they are in control of their own destiny. At the heart of this example is the insight that collective control is important to the capacity to appropriate elements from other cultures and ways of life without feeling that this threatens the group itself.

3.6. Four Criticisms of the Above Conception of 'People'

In this section, I consider four criticisms of the above conception of 'people'. The first two suggest that it is under-inclusive; that it unfairly excludes some groups from exercising territorial rights. The third criticism suggests the opposite, that it is over-inclusive and leads to an account that endorses too many, incompatible territorial right-holders. The fourth criticism presses on the relationship between individual interests and group interests, individual rights and group rights.

The first two criticisms are concerned that my conception of 'peoples' excludes groups that should be included. One version holds that such groups have been oppressed in the past; as a result, they no longer possess any territory, and it is unfair to deprive them of rights that they would otherwise have on this basis. Another version is that either oppressed groups cannot mobilize or the members of these groups have developed adaptive preferences as a result of prior unjust treatment, and, as a result of adaptive preferences, they do not seek self-determination as a group because their circumstances are such that this seems hopeless. It might be argued that this is both unfair and gives rise to perverse incentives.

It is true that the requirement that a territorial right-holding group must occupy a territory seems to exclude groups that have been treated unjustly in the past and have had their territory taken from them. The concern is that this is unfair; that it begins from an unfair starting point. This is a serious worry, which I will postpone until chapter 7. I argue there that that would represent a serious injustice—a denial of their individual residency rights, their collective occupancy rights, and their rights of self-determination. There is a strong case for corrective justice in such cases, and I also try there to address the further criticism that this requirement could give rise to a perverse incentive (to steal territory).[39]

The second, unfairness criticism can be interpreted in two different ways. On one interpretation, what is unfair is that the very definition of a people may exclude groups that have the aspiration for collective self-determination but are too oppressed to demonstrate it. Here the problem seems to be partly an evidentiary one. The conception of the group in question is not ascriptive, and so requires some evidence of will or mobilization. I do not confine the evidence of an aspiration to exercise collective self-determination to the results of democratic elections, for that *would* be deeply unfair: oppressed groups typically do not have the democratic means to make their aspirations known. There are, however, other mechanisms of resistance that oppressed groups, seeking self-determination, can employ. I am doubtful that there are cases where there is no evidence at all of any such aspiration, while at the same time the group is actually characterized by these aspirations.

It is, however, possible that an oppressed group does not have the aspiration to self-determination and that the explanation for this is that people have adapted to their oppressed state. On this interpretation, they have adapted to their oppression, just as a housewife in a patriarchal society may have preferences to keep her house clean, to make sure her husband is happy and his meals are cooked properly. The adaptive-preference criticism suggests that, because preferences are often formed in relation to unfair social contexts, preferences should not be taken as morally basic.

My response to this criticism is that it is not part of my argument that people must be self-determining as group X rather than as a part of another group, Y, as long as group Y is one in which they can also be collectively self-determining in the sense outlined here. This means that relying on an existing aspiration to collective self-determination is not analogous to the standard (oppressed housewife) case of adaptive preferences, because the aspirations in question are only directed at *which* self-determining group the individuals are members in, not the basic entitlement to be part of a self-determining collective group.

A third, and in a way opposite, criticism is that the definition of 'peoples' is too capacious, that it could potentially be met by people defined by states, people who belong to indigenous groups, people who comprise minority nations, people who have organized into a enduring resistance movement against imperialism. I agree that the definition of 'peoples' is capacious; indeed it is meant to be so. There are things about living together under a shared institutional structure that explain why people have the identities and aspirations and relationships that they do, but living together in a state is not fundamental at the justificatory level and so my definition could potentially extend to groups that are not defined by states or state-like institutions. Cultural groups, which share a language or religion or cultural patterns, may also seek to be collectively self-determining, and meet the other requirements for jurisdictional rights. This means that the conclusion of my argument may be aligned with the judgements that a cultural nationalist would make, mainly because culture also is an important axis of national group membership, on which peoplehood can be based. But again this is an explanation for why the group has developed a collective identity of a certain kind, not a justificatory argument for the group's exercise of jurisdictional rights. The same is true of indigenous groups or people who have united together over time to fight for independence against imperialism. All these different types of groups are potential territorial right-holders.

Is the account *too* capacious? To address this worry, note that the 'capacity' condition and the shared history of cooperation condition together have the effect of reducing the number of territorial right-holders. It is not sufficient simply to aspire to be collectively self-determining; members of the group must be in a temporally extended relationship with one another which involves political cooperation. Moreover, since creating and maintaining political institutions, rights, and rules is a non-trivial matter, it is important that the group has the capacity to perform the necessary functions of government. This means that a group with limited capacity cannot acquire the full set of territorial rights, but have more limited forms of self-determination, consistent with the group's capacity, including its ability to defend itself. This is justified in terms of realizing the moral goods or moral value of self-determination.

However, this still leaves the problem of whether my account will fail to determine who is the appropriate territorial right-holder when different groups each claim rights over the very same territory on the grounds that they are a people. I postpone discussion of this issue until chapter 6, where it is treated at length.

Finally, my account might be criticized for ignoring the rights and claims of individuals who do not share the political identities and political aspirations of the group, but who live within the territory of a political community. Call this the problem of the individual dissenter. The critic could claim that my account seems to assume that all residents of a contiguous area share the same broad political identity and political aspirations. In response, let me make begin by emphasizing that I do not assume that all individuals share in the same political identity. I have argued that territorial rights are the kind of rights that are held by collectives, not by individuals. Other rights are rights held by individuals: I have elaborated on the individual moral right of residency; and I also think that all people have basic human rights, such as the right not to be tortured, a right to a decent life, and so on. Since territorial rights are collective, the individual is not the bearer of such rights, so the individual is not being denied a right simply by not having territorial rights extended to him/her.

Perhaps, though, we can reinterpret this criticism. Perhaps what underlies this objection is an anarchist or libertarian position on the justifiability of coercive political authority. On my account, while a people (conceived as a non-statist group) are the fundamental holders of territorial rights, they can be so only by erecting a common political authority, and so creating a political order that implements common rules to regulate their lives together, and it is this aspect of territorial rights that is being objected to. It is the libertarian or anarchist worry that political authority is unjustified or unjustifiable, that it is inherently coercive, a violation of basic freedom, and could be justified only by the consent of the individual himself or herself, a position that only the individualist Lockean account of territory adequately incorporates. There are two things to be said to this underlying worry. First, the account I've been presenting is an account of how territorial rights arise, not an account of how political authority over individuals arises. There is a rich debate in the political-obligation literature that is designed to address the anarchist objection, and I am on the side of those who think that political authority can be justified.[40] The problem of individual dissenters is a problem only if we believe that for a political authority to be justified it must achieve unanimous consent—a condition which no state achieves and no state is likely to achieve—but this is not a position that I hold. Indeed, I believe that it is only by erecting a political authority that subjects everyone to the same rules that we can achieve the conditions in which no agent is dominating another. To the extent that this objection stems from a worry about the justification of political authority itself, it is based on a misunderstanding of my project, which is focused on how territorial rights arise.

3.7. The Value of Collective Self-Determination of Peoples

The key elements in my account of the 'people' are its focus on (1) group-based identities (2) that are based on relationships between people which persist over time and are conceived of as valuable, and therefore give rise to moral reasons for action, and (3) that involve aspirations to control the basic institutions that govern the collective conditions and physical location of people's lives. In this final section of this chapter, I explain and justify why collective control over institutional life is important to collective identities and connect this to jurisdictional authority over territory in the case of a 'people'. The right of self-determination of peoples is enshrined in article 1, paragraph 2, and article 55 of the United Nations Charter.[41] I assume however that there is also a moral (not merely legal) right to collective self-determination. This is connected to the moral value implicit in the relationship that obtains among a 'people', which depends in part on the kind of relationship that it is. To explain why political self-determination is important, I need to begin by saying something about personal relationships generally, and the special value that they create.

Relationships imply enduring interactions that are substantive in content and mutual in the sense that they are orientated to the other participants in the relationship.[42] This is true of friendship and the various things that friends do together. It is also true of participants in the relationship that I have termed 'peoplehood' because this requires both subjective definition or subjective identity as a member of the group, recognition of others as also engaged in or aspiring to be engaged in a political project with one, and actions orientated towards achieving that end, or sustaining that relationship, in cases where the group already enjoys substantial institutional self-government.

Participants in relationships are active agents: they maintain relationships through their actions. There are often significant goods in relationships, so that participants are not just agents but also beneficiaries. Significant relationship goods are coproduced by the relationship and often partly constitutive of the relationship. Following Seglow, there are two kinds of relationship goods: relationship-independent goods and relationship-dependent goods.[43] These correspond to the interests that the relationship serves. Relationship-independent interests are interests that a person has, which require some kind of relationship to be met, but do not require that the relationship is with a particular person or set of persons. Children have relationship-independent interests in being cared for and clothed and educated; these are not interests they can meet on their own, so whether these interests are met often depends on the child's relationship with significant others, usually parents, in their lives. However, a child's interests in food, shelter, and clothing could be met by another party.[44] Similarly, a group's interest in being governed by a rule-governed procedure and/or institution, in which human rights are respected and people are treated impartially, is a relationship-independent interest: it is an interest that can be met only within a political and legal organization, but it does not require that the relationship is with particular people or groups of people. Most justifications of the state are of this kind, pointing to the various interests that are served by the creation of a rule-governed political order.

Some of the moral value embedded in relationships reflects our relationship-dependent interests. These are goods which are distinctive to the relationship itself. While children can be fed and housed and clothed by anyone, it enhances the parent–child relationship if that someone is a parent, if that kind of care and concern is exemplified by the parent for the child. Think of relationships that realize the following intrinsic goods or benefits: love, intimacy, mutual affection, concern, just the sheer joy sometimes of spending time together. In many of our relationships—think here of intimate relationships or close friendships—goods can be realized only by particular others, and cannot be met satisfactorily by assigning a substitute. I cannot pay someone to be a confidante to my friend, if she wants to talk to me about some pressing concern and I am very busy; presumably she wants to confide in me. The good of intimacy cannot also be met by asking an acquaintance to be physically intimate with my lover; or to visit my sick mother in hospital. Hopefully both want to be intimate with *me* and visited by *me*.

There are analogies here with the kind of relationship that constitutes peoplehood, for this involves not simply creating rules of justice, but doing so with particular others—co-citizens, co-nationals, other indigenous people—with whom I have an ongoing commitment and a shared collective identity, as a member of a particular people. There are a number of moral values connected to the relationship, not only the relationship-independent interests that we can think of, which are realized by the creation of a just state order, but other kinds of agency goods, which are achieved by shared activities and by co-creating the rules and practices that govern the collective conditions of their lives together.

The relationships that mark both aspirant and realized political communities are morally valuable in part because they are characterized by agency goods. They are spaces in which members co-create their own political project and together implement their own conception of justice. Institutions of political self-determination give expression to the communities in which people live; they express people's identities; and they are an important forum in which collective autonomy can be expressed, and people can shape the context in which they live, and realize their political aspirations, free of external domination.

The moral value of self-determination does not inhere in the fact that through it people create objective justice, although sometimes they do, and when they do, that is an additional good. But I've also emphasized that, in addition to relationship-independent goods, there are relationship-dependent agency goods: the process of making the rules that govern a people's collective existence is itself morally valuable. People who exercise collective self-government have the institutional mechanisms to shape the conditions of their existence, and their future together, and are thereby more autonomous— or experience a different (collective) dimension of autonomy than is involved in most liberal accounts of autonomy, which are mainly focused on protecting autonomy through protecting the individual private sphere.

The reason why collective autonomy is valuable mirrors some of the considerations or arguments underlying the value of personal autonomy, as one would expect, given that it too is an agency good. The central ideal of personal autonomy is that people should make their own life, and control their own destiny, shaping the course of their life through successive decisions over its course.[45] Of course this central idea of control is difficult to operationalize: what counts as enough control to be autonomous? It is usually thought that personal autonomy requires an adequate range of choices, though not the existence of any particular choice, and that most choices do close off some options and open up some others, and that this is fine, as long as the agent is in a position, at various stages of his or her life, to make decisions from among this acceptable range. If we have only personal autonomy but no say in the collective conditions in which we live, and among which our options are made, then it's clear that the extent to which we are in control of our life is diminished. If it is valuable for the individual to be in control of his or her life, then it is also valuable to have control as a member of a collective, in which the collective itself has a range of powers from which to choose. We do not need to endorse personal autonomy to see that collective autonomy is valuable but certainly if we do think that individual control over the shape of his or her life is important, then this holds, not only in the narrower, private sphere, but also in our capacity to affect decisions, and to participate in a collective group that itself exercises control, and has the capacity to shape the broader canvas from which we make choices.

Collective autonomy is realized through institutional mechanisms, such as a state or state-like structure. On my account of the territorial right-holder, a people is a collective agent that has persisted over time, in which the interactions of its members have sufficient continuity that the people see themselves as participants in an ongoing political relationship with one another, and share a political identity as members of a group. In relatively large-scale groups it is often hard to maintain these relationships and group-based identities without institutional mechanisms of control and decision making, and especially control over the institutional mechanisms by which group identities are reproduced and group boundaries are maintained. Through making decisions within the institutional structure, a people can realize the moral value of collective freedom or collective self-determination.

3.8. Conclusion

In this chapter, I set out a collective self-determination theory of territorial rights, in which territorial rights are attached to a non-statist group that I call the 'people'. One aim of this chapter has been to address the attachment problem, that is, to explain how particular states can legitimately exercise territorial rights over a particular area of land. It did this by identifying the kind of group that can be the ultimate source of territorial rights.

Stated formally, the argument of the chapter is as follows:

1. State S holds territorial rights by acting as a vehicle of self-determination of group G.
2. Group G is a group of the right kind to be the ultimate source of territorial rights.
3. Group G legitimately occupies territory T (territory here understood as geographical space).

Therefore, state S legitimately holds territorial rights over territory T.

To defend this argument, I explained what's involved in a group occupying T, why physical presence is important, and the kind of relationships that can develop between a people in a group, and between people and land. I also argued that not every group that is in occupancy of territory is the 'right kind' of group to hold territorial rights, and I defined the group in terms of the possession of three conditions: political identity, political capacity, and political history. I showed why this is the right kind of group, argued that it is distinct from either a statist account or a cultural account, and suggested that these elements are both important for the exercise of territorial rights, and that territorial rights (rights that attach to the group to exercise jurisdictional authority over that territory) are morally valuable.

In the next two chapters, I extend my argument for this theory of territorial rights by showing, through a comparative examination, that it avoids the problems associated with the two other prominent accounts of territorial right-holders: cultural nationalist accounts and statist accounts.

Notes

1. Historical arguments often fail this test. One problem is which point in history one begins from and takes as authoritative for the purpose of adjudicating rival claims to territory. Historical arguments will fail this test if they are framed in terms of a direct appeal to a particular version of history, where the salience of particular events is determined in a way that is internal to the particular group's perspective. They have to be constrained by the

recognition that there is often a problem of disagreement about history itself, and rival claims, so the justification has to be one that all people can understand at least in general terms.

2. For a typology of 'territorial rights', see Simmons, 'On the Territorial Rights of States', 300–326.

3. Cited in Michael Walzer, *Spheres of Justice: A Defense of Pluralism and Equality* (New York: Basic Books, 1983), 43.

4. David Miller, *National Responsibility and Global Justice* (Oxford: Oxford University Press, 2007), 217; Tamar Meisels, 'Liberal Nationalism and Territorial Rights', *Journal of Applied Philosophy*, vol. 20, no. 1 (2003), 31–43; and Tamar Meisels, 'Can Corrective Justice Ground Claims to Territory?', *Journal of Political Philosophy*, vol. 11, no. 1 (2003), 65–88.

5. Annie Stilz grounds the moral right of occupancy in a more fundamental appeal to autonomy. 'Occupancy of territory', she writes, 'is connected to autonomy because it plays an important role in almost all of our plans. We build our lives on the assumption that our goals, relationships, and pursuits will not be unexpectedly destroyed through forced displacement'. Stilz describes a people's right of occupancy as 'an aggregated bundle of individual occupancy rights'; Stilz, 'Nations, States, and Territory', *Ethics*, vol. 121, no. 3 (2011), 572–601, at 579, n. 15. See also Nine, *Global Justice and Territory*, 90–92.

6. One could argue that the reason why 'ethnic cleansing' is regarded as so wrong is simply because it involves the aggregation of many individual rights violations.

7. A moral right of residency could have important implications for how we think about tenants' rights. However, in my view, place-related rights have to be limited by other kinds of rights or legitimate interests. If we apply a right of residency straightforwardly to tenants who do not pay their rent—permit them to stay in spite of their failure to pay rent—this is not compatible with a market-based economy in rental housing. This is a case where rights need to be balanced. I take the view that markets are a third-best non-ideal institutional arrangement, justified almost entirely for the reasons offered by Joe Heath (that is: not on liberty grounds, but in terms of efficiency understood in terms of the normative principle of Pareto optimality). A strong residency right that simply allowed non-paying tenants to reside in a place forever cannot be reconciled with market arrangements. I do not think of markets as moral-free zones; normative principles underlie market arrangements and justify them. For this reason, a moral right of residency ought to lead to strengthened tenant rights in various ways, but I would argue that it should be construed in a way that is compatible with some sort of market arrangement in rental housing, which, I also believe, can be justified morally. See Joseph Heath, *Morality, Competition, and the Firm* (Oxford University Press, 2014), chapter 7.

8. This disastrous policy was recognized as such in numerous studies conducted by the Royal Commission on Aboriginal People, 1994, and culminated in a public monument apologizing for this displacement in August 2009. See Royal Commission on Aboriginal Peoples (RCAP), *The High Arctic Relocation: A Report on the 1953–55 Relocation* (Ottawa, ON: Minister of Supply and Services, 1994). Commissioned RCAP research papers on this subject include Carol Brice-Bennett, *Dispossessed: The Eviction of Inuit from Hebron, Labrador* (Ottawa, ON: Minister of Supply and Services, 1994).

9. There are also social-justice implications of a moral right of occupancy. It suggests that governments should be prepared to shoulder some additional costs to provide services to remote communities, but that it is not similarly incumbent on governments to bear extra costs for people who move voluntarily to remote areas. For an excellent discussion of some implications, see Margaret Kohn, 'What is Wrong with Gentrification?' *Urban Research and Practice*, vol. 6, no. 3 (2013), 297–310.

10. This includes the Mi'kmaq of Nova Scotia in the 1940s, the Gwa'Sala and 'Nakwaxda'xw of British Columbia in 1964, the Mushuau Inn of Labrador (who were moved to Davis Inlet on Iluikoyak Island), the Inuit of Hebron Labrador, the Sayisi Dene in northern Manitoba, and the Yukon First Nations, all in the 1960s. See RCAP, *Report of the Royal Commission on Aboriginal People*, vol. 1, *Looking Forward, Looking Back* (Ottawa, ON: Minister of Supply and Services, 1996), 398 (http://caid.ca/RRCAP1.11.pdf). There are similar stories about other disastrous relocations of indigenous peoples typically to

worse (and unfamiliar) areas in other parts of the world: Emily Benedek, *The Wind Won't Know Me: A History of the Navajo-Hopi Land Dispute* (New York: Alfred A. Knopf, 1992); and for an excellent account of similar Australian dislocation, see Paul R. Wilson, *Black Death, White Hands* (Sydney: George Allen and Unwin, 1982).

11. RCAP, *Report of the Royal Commission*, vol. 1, 400.

12. Donald Calimont and Dennis William Magill, *Africville: The Life and Death of a Canadian Black Community* (Toronto: McClelland and Stewart, 1974); CBC News, 'Halifax apologizes for razing Africville', 24 February 2010 (http://www.cbc.ca/news/canada/nova-scotia/halifax-apologizes-for-razing-africville-1.894944); and https://www.youtube.com/watch?v=_gSrNH5_nk0 ('Broken Homes and Broken Hearts').

13. Danny Dorling, 'Overseas Property Buyers Are Not the Problem: Landlord Subsidies Are', *The Guardian*, 10 February 2014.

14. This is practised in many jurisdictions in Canada: for example, under the Ontario Landlord and Tenant Act, landlords are restricted in the annual increase that they can charge to sitting tenants (tenants who have been on a tenancy for more than twelve months), and often this cap is quite small and tied to general inflation rather than the more volatile house price market.

15. However, a state may be composed of a people who meet the criteria set out for territorial rights, and also some groups that have occupancy rights but do not meet the conditions for full territorial rights. Think here of some indigenous groups that cannot exercise the forms of authority that we associate with a state but are prepared to throw in their 'lot' within a state that recognizes their rights, including their occupancy rights, and perhaps ensures that they have local forms of jurisdictional control over land that they occupy. In that case, the state territory is in the right relationship to land to justify authority over it. This in fact is one way to think of 'coming together' federations.

16. The account of the moral value of collective self-determination advanced in this chapter is consistent with Joseph Raz's definition of value-individualism, namely, the basic claim that 'the explanation and justification of the goodness or badness of anything derives ultimately from its contribution, actual or possible, to human life and its quality'; Joseph Raz, 'Rights-Based Moralities', in Jeremy Waldron, ed., *Theories of Rights*, 182–200 (Oxford: Oxford University Press, 1984), 183.

17. Christian List and Philip Pettit, *Group Agency: The Possibility, Design, and Status of Corporate Agents* (Oxford: Oxford University Press, 2011).

18. John Searle, 'Social Ontology and the Philosophy of Society', *Analyse & Kritik*, vol. 20, no. 2 (1998), 143–158.

19. Margaret Gilbert, *On Social Facts* (Princeton: Princeton University Press, 1989); see also Larry May, *Crimes against Humanity* (Cambridge: Cambridge University Press, 2005), who also advocates a similar theory of what distinguishes a group for purposes of talking about group action.

20. Raimo Tuomela, 'We-Intentions Revisited', *Philosophical Studies*, vol. 125, no. 3 (2005), 327–369.

21. Similarly, the freedom of collective agents is not reducible to the freedom of their individual members. Adapting from Cohen's example of the proletariat being subject to collective unfreedom, Frank Hindriks has argued that a soccer team that is shipwrecked on an island—which, in his example, is beautiful and sunny, with plenty of food and water—and which has the material for building a solo canoe, but nothing larger, is one in which the individuals are individually free to leave but collectively unfree. They cannot leave *as a soccer team*, as a group that seeks to engage in collective or joint actions. G. A. Cohen, 'The Structure of Proletarian Unfreedom', *Philosophy & Public Affairs*, vol. 2, no. 1 (1983), 3–33; Frank Hindriks, 'The Freedom of Collective Agents', *Journal of Political Philosophy*, vol. 16, no. 2 (2008), 165–183.

22. See here David Copp, 'On the Agency of Certain Collective Entities', *Midwest Studies in Philosophy*, vol. 30 (2006), 194–221; and Philip Pettit, 'Responsibility Incorporated', *Ethics*, vol. 117, no. 2 (2007), 171–201; and Anna Stilz, 'Collective Responsibility and the State', *Journal of Political Philosophy*, vol. 19, no. 2 (2011), 190–208, at 192–193. The supervenience criteria are identified by List and Pettit: they draw on epistemic and

methodological difficulties in deriving group-based facts from individual-based facts to explain why the agent is collective but not mysterious; List and Pettit, *Group Agency*, pp. 64–72.

23. This is more contentious because it is not clear that being a collective in that sense gives rise to much in the way of rights or obligations. See David Miller, Review of Margaret Gilbert's *A Theory of Political Obligation*, *Philosophical Quarterly*, vol. 58, no. 233 (2008), 755–757.

24. Miller, Review of Gilbert, 756.

25. One of the difficulties with the generic analysis in terms of shared intentional states or cooperative activity on behalf of a plural subject is that it is difficult, in the absence of an institutional decision-making structure, to be sure when there are these shared aspirations and shared recognition of membership. Elites acting on behalf of a group, or claiming to be representative of the group, will claim that there is this shared sentiment underlying the group, which they represent. To address this problem, we interpret the first condition as requiring that there be strong, persistent, empirically verifiable evidence that they either exercise and value collective self-government or aspire to collective self-government. This does not mean that it collapses into a purely plebiscitary account of self-determination. Although the evidence for we-intentions might involve examining the way in which people vote, this account is not equivalent to Wellman's plebiscitary method, which is an aggregate account in the sense that it aggregates people in accordance with their voting patterns. See Christopher Heath Wellman, *A Theory of Secession: The Case for Political Self-Determination* (Cambridge: Cambridge University Press, 2005).

26. Voting patterns here simply supply evidence to support the claim that there is a social group, which acts in concerted ways to achieve self-government. It is meant to challenge or support elite claims, but only represents one kind of evidence of the existence of a social group.

27. James C. Scott, *Domination and the Arts of Resistance: Hidden Transcripts* (New Haven: Yale University Press, 1990); see also Maria Lugones, 'Multiculturalism and Publicity', *Hypatia*, vol. 15, no. 3 (2000), 175–181.

28. Bhikhu Parekh, *Rethinking Multiculturalism: Cultural Diversity and Political Theory* (Cambridge, MA: Harvard University Press, 2002); Uma Narayan, 'Essence of Culture and a Sense of History: A Feminist Critique of Cultural Essentialism', *Hypatia*, vol. 13, no. 1 (1998), 86–103.

29. John Rawls, *The Law of Peoples* (Cambridge, MA: Harvard University Press, 1999).

30. My position here contrasts with the plebiscitary-rights argument, endorsed by Christopher Wellman in his book *A Theory of Secession*, in which he proposes that any collection of individuals who freely seek to associate (politically) with one another and can perform the functions of the state has a right to do so (to be a territorial right-holder). The difference between my account and Wellman's account, which is more focused on subjective aspirations but does not require a shared history of cooperation, is analogous to the difference between a long-standing friendship and my relation to someone I just met who seems like they might make a good friend in the future. I have associative ties and reasons for action with respect to the long-standing friend that I do not have with respect to the person I just met. These reasons for action include the fact that, through past cooperative activity, my interests and that of my friend have become intertwined (I am grateful to Annie Stilz for suggesting this analogy).

31. I am grateful to Annie Stilz for pressing me on this point.

32. Aristotle, *Politics*, Bk I, ch. 1 and Bk III, chapter 4 (Harmondsworth, Middlesex: Penguin Books), p. 25, 107.

33. Indeed, more generally, I argue that most identity groups value control over the relevant domain (religious groups over religion; families over family life, etc.) of their identities and shared relationships.

34. Ethnic groups, like nations, are social groups—characterized by myths of common descent, some common culture and mutual recognition, and complex rituals regarding boundary maintenance—but they are not coextensive with nations because they lack the political self-consciousness that is usually associated with national communities.

35. Iris Marion Young, *Justice and the Politics of Difference* (Princeton: Princeton University Press, 1990), p. 46.
36. This is similar to the argument that Alan Patten makes in developing his distinctive institutional account of cultural groups. He claims that his account avoids objectionable essentialism: it does not identify groups with some fixed 'essence' or require us to examine a subjective mental state, but only to associate groups (for him, cultural groups) with subjection to common institutions, allowing us to individuate the groups by examining the continuity of these institutions, which have a formative influence on people's lives (or on my account, structures their relationships); Alan Patten, 'Rethinking Culture: The Social Lineage Account', *American Political Science Review*, vol. 105, no. 4 (2011), 735–749. It is also defended in Alan Patten, *Equal Recognition: The Moral Foundations of Minority Rights* (Princeton: Princeton University Press, 2014).
37. This example was initially deployed by Will Kymlicka, *Multicultural Citizenship* (Oxford: Oxford University Press, 1995), to distinguish between the structure of a culture and the character of a culture. I do not think this terminology is very helpful, but he was trying to capture the problem of explaining how identities can persist even when they are subject to unremitting change in values, practices, and traditions.
38. Margaret Moore, *Ethics of Nationalism* (Oxford: Oxford University Press, 2001), 70–71.
39. This is discussed in chapter 7.
40. See here Richard Arneson, 'The Principle of Fairness and Free-Rider Problems', *Ethics*, vol. 92, no. 4 (1982), 616–633; Richard Dagger, *Civic Virtues: Rights, Citizenship, and Republican Liberalism* (New York: Oxford University Press, 1997); Richard Dagger, 'Membership, Fair Play, and Political Obligation', *Political Studies*, vol. 48, no. 1 (2000), 104–117; William Edmundson, *Three Anarchical Fallacies* (Cambridge: Cambridge University Press, 1998); John Horton, *Political Obligation* (London: Macmillan, 1992); George Klosko, *The Principle of Fairness and Political Obligation*, 2nd edition (Lanham, MD: Rowman and Littlefield, 2004); David Lefkowitz, 'Legitimate Political Authority and the Duty of Those Subject to It: A Critique of Edmundson', *Law and Philosophy*, vol. 23, no. 4 (2004), 399–435; and Jeremy Waldron, 'Special Ties and Natural Duties', *Philosophy & Public Affairs*, vol. 22, no. 1 (1993), 3–30.
41. This principle has potentially far-reaching consequences, and so is qualified by numerous other articles in the UN Charter affirming the sanctity of the principle of the territorial integrity of states and denying the right of the UN or its member states to intervene in the internal affairs of recognized states. See Rupert Emerson, 'Self-Determination', *American Journal of International Law*, vol. 65, no. 3 (1971), 459–475.
42. See Jonathan Seglow, *Defending Associative Duties* (New York: Routledge, 2013), 38. I am indebted here to the many complexities outlined by Jonathan Seglow in this book, but especially his discussion of relationships and the way he distinguishes them from other similar notions, like relations and other interactions.
43. Seglow, *Defending Associative Duties*, 34–35.
44. This example is from Seglow, *Defending Associative Duties*, 34.
45. Joseph Raz, 'Autonomy, Toleration, and the Harm Principle', in Susan Mendus, ed., *Justifying Toleration: Conceptual and Historical Perspectives*, 155–175 (Cambridge: Cambridge University Press, 1988), 156.

4

Non-Statist Theories of Territory

In this chapter and the next, I argue for the superiority of my political self-determination theory of territory through a comparative examination of the two dominant theories of territory: cultural theories of Miller and Meisels (and here I also include Kolers's ethnogeographic account); and functionalist or statist theories associated with Hobbes and Kant, Sidgwick, and their contemporary heirs, largely Kantian-inspired, such as Buchanan, Waldron, Stilz, and Ypi.

Statist theories of territory, which I will discuss in chapter 5, typically involve describing the relationship between people and the state, and then arguing that rights to particular territories and different kinds of rights associated with territory will simply fall into place. The strategy adopted in this book and in the cultural nationalist theories examined here has a different structure. The problem of relating authority over people and authority over land is solved at the same time, through a more complete analysis of the relationship between the group and the land and between people in the group. These non-statist theories are similar in that they link people and land together prior to or independent of the argument for the state. In this chapter, I examine the ethnogeographic theory of Avery Kolers and the cultural nationalist theory advanced by Meisels and Miller, mainly focusing on Miller. I argue that while they are similar in certain respects, Kolers's theory does not offer a sufficiently determinate account of the territorial right-holder; and Miller's account overstates the conditions for holding territorial right. In both cases, this leads to difficulties in their account of how to 'attach' the group to the territory.

My theory is clearly distinct from its rivals. It is distinct from the statist account because it does not assume that the territorial right-holder necessarily corresponds to a state. It is distinct from cultural nationalism because it does not rely on the idea of culture to identify the relevant group. Nor, as I will explain, does it identify the right-holder with an ethnogeographic community, as Kolers does. Situating my theory in this comparative context is an important part of the argument for it. In the previous chapter I argued for a non-statist, non-cultural account of the collective agent that is entitled to territorial right, but the arguments were presented abstractly, without the benefit of comparing my argument with other theories of territory. I argue in this chapter that my theory offers a more plausible account of the fundamental holder of territorial rights than either of these two theories.

4.1. Kolers's Ethnogeographic Communities and their Territorial Rights

In this section, I examine a theory of territorial rights that has recently received considerable attention in the literature: that of Avery Kolers in *Land, Conflict, and Justice*, in which he ascribes territorial right to what he calls 'ethnogeographic' communities. The structure of the argument is similar to that of my theory and cultural nationalist theory in that we all rely on a non-statist conception of the territorial right-holder. In this section, I'll explain the problems with Kolers's theory, in part as an attempt to explain how my theory offers a better account of the territorial right-holder.

Kolers's theory is one of the most innovative and interesting recent theories on territory and territorial right. The structure of the argument—in particular, the fact that he identifies the territorial right-holder with a group that is already in a relationship to a particular piece of land—is similar to mine and to the cultural nationalist theories of Meisels and Miller, which I will consider in section 4.2. However, in contrast to Meisels and Miller, Kolers identifies the territorial right-holding group with a group that has a particular ecological and environmental relationship to land (rather than a cultural one). He argues that an ethnogeographic group (which, on his account, has rights to jurisdictional authority) is defined by (1) its specific social ontology of land, and (2) its distinctive pattern of land use. Because his account of the right-holder is already defined in terms of a particular relation to land, Kolers seems to have no difficulty solving 'the attachment problem': the account of the territorial right-holder already contains within it an account of what makes that group particularly appropriate to hold jurisdictional authority over the particular area that they distinctively use and have a particular theory about (in Kolers's terms, their 'social ontology'). This is important to his theory of how that group is attached to land. He also offers an original criterion to decide between rival claims to the same territory, which he calls 'plenitude'.

Kolers's concept of territorial right is itself relatively uncontroversial. It is defined as the right of a group to control (or possibly share with other groups in controlling) the legal system of a political and juridical territory.[1]

The appropriate right-holding group—the ethnogeographic community—is defined as a 'group of people who share an ontology of land', by which he means 'a culturally specific conception of land, what land is, what about it is valuable, and how humans interact with it'.[2] Another requirement for counting as an ethnogeographic community of the relevant kind is a material one: their 'land-use practices densely and pervasively interact'.[3] The two criteria are described as interlinking: Kolers emphasizes for example that modern industrial economies often tend to be supported by relatively coherent belief systems about the relationship of people to land, such that natural resources should be exploited in the most efficient way possible.

Kolers also addresses the situation where two or more rival ethnogeographic communities will claim rights over the same land. He addresses squarely the problem of how to arrive at a value-neutral mechanism for deciding between rival claims, and he develops his own original criterion, that of 'plenitude', which I will discuss in more detail in chapter 6.[4] In this section, I will focus on the applicability of his model to many cases of territorial conflict, where the concern is not with the adjudicating mechanism, but with his conception of an ethnogeographic community. Kolers argues that the ethnogeographic community is the fundamental holder of territorial rights, but it is, I argue, insufficiently determinate and implausible in its implications. I also think that, since there is indeterminacy embedded in his very conception of the territorial right-holding agent, the attachment problem, which would seem to be solved by this method, is actually not resolved.

Let me turn first to the problem of defining the appropriate holder of territorial rights. Recall that Kolers defines the ethnogeographic community in two distinct ways. They are a group of people who share an ontology of land, which means that they have a specific conception of land—what makes it valuable and how humans interact with it.[5] He also describes the group in terms of their material (rather than subjective) relationship to land: this group can be distinguished from other groups by their land-use patterns. These are two distinct criteria, which can come apart in particular cases, and the reader is uncertain whether the crucial criterion to be an ethnogeographic community (and thereby holder of territorial right) is the shared *ontology*, or theory, of land *or* the material pervasiveness of the land-use patterns *or* whether they are jointly necessary and sufficient conditions. This is important because, by conveniently assuming that the two criteria will always coincide, Kolers does not confront directly the more difficult cases where they press in opposite directions. And the two criteria can suggest quite different views of the territorial right-holding agent. To the extent that Kolers emphasizes the first criterion—the shared social ontology—his account seems to be much closer to a cultural nationalist account, such as that defended by Miller and Meisels, because we can imagine that those groups which have different poems about the land, different cultural and symbolic meanings attributed to the land, are what we would normally think of as different cultural groups. To the extent that Kolers emphasizes the second criterion—the pervasiveness of the land-use pattern— his theory seems to track economic and functional considerations.

At crucial points Kolers shifts the emphasis he places on the two criteria. For example, when he confronts the problem of dissident individuals, by which he means individuals who do not share the dominant or hegemonic conception of land (a problem which any collectivist account has to deal with, in some form), Kolers is careful to note that he does not assume that all people share the same view. His is not a homogenizing conception: ontologies (of land) are shared because they are viewed as natural by most members of the group. There may be some people who do not share them—Kolers cites ecofeminism and agrarianism as dissident ontologies in the American context—but, he argues, this doesn't affect whether they're shared because the material relationships in which people are situated force them into a particular kind of relationship to land. Here it seems that Kolers shifts from the first criterion—the extent or degree to which a theory (or 'ontology') is shared or assumed to be natural—to the second criterion, which is the material relationships in which people are situated.

The problem with this is not simply that it is unclear which criterion is fundamental. There is also the problem that we get different results, or different ethnogeographic communities, depending on how generally or abstractly we apply the criteria. If we take a macro view of the situation, we might say that all people in North America share a pervasive and dense land-use pattern, that we are locked in a North American economic zone, and share roughly similar views about the economy, about land, and about overall values. From a micro perspective, we might acknowledge that the land carries with it different symbolic meanings: the Plains of Abraham, for Quebec nationalists, represent the location of their defeat in North America and forcible incorporation in an English political and cultural project. For English Canadians, it does not (I hope!) have the sweet smell of victory lingering on it, but is now viewed mainly as a tourist destination, as located in one of the most attractive (in architectural and culinary terms) cities in North America. Whether these are the same or different ontologies of land, described in terms of the symbols and belief systems governing the people's relationship to the land, depends on whether we zoom in and examine micro considerations, or whether we zoom out and examine the broad picture. The problem of the appropriate level of generality or specificity in applying the criteria is a problem regardless of which criterion we interpret as fundamental, or whether we think that both have to be in place, as necessary and sufficient conditions (although the possible ethnogeographic communities can multiply depending on the configurations between these elements).

In the applied parts of his book, Kolers offers examples of territorial conflict which help to elucidate his understanding of how exactly the relationship to land can mark out the ethnogeographic community. Here, he seems to apply his criteria with a fairly broad brushstroke, which ends up placing emphasis on the material relationship of people to land. As a result, I argue below, his theory does not pick out many of the groups that we might think of as engaged in a territorial conflict with another group, which limits the usefulness of his analysis and, more seriously, undermines the plausibility of his account of the territorial right-holder.

Many of the conflicts that we often think about as territorial in nature are cases where two different groups seek to use the land in the same way, for the same purpose, and where two groups share a similar densely interacting and pervasive pattern of land use. In some sense, then, one could say that they have a similar ontology of land and also share a similar pattern of land use—though they just have different ideas of who (which group) is entitled. This does not, for Kolers, represent a territorial dispute: this is a mere boundary dispute. He writes:

> Territorial disputes are distinctive because they involve parties that are not working from a shared conception of land. It may be helpful to distinguish between territorial disputes proper and what we might call mere boundary disputes. . . . Mere boundary disputes occur because two conflicting parties want a piece of land for the same reason—a tax base, national security, a source of natural resources, or even a shared conception of sacredness. Territorial disputes proper are at their core disputes between conflicting ontologies of land, or as I call them, ethnogeographies.[6]

Consider first the implications of this distinction and the kinds of disputes that become interpreted as boundary disputes. First, it would seem that boundary disputes, as Kolers defines them, are pervasive and not very tractable. For example, the conflict in Northern Ireland, which in its most recent form lasted from 1969 to 1998, would almost certainly be described by Kolers as a boundary dispute. Protestants and Catholics in Northern Ireland share similar land-use patterns and even similar views about what the land is for; they just differ on which group is entitled to use the land for that purpose. Of course, there has been residential segregation in Northern Ireland, with Catholics confined to the wilder glen areas and Protestants farming the more lush valleys, since the Protestant Plantation. The Troubles, which broke out in 1969, increased the social and residential segregation of the two communities, but, despite this, both Catholics and Protestants broadly shared a view about the basic relationship between land and people, and both were engaged in commercial farming for the same (local urban and English) markets. There were small cultural differences, some of which involved different meanings attributed to the land: the contesting parties had different 'sacred geographies' based on community deaths, battles won or lost, parade routes, but those cultural and historic differences match up, and weakly so, to only the first criterion for counting as an ethnogeographic community. Northern Ireland, then, on Kolers's criteria, is not a territorial conflict: the two groups do not seek to use the land in different ways, do not have different land-use patterns; it's not even clear that they have different ontologies of land (in the sense that both communities basically ascribe the same meaning to the land). In Kolers's view, this is a boundary dispute, not a territorial dispute.

Quebec—a case that Kolers does discuss at length—also does not count as a distinct ethnogeographic community. In a revealing passage, Kolers argues that, 'whatever was the case prior to the Quiet Revolution of the 1960s, Quebec is now not a distinct ethnogeographic community. According to the 2001 Census, Quebec matches Canadian rates of urbanization, a roughly 80/20 population split, with Quebec slightly higher than Canada as a whole), and closely mirrors Anglophone Ontario in issues such as commuting to work and household organization'.[7] Thus he concludes that Quebec does not constitute a distinctive ethnogeographic community: in his terms, 'Québécois currently lack any distinct eligibility to lodge a territorial claim against that of Canada'.[8] Interestingly, Kolers thinks that indigenous peoples within Quebec, such as the Cree and the Mohawk, *do* constitute distinct ethnogeographic communities, with territorial rights, because they do have an ontology of land and material way of life in relation to that land that is distinct from the surrounding Francophone community.

But if this is true of Northern Ireland and Quebec, isn't it also true of Israel/Palestine? There is a genuine and deep conflict between nomadic and settled people in Israel/Palestine, to which Kolers's theory is clearly relevant, for there we have disagreement about what land is for, as well as different land-use patterns. Kolers's conception of an ethnogeographic community certainly applies to distinguish Bedouin from settled people. The conflict between these two groups is interesting and important, but it is not the political struggle that is gripping the area today. And it is not easy to make the first kind of dispute (about what the land is for) map neatly on to the second kind of dispute (about who gets to control the land). It's just false to identify Palestinians as agrarians and Israelis as urban dwellers, since many, many Palestinians live in urban areas, and are involved in a very dense web of interaction with Israelis, and many Israelis live in rural areas, while the Bedouin are a very small and distinct proportion of the Arab community there. Kolers spends a whole chapter discussing the Israeli case, but he seems simply to assume that the Israeli-Palestinian conflict is a territorial dispute, and so spends most of the space discussing how the concept of 'plenitude' applies to adjudicate it, not the prior question of how to identify distinct ethnogeographic communities there. I do not deny that the conflict between nomadic and settled is both significant and interesting, but if Kolers's theory implies that the real struggle is between the Bedouin and everyone else, it is much less pressing, much less important to live political issues, than it purports to be. The cases where Kolers's theory seems most fitting are those of deep cultural conflict between nomadic and settled peoples, indigenous and people of European origin, in the Americas and Australasia and so on.

Kolers is surely right that there is something different about a disagreement over what land is *for*, and disagreement over *who* is entitled to use land for an agreed purpose (who gets to exploit the oil, for example). The first constitutes, for him, a *territorial dispute*; the second, which he calls a *boundary dispute*, is less fundamental. However, while we might think there is a distinction here, it is not one that is particularly useful to draw. For one thing, as the cases above illustrate, what Kolers calls a boundary dispute can presumably be just as intense and destructive as what he calls a territorial dispute. Indeed, the term 'boundary dispute' is a bit misleading, because it suggests two groups disputing over where precisely a particular line should be drawn, whereas in fact it might encompass pretty much the whole of the territory in question.

In short, although Kolers seems to think that his argument applies to territorial disputes of the sort that we would normally consider to be such—he gives such examples as conflicts between Jews and Palestinians in Israel/Palestine, between people of European and native descent in the Americas and Australasia, and the claims of Kurds, Québécois, Basques, and others in relation to the state[9]—most of the argument proceeds abstractly, using his distinctive terminology. The relation between the terms that he uses to describe the right-holding groups (ethnogeographic communities) and the groups that we normally think of as the type that might be in a territorial conflict do not clearly match up. But this is not simply a problem of application: it is, as I've shown, connected to indeterminacy in his account of the territorial right-holder, an indeterminacy which makes it difficult for him to identify such right-holders clearly, and hence demonstrate conclusively which groups are attached to which pieces of land. And a crucial distinction that flows from his account of the territorial right-holder (the ethnogeographic community)—the distinction between boundary and territorial disputes—appears to be unmotivated. It does not track the kinds of arguments and values that people themselves apply to land and their relationship to it.

4.2. Cultural Accounts of the Territorial Right-Holder

Philosophical liberal nationalists have been at the forefront of examining territorial rights, and have advanced a number of arguments to justify the nation's rights over a *particular* land.[10] This section of the chapter focuses on Miller's cultural nationalist theory, which is based on a complex argument about the interrelationship between three elements: group culture, land, and state territorial rights.[11] It is not the only prominent cultural nationalist argument about territory: Tamar Meisels too has written on this topic.[12] Nonetheless, their theories are similar in certain ways and so I will focus on Miller.

His is a cultural nationalist account, in which the nation is defined as having objective cultural features (connected to a particular territory, marked off from other communities by a distinct public culture, and extended in history) along with subjective features, such as shared beliefs and mutual commitments. I will argue in this section that Miller offers a too thick account of the territorial right-holding group, and that this is also problematic when he discusses the other element of the nexus—the link between the cultural group and state territorial rights.

Before we can talk about a cultural nationalist account of the territorial right holder, it is important to acknowledge that there is considerable disagreement about what is meant by the term 'culture' or 'cultural nation', and relatedly, disagreement about how to individuate distinct cultures. This is partly because there are no clear necessary and sufficient conditions to be a distinct culture or nation; and any attempt to enumerate such a list typically encounters a couple of important exceptions. The usual strategy in such cases is to view 'culture' and 'cultural nation' as a family-resemblance concept, to identify a number of features which typically mark groups that we think of as constituting a 'cultural community' or 'cultural nation' and then use these characteristics to individuate nations. This strategy was deployed by Margalit and Raz in an early argument for national self-determination, in terms of characterizing the groups that, they contend, have this right. They suggest that, among the most important features of these groups are: (1) they have a common character and common culture, which encompasses many important aspects of life; (2) membership in the groups is an important identifying feature for each person; and (3) the groups are large and anonymous, and mutual recognition is secured by possession of the group's general culture and other aspects.[13] These are discussed in a somewhat open-ended way, but the possession of these three features is thought to identify the group accurately enough without further specifying which of them is more or less important.

In a rather similar vein, but with a more detailed argument, David Miller in *On Nationality* lists five elements that together constitute a nation: it is, he writes, 'a community (1) constituted by shared belief and mutual commitment, (2) extended in history, (3) active in character, (4) connected to a particular territory, and (5) marked off from other communities by its distinct public culture'.[14] The fifth characteristic—distinct public culture—makes this a 'cultural nationalist' account, although the official definition accords just as much weight to subjective identification and mutual commitment, thus sharing with my account the idea of subjective identity and an ongoing relationship on behalf of a shared commitment (which, in my case, is a political project). I will say more about this point below.

This account clearly meets the most important *desiderata* of a theory, discussed in chapter 2. It attributes rights over territory to a non-statist group that can be identified on the basis of the possession of these five features. It avoids the problem of circularity, which, we will see, potentially plagues statist accounts, where the group has a right to territory only if it is already a state, which, by definition, involves a right over territory. It also has the merit of providing an account that clearly explains the relationship between the group (characterized by shared culture) and the right to territory (which, as I will go on to show, is marked by that culture, and informs the culture). In this way, it is a coherent and plausible non-statist account of the territorial right-holder, which, at the same time, helps to identify clearly the right-holding group.

There is however a potential difficulty with Miller's account of the territorial right-holding group, which bears on his solution to the attachment problem. Above, I characterized Miller's account as a cultural nationalist one, because the possession of a shared culture is key to his argument for jurisdictional authority over territory. But in fact he has several different criteria in his account of a cultural nation, including elements that are also shared with my non-cultural account, and it's important to first clarify what I see as the key differences between our two accounts, before suggesting that Miller shifts between these characteristics in dealing with concrete examples, sometimes relying just on political identity rather than a cultural account.

Let me clarify the relationship between my account and Miller's cultural nationalist account. On my theory, the territorial right-holders are groups or collective agents that are neither necessarily cultural nations, nor necessarily states, but are defined by their common political project and that seek to be institutionally organized either in a state or in ways less formal than states. They are collective agents with a shared political identity. The key feature in constituting the group as a collective agent is mutual recognition and shared political identity, shared aspirations to be collectively self-governing as a group of that kind. I do not deny that there may be some degree of correlation between a shared culture and a shared political identity: many cultural groups share a common political identity and are collectively mobilized as a political community, and so can meet my criteria for having territorial rights. However, I am not making a normative argument for the view that cultural groups have special entitlements that other groups do not have.

The problem is that Miller, like many cultural nationalists, obscures the difference between identity-related accounts and culture-related accounts by using the term 'nation' to refer to cases where groups share a common culture constituted in part by shared beliefs and to cases where they share a common identity constituted by shared sentiments. This failure to distinguish between shared cultural features and shared political identities is ubiquitous, reaching back to Miller's argument in *On Nationality* about 'a common sentiment of nationality . . . co-exist[ing] with linguistic and other cultural differences'.[15] In Miller's argument, it is embedded in the five features that he originally identified, the first of which emphasizes subjective identity; the third of which obliquely suggests political aspirations; and the fifth of which to a shared culture. If all of these are present, then the political identity component is a necessary but not sufficient condition. It serves to distinguish a national community from a mere ethnic group, but the cultural markers between groups (condition five) is also presented as necessary.

The problem with the cultural account, at least for liberal nationalists (which is how Miller is widely perceived) is that there are several key examples of groups that we think are nations (or potential territorial right-holders), but which do not seem to share a culture as that is normally understood. In my previous work, I referred to my native country, Canada, and argued that Canadians do not have a culture sharply distinct from Americans, or at least, it's not clear that the cultural differences between Canadians and Americans is greater than the cultural differences within Canada or within the United States. Nevertheless, there is a quite distinct *political* identity in Canada, with distinct political aspirations.

Anthropologists, sociologists, and political scientists who study nationalist conflicts often remark that national (and ethnic) identities require some 'cultural marker', some mechanism for mutual recognition of members (and so implicitly a method for recognizing outsiders) but these do not necessarily correlate with sharp linguistic or cultural differences.[16] Consider, in support of this contention, cases which we might think of as conflicts between different cultural communities—Northern Ireland from 1969 to 1998, Rwanda in 1994, and the former Yugoslavia in 1992–95. In these cases, the level of violence involved in the conflicts was significant, and yet members of the antagonistic communities spoke the same language and had broadly similar cultural values. Moreover, this cultural similarity is often recognized by members of the antagonistic groups themselves. For example, in Northern Ireland, where there are two distinct and mutually antagonistic political-identity communities on the same territory, the conflict between the two groups is not about some objective cultural difference. Despite a common misconception, it is not religious in nature. The groups are not arguing over the details of doctrinal interpretation. Religious leaders (priests, nuns, ministers) are not targets for violence, as they were in the Reformation period, when conflict was genuinely religious.[17] Nor is the conflict about sharp *cultural* differences. A 1968 survey of cultural similarity in Northern Ireland revealed that 67 percent of Protestants thought Northern Irishmen of the opposite religion were about the 'same as themselves', while only 29 percent thought the same about Englishmen. Of Northern Irish Catholics, 81 percent regarded Ulster Protestants as about the 'same as themselves' but only 44 percent thought this about southern Catholics.[18] This supports anthropological findings that suggest that, despite social segregation of the two communities in Northern Ireland, there was a 'considerable area within which Catholics and Protestants shared a common culture'.[19]

Analysts of the conflicts in the former Yugoslavia almost universally emphasize the cultural similarities between the different groups.[20] Part of the fascination underlying the breakup of Yugoslavia, and subsequent war, is that many analysts have noted that, prior to the conflict, Serbs, Croats, and Muslims shared a common life, language, physical appearance, and a lot of history. The Muslims were among the most secularized Muslims anywhere in the world. One of the primary divisions was between urban and rural communities, which meant, in effect, that an urban Serb would have more in common with her urban Croat neighbour than with rural Serbs. In short, the groups themselves were culturally very similar; and cultural variation was as great *across* groups as within them. There were clearly distinct political identities but this is not the same as having distinct cultural characteristics, at least as this is normally understood.

This suggests that we should avoid the view that divergent political identities can be equated with divergence in substantive culture and language.[21] Of course, in some cases, political identities *do* correspond to cultural differences, but in some key cases—Canada, Northern Ireland, and so on—cultural differences do not match up easily with political identities.

It would be a serious flaw for a conception of nation—which in Miller's theory is the candidate territorial right-holder—if it could not explain or account for cases that we think of as central cases of nations. And indeed it is noteworthy that when Miller does deal with such cases, he shifts to emphasizing the first condition, rather than the more strictly cultural condition: he emphasizes the fact that people in that community have a shared aspiration to be collectively self-governing, or a shared political identity. It's not merely that in some cases one feature is more important, and in other cases, another feature is more important, but that all are to some degree present—a family-resemblance conception of cultural nation is sufficiently flexible to deal with that. Rather, it seems that shared political identity is an absolutely crucial condition, and indeed necessary in a way that shared culture, as that is ordinarily understood, is not. If that's right, then, while Miller's view is coherent and well argued, there is the difficulty that some central candidate territorial right-holders do not seem to be distinct cultural communities at all, but certainly do seem to be political communities in my sense.

Let me turn, now, to the other key element in a theory of territory: Miller's (and Meisels's) solution to the 'attachment problem'. The relationship between group culture and land is established through an argument that emphasizes the symbiotic relationship between them.[22] In Miller's view, the people who inhabit a certain territory shape the land that they occupy; their culture is mixed with the physical characteristics of the land, and the physical characteristics shape the culture that they develop. Through custom and practice as well as by explicit political activity they create laws, establish individual or collective property rights, engage in public works, shape the physical appearance of the territory. Over time this takes on symbolic significance as they bury their dead in certain places, establish shrines or secular monuments, and so forth. There is a sense in which the cultural national community can come to have 'rights' to land by mixing its culture with it. Miller writes:

> Consider a nation that over a long period occupies and transforms a piece of territory and continues to hold that territory in the present. This unavoidably has a number of consequences. First, there is a two-way interaction between the territory and the culture of the people who live on it. The culture must adapt to the territory if the people are to prosper: it matters whether the climate is hot or cold, the land suitable for hunting or agriculture, whether the territory is landlocked or open to the sea, and so forth. But equally the territory will in nearly every case be shaped over time according to the cultural priorities of the people, as fields are marked out and cultivated; irrigation systems are created; villages, towns, and cities are built; and so forth, so that eventually the face of the landscape may be changed beyond recognition. It has become the people's home, in the sense that they have adapted their way of life to the physical constraints of the territory and then transformed it to a greater or lesser extent in pursuit of their common goals. It does not matter here that the transformation may

not be coordinated or consciously intended by the participants, so long as it reflects their shared cultural values.[23]

Tamar Meisels, too, emphasizes the symbolic significance of the land for the people living on it, and her language also strongly evokes Lockean mixing of culture with land and the transformation of the land through labour. People make decisions about the use of their territory or land that reflects their culture: 'they must . . . choose between various modes of architecture . . . build churches or synagogues or mosques,' or erect monuments with historical and cultural significance, she writes.[24]

The interrelationship between culture and land gives rise to a second type of claim to attachment: this is the argument that the land has, in addition to universal value, particular value: it is important to the culture and identity of the group in question. Miller writes:

> Living on and shaping a piece of land means not only increasing its value in an economic sense, but also (typically) endowing it with meaning by virtue of significant events that have occurred there, monuments that have been built, poems, novels and paintings that capture particular places or types of landscape.[25]

All of these activities give them an attachment to the land that cannot be matched by any rival claimant.[26] It is not simply that the land is shaped by the culture, but also—a point particularly emphasized by Meisels—that this process leads people to become attached to the land in such a way that it becomes a crucial feature of their group identity and the land has subjective value for them.

While this argument suggests that particular land is important for particular groups, this does not yet constitute a justification of territorial right. This brings us to the third element of the culture-land-territorial right nexus. Miller argues:

> Rights of jurisdiction are relatively easy to defend. . . . Rights of private property alone will not serve [to protect this added cultural value] because (1) such rights are always susceptible to being redrawn by whoever holds rights of jurisdiction and (2) much of the embodied value that the group has created is likely to be located in public space—in public architecture, landscapes of historic significance, and so forth. The group needs to maintain overall control over the territory in order to secure that value over time, and for that it needs rights of jurisdiction such as those normally exercised by a state.[27]

There are three basic criticisms of this element of the cultural national-ist account: the agent-indeterminacy criticism; the territorial under-inclusive criticism; and the group over-inclusive criticism. All three have been articu-lated most forcefully by Annie Stilz, who has questioned the extent to which the cultural nationalist account, which she associates primarily with Miller's work, grounds territorial (jurisdictional) right, as we know them. I do not think that two of the criticisms succeed, but I will rehearse them here to clar-ify why and then focus on the third, which I think is troubling for this account.

The agent-indeterminacy criticism questions the criterion for determin-ing whether an action belongs to an individual agent or the collective agent of which the individual agent is a member. 'Much of the improvement of land that goes on within a national territory—the construction of homes, churches and the like—is not carried out by the nation, but by individuals or private associations. "The nation" does not mix its labor with those objects in any sense except metaphorically, so why shouldn't the individuals who actu-ally labored on the objects in question gain private property rights in them?'[28] There is no tension of course between an argument that supports individ-ual private property for labour and territorial rights for groups. We do not need to choose between them. Her argument—expressed in that rhetorical question—rests fundamentally on a denial of the very idea of a collective agent, of people acting in terms of their group identity, which of course can coexist with their individual identities, and that these collectives (groups) can hold rights. It is not just an argument against Miller's theory but suggests a strongly individualist account of all human actions. As such, her criticism is also relevant to my own argument, which similarly confers rights on a collec-tive agent. I think the correct response is to agree that at some level of course only individuals can labour (and have experiences) but then to point out that we can nevertheless attribute actions, aims, and identities to groups too, and indeed it would be a very impoverished and empirically odd view of the social world if it was devoid of any collective agents or collective identities. They are often central to the explanations of individual actions. And it is not psycho-logically difficult to imagine that where individuals do alter land in the way described by Miller, and the type of landscape and environment is celebrated in their literature and culture generally, that land would be particularly valu-able to them. It would be valuable to them as individuals, but also as members of the group, in cases where they have a group based identity. Stilz's objection, in other words, represents a coherent position, but it certainly involves a rejec-tion of far more than Miller's or Meisels's cultural nationalism, and thereby runs into other problems: such thoroughgoing individualism has a difficult time explaining social phenomena which involves recognition of group iden-tities, group mobilization, and so on.

The second criticism—the territorial under-inclusive criticism—presses on the problem of undeveloped areas. '[I]f the only explanation for the acquisition of jurisdictional rights is that land has been labored, then the state cannot have jurisdiction over undeveloped areas'.[29] The problem here is under-inclusiveness of territory, and, if this criticism goes through, it raises questions about whether this argument can generate a theory of territorial right as we know it. There are two things to say about this objection: the first is that it focuses on a very narrow understanding of the cultural nationalist position. The cultural nationalist position isn't focused only on labouring, so is not in danger of creating a patchwork of jurisdictional authorities corresponding to specific acts of labouring by specific people: it presupposes acceptance of a collective ontology and a general picture of a land that is linked in important ways to a particular culture. It can successfully link cultural groups to specific geographic areas. But, even with this more sympathetic understanding of the argument in play, there is an important sense in which the cultural nationalist picture can only attach people to geographical areas: it reveals 'heartlands' of particular groups, but does not give us an account of boundary-drawing specifically. But this difficulty is shared by all the accounts on offer, including Stilz's and my own. Stilz introduces arbitrariness into her account through relying on (arbitrary) state borders. My account, like Miller's, solves the attachment problem in being able to link particular areas to particular groups, but there is a certain degree of indeterminacy at the borders, in part because groups are not homogeneous entities, hermetically sealed on particular lands, so it is necessary to supplement accounts like this with further, subsidiary principles to delineate boundaries. And, to the extent that Stilz's account, like mine, relies on right of occupancy, it is subject to the under-inclusive criticism. More needs to be said about what it means to occupy a land, if the individual is not physically taking up room in the land: how should we deal with land on which no members of the group are currently resident? This is the subject of chapter 6.

The third criticism, which I think is the most telling because it is specific to the cultural nationalist argument, focuses on the cultural component of the nationalist (or Miller's nationalist) definition of the nation. Cultural nationalism, Stilz complains, 'seems to grant territorial jurisdiction to any group that constructs a culturally marked infrastructure, including immigrant groups', and cites the case of Little Havana in Miami.[30] At this point, Miller might object that this criticism misses its mark, since he distinguishes national groups from immigrant groups in his account of the five components that are necessary to qualify as a 'nation'. However, since his account of the relationship of culture to land (cultural infusion) and the relationship of that to territorial rights (or at least rights of jurisdiction) is doing most of the philosophical work 'attaching' people to land, it is not clear why only nations, and not also other cultural groups with the right sort of identity and land-transforming capacity, are entitled to jurisdictional rights.

I think that Miller's argument could address this criticism in one of two ways. He could introduce a further criterion to the effect that only cultural groups that have the functional capacity to exercise robust political authority are entitled to do so, and so deny jurisdictional authority to small Spanish-speaking enclaves in particular cities and other similar cultural communities. However, on his own account, these sorts of limitations would be ad hoc and would represent an uncomfortable (non-normative) compromise with reality; it would be a compromise, since in other respects such groups would have the right sort of relationship with land, and would justifiably want to be able to protect its value through the exercise of jurisdictional authority. Alternatively, Miller could modify his account in the direction of mine, and minimize its reliance on culture as a vehicle to attach groups to land, and to demarcate distinct groups.

In short, I think that Miller's position would benefit from moving in the direction of mine. Moreover, I think my account captures what is attractive about both Meisels's and Miller's positions. On my account, the overwhelming argument for having a right to territory, a right to jurisdictional control over a particular piece of land, follows from the value of collective self-determination, and the locus of that self-determination is determined by having a relationship both with other persons and with the land itself, on land that is occupied not unjustly. The very plausible story that Meisels and Miller tell—of transforming the land and being transformed by it—will happen naturally through living on the land, using it as a source of food or shelter or water and interacting with the environment. It is not necessary to require the transformation of the landscape by the culture, since some cultures might value non-transformation of (some of) the land and value different kinds of relationships to land. In other words, I think the principles that Miller and Meisels point to—the use of the land for subsistence, the effect on the landscape of the people's culture, and the cultural choices that they make in transforming the land—follow naturally from people occupying land. There is no need to make a special appeal to these kinds of considerations at all. At best, they might be thought of as empirical evidence to show that people are settled there. Moreover, it would seem that there are many distinct cultural groups within a society that add subjective and objective value to the land; and if this is the key element in creating jurisdictional authority, then the argument seems to include many territorial right-holders beyond the ones that we normally think of as nations.[31]

Notes

1. Avery Kolers, *Land, Conflict, and Justice: A Political Theory of Territory* (Cambridge: Cambridge University Press, 2009a), 10.
2. Kolers, *Land, Conflict, and Justice*, 3–4.
3. Kolers, *Land, Conflict, and Justice*, 3–4; see also 86.
4. 'Plenitude' is described in terms of a number of elements: (1) internal diversity, (2) external distinctness, and (3) feasible plans for maintaining these in perpetuity, with the further specification that the first two elements are each determined from the perspective of the claimants. The advantage of this criterion is that it is value-neutral in the sense that it does not rest on a normatively contested theory of appropriate use, as the 'efficiency' criterion is often thought to do.
5. Kolers, *Land, Conflict, and Justice*, 3–4.
6. Kolers, *Land, Conflict, and Justice*, 14.
7. Kolers, *Land, Conflict, and Justice*, 90.
8. Kolers, *Land, Conflict, and Justice*, 90.
9. Kolers, *Land, Conflict, and Justice*, 11.
10. On this view, the fundamental holder of the right is the nation, and the relationship between the nation and the state is similar to a limited trust, where the institutions of state perform the functions on behalf of the nation; Miller, 'Territorial Rights', 251.
11. Tamar Meisels also endorses an identity argument, in which the importance of the land in the identity of the people is primary; Tamar Meisels, *Territorial Rights*, 2nd edition (Dordrecht: Springer, 2009), 95.
12. Meisels, *Territorial Rights*.
13. Avishai Margalit and Joseph Raz, 'National Self-Determination', *Journal of Philosophy*, vol. 87, no. 9 (1990), 439–461, at 443–446.
14. Miller, *On Nationality*, 27.
15. Miller, *On Nationality*, 98. Arash Abizadeh accuses David Miller of just this move in 'Does Liberal Democracy Presuppose a Cultural Nation? Four Arguments', *American Political Science Review*, vol. 96, no. 3 (2002), 495–510. It is, however, clear that Miller has a thin but substantive cultural nationalist argument; and he is mainly thinking of cases where the different meanings of the term coalesce. Miller's strategy is to avoid the charge of essentialism by identifying several features—which bear a family resemblance—of the usual concept of 'nation', even if no single feature is essential.
16. Walker Connor, *Ethnonationalism: The Quest for Understanding* (Princeton: Princeton University Press, 1994), 32–36; Donald L. Horowitz, *Ethnic Groups in Conflict* (Berkeley: University of California Press, 1985), 36–54; Thomas Hylland Eriksen, *Ethnicity and Nationalism: Anthropological Perspectives* (London: Pluto, 1993), 38–46.
17. John McGarry and Brendan O'Leary, *Explaining Northern Ireland* (Oxford: Blackwell, 1995), 171–213.
18. Richard Rose, *Governing without Consensus: An Irish Perspective* (London: Faber, 1971), 218.
19. Rosemary Harris, *Prejudice and Tolerance in Ulster* (Manchester: Manchester University Press, 1972), 131.
20. Michael Ignatieff, 'Nationalism and the Narcissism of Minor Differences', *Queen's Quarterly*, vol. 102, no. 1 (1995), 13–25, at 13; Paul Mojzes, *Yugoslavian Inferno* (New York: Continuum, 1995), xvi; Noel Malcolm, *Bosnia: A Short History* (New York: New York University Press, 1994), 282; Christopher Bennett, *Yugoslavia's Bloody Collapse: Causes, Course and Consequences* (New York: New York University Press, 1995), 247.
21. In my previous work, I somewhat misleadingly called political identities 'national identities', but I did not mean that the nations had to be culturally distinct nations, which is what I here refer to as a cultural account.
22. One potential difficulty with the two-way relationship between culture and land argument is that it is not specific on which exactly is primary. It is true that they are often in

symbiotic relationship, and in the paradigmatic example, people who occupy land naturally transform it *and* become attached to it.

23. Miller, *National Responsibility and Global Justice*, 217–218.
24. Meisels, *Territorial Rights*, 95.
25. Miller, *National Responsibility and Global Justice*, 218.
26. In one of the early formulations of this argument, Miller suggests that this in turn justifies their claim to exercise continuing political authority *over that territory*; David
Miller, 'Secession and the Principle of Nationality', in Margaret Moore, ed., *National Self-
Determination and Secession*, 62–78 (Oxford: Oxford University Press, 1998), 68; the italics are mine.
27. Miller, 'Territorial Rights', 263.
28. Stilz, 'Nations, States, and Territory', 577.
29. Stilz, 'Nations, States, and Territory', 577.
30. Stilz, 'Nations, States, and Territory', 577.
31. The tripartite argument culture—value in land-jurisdictional rights—may also be potentially exclusionary of some kinds of settlement patterns, and provide a perverse incentive
for erasing a people's cultural impress on the land—by changing place names or defacing
cultural monuments to ensure that only one's culture is impressed on the land. On this
last point, I must admit that an occupancy principle provides a perverse incentive too—to
expel people from land that they occupy. This will be discussed in chapter 7.

5

Functionalist and Statist Theories of Territory

This chapter takes up the second part of the challenge of defending my theory on the grounds that it offers a better account of rights over territory than its principal rivals. In this chapter I examine functionalist and statist theories of territory, which begin from the widely held view that a state that is able to impose order in any region thereby gains territorial right. This position has the practical advantage that establishing who has territorial rights is relatively easy whenever there is an effective state available to be identified.

It also justifies territorial rights straightforwardly in terms of the goods that the state achieves. It relates claims to political authority over persons and claims to rights over territory through an argument that takes the question of political authority as having logical priority: we explain how the state can have legitimate authority and then states' secondary rights over territory fall into place. That strategy, familiar to us in the works of Hobbes and Kant and many others, links jurisdictional control over land with the fulfilment of the purpose of the state (the achievement of peace, in Hobbes's theory, or justice in Kant), which makes territorial right contingent on the achievement of these goods.

I've already indicated that I regard this basic strategy as deeply problematic: I do not think that an argument justifying authority over people can generate authority over territory. In this chapter, I try to show the limits of this strategy, both in terms of linking the state with particular bits of territory and in terms of its counter-intuitive implications.

Statist theories of territory come in two main forms: a Hobbesian version, which identifies the achievement of peace, stability, coordination, and order as the function of the state and then justifies territorial rights as necessary to an effective state order; and a more moralized version, which links the state with the achievement of justice, and argues that territorial rights should be accorded to a just (or legitimate) state. In this chapter, I discuss each of these versions in turn. I argue that the Hobbesian version suffers from indeterminacy in isolating territorial right-holders prior to their actual exercise of jurisdictional authority; that it has status quo bias; and has counter-intuitive consequences. The Kantian argument for a statist holder of territorial rights can solve many of the problems inherent in the Hobbesian version, by linking the idea of justice with the state as locus of sovereign authority. It does this by linking tightly the normative arguments for the state with the exercise of territorial right. However, I argue that while this version solves some of the problems associated with the Hobbesian version, it is nevertheless problematic in two ways: first, it does not provide a convincing story of attachment, that is, a response to the problem of attaching particular bits of territory to particular states; and second, it is too demanding, and fails to justify territorial rights in many cases, which makes it counter-intuitive. In my view, the tight link it draws between justice and the state does not pay enough regard to the moral value of self-determination, which, I argued in chapter 3, ought to be at the heart of the case for territorial rights.

5.1. Hobbesian Statist Theories of Territory

Hobbes argues that human beings create political community to protect themselves from each other. He argues that, without government, people would be in a state of conflict: they would regard each other with diffidence and suspicion, and the resulting state of affairs would be a state of 'warre, as is of every man, against every man', where 'warre' consists not necessarily in actual fighting, 'but in the known disposition thereto, during all the time there is no assurance to the contrary'.[1] In order to escape this state of affairs, in which life is 'nasty, brutish and short', individuals must unite together in a political community, and create a sovereign authority that can keep peace and order and protect people from one another. On this formulation, individual persons establish sovereign authority through a contract in which they transfer all rights to a sovereign authority, which he calls Leviathan. Leviathan creates the people: it represents the will of those who had alienated their rights to it; and it is Leviathan, the sovereign authority, which creates the basic rules of society, including what counts as just and unjust, lawful and unlawful. On this view, being a state in the minimum sense of creating or maintaining order is sufficient to justify territorial rights. There is no logical limit to the state's boundaries: people unite out of fear, rather than a sense of affinity or cultural ties, and indeed they need the sovereign to create order, to give content to the ideas of justice and injustice, as well as other moral ideas. There is no pre-political basis for order, other than the coercive authority embodied in the sovereign. Territorial rights are necessary to the functioning of the sovereign authority, but there is not, on this view, a natural limit to the sovereign state: indeed, the sovereign usually exerts authority where it can, and then runs up against another sovereign authority, which has managed to secure order in another geographical area. There is no barrier to conquest on this view, provided it is effective in maintaining order. The international order is itself conceived as a state of nature, characterized by diffidence, suspicion, and glory-seeking, and while there is no theoretical reason why we couldn't have a global political order, to escape fully and finally the state of nature, this is not the world that we know, which is characterized by a plurality of such entities. Each one has territorial rights over its geographical domain, because this is necessary to achieve stability and order within its borders.

Two hundred years later, Sidgwick sought to show that rights over territory, which we take as straightforwardly related to the exercise of state sovereignty, were justified because necessary to the good functioning of government, which in turn was related to the ultimate utilitarian standard of individual happiness. Like Hobbes and most modern international lawyers, Sidgwick defined the state in terms that make control over territory integral: the modern state, he wrote, is 'a determinate and stable group of human beings, whose government has a practically undisputed right of regulating the legal relations of human beings over a determinate portion of the earth's surface'.[2]

Sidgwick addressed the justification of territory directly. In his view,

> the main justification for the appropriation of land to the exclusive use, either of individuals or groups of human beings, is that its full advantages as an instrument of production cannot otherwise be utilised; the main justification for the appropriation of territory to governments is that the prevention of mutual mischief among the human beings using it cannot otherwise be adequately secured.[3]

Although Sidgwick, as a utilitarian, could have adopted a much more demanding standard for state rights over territory (namely, that the state performs better by the utility criterion than any likely alternative), in fact he adopts a minimalist standard, similar to Hobbes, of requiring effective and continuous jurisdiction over a territory. This is clearly the implication of his argument in relation to competing territorial claims: when discussing claims to secession, he argues that such claims have force only when the secessionists can demonstrate 'some unjust sacrifice or grossly incompetent management of their interests, or some persistent and harsh opposition to their legitimate desires'.[4] There is a performance standard that the state must meet, and presumably some states will fail to meet it, and will not be entitled to exercise rights over territory, but this standard is met by the simple exercise of effective control over the territory in question.

There are three serious problems with this type of statist conception of the holder of territorial right, where states are identified principally with the ful-filment of the minimal functions of maintaining order and effective govern-ment across a contiguous territory. The first difficulty is connected to the view that territorial right—the right to make rules within the territory—*follows from* effective control. This means that it is impossible to determine in advance whether any particular state is the proper holder of territorial right until it demonstrates that it is able to exercise control over the said territory.[5] This is not satisfactory in cases where two groups are contending for state control: it means that the right cannot be determined in advance of the actual exercise of control.

A related difficulty is that it appears that when a state is able to exercise con-trol, challenges to that, by movements for autonomy or independence or rebel-lion, must be resisted, because the exercise of control alone seems to carry with it territorial right. For Hobbes, only if the state is grossly incompetent—that is, a failed state—do other sorts of claims have force. It appears then to be not only statist but also supportive of the status quo, even if there are other mobi-lized groups that would be better at exercising control, realizing justice, and governing according to the wishes of the people.[6]

Finally, since, on the statist view, territorial right is held by the state and not the people, it has counter-intuitive consequences in cases where a regime or other state exercises control over an area previously under the jurisdiction of a failed state. Let us suppose, for example, that Somalia is a failed state. The government does not exercise authority throughout its territory; indeed, huge swathes of land are in the control of lawless bands of criminals. Since the government does not fulfil the functions of a state, it does not have territorial right.[7] It follows that any state or group that is able to exert order, to impose a system of control over the land, would thereby gain territorial right. If Ethiopia or some other adjacent state, or even some distant imperial power (such as the United States) went in to the area with overwhelming force and were able to impose order and state control, it would seem that it would thereby gain terri-torial rights. This does not accord with our intuitions about conquest nor with international law on the rules of intervention.

Moreover, are we to understand that the adjacent state or imperial power would thereby gain rights, not only: (1) the right to jurisdictional authority, but also (2) rights to control entry and exit, and (3) rights to regulate, sell, and extract natural resources within the ground? It is simply unclear how 'the prevention of mutual mischief' among the human beings who inhabit a ter-ritory should give the state either the right to exploit the resources that the territory contains, or the right to control immigration and emigration. A utilitarian could explain why somebody should exercise these rights—for example, the reasons why stable and secure ownership of resources is prima facie desirable—but not why that must be the same agency as the one that regulates the behaviour of persons. In that sense, it cannot explain and justify territorial rights as we would normally understand them, which of course was Sidgwick's initial intention.[8]

5.2. Legitimate-State Theories of Territory

The quest for a more robust account of territorial rights—one rooted in justice and mutual recognition—leads away from Hobbes to Kant. The Kantian view justifies territorial right in terms of the more demanding standard of justice. For Kant, the sovereign authority is also defined in terms of a contract, but the state is not conceived of as 'above' the law, or as creator of 'right' and 'wrong', just and unjust. Rather, the state is legitimate because it is required by justice, by the requirement to exercise power in accordance with Right.[9] This Kantian account of sovereign authority has a number of contemporary defenders, who have put forward sophisticated and nuanced arguments in its favour, notably, Allen Buchanan, Anna Stilz, Jeremy Waldron, Lea Ypi, and to some extent Cara Nine.

Kant's main contribution to our understanding of the relationship between territory and the state is through putting forward an account of the territorial state as required by justice. According to Kant, individuals have a permissive claim to be in occupancy of land[10] and to obtain objects, and both activities are justified by the exercise of their freedom. However, these acts are permitted only as long as individuals also endeavour to leave a state of nature, that is, a condition with no political authority and therefore lacking in justice, and submit to a common jurisdictional authority. This obligation is initiated by the possession of things, which is justified in one sense as an extension of individual freedom[11] but which also contradicts (other people's) freedom, since removing things from common use prevents other people from enjoying the object in question.[12] Since the exercise of my freedom seems unavoidably to involve restrictions on the exercise of someone else's freedom, the dilemma can be resolved only by reciprocal recognition of everyone's obligation to respect the fundamental principles around the acquisition, transfer, and use of objects in the external world, which we normally think of as 'rights of property'. This reciprocal recognition involves creating a civil condition, which ensures that my freedom will be respected and that others' freedom will be respected, an assurance that cannot be met in the state of nature. Such a change transforms the use of these external things from the coercive will of one person to the general will of a jurisdictional authority, because it provides a framework of general rules, which is the foundation of civil society.

Drawing on Kant, and consistent with the reasons above for conferring territorial rights on states, legitimate-state theorists advance a normatively laden version of statist theory. Lea Ypi argues that the creation of a collective political authority is justified because it is necessary to adjudicate claims impartially, consistent with principles of equal freedom. In Buchanan's theory, the state is legitimate if it upholds human rights, by which he means acts in ways consistent with human rights, and, furthermore, acts to defend human rights more generally. Buchanan emphasizes the need for mutual recognition of territorial rights by other states and established standards of recognitional legitimacy. Both theories draw on Kant's basic idea that rights to territory are second-order rights, which follow because territorial jurisdictional authority is necessary to the proper functioning of a state and just relations among people within states.[13]

Cara Nine's argument in *Global Justice and Territory* combines elements from three very diverse theories in an innovative way, and the key question is whether this combination is coherent.[14] Although there are different strands in her work, I discuss it here, because she shares with legitimate-state theorists a defence of justice as the central moral ideal underlying territorial rights. In her view, the right to territory—defined as a right to jurisdictional authority over people and resources—can be justified because it is necessary for the provision of individual needs. Meeting individual needs requires coordination amongst people who share the land with regard to resources and so they are justified in implementing 'rules of justice' to do this. The territorial right-holding agent is identified as a people, a collective, that 'must (1) demonstrate the capacity to meet minimal standards of justice (to provide secure access to the objects of basic human needs for members and to respect the basic human rights of all persons), and (2) have members who share a common conception of justice'.[15] The second condition suggests a more relativist position than the first, though perhaps it's meant only to suggest that different communities meet human rights and basic needs differently—and that the rules count as rules of *justice* as long as they contribute to human needs and are consistent with respect for human rights. Setting aside the problem that it is unclear what it means to apply the success condition—justice—to *societies*, and how that relates to the relative justice of the regimes or states, what is important here is that the crucial normative argument for jurisdictional rights over territory is in terms of the importance of justice, defined in terms of meeting basic needs justly, and so, I will argue below, this theory has implausible implications in many of the same cases as the other (justice-based) theories.

There are three elements to most legitimate-state theories (only the third is shared by Nine). The first element is identifying the state as the fundamental holder of territorial right. The second is there needs to be some way to move from the general claim to (some) territory to a claim to particular territory and this means that there has to be some principle to attach particular states to particular territories. The third is the normative criterion—that of justice—that is employed to justify rights over territory. Each of these will be discussed in turn.

5.2.1. The State as Territorial Right-Holding Agent

The first component of legitimate-state theory involves the claim that the state is the fundamental holder of territorial right. Why should we adopt this view? There are two clear practical advantages. One is that there is no difficulty conceiving of the state as the right kind of collective agent: it has a clear, unified decision-making structure which is distinct from the separate wills and decisions of the individual members of the state. Second, we can readily identify territorial right-holders: they are the states that exercise jurisdictional authority over an area.

In addition to these practical advantages, there are theoretical arguments, derived from or congruent with an analysis of Kant's theory, which explain why the Hobbesian treatment of states is inadequate. The most compelling argument for this view is advanced by Allen Buchanan, who writes:

> The chief moral purpose of endowing an entity with political power is to achieve justice. Given the state's coercive and monopolistic character and the fact that it necessarily involves inequality of power, nothing short of this could justify creating an entity so capable of causing harm, infringing freedom, and creating or maintaining inequalities. A wielder of political power that does a credible job of achieving justice is morally justified in wielding that power, if it provides a reasonable approximation of justice through processes that are themselves reasonably just.[16]

Anna Stilz also explains why the state is uniquely appropriate to possess territorial rights. She defines her theory in central contrast to cultural nationalist theory. She writes: 'on the legitimate state theory, the "people" are made into one collective body by being subject to state institutions and by participating together in shaping these institutions. In order to account for territorial rights, we do not need to invoke a cultural nation that pre-exists the state. On my view, the state instead defines the citizenry that is subject to it. Over time, as we shall see, this initially unconnected group of citizens may be made into "a people" by cooperating together in shared institutions'.[17]

Stilz pursues this argument by reflecting on reasons why Kant thought that only states are appropriate holders of territorial rights. There are two problems involved in any exercise of jurisdiction by non-state actors: the problem of unilateral interpretation and the problem of unilateral coercion. The problem of unilateral interpretation is mainly referred to in cases of conflict over property, where an individual's right to property is subject to questions of interpretation and enforcement by actors, who might not agree on the bounds of property and the limits of property rights. Even if we agree on the limits of our property (and so there is no problem of interpretation between us) there is still a problem of unilateral coercion, because you depend on me to continue to agree with your interpretation. As Stilz writes: 'You might respect my rights now, but your will could change, and so you retain the *power* of interference with me and my rights, even if you do not in fact exercise that power. To be fully independent, though, I must have a mechanism to *assure* me that my rights will be guaranteed, no matter what the condition of your will. The proper mechanism of assurance is the state's framework of lawful coercion'.[18] This of course explains why a state is required. Many non-anarchists (including myself) would agree with this: a state, or state-like entity, is necessary to secure everyone's independence, and since we have a basic or fundamental duty to respect each other's independence, we do not have to consent to the state to be bound to it. This is in fact a standard non-libertarian view, widely held across the political spectrum, by liberals, conservative, social democrats, and others.

The argument that is meant to justify the state as the holder of territorial rights (or at least jurisdictional authority over territory) is simple: the state is necessary to the interpretation and enforcement of rights, especially rights to property; and this helps to explain why states and only states can claim jurisdiction over territory. However, even if we accept the view that states are necessary to solve the problems of unilateral interpretation and unilateral coercion, one might still think that there are even more fundamental claims, held by the people on whose behalf the state is operating. On this rival understanding— which is the view held by the non-statist theories, discussed in chapters 3 and 4—the state may be the appropriate *mechanism* through which rights, vested in the people, are exercised, but the people are the fundamental holder(s) of territorial rights. In response to the statist claim that territorial rights require some kind of agent similar to the state, which can solve these two problems of unilateral interpretation and unilateral coercion, the non-statist could reply that it's just not true that states are the only agent who might be entitled to exercise territorial rights. Indigenous groups, substate groups, suprastate groups might also in principle qualify. Of course, there would need to be some mechanism, some institutional apparatus for such groups to be effective in making rules over a geographical area, but this doesn't mean that states, rather than the group(s), are the fundamental holder of territorial rights.

Many versions of legitimate-state theory obliquely recognize that the claim that a state or state-like entity is necessary to solve problems in a state of nature is insufficient to show that territorial rights are held by states. After all, one could conceive of the state as a necessary mechanism by which a group of people exercise their rights, while the people themselves are the fundamental territorial rights-holding agent. To complete the argument, it is necessary to criticize the alternative, which is often taken to be the cultural nationalist theory of territory. Unfortunately, statists tend to describe the nationalist view in a caricatured way, foreclosing other possibilities. Jeremy Waldron exemplifies this strategy: he distinguishes between (1) affinity theories, which he associates with nationalism and which, he claims, ignore the problems of conflict, contest, and disagreement; and (2) statist theories, which are built on the idea of conflict as endemic to society.[19] Unfortunately, this way of setting up the problem seems to ignore the possibility of a combined approach: jurisdictional authority is necessary to solve conflict and disagreement and provide mechanisms for making social choices; but some pre-existing affinity, some commitment to operating this institution with particular people, is necessary to ensure that people are prepared to resolve conflicts through setting up this procedure, and to agree to the norms underlying it.

Stilz, too, defines the central alternative to legitimate-state theory as a particular type of 'nationalist view', which is necessarily committed to regarding 'the people' as an ethnic or cultural community. This is arguably true of the two theorists that she examines at some length[20] but it is not generally true (and I would argue not even true of them). In this book, I've advanced a non-statist conception that is not tied to culture. And even theorists that we might think of as cultural nationalists, such as Miller, do not espouse an essentialist or static view of culture: he has a fairly thin and flexible view of culture, and is careful to distinguish national identity from mere ethnic or cultural identity.

5.2.2. The Attachment Problem

Since Kant's argument is directed, in the first instance, at demonstrating why *in general* states are necessary for justice, and why individuals are obligated to submit to a state rather than remain in a state of nature, it is able to justify territorial rights in general, but has difficulty explaining how particular states can have authority over particular territories. Indeed, the logic of the account is distinctly cosmopolitan: there is no reason internal to the theory why the jurisdiction should not be universal, why we would not end up in a global state.

Kant himself tries to avoid this conclusion by appealing to considerations which fall outside of Kantian theory normally understood, such as that people tend, as an empirical fact, to be naturally grouped into linguistic or religious collectivities and that membership in these cultural groups helps to define the particular jurisdictional domain.[21] Some legitimate-state theorists—such as Lea Ypi—are probably happy enough with this cosmopolitan conclusion, viewing the state as instrumentally valuable, in whatever configuration that it presents itself, as long as it is conducive to the realization of cosmopolitan justice. However, this means that there are many issues about which questions of justice arise that legitimate-state theorists do not have the conceptual resources to address: they cannot effectively tackle boundary drawing, secession, defensive war, immigration, and control over resources. They can consider these only indirectly, in terms of the relative justice of the entities that are making these claims.

Most legitimate-state theorists, however, recognize that the failure to address the attachment problem—that is, the failure to explain the attachment of particular states to particular territories—is a serious deficiency, not only theoretically, because it represents a less complete theory of territory, but because it means that this account has counter-intuitive implications in many situations in the current world order. Recently, Stilz has defended a modified version of legitimate-state theory that aims to solve the attachment problem *and* to address these non-ideal situations in a coherent and morally persuasive way, and is therefore worth examining in some detail.

One distinctive feature of Stilz's account is her emphasis on moral rights of occupancy (defined differently than mine), which has two functions in her theory. First, it helps her account explain in a non-circular way the usurpation condition; and, second, it helps to tie the state to a certain geographical domain. If her argument is successful, she will have developed a legitimate state argument that addresses the attachment problem.

Stilz argues that a state 'has rights to a territory if and only if: (a) it effectively implements a system of law regulating property there, (b) its subjects have claims to occupy the territory, (c) its system of law "rules in the name of the people," by protecting basic rights and providing for political participation, and (d) the state is not a usurper'.[22] Only condition (a) refers to the performance of *state* functions. Condition (b) refers to whether *the people* have a right to legitimate occupancy; and condition (c), in invoking the idea of *legitimacy*, refers to the idea that the state itself ought to function in the interests of the people, and indeed that it is through the protection of their fundamental interests that the state is legitimate at all. Condition (d)—the non-usurpation condition—refers to the case where one state takes over the territory of another.

Here, I want to focus on the role of moral occupancy both as a condition in its own right for a legitimate state, and as a means for thinking about usurpation, in one sense at least. Although many theorists have appealed to moral rights of residency or occupancy, as I have done in chapter 3, Stilz's appeal to a version of that principle in the context of legitimate-state theory is innovative, since it functions both to locate territorial rights (they apply only where members occupy the territory) and to explain her non-usurpation condition. What Stilz needs to do if this is to be a separate condition for holding territorial rights is to give us a non-circular understanding of just and unjust occupancy. Unfortunately, however, she fails to avoid the problem of circularity, because she tries to remain faithful to the requirements of a statist theory. When she specifies the conditions of a legitimate state (to which moral rights of occupancy are central), she defines occupancy thus: 'A person has a right to occupy a territory if (1) he resides there now or has previously done so, (2) *legal residence* within that territory is fundamental to the integrity of his structure of personal relationships, goals, and pursuits, and (3) his connection to that particular territory was formed through no fault of his own'.[23] The reference to legal residence preserves the statist dimension of her argument, but it means that her argument is in fact circular, because the legitimacy of the state is partially defined by the occupancy principle, which in turn is defined in terms of *legal* rights (of residence) in a legitimate state. What looked like a pre-political principle that a rightful authority should uphold is converted in her statist account into a political status that the state confers on its members.

5.2.3. The Demanding Standard of Justice for Territorial Rights and Its Counter-Intuitive Implications

An even more serious problem is that legitimate-state theory is too demanding, and this leads to counter-intuitive consequences in many cases. This criticism also applies to Nine's theory in so far as it justifies rights over territory in terms of justice.

What is the problem with relying on justice as a justificatory argument for state control over territory? The appeal of the argument is that, by establishing a tight link between the state, territory, and justice, it seems fully to justify the state's political authority over persons. Yet it imposes a very demanding standard. If we identify justice with the impartial application of rules (the rule of law), the protection of human rights, and/or distributive justice within a community, then most states in existence today are not just. Most states in the past were not just. Since most countries that exercised jurisdiction over territory were not just, the exercise of their jurisdictional authority was not justified. But—do we really believe this? Do we think that France in the seventeenth century had no territorial rights, nor Morocco in the eighteenth century, nor many of the principalities in India prior to British rule?[24] Most people think that they were not just, but that they still had rights over territory.

This intuition can be explored in relation to the wrong of colonialism. Most people think that the wrong of colonialism isn't captured just by the fact that the imperial authorities failed to include the colonial peoples fully in their political projects, and instead erected forms of political and legal domination over them. By 'domination' here, I mean that the colonized subjects were not granted any share of political power, so they were dominated in the same sense in which, say, serfs under feudalism were dominated. This was part of the problem, to be sure, but we also think that a significant part of the problem was that the imperial powers were involved in the taking of territory. We think that colonialism was wrong in two separate ways: one is that these were forms of political domination; but the second is that the imperial power was involved in the taking of territory. The imperial powers were extending jurisdictional authority over people and so claiming territorial rights over the land, despite the fact that the people did not want to be included in that political project.[25] The problem with colonialism wasn't simply the violation of the equality condition (equal treatment of persons); it was that the imperial power was engaged in taking territorial rights from another people, through extending political authority (rules of justice) over them.

The same difficulty extends to contemporary cases, which I will consider below. Legitimate-state theory has counter-intuitive consequences in cases of annexation, injustice, and state failure. In cases where a state is annexed by another state but the second state is more effective in securing justice, it would seem to license the aggressor in thereby gaining territorial right. In cases where the state is unjust, it would seem that another state can gain control of the territory and implement a more just order, and thereby gain territorial right. And in cases where a state is failed—by which I mean that it fails to exercise authority throughout its territory, where large swathes of land are in the control of lawless bands of criminals—it would seem that an effective state, which is able to implement rules of justice, can thereby gain rights over the territory. These results are counter-intuitive, as I will argue below; and they also do not correspond to international law, which is clear that aggression should not be rewarded and that intervention in an emergency, such as when the state is failed, can be justified only for the minimum amount of time necessary to return a functioning order to the people living on the territory.

As a response to the problem of demandingness, legitimate-state theories attempt two distinct strategies. The first is to try to reduce the dependence on justice and rely on a more minimalist standard—that of legitimacy—which is not the same as justice, and which brings the theory much closer to the

Hobbesian or Sidgwickian position than it at first appears. The second is to modify legitimate-state theory in the direction of non-statist theories, to deal with these specific, counter-intuitive implications generated by the lack of link with particular territories.

The first strategy is clearly seen in Allen Buchanan's work, principally as it applies to secession, a situation that he has considered at length. Consistent with Buchanan's justice theory of the state, he has argued for a just-cause theory of secession, according to which there is a remedial right to secede for groups that live in unjust states.[26] One advantage of this type of theory is that it suggests a strong internal connection between the right to secede and human rights, and so grounds arguments in the ethics of secession within the generally accepted framework of human rights and a generally accepted theory of state legitimacy. It might seem that this not only has the advantage of being continuous with credible understandings of justice, human rights, and state legitimacy, but that it is relatively easy to apply. It requires only a backward-looking assessment of the policies and practices of the state, and the veracity of claims made by the would-be secessionist group concerning violations of human rights, torture, and unjust killing. To avoid the problem of disagreements about what justice requires, Buchanan focuses only on those egregious violations of human rights that are generally accepted as deeply problematic both in the philosophical literature and the international legal order.[27] These are those human rights commonly thought to protect fundamental human interests, such as the right not to be tortured or the right not to be unjustly killed.[28]

However, a more careful analysis of the structure of Buchanan's argument reveals that Buchanan waters down the justice-based argument in important ways, which has the effect of granting territorial rights to many entities that are far from just. This brings Buchanan's theory, at least as it applies to territorial rights, perilously close to a Hobbesian or Sidgwickian theory, in which justice almost drops out of the picture.

In his book *Secession*, Buchanan argues that the desires and claims of the secessionists have to be weighed against the claims of the state, which, if it is a just state, is the 'trustee for the people, conceived as an intergenerational community'.[29] The just state, therefore, has an obligation to protect all (existing and future) citizens' legitimate interests in this political and territorial community. Secession is permissible only when the state forfeits its claim to being a legitimate trustee by failing to fulfil its justice-based obligations. One interesting feature of the structure of this argument is that it doesn't require that the would-be secessionist group itself be the victim; rather, it requires only that the state that is being dismembered is the perpetrator of injustice.

An even more interesting question is raised by Buchanan's invocation of the role of the state, as distinct from the regime. His theory raises the question: at what point do we regard *the state itself*, as opposed to a particular regime, as unjust? In his 2004 book, *Justice, Legitimacy, and Self-Determination*, he elaborates on the distinction between *state* acts of injustice and particular *government*'s acts of injustice.[30] Buchanan defines a 'state' as an enduring structure of basic institutions for wielding political power, where this structure includes roles to be filled by members of the government.[31] The 'government' can be thought of as the human agency by which the institutional resources of the state are employed. If the state is illegitimate, its government is illegitimate. But the reverse need not be true.

If unjust acts are committed by a particular government, then the logic of the analysis is that they can be rectified by a change in government. We are then in the realm of revolution, as John Locke argued in his Second Treatise of Government.[32] Buchanan argues that remedying the flaws of an illegitimate state involves more than a change of character in the government: it requires profound constitutional changes that transform the state itself. An example of such a profound constitutional change is secession. And of course secession is justified only if the *state* is illegitimate, because by definition the state does not deserve the rights (to territorial integrity) that it has had conferred on it by the international community. On Buchanan's account of the distinction between 'state' and 'government', there are potentially two distinct categories of unjust (or just) entities. The category 'unjust government' is over-populated, encompassing all governments who have engaged in unjust conduct. The category 'unjust state' is seriously under-populated. Buchanan cites only two examples: Apartheid South Africa and ante-bellum United States.[33] The first of these is a curious example, since the remedy for the constitutional flaws of the state involved principally a change in government.[34] Nevertheless, it certainly suggests that the line between state and government is much more fluid than Buchanan's distinction implies. Secession is legitimate only if the entity in question falls into the category of 'unjust state', which is highly unlikely, since repression, torture, and killing at the behest of the government is not sufficient to render a state as 'unjust'. Indeed, it seems that this line of argument doesn't really constitute a theory of legitimate secession, since there are practically no instances of secession that would be justified.

What is interesting for our purposes, however, it not whether the distinction between just government and just state is compelling in itself, or as it applies to the ethics of secession, but that it serves to significantly lower the bar in assessing whether a state can lose territorial rights. On the one hand, justice is the main justificatory argument for having rights over territory, but on the other hand, it seems that many kinds of injustices do not have any consequences for the state's rightful control over territory; that people could suffer distributive injustices, violations of their human rights and neglect of their interests, but that this would be conceived as the consequences of an unjust *regime*. The state would thereby pass the standards of legitimacy. It turns out then that the standards set—through this distinction between just and unjust state and regime—are extremely minimal, such that almost any state, past and present, would meet it.

A second strategy is to modify the conditions that a state must meet in order to have rights over territory. In the original Kantian story, these conditions were spelled out primarily in terms of justice. Anna Stilz emphasizes that the standard does not have to be perfect justice, but a lesser standard: that of legitimacy. Moreover, she does not just present this in an ad hoc way, as some kind of approximation of justice. She spells out the conditions that must be met if a state is to qualify as legitimate, which helps to respond to the attachment problem, and address some of the counter-intuitive consequences of a theory of territory rooted in justice. These are: (1) the legitimate-occupancy condition, and (2) the non-usurpation condition. In section 5.2.2, I have examined the legitimate-occupancy condition, which is based on people's right to live in a place and pursue plans and goals. To preserve the statism of her theory, Stilz argues that states have territorial rights over the geographical space where the people live and have legal residence. I have already shown that this condition is (viciously) circular.

I focus now on the non-usurpation condition, which specifies that only states that are not usurpers can have rights to territory. What does it mean for a state to be a usurper? How should we understand the concept of usurpation? We might think of usurpation as involving taking over the territory of another state and expelling people from that territory. This would seem to be ruled out by Stilz's understanding of rightful or just occupancy (condition 2 above). Alternatively, we might not think of usurpation as referring to a case where one state takes over the territory of another, with no change of occupancy, and in that case, the crucial feature is whether the previous state was indeed a just state, which in turn is centrally related to whether the usurping state committed an injustice. (If the previous state was murderous and unjust, the displacing state could not be conceived of as *usurping* its rightful authority.) Usurpation by definition seems to exclude the new power from being the holder of territorial rights. On this view, it would be a violation of justice (and of legitimate-state theory) to displace another justice-enforcing state.

On legitimate-state theory, then, states have rights to territory if they are effective and rights-respecting, and this includes respecting the usurpation prohibition. Let us now consider a case where a state conquers an aggressive and unjust state (that is, the conquering state did not violate the

non-usurpation condition because the defeated state was unjust). An example of this is the Allied defeat of Nazi Germany in 1945. It would seem that
legitimate-state theory has to take the view that there would be nothing wrong
with the occupied powers gaining territorial right by imposing a system of just
laws and rules over German territory and incorporating that territory into
their own. Yet, this seems counter-intuitive. We might agree that the Nazi state
was illegitimate, but we do not thereby think that the German people should
lose their previous capacity to make rules to govern their collective life, and be
thereby collectively self-determining. (Of course, for legitimate-state theory
of territorial right, the German people do not *lose* this right, since it is held by
the state, not the people.)

In order to respond to the potentially counter-intuitive implications of
her theory in this case, Stilz modifies the non-usurpation condition so that it
does not simply refer to the non-usurpation of a legitimate *state*. There is, she
notes, a 'widely shared intuition that for such an annexation [the United States
annexing German in 1945], there must be some expression of collective consent on the part of the annexed group'.[35] She notes that this is a difficulty for
her theory since it denies that there is a pre-political nation independent of the
state, and it denies that consent is necessary for state legitimacy. Nevertheless,
she argues that 'unilateral annexation [of Nazi Germany by the United States]
would infringe the residual right of the German *people* in their territory. This
gives the German people a claim against annexing states even when their
own state fails or becomes illegitimate'.[36] How can a statist analysis possibly
explain these residual rights to territory? Stilz answers that she does *not* rely
on a pre-political 'nation'; indeed, if she did, it would mean that her argument
has just collapsed into the cultural nationalist one. She writes: 'Recall that on
the legitimate state theory the people are made into one body by being subject
to common institutions and by participating together in shaping those institutions'.[37] On her view, while a people can be created only by being united into
a state, once a people have been so created, through the coordinated social
behaviour that marks a state, they develop moral bonds that persist even
when the state fails or becomes unjust. This enables Stilz to reach an attractive
conclusion, but to do so she relies on an implausible empirical claim to maintain a purely statist account, where she claims that 'only a history of sharing
a state demonstrates the existence of the moral bonds that support political
authority'.[38]

At this point, it might be helpful to reflect on the ways in which my
self-determination theory of territory deals with such cases: it does not
emphasize justice nor (in contrast to the cultural nationalist) the preservation
of value in land, but the moral value of self-determination. It has intuitively
plausible consequences for a range of justified action at the international level,

including a better account of territorial rights for failed states and the conquest of an unjust state.

Consider first the case of a failed state. Legitimate state theory reasons from the fact of no effective state and therefore no justice to the conclusion that failed states ought not to have territorial right.[39] On my account, advanced in chapter 3, the people in a failed state, such as Somalia, may be the appropriate territorial right-holding agent if they share a political identity, have political capacity, and have a history of political cooperation. Let us suppose that the first and third conditions are met; there is still an important empirical question whether the people are capable of exercising collective self-government. The fact that they do not have an effectively functioning state raises questions about whether they satisfy this condition. And here the capacity condition is revealed as having a number of different dimensions, referring sometimes to the ability or capacity (or lack thereof) of the group to govern themselves, by erecting shared institutions and cooperating together to achieve shared aims; sometimes, to material conditions, such as poverty and lack of infrastructure and institutions, which make it difficult for the group to govern themselves; and to a hostile environment, where the defence of territorial rights is particularly costly (any such people must have the capacity to defend their territorial project). I argued in chapter 3 that, if the reasons behind lack of capacity could be corrected through just means, through redistribution from rich to poor countries, then there was an obligation on the part of third parties to assist the Somalis in building capacity and so realizing the moral value of self-determination. On my account, the central question in cases where a people (e.g., the Somalis) have conferred on them by the international community jurisdictional authority over their territory, but they are unable to exercise that authority effectively, the important question is: why? If they are *incapable* of doing so, then the exercise of territorial rights should fall to some other agent. But we should not infer from the empirical fact of a failed state that Somalis are incapable of creating a viable political order. They have many of the conditions necessary to exercise territorial self-government: they are geographically concentrated on territory that they occupy not unjustly; they do not seek to be part of another state or ruled by an external power, so we can assume that they wish to exercise collective self-government as Somalis. And if this is so, then, the right conclusion is to assist the Somalis in their endeavour to create a functioning self-governing community, both through respecting principles of non-intervention, so that they can exercise control over their own affairs, and by facilitating the creation of what Rawls called 'favourable conditions' to ensure that they can be collectively self-governing. This is also in accord with accepted international norms, which, under certain conditions, justify intervention, but it also argues that intervention should be as minimalist or as temporary as possible, because the ultimate aim is to restore jurisdictional authority to the people living on the land.

What about the case of an aggressive and unjust state that has been conquered, as with Nazi Germany? My theory, which emphasizes the moral and legal right of self-determination of peoples, provides a non-consequentialist explanation of the wrong of conquest. The problem with conquest is that it violates peoples' right to be self-determining. It is not about the stability of rules of the international order, nor imposing a non-usurpation condition on the exercise of territorial right to avoid perverse incentives, although all this is true, but that conquest violates self-determination. Since, on my view, the territorial right-holder is the people, it's not possible to acquire the moral right to exercise authority over territory *from the people* as a result of conquest of *the state*, because the people are the territorial right-holder and as such have the moral rights to reconstitute themselves in a political community.

What about Stilz's claim that statist theory can still be vindicated because only a state has the capacity to create a people, and so we can describe a people (who were once united in a state) as having meta-jurisdictional authority? This enables her to respond to legitimate-state theory's counter-intuitive treatment of the Nazi Germany case, but is it correct?

If this is intended to be an empirical claim, about what kinds of ties are necessary to forge a 'people', it is implausible, since there is ample evidence of state failure to 'nation-build', to build a single people, and some evidence of state success in units that did not have prior institutional recognition.[40] Israel is of course a paradigmatic example of the latter, but many countries were carved out of the defeated (Austro-Hungarian, Ottoman, and German) empires after the First World War and went on to be successful states, even though they had no prior history as states. It is not true that only groups that had previously had statehood conferred on them have the right kind of unity to justify according them territorial rights. There are empirical examples of political communities that seek to be self-determining from a state, as I will discuss in chapter 6, in relation to secessionist claims, and also many examples of states which have failed to develop the right kind of unity and identity. Consider for example the case of Ireland, which sought collective self-determination (from Britain) without any form of institutional differentiation. Ireland was an integral part of the United Kingdom, electing MPs to the Westminster parliament since 1801, but this internal representation was insufficient, as they still sought to be self-governing as a separate people or island. Of course, living in a state can help to underwrite institutional reciprocity and practices of cooperation, but these can also be developed in other ways, such as through cooperation and mobilization designed to affect liberation against an imperial order or large

majority-dominated state. It is possible—conceptually possible and empirically true too—that a history of cooperation against a state or against a usurper
or a settler group might also forge the moral ties that could sustain institutions
of government.

5.3. Conclusion

In conclusion, let me briefly review the ways in which statist theory is flawed.
Purely functionalist accounts, such as advanced by Hobbes, were subject to
three serious problems: they were unable to identify territorial right-holders
prior to actually exercising jurisdictional authority; they exhibited status quo
bias; and they had counter-intuitive consequences in cases where the account
confers rights on a state that is effective but unjust.

Legitimate-state theories, derived from Kant, justify political obligation
(and thereby ostensibly territorial rights) when the state is both functional and
just, and the latter is usually defined in terms of adhering to the rule of law,
democratic governance, and the protection of human rights. However it has
counter-intuitive consequences for rights to territory in cases where the state
is either a failed state or cannot meet the high bar of justice. It renders almost
all past states and most (or even all) current states without rights over territory. Justice theories address this problem in two ways. One way is by watering
down the justice requirement: this is done by Allen Buchanan's distinction
between an unjust state and an unjust regime, which has the effect of bringing
the theory perilously close to the Hobbesian version, and conferring territorial
rights (against secessionists) to many entities that are governed in radically
unjust ways. A second strategy is to modify legitimate-state theory by add-
ing extra conditions designed to deal with some of the most counter-intuitive
implications of the justice requirement. In this way, justice theories can focus
on the lesser requirement of legitimacy (which functions as a threshold condition) but instead of being ad hoc, there is an argument for these particular conditions. The problem with the latter move, as it is found in its most developed
form in Stilz's writings, is that it is not coherent. First, her theory is circular, in
defining moral occupancy in terms of legal residence; and second, the two conditions cannot be simply added to a Kantian analysis because they work only if
we assume that the appropriate right-holder can be defined without reference
to the state. These 'conditions' cannot be ad hoc modifications of a basically
Kantian position: they go to the heart of who holds territorial rights. Perhaps
Stilz can respond that she is not trying to vindicate Kant but to offer her own
original account, but, for this, she needs to define and defend the collective
entity in terms that don't appeal to the state. At present she relies on the state

to define who counts as a people, but then, incoherently, moves away from that position to address the Nazi Germany case.

Notice that these cases (failed states, unjust states, unjust and aggressive conquered states) are not a problem for my account, in which territorial rights are justified by reference to the moral value of ensuring that members of the political community can have control over the collective conditions of their lives. Injustice is a terrible thing, and it should be met by resistance, rebellion, or revolution, but it is counter-intuitive to argue that people who suffered injustice at the hands of their governing regime should thereby also be denied the possibility of exercising collective self-government at all because some other justice-producing entity can thereby be entitled to govern the territory. That result would be deeply counter-intuitive and suggests a very passive view of the relationship between the government and its subjects. My view, in short, corresponds to our intuitions about the importance of self-determination and the correct relationship between that value, justice, people, and land.

Notes

1. Thomas Hobbes, *Leviathan*, ed., with an introduction, by C. B. Macpherson (Harmondsworth: Penguin, 1968), 88–89.
2. Henry Sidgwick, *Elements of Politics*, 3rd edition (London: Elibron Classics, 2005), 208.
3. Sidgwick, *Elements of Politics*, 227.
4. Sidgwick, *Elements of Politics*, 205.
5. This objection is from Miller, 'Territorial Rights', 252–268.
6. Sidgwick's position is more nuanced: because he's a utilitarian, he has to allow that states that fail to satisfy the 'legitimate desires' of a significant part of the population may lose their claims to territorial rights.
7. There are complex questions here about the existence conditions for a state. In this section, I mean that a state that has external recognition as a state, by other states, can be called 'a state' for my purposes but that it would fail to qualify for territorial rights.
8. I am indebted to David Miller for this point.
9. Arthur Ripstein, *Force and Freedom: Kant's Legal and Political Philosophy* (Cambridge, MA: Harvard University Press, 2009), chapters 1 and 4.
10. Kant articulates a right of occupancy, noting that the earth is limited and that people can and must inhabit a specific part of the globe. 'Through the spherical shape of the planet they inhabit, nature has confined them all within an area of definite limits. Accordingly, the only conceivable way in which anyone can possess habitable land on earth is by possessing a part within a determinate whole in which everyone has an original right to share'; Immanuel Kant, 'The Metaphysics of Morals', in H. Reiss, ed., *Kant's Political Writings* (Cambridge: Cambridge University Press, 1970), 172. Kant is clear, however, that the right of occupancy does not extend to occupying land that is already occupied by other peoples: 'This does not, however, amount to a right to settle on another nation's territory, for the latter would require a special contract'; Kant, 'Metaphysics of Morals', 172.
11. Property can be viewed as an extension of freedom in the sense that people are permitted to make free choices and to use objects in the external world for their freely chosen aims but have a duty to try to render that permission fully consistent with the rules of Right. See Lea Ypi, 'A Permissive Theory of Territorial Rights', *European Journal of Philosophy*, vol. 22, no. 2 (2012), 288–312.

12. It is thus not consistent with Kantian doctrine in so far as Kant claims that our innate right to freedom must 'coexist with the freedom of every one in accordance with a universal law'; Kant, 'Metaphysics of Morals', 133 and 137–138.

13. Ypi, 'Permissive Theory of Territorial Rights', 8.

14. First, like my argument in chapter 3, she identifies the territorial right-holder with the people, understood as collective group, which she claims seeks to erect rules of justice over its life. (It should also be mentioned, just to avoid confusion, that this is different from her previous work which was explicitly statist.) Second, she offers an acquisition theory to explain the attachment between the collective and the land, which is explicitly Lockean in inspiration, but the value created accrues to the group, not the individuals. Third, she develops a justice account to explain why the people, who are the fundamental holder of territorial rights, should be entitled to rights over territory. It is because of the third aspect of her theory—the focus on justice—that I include her here.

15. Nine, *Global Justice and Territory*, 67.

16. Buchanan, *Justice, Legitimacy, and Self-Determination*, 247.

17. Stilz, 'Nations, States, and Territory', 579–580.

18. Stilz, 'Nations, States, and Territory', 581.

19. Jeremy Waldron, 'Proximity as the Basis of Political Community', paper presented at Workshop on Theories of Territory, King's College, London, 21 February 2009.

20. Miller, *National Responsibility and Global Justice*; Miller, 'Territorial Rights'; Meisels, *Territorial Rights*.

21. Kant, 'Perpetual Peace: A Philosophical Sketch', in Reiss, ed., *Kant's Political Writings*, 11; cited in Miller, 'Property and Territory', 104.

22. Stilz, 'Nations, States, and Territory', 584.

23. Stilz, 'Nations, States, and Territory', 585. Italics are mine.

24. See Ayelet Banai, 'The Territorial Rights of Legitimate States: A Pluralist Interpretation', *International Theory*, vol. 6, no. 1 (2014), 140–157.

25. This reminds me of the scene in *Monty Python's Life of Brian* (1979), where the crowd is asked 'What have the Romans ever done for us?' and numerous answers follow from the crowd: aqueducts, sanitation, roads, wine, and so on. My contention is that this was the wrong question: there might be functional benefits to the existence of a particular state, but that the state may nevertheless wrong people by establishing a jurisdictional authority over them that denies their collective self-determination.

26. Allen Buchanan, *Secession: The Morality of Political Divorce from Fort Sumter to Lithuania and Quebec* (Boulder, CO: Westview, 1991). Included amongst these injustices are prior occupation and seizure of territory (a condition which raises the question of whether we can explicate just and unjust occupation in terms that do not rely on the existence of a just state in the first place) but also serious violations of human rights.

27. This doesn't need to be regarded as a purely pragmatic decision. It might be thought that the gravity of the situation, or the remedy sought, might necessitate a greater degree of determinacy both about the justice violation and the consequences attached to rectifying it. See Allen Buchanan, 'Are Human Rights Parochial?', paper presented to the Political Philosophy Group, Queen's University, Kingston, Ontario, October 2005; *Philosophy & Public Affairs* (forthcoming).

28. These are also embodied in the major international human rights conventions, such as the Universal Declaration of Human Rights, the International Covenant on Civil and Political Rights, and the International Covenant on Social, Cultural and Economic Rights—although these international conventions are also more extensive than the minimalist list I provide.

29. Buchanan, *Secession*, 109.

30. Buchanan, *Justice, Legitimacy, and Self-Determination*, 281–288. Here Buchanan is principally concerned with the issue of legitimacy as it applies to state recognition policy (recognitional legitimacy), but this question (of who should be the object of recognition (with all the rights and obligations that that entails) is another way of posing the question of the legitimacy of secession.

31. Buchanan, *Justice, Legitimacy, and Self-Determination*, 281–283.

32. Locke considered the possibility that 'either the Executive, or the Legislative, when they have got the Power in their hands, design, or go about to enslave, or destroy them [the people]. The People have no other remedy in this . . . but to appeal to Heaven.' Locke was clear that this constitutes a right to revolution, although he was careful to argue that it should be exercised judiciously. 'Nor let any one think, this lays a perpetual foundation for Disorder: for this operates not, till the Inconvenience is so great, that the Majority feel it, and are weary of it, and find a necessity to have it amended'; Locke, 'Second Treatise of Government', bk II, chap. XIV, para. 168; in Laslett, ed., *Two Treatises*, 379–380.

33. Buchanan, *Justice, Legitimacy, and Self-Determination*, 282–283.

34. However, some might regard the negotiations between the National Party of South Africa and the African National Congress, under the leadership of Nelson Mandela, and the 1994 transition to majority rule as involving a 'bloodless revolution'.

35. Stilz, 'Nations, States, and Territories', 590.

36. Stilz, 'Nations, States, and Territories', 591; emphasis in original.

37. Stilz, 'Nations, States, and Territories', 592.

38. Stilz, 'Nations, States, and Territories', 593.

39. Stilz accepts this logic, arguing that failed states indicate lack of capacity to dispense justice. She writes: 'Consider severe failed state cases, such as present-day Somalia. My interpretation of the "facts on the ground" in Somalia may be contestable: but let us assume for the purposes of the argument that there is now no collective agent in Somalia capable of organizing and sustaining a legitimate political authority. Then it may not be wrong for another state to annex the territory, if their invasion was just and they can commit to ruling legitimately. The purpose behind a people's self-determination is the provision of justice for its members: where there is no collective agent on the territory capable of sustaining a legitimate institution, this purpose must be fulfilled in some other way'; 'Nations, States, and Territories', 598.

40. If, on the other hand, Stilz's argument is intended to be a normative claim, we need to be given reasons to exclude forms of political mobilization that are not institutionalized in a state but which express strong ties and cooperative practices.

6

Heartlands, Contested Areas, Secession, and Boundaries

This chapter draws out the implications of the argument set out in chapter 3 for adjudicating between rival claims to territory, drawing boundaries around jurisdictional units, and for secession. It does this by exploring the implications of the collective moral right of occupancy in establishing heartlands of groups, which, I argue, are useful to demarcate boundaries between self-determining peoples and territories.

I begin in section 6.1 by considering the claim that neither democratic theory nor justice theory can be usefully applied to the issue of drawing boundaries. I then turn in section 6.2 to examine the issue of boundaries by extrapolating from the occupancy principle. In this section of the chapter, I consider a difficult question: what does it mean to occupy land? What is the scope of occupancy? How much land can a group claim as occupied? I argue that the moral occupancy principle can identify 'heartlands' of groups but is indeterminate at the edges and in certain cases. In section 6.3 I consider three different hard cases, in which the neat picture of peoples attached to territory that some may have thought was presupposed in chapter 3 does not apply. First, there are cases where land is claimed by two rival states and the people living on the land, typical of many borderland people, identify with one or other of the contending adjacent states and are demographically intermingled, such that it is not possible to draw a neat boundary between the two groups. This was historically the case with Northern Ireland, where Protestants and Catholics had a British and Irish identity respectively, but relatively few held a Northern Irish identity, at least not if this was interpreted in terms of claiming full territorial rights over Northern Ireland. Second, there are cases where land is claimed by rival states, such as India and Pakistan, but the people who live on the land, in this case Kashmir, have different identities: some identify as Indian; some as Pakistani; and some as Kashmiri. Finally, there are cases where land is claimed as an integral part of a state but the people living on the land do not identify with the state, or the nation created by the state, but think of themselves as a distinct kind of people, and aspire to their own collective self-determination project. I discuss this in terms of the claims and aspirations of the Kurdish population in northern Iraq. I argue that my theory, despite its main focus on 'heartlands' rather than on boundaries specifically, has implications even for these hard cases.

In section 6.4, I consider the issue of secession. The number and violence of secessionist movements across the globe make it vitally important to consider and develop principles and processes to regulate secession. Some might think that the arguments made thus far, in terms of territorial rights and self-determination, apply directly to legitimate secessionist projects (as long as the group meets the requirements of a 'people' and is territorially concentrated on land that it occupies not unjustly). Here, as with the discussion of intermingled populations and contested land, I argue that independent states on the Westphalian model, and secession to create these, aren't the unique institutional corollary of the defence of self-determination that I've presented in this book.

I argue that secession is often problematic, because it does violence to the institutionally mediated relationships amongst people. At the core of the theory of political self-determination is a belief in the importance of obligations that arise from people's relationships, and this is relevant too when relationships are broken or altered.

Finally, a *caveat* is in order. I do not discuss in this chapter cases of territorial disputes over *unoccupied* land. This is not because my theory has nothing to say about such cases: on the contrary, I devote half of chapter 8 to them. But I think that these kinds of cases are wrongly conceived of as territorial disputes connected to self-determination projects. In cases where land is claimed by a particular group but is not occupied by the group in question, the group (or its representatives) is typically viewing the land instrumentally, as a kind of property. I argue that what is needed in such cases is the creation of jurisdictional authority to regulate property claims. It makes sense to discuss this in the chapter on natural resources, because land is also a kind of resource.

6.1. Boundaries: Democratic and Justice Theories

6.1.1. The (Il)legitimacy of Boundaries and Democratic Theory

Boundary drawing is a difficult issue. Many people have argued that democratic theory cannot help us in solving the boundary problem—that is, the problem of determining the boundaries within which democratic decisions are taken.

This point has been put forcefully in terms of a paradox of 'national self-determination' and a paradox of democracy. The paradox of national self-determination was articulated forcefully by Robert Lahnsing, under-secretary of state to US president Woodrow Wilson, when he commented on the difficulties of institutionalizing the principle of national self-determination in the wake of the carve-up of the (defeated) German, Ottoman, and Austro-Hungarian empires in 1919: 'The people cannot decide unless somebody decides who are the people'.[1] The principle of national self-determination, though, suggests at least one solution to the problem of determining the boundaries of the state, unit, or *demos*: this is to invoke considerations external to democracy, considerations that are pre-political, such as that of shared ethnicity and language, as components of cultural nationalism. The 1919 map drawers tended to invoke ascriptive criteria of this kind, although the story is complicated by the fact that they did not do so consistently: they were also anxious to punish the conquered peoples and to reward the victors. Lahnsing's point, though, was not just that this might be contentious, but that this is not a democratic process: the seeming convergence of democratic and national self-determination criteria is exposed at the very point of determining the domain of democratic decision-making.

The problem to which Lahnsing pointed is, however, also a problem for democratic theory; indeed, Lahnsing's point gains plausibility only because he seems to assume that democratic principles are the only appropriate principles to legitimate the contours of the demos or the state. This problem has not gone unnoticed by a number of democratic theorists. Both Joseph Schumpeter and Robert Dahl were aware that democratic authorization is important to the legitimacy of the social choices that are made, but Dahl argued that 'we cannot solve the problem of the proper scope and domain of democratic units from within democratic theory itself'.[2]

Normative theorists are unlikely to be satisfied by the view that the domain of decision making is simply taken as fixed, nor by an appeal to pre-political or ascriptive criteria, which is implicit in at least one type of appeal to the principle of national self-determination (understood to involve distinguishing between cultural nationalist groups on the basis of language or ethnicity). The former argument counsels that we should simply accept that the boundaries of states are arbitrary, that they are entirely a product of history and coercion, but cannot be tampered with because this would lead to instability. This indeed is one of the staple arguments for the current dominant approach to boundaries in international law, the *uti posseditis* principle: that territory is entitlement based on what one possesses, without requiring further inquiry into the unacceptably coercive and fraught history that brought about that possession. Nor are normative theorists likely to endorse an appeal to pre-political, cultural features, as a basis for drawing boundaries. This, too, would conceive of the most fundamental questions, of the very contours of the state, and of the demos, as part of our circumstances, rather than our choices. It would render the most fundamental constitutional question of citizenship, of belonging, and of democratic decision-making as based on unchosen, largely ascriptive features of ethnicity or language.

Are there any better normative positions on the issue of drawing the bounds of the demos? One view is to invoke what seem to be non-political considerations, but to argue that they are not purely empirical, external, and arbitrary characteristics: they are relevant to democracy. This is the position taken by David Miller. He contends that the substantive normative principles of democracy can be applied to the drawing of boundaries, not as a direct application of the democratic procedure, but in terms of the likelihood of a certain configuration being conducive to democratic decision-making and democratic stability. Indeed, he argues that what view one takes of democracy—whether a republican democratic or liberal democratic view—makes a difference to how we should conceive the demos and therefore the appropriate principles for demarcating between different demoi, with the liberal democratic model suggesting a much thinner, more flexible and inclusive demos, and the republican democratic model requiring a more substantial level of agreement on the animating values of the particular political community. The main point though is that the boundaries are legitimated by applying substantive democratic values, though not through a democratic procedure. (He also, incidentally, sees this argument as complementary to the main argument he makes about territories applying to cultural national groups. The link between the two kinds of arguments is an empirical claim that groups that share a culture are also likely to foster trust and important kinds of solidarity that are instrumentally helpful to a well-functioning democracy.)

What can be said of this sort of argument? Arash Abizadeh rejects this position as instrumental, and presses his cosmopolitan democratic alternative.[3] However, it's not clear why this amounts to a *rejection* of Miller's view. After all, being an instrumental justification doesn't make it wrong. Moreover, it's clearly a *normative* argument in the sense that it assesses different boundary configurations in terms of normative commitment to realizing democracy.

What of the argument, associated with the work of Abizadeh, that there is in principle no limit to the demos? This argument is initially developed in terms of a cosmopolitan challenge to the state's right to control immigration, where Abizadeh argues that immigration controls represent coercion against prospective migrants.[4] Abizadeh begins with the normative democratic principle of political legitimacy, namely that the coercive exercise of political power be democratically justified to all those over whom it is exercised. Abizadeh then argues that the regime of border control subjects both members and non-members to the state's coercive exercise of power and this means that justification is owed to both members and non-members.[5] He concludes that the state does not have the right to exercise coercion over border entry. The argument that is developed is not simply about the justifiability of immigration controls, but it raises the larger question of the legitimacy of boundaries themselves, since the legitimation of state coercion requires democratic assent of all affected people to the border regime itself. The implication of the argument is that that the demos is global in scope, and that boundaries can be legitimate only from the point of view of the global demos.

However, Abizadeh, like most cosmopolitans, is not actually endorsing a world state: he suggests that this argument is compatible with the drawing of boundaries by a legitimate global demos. This would make all boundaries akin to the federal boundaries of India, where, unique among federations in the world, the boundaries of subunits are drawn by the central government, albeit often in consultation with local groups.

Three problems with this position suggest themselves immediately. One is that Abizadeh is unable to provide any normative principles to guide the drawing of internal but, one can presume, still significant boundaries. They are rendered legitimate only because decided upon democratically, but there are no substantive normative principles to guide the drawing of the boundaries: they are presented as arbitrary in substance. This seems deeply unsatisfactory, indeed more unsatisfactory than applying an instrumental normative justification to the drawing of boundaries, such as that endorsed by Miller. Second, it is not a realistic approach to the drawing of boundaries. While in ideal theory, we might be able to imagine a global demos drawing legitimate boundaries within itself, it renders all existing boundaries, and all boundaries in the immediate future, unjustified and illegitimate. This does not show that the argument is wrong in itself, but we might want some further account of how to think about borders in the world that we live in.[6] Finally, the solution that Abizadeh offers— the appeal to the global demos—is itself deeply problematic and, some might argue, has a serious over-inclusion problem in that every border, every boundary, is potentially coercive in Abizadeh's sense and so would seem to require global democratic legitimation. Within federations, there is a significant, normatively fraught question of whether a referendum (on indigenous self-government, say) should be held by indigenous people, deciding for themselves, or by all the voters in the unit from which they were planning to secede. This problem has been much discussed in the secessionist literature, and is a live political issue in Canada today, where, for example, the Nisg'a tribe in British Columbia, which seeks to be collectively self-governing on territory that it historically and currently occupies, has negotiated a treaty with the province of British

Columbia. Any treaty which grants significant powers of self-government to this group will affect all the citizens of British Columbia, indeed, arguably all citizens of Canada. There are however reasons to think that a referendum of all the citizens in the entire (white-dominated) province (or the country) is not the appropriate method to decide this issue. After all, the Nisg'a constitute a community of interest, with their own history and identity and aspirations to be collectively self-governing, aspirations which are precisely what a referendum by the whole country or the whole province denies. Including all people in the decision represents a denial of their central claim that they constitute a community that is entitled to be collectively self-governing in the first place. Part of the problem here is with Abizadeh's thin account of coercion, which suggests that everyone who is potentially subject to the rule is coerced by it and so entitled to decision-making authority. This is insensitive to the various ways in which people are subject to the exercise of coercive power: it seems unjust to give people who are only potentially subject to a rule an equal voice in the decision itself. The more serious problem is that this principle assumes that there is no legitimate collective life of the groups of people in the state. If individuals' well-being and interests and identities are bound up in their membership in certain groups, over which they seek to be self-governing, then, the problem is that the global-demos argument implies that these groups have no legitimacy at all, that the aspirations of people who seek to be collectively self-governing over significant areas of their lives is entirely without warrant. But this of course is precisely what is in contention.

In the section that follows, I suggest that Abizadeh's argument rests on a mistaken belief: he wrongly assumes that the only source of legitimacy for borders is a democratic one. Why should we assume that democracy is the only method, the only procedure, to legitimate borders? Democracy is an important source of legitimacy, to be sure; it ensures that decisions made by government are authorized by the people who are thereby governed, but it is not clear that it is appropriate in all domains. We do not have to subject every institution, every policy, to a *democratic* legitimacy test in order for it to be justified or legitimate. Justice constitutes a standard of legitimation too. Consider, for the moment, practices and institutions that we associate with the rule of law, such as rules regarding the presumption of innocence, rules surrounding the gathering of evidence, and appropriate forms of interrogation. These are not justified democratically: we do not adhere to them because we, as a people, have determined, through a majoritarian or super-majoritarian procedure, that that is the appropriate way to proceed. They are justified on justice grounds, because we have reason to believe that these procedural rules are connected to ensuring that justice is done, where justice is connected to the punishment of the guilty, and with a special requirement that the innocent not be wrongfully convicted. If it became clear that a particular procedure or particular rule was likely to lead the innocent to be wrongfully convicted, we would have good reason to change that rule. We should change it even if the rule was endorsed democratically.

What is needed to motivate Abizadeh's global-demos argument is a prior argument that boundaries can *only* be legitimated democratically, and he does not provide this. This chapter suggests that there are normative principles that can apply to the drawing of boundaries, and also sources of legitimacy besides that of democratic assent.

6.1.2. Boundaries and Justice Theories

What, then, of a justice-based strategy as this applies to drawing boundaries? Many justice theorists have largely ignored the issue of territory, preferring instead to focus on the relationship between state and citizen, and abstract from the obvious fact that states are territorial entities. In the previous chapter, I argued that statist theories have a problem in being unable to explain precisely which land should attach to which state. They do not have a problem conceptualizing boundaries or explaining why they are necessary. If there are states, there are boundaries that delimit their extent. But if the boundaries themselves are arbitrary, in the sense that there are no principles to govern where boundaries are drawn, the differential opportunities, resources, well-being, and wealth on different sides of a boundary may be a deep embarrassment for these theories rooted in justice (depending of course on what their conception of justice is).

Cultural nationalist theories are a little different. Activist nationalists typically appeal to a homeland of the nation, and often the boundaries of that homeland are imaginatively fixed in the literature, history, music, and folklore of the particular national group. The problem for philosophical cultural nationalists is that they cannot rely on these claims to determine the boundaries of political units: in many cases the same land is an important element of more than one national community and so some more impartial principle or rule or procedure is necessary to deal with conflicts.[7] My account, rooted in a group occupancy principle, is distinct from either of these: on the one hand, it escapes the arbitrariness of simply appealing to state borders, however they have been arrived at, that infects statist theory; and it can give reasons that serve to distinguish between different kinds of claims, unlike many versions of cultural nationalist theory.

The strategy adopted in this book is to bring together two distinct kinds of boundaries: it brings together territorial boundaries between political or jurisdictional units, and social boundaries, which delimit different kinds of social groups. It does this by invoking the occupancy principle, which argues that borders should be drawn *around* groups that meet the criteria of people-hood: groups that are territorially concentrated on land that they occupy not unjustly; that aspire to or aim at significant forms of self-determination to gov-ern their collective lives; and that have a history of cooperation together. Since the definition of peoplehood includes a reference to their territorial concentra-tion on land that they occupy, it should be possible to apply the occupancy principle in most cases to delimit geographical domains of jurisdictional authority. This principle, however, does not decisively determine boundaries, in part because most groups are not hermetically sealed and homogeneous, and their residency and relationship patterns in the land are variable, but it does offer progress in thinking about the appropriate domain for territorial rights.

6.2. Moral Occupancy, Heartlands, and Drawing Boundaries

Let me draw out some implications of the moral right of occupancy for some cases discussed in chapter 1, including cases of territorial conflicts. It's clear where members of a group are physically present on a piece of land that they occupy at least some of it, but what is the extent of that occupation? In the case of a group that is said to be occupying territory, what does the occupancy prin-ciple imply? How expansively should we interpret the domain of occupancy?

I suggested earlier that Sir George Somers, who landed with prospective colonists and sailors on Bermuda in 1609, was at liberty to go ashore and settle there, as the land had been unoccupied for several centuries. But what counts as unoccupied? The Bermuda case is relatively simple, because islands are geographically bounded by water on all sides. If the whole island is bereft of human beings, that is a clear case. However, suppose that Sir George Somers had landed on the island in 1609 and the following year a second group, from Spain, had landed there too. Would they be entitled to settle on the land? On my account: it depends. If they landed on the island and tried to forcibly remove Sir George Somers and his community, they would be in violation of the Somers's group's moral rights—their individual moral rights of residency and their group rights to occupy the island. But the collective moral right of occupancy does not simply involve a right of non-dispossession: it also involves a right to control the collective conditions in which the group lives. The question then is whether the people on the Spanish ship, who are seeking to establish a colony somewhere, are at liberty to do so in Bermuda, after Sir George Somers's group had already established a colony. This is an important question, the answer to which will vary depending on the group and its relationship to the land. If a later group tried to settle on land that was on precisely the site taken by the English settlers, next to their homes and churches and in their central public square, this would be regarded as already occupied and the attempt to establish a settlement there as a violation of the English settlers' right of occupancy. (Here I am setting aside the case where the Spanish ship is in desperate straits, has run aground, and the sailors are seeking refuge on the island. The right to refuge is not the right to settle: I discuss the first right in chapter 9.)

What if they had landed on the *opposite* side of the island, and set up a community there? Does a small village on one part of the island constitute occupancy of the whole island? We can imagine circumstances where the Spanish would be at liberty to occupy their part of the island, because it would be, for the purposes of the collective occupancy principle, unoccupied. This would be the case if Sir George Somers and his group had only just begun to establish themselves, and their projects and relations and connections did not extend to the other part of the island (or they had been there a long time, but the island was a big island). We would say then that the rest of the island was not only unoccupied, but that there was no significant relationship between the community that he had established and the other group or the other part of the island.

This does not mean that it is necessary to have people spread evenly throughout the island in order to establish occupancy. Indeed, in many real-life cases, people settle first and primarily along the coast and along major rivers, as often the interior is thick jungle or forest or desert unsuitable for human habitation. But the interior might still be occupied in the relevant sense, if the people have projects and relationships and attachments that presuppose access to and control over that territory. The occupancy principle in other words doesn't require that every square kilometre of land be literally occupied by a human being. Indeed, we should expect that a people might want to leave some areas as green land, or unimproved mountains, or rainforest. It is sufficient that the land be an integral part of the collective self-determination project of the group. Thus, the group might rely on resources from parts of an island that they do not inhabit, but which are nevertheless central to their way of life, or they may regard some part of that island—say, a strikingly beautiful mountain—as having symbolic or even religious significance, or they might view parts of the land—sand dunes that are host to rare plant and animal life—as protected land, and the people as stewards of the area. As long as they can argue that their way of life is still bound up with access to and control over the area, the group occupies it in the relevant sense. The relevant sense here is that it represents the location of their aims and projects, and is central to their way of life.

These considerations are relevant to determining borders and also in fixing a geographical domain which might include relatively uninhabited areas, which are nevertheless important to a people.

The appeal to occupancy, then, is useful in identifying *heartlands* of groups. Since the 'test' of the occupancy principle is whether the location is central to the aims and projects and relationships of the group, the occupancy principle requires some empirical investigation to verify that places are indeed central or integral to the way of life of the group. While this criterion represents progress in linking peoples and places, at the edges there is indeterminacy, so three further points of clarification are needed.

First, arguments about religious or sacred sites, or places that are central to the culture, identity, or projects of the group are helpful in clarifying place-related interests, and are useful for drawing boundaries around a location in cases where the group in question is the only claimant. In many cases, groups claim land because they see it as infused with religious or symbolic significance for them. Serbian nationalists, for example, often describe Kosovo as the 'cradle' of their nation and they point to the monasteries and ancient battlefields and Orthodox churches there as indicative of a strong historical Serbian presence, to which they are deeply attached.[8] Jerusalem, too, has emotional and symbolic significance for Jews, Muslims, and Christians, and in the case of the first two groups, these arguments are often used as part of an argument for jurisdictional authority over it. On my account, these claims are relevant in cases where we are considering the inclusion of an *uninhabited* area within the bounds of a political community, but are overridden in cases where the land is literally inhabited or occupied by a different group, who have moral occupancy rights on the land, and who also seeks rights of self-determination.[9] It is hard to see how religious or cultural or historic attachment to a place can justify jurisdictional authority over people who seek to exercise their own forms of collective self-determination. At best, attachment to places of religious significance by itself (when not conjoined with physical occupancy) might give people a right of access, or even some kind of jurisdictional authority, in a power-sharing arrangement, only over their places of significance, in cases where the area is of significance to more than one group.

Second, it is very likely that claims to uninhabited areas will not be exclusive. Where two groups live on different parts of the same island, they may make rival claims to the same unoccupied places. In that case, these claims have to be assessed comparatively. Which group has a better claim? Which group can marshal evidence that they have historically rooted attachment to the area, or that the resources are of importance to the collective well-being of the political community, and so on? It might well be that two different groups can provide evidence to support a claim to uninhabited areas. This is for the obvious reason that that area might have connections to more than one group. In that case, any division of the territory between two groups will be arbitrary in the sense that the line drawn represents a compromise between two rival heartlands, identified by two different groups. In other cases it might give rise to soft jurisdictional borders or to power-sharing arrangements over key areas, such as holy sites; or rights of access to areas of significance; or self-determination without partition, where each group gets some jurisdictional authority, some territorial rights over a geographical domain, but this is combined with power-sharing also on important common matters in cases where the groups cannot be wholly separated.

Third, it might be thought that I ought to be able to do better than a comparative evaluation of the relative strengths and weaknesses of various claims in these sorts of cases, and that at the least I should offer some kind of priority with respect to the different sorts of claims. This is the solution proffered by Avery Kolers in his book *Land, Conflict, and Justice*, and it certainly seems more attractive because more determinate than what I am offering here. I do not think that his argument works, however, for reasons that will become clear shortly; but here suffice it to say that my decisive criterion is (not unjust) occupancy of land. It has priority over all other sorts of claims, and these other, weaker claims can often be addressed through mechanisms other than territorially delimited full jurisdictional authority. The appropriate solution very much depends on the empirical details of the case, as I will demonstrate in section 6.3, with respect to my three hard cases: Northern Ireland, Kashmir, and Kurdistan.

With respect to the advantage of Kolers's theory, let me say here that he claims to deploy the value-neutral metric 'plenitude' in order to assess rival claims to the same territory. What, though, does it mean to 'achieve plenitude'? This is not easy to answer, because he incorporates a number of diverse things into the criteria of plenitude. It involves, he writes: (1) internal diversity, (2) external distinctness, each from the perspective of the claimants, and (3) feasible plans for maintaining these in perpetuity.[10] Plenitude is claimed to be value-neutral in the sense that it does not rest on a normatively contested theory of appropriate use, and is compatible with an ecologically sensitive approach to land as in tune with nature. But this is achieved at some cost, because it fails to provide a mechanism that authoritatively decides between different claimants, each of whom can claim plenitude with respect to the land. The problem here is that different groups might see the same area as having plenitude for them—they both might have plans for the area; they both might see the area as externally distinct and have a distinct historical or cultural narrative with respect to the land, and both might be able to identify various kinds of internal diversity with respect to it. Since 'plenitude' is presented as a single criterion, it has the illusion of being able to decide between rival claims, but in fact a number of distinct elements are incorporated into it. It is possible that more than one group meet all three, or that one group might meet the first but not the second, or another group the second but not the third and so on. Although Kolers's theory has the structure of an account which reduces all elements to a common metric ('plenitude'), he does not tell us how to measure the various different dimensions of 'plenitude', and so in fact is no less precise than my account. Indeed, I would argue that my account has the considerable virtue of offering good reasons in support of the considerations that I adduce.

Finally, the emphasis on the moral value of relationships in explaining the collective right of occupancy can explain why we think that children born on the island have a right to reside there, and to participate in forms of jurisdictional authority, but not necessarily people on other ships who are passing by the island and think that it might be a nice place to live. The child is related in morally important ways to the members of the group who enjoy rights of occupancy on the island, so this collective account can explain why we often think that there are place-related rights that attach to children of people who legitimately reside on the island, which do not necessarily apply to others, even though they would choose the island as a good home. It can also explain how occupancy rights apply intergenerationally. The group that has rights of occupancy—a people—are, after all, an intergenerational community, with a past, present and future, and is composed of people from a number of different overlapping generations. By contrast, a purely individualist account—which discusses the relationship between land and individuals in terms of the background conditions for the exercise of autonomy, for example—cannot explain why we might think that different rights attach to born people in the group and people born outside the group.

6.3. Hard Cases: Northern Ireland, Kashmir, and Kurdistan

Even if one accepts that the argument above can identify heartlands of groups, which are relevant to their legitimate territorial claims, it might be claimed that this is not really much of an achievement, since in many cases of conflict, the problem arises at the borderlands, in the area where two different rival groups, both claiming territorial rights, both seeking to exercise jurisdictional authority, are in dispute. This section examines three different sorts of territorial disputes, all of which reflect contemporary or recent conflict zones—Northern Ireland, Kashmir, and the Kurdish area of Northern Iraq—and argues that the underlying moral principles can be usefully applied to these cases too.

The first case—Northern Ireland—is a borderland region, inhabited by people who identify with two rival political communities, who are so thoroughly intermingled that it is impossible to draw a line on the map, or demarcate territorial zones, which roughly corresponds to the different self-determination projects. Their rival national identities as British and Irish correspond fairly closely to their religious identities as Protestant and Catholic. The two communities are not quite of equal size: approximately 60 percent of the population is Protestant, 40 percent Catholic, although that balance is changing rapidly, with greater out-migration (to England) of Protestants, and a higher Catholic birth rate. Their conflict was not essentially religious: the basis of the dispute was never the finer details of Catholic or Protestant theological differences but which (British or Irish) self-determination project Northern Ireland should be included in.[11] This could not be resolved by either applying democratic or justice considerations to the matter, but, it would seem, the moral occupancy principle is also helpless to decide the issue, since it is impossible to draw geographical boundaries around the groups.[12] While this might be true, the appeal to self-determination, which is at the heart of this book, can be applied to cases of this kind.

We have in this case two rival self-determination projects, two different 'peoples', but neither can exclusively exercise jurisdictional authority over the territory. I have offered reasons why we might think of these people, these collective agents, as embedded in relationships that have moral significance, and why we might think that their collective self-determination is morally valuable. This gives us reasons why one community should not dominate the other. In cases such as this, an obvious non-territorial solution is to give recognition to both communities, to have institutional mechanisms in which each community can exercise some kind of control over its collective life; but, over most spheres where coordination is necessary (these are substantial, given the extent of territorial intermixing), power-sharing is necessary. The argument advanced here gives us reasons to think that the fair and appropriate institutional solution was precisely what emerged from the 1998 Good Friday Agreement: the joint creation of a jurisdictional authority in which the two communities are coequals, sharing power so that neither group is excluded from its exercise, and both can see the territory of Northern Ireland as one in which their collective aims, aspirations, and identities are reflected.[13]

At this point, we are in the realm of complex institutional design rather than moral principles, but there is a substantial literature to draw on in such cases. The most developed literature is in the consociational (power-sharing) democracy tradition. Although I cannot do justice to the complexity of either the normative issues or issues of institutional design here, it might be useful to reflect on the applicability of the basic principles of consociational democratic theory to a case such as this, to show that it is consonant with the basic moral principles that I have outlined. In this theory, the collective agency of groups is the pillar on which democratic forms are built, thus giving recognition to the moral value of the relationship among group members. The main features of consociational democracy, according to the political criteria laid down by its most famous exponent, Arend Lijphart, are: (1) cross-community executive power-sharing;[14] (2) proportionality rules throughout the governmental and public sectors;[15] (3) (territorial) self-government or political autonomy;[16] and (4) veto rights for minorities, so that each is able to prevent changes that adversely affect their *vital* interests. If we think of this, not as a precise map or blueprint of institutional design, but as encompassing any institutional arrangement organized according to these four very basic principles, we can see that it is possible to develop forms of self-determination appropriate to the governance of territorial intermixed communities with rival political identities. Consociational institutions are appropriate if people in this context value their political identities and their relationships with co-members of the same political community, if they seek some protection of their legitimate communal life, and if they seek jurisdictional power or authority to ensure (some degree) of collective self-government. The case of Northern Ireland is further complicated by the fact that its two main political identities are not internal to the province, but are connected to two adjacent states. This means that any fair democratic institutional arrangement over the territory cannot comprise simply internal power-sharing among Protestant–British, and Catholic–Irish communities within the province, for this would ignore the significant national dimension of these two identities. In other words, if the province remained simply a part of the United Kingdom, it would not be a fair compromise between the two political communities. What is required to be fair to both identities, to both political communities, is recognition of the significant external dimension of their identities, in the form of an imaginative British–Irish international arrangement in addition to an internal (consociational) power-sharing arrangement. Interestingly, this is exactly what is provided for in the terms of the 1998 British–Irish Good Friday Agreement, which created a North–South Ministerial Council, with significant British and Irish government dimensions.

Let me turn next to the case of Kashmir, which is similar in so far as it also involves rival (Pakistani and Indian) political claims over the province and territorially intermingled communities with very different political identities.[17] To understand the complexity of the Kashmir case, some historical context is in order. When India gained independence, the princely state of Jammu and Kashmir was not part of British India, but the princely kingdom was not independent of British sovereignty either, being subject to the doctrine of paramountcy through various treaty and political arrangements in force. In October 1947 Pakistan backed armed incursions into pro-Pakistan parts of Jammu and Kashmir, which led the Hindu princely ruler to request military aid from India, which, in turn, requested that the state of Jammu and Kashmir accede to India prior to sending troops. This led to the signing of the Instrument of Accession on 26 October 1947, which was accepted by Lord Mountbatten, the viceroy of India. However, in a letter accompanying the Instrument of Accession, Lord Mountbatten stipulated that the decision over territorial control of the princely state could not simply be taken by the prince and another state (India) but should be ultimately decided through a plebiscite of the people in the territory of Jammu and Kashmir. Let us set aside for the moment the issue of the plebiscite, and the implicit view of the legitimate territorial right-holder. The operative assumption in the request by India and the prince's accession to that request is that the existing state had the authority to make that kind of decision, that it was the fundamental holder of territorial rights and could transfer those rights—rights not only to legislate across the domain, but also decide the terms and structure of the entity with jurisdictional authority—without regard for the people who live on the land. This however was not a hegemonic view, as the requirement to hold a plebiscite indicates: that suggests that it was not obvious, even then, that the Hindu prince and/or the British had the authority to decide the sovereign future of a majority Muslim province.[18] One lesson from the Kashmir case is the problem created by lack of international consensus on the appropriate norm governing territorial rights and territorial transfers, which is precisely the subject of this book. There are rival norms that different groups appeal to, with each side convinced that its view has normative authority.[19]

The main question raised in the case of Kashmir is: who ought to hold territorial rights? What kind of entity should have jurisdictional rights over territory? This first question is raised at a very specific level, because there are a number of possibilities. Kashmir is currently divided between India and Pakistan (and there is also a small, relatively unpopulated part within China, a point that I bracket here). This means that first we have to consider, generally, whether Kashmir should remain divided or be reunified, and in the latter case, whether it should be part of India, part of Pakistan, or independent. The answer to these questions depends, at least to some extent, on more general understandings of what kind of entity ought to hold territorial rights, and the relationship of that entity to the people living there. The Kashmir case is further complicated—and here it is even more complex than that of Northern Ireland—because it is extremely heterogeneous, with Sunni and Shia Muslims, Hindus, Buddhists, and Sikhs all forming majorities in different areas. The different communities support different territorial solutions, such as inclusion in India, inclusion in

Pakistan, and an independent Kashmir. It's clear, however, that, given the territorial and ethnic patchwork, none of these on their own would be fair to these rival political identities, so that, like Northern Ireland, the only fair solution would be a complex one, which involves imaginative forms of power-sharing amongst these different groups, and some kind of links to the respective 'parent' states (Pakistan and India), which is of course unlikely given their disputatious history.

While one might think that a referendum or appeal to a referendum is the obvious institutional principle for the argument I've made in this book—that the people are the ultimate or fundamental holders of territorial right—in fact, a referendum is a very crude instrument,[20] and there may be better mechanisms, or superior public policy approaches in such cases.[21] It's very difficult for the people in Kashmir to know what they want, even if they have a sense of all being Kashmiri, because they have been divided by the line of control, prevented from developing cooperative and reciprocal political arrangements that would have been helpful in determining what kind of society they wanted to create. The emphasis on the importance of existing political relationships discussed earlier, and not just voluntarist will, suggests that a good, stable public policy prescription in Kashmir would involve not just the withdrawal of a heavy Indian army presence and a referendum, but military withdrawal combined with the creation of political space in which Kashmiris can develop relationships and understandings amongst themselves about what kind of relationships they want, both amongst themselves and with the kin political communities (India and Pakistan). It would be a process, not a single one-off referendum, and the process should, I've argued above, involve power-sharing, not just at the elite level, but the kind that makes possible the development of relationships and forms of reciprocity and dialogue within the various communities.

The third case of contested territory that I shall discuss is the Kurdish-dominated area in northern Iraq. This is also a case of contested territory and contested secession, where the people living on the territory do not have an Iraqi identity: as far as we can tell, they think of themselves as Kurdish, and the territory as Kurdistan, which should be decided by the Kurdish people who occupy the area. Typically, it is difficult to gauge the extent of mobilization behind a particular political identity, especially in the context of a repressive and undemocratic regime, but there is strong evidence that the population is mobilized along national, and also clan, lines, but not as Iraqi (civic) nationalists. Although neither of the two major political parties—the Patriotic Union of Kurdistan (PUK) and the Kurdistan Democratic Party (KDP)—calls for independence, most analysts argue that this 'preference' is strategic: they recognize that the United States would not support Kurdish independence (at least not in the current context) and the Kurds need American support.[22] Indeed, most Kurdish political leaders and outside observers contend that the major political parties act as a restraint on the population, which is strongly mobilized behind independence, as the 2005 referendum result indicated.[23] This is often expressed in very strong language. According to Peter Galbraith, a former US ambassador, 'the people of Kurdistan equate Iraq with repression and genocide. Almost no one in Kurdistan would choose to be part of Iraq if there were an alternative'.[24]

Support for independence, or lack of support for continued inclusion in Iraq,[25] is hardly surprising, since the previous Ba'athist regime was ideologically associated with pan-Arabism, which was used to justify oppressive and genocidal policies against the non-Arab (Kurdish) population. The oil resources were not used to the benefit of the Kurdish people of northern Iraq, on whose territory the oil was found, nor even fairly across the state as a whole, but disproportionately benefited the Sunni community, concentrated in a triangular area in the centre of the country, who formed the bedrock of the Saddam Hussein regime. The regime was also not rights-respecting.[26] The history of unjust treatment is sometimes very strongly correlated with sentiments of minority nationalist mobilization. In such cases, and even without reference to the previous history of unjust treatment, it's clear that, if the Kurdish population meets the 'tests' of a people that I set out in chapter 3—they share a distinct political identity, with aspirations to be politically self-determining as a group; they have the capacity to be self-governing, and particularly to maintain institutions of legal and political governance on the territory; they have a history of relations of cooperation; and they are geographically concentrated on land which they occupy not unjustly—then they are the appropriate holders of territorial right. They ought therefore to decide the future of the political entity that they co-create, maintain, and are governed by. The occupancy principle, in other words, can justify secession in such cases, in the region which is most clearly identified with the Kurdish people, if we have strong reason to believe that this is indeed reflective of the collective aims and aspirations of the people living there.

At this point, however, we again face the limits of the occupancy principle as a principle for drawing borders. Most of the Kurdish territory is not in dispute, with the exception of Kirkuk, which was historically Kurdish, but there was, under Saddam Hussein, a considerable movement of Arab population into the region, which makes the application of the occupancy principle difficult (a complication which will be discussed in chapter 9 on corrective justice). There are claims (put forward by the Kurdish leadership) that Kirkuk (the city, as well as the region) has been an historically Kurdish area, and that some (Arab) members of the existing population, who are entitled to vote in a referendum on Kirkuk (which is actually provided for in the Iraqi Constitution, but has never been held), have moved into an area as a result of state-directed population movements.[27] In that case, there may be corrective-justice arguments for including Kirkuk as part of the Kurdish region. (Kurds claim that, notwithstanding this Arabization campaign, the existing population is still majority ethnic Kurd.)[28] The heterogeneous nature of the population of that region also gives us reasons to consider local and inclusive forms of power-sharing to govern the region, similar to the ones suggested with respect to disputed lands in Northern Ireland and Kashmir.

One of the reasons why this area is so contentious is that it sits adjacent to a large oilfield: whoever controls Kirkuk, on the current understanding of territorial control (where control of territory involves control of resources), also controls access to, benefit from, and taxation of this huge source of wealth.[29] This of course depends on what view we take of the relationship of jurisdictional authority over territory to control over resources, which is the subject of chapter 8. At this point, suffice it to say that we need to think imaginatively about sharing the resources within a fair, federal Iraq, if that were indeed the constitutional dispensation that the different communities agreed to.

6.4. The Theory of Secession Implicit in this Account

One common worry about secession is that it is potentially destabilizing to the secessionist region and the international order, though, of course, this is as much a result of the state's response to secession as of those who mobilize in favour of secession. Most theorists interested in the ethics of secession accept that secession from unjust states is nevertheless justified. They frequently express the worry that secession is sometimes not a response to injustice, but the product of unjust motivations or 'vanity secessions'.[30] As an example of this, theorists writing about the ethics of secession often assume that this is the principal motive in cases in which rich regions seek to secede from a relatively poorer state. Rich regions that have no just cause to secede—they cannot point to historical grievances or injustices—are assumed to be mere 'vanity secessions', the product of politically opportunistic elites who seek to capitalize on unjust greed, hoping that all the wealth of their unit can be kept within a smaller group.[31] Thomas Pogge, in his discussion of secession, assumes that most secessionist movements in rich regions are unjustified. He argues that 'many such [secessionist] conflicts are motivated by morally inappropriate considerations', and he cites both competition for valuable or strategically important territory and attempts by the more affluent to separate themselves

from poorer regions, 'in order to circumvent widely recognized duties of distributive justice among compatriots'.[32] It is an implication of this argument—
and especially the assumption that people in richer subunits are motivated to
secede in order to avoid duties of justice—that these richer regions should *not*
be permitted to secede, or are *not* justified in seceding, from units to which they
are attached.[33] This assumption is questionable. The aspiration for secession
might not be motivated primarily by the desire to escape obligations of distributive justice; indeed, many groups have expressed, as groups, a desire for collective self-determination, even in contexts where the self-determination will
not contribute to their wealth or well-being on other fronts. While the account
of the motivations behind secession advanced by Pogge and Norman might
explain Slovenia's secession from the former Yugoslavia, in terms of its relative wealth, it couldn't explain why Kosovars, the poorest group in the former
Yugoslavia, were mobilized to seek collective self-determination even prior to
the 1999 expulsion of Kosovar Albanians from the territory.[34] It seems unfair
to deny self-determination to the richer regions, while allowing it to the poorer
regions, since they might be motivated by exactly the same considerations.

My account gives normative significance to the relationships among people
who aspire to be collective self-determining, but it also, consistent with this,
acknowledges that in many cases there are good reasons to think that seceding
units have obligations to provide additional resources to the remainder state
following secession. The dissolution of states and/or the secession of particular
regions from a larger state raise important questions about the kind and extent
of duties that can arise from a long-standing historical relationship between
different parts of a state, and the continuing obligations that may arise in this
context. In this final section of the chapter, I argue that in many cases there are
special obligations of support or compensation, which arise when a rich region
(either a region rich in natural resources or a region with a more developed
economic infrastructure) seeks to secede from a state. This is relevant to the
'unjust motive' charge and it would seem to be a possible stabilizing element in
an international order that regulates secession.

In addition to the responsibilities that each of us has towards people as
such, regardless of whether or not we have institutions or practices of cooperation in place—such as duties of assistance, duties not to harm, and so
on—common-sense morality holds that there are additional, and often quite
burdensome, responsibilities that members of significant social groups and
participants in close personal relationships have to each other.[35] I am interested in the type of duties that arise from ongoing reciprocal cooperation over
time, which I will call here 'duties of reciprocity'.[36] I will argue that, when the
previous state order involved institutionalized reciprocity, there can be duties
of reciprocity, which apply even after a successful secession.

In order to discuss specific duties arising from reciprocity, it is necessary to have a precise understanding of what 'reciprocity' means. Reciprocity appeals to the idea of mutual benefit, but this requires that we specify the baseline for measuring mutual benefit. In the case of a relation between two people, we might say that their relation is characterized by reciprocity if they take turns, helping each other out when need arises. If my neighbour Sandra looks after my daughter when I am unavoidably detained at work, and I do the same for her when she is unavoidably detained, then we might say that our relation is imbued with the principle of reciprocity. The relation has the vital character-istic of being mutually beneficial.[37] In small, voluntary relationships, such as between friends, we could define mutual benefit in comparison to a state of nature (no interaction). All that is required to describe the relationship as 'mutually beneficial' is that the participants are better off than they would have been had there been no interaction at all: it doesn't require a fair division of the benefits of cooperation. This relationship could be duty-creating: in the con-text of ongoing cooperation, I would be violating my duties of reciprocity if my neighbour Sandra rang and asked me to take her child as she was unavoidably detained, and I answered simply that I was too busy at the moment, as I was just going to dash out to get a much needed double espresso. That would have been a perfectly reasonable response if there had been no prior cooperative practices: it might not be altruistic, but it violates no duties. However, in the context of our relationship, and the reciprocity that has characterized it, that response would violate my duties. The point here is that ongoing shared coop-erative practices can create obligations in the future.

When we transfer the idea of reciprocity from small, face-to-face rela-tionships to relationships that are mediated by institutions, which in turn instantiate reciprocity, the idea of reciprocity changes in two ways. First, the minimalist conception of mutual benefit (as defined against a baseline of no interaction) is not appropriate. It makes sense of individual bargains, where people would agree to the bargain only if they expected benefit (else why would they agree?) but it is less applicable to a political entity, where no one has consented to the state order but where we are forced to live in one. If we apply that conception of mutual benefit to institutional structures, it could license very unequal power relations, and so it would be impossible to distin-guish between a 'reciprocal' order and an order of domination and subordi-nation. The idea of reciprocity, based on mutual benefit, which is appropriate in political and institutional arrangements, requires us not to take advantage of differences in bargaining power; instead, we should seek to benefit equally from cooperation, unless all can gain from an unequal division of benefit. This is, broadly speaking, Rawls's account of mutual benefit in *A Theory of Justice*.[38] This is not an impossible standard to meet, since, typically, riches in one area do serve to advantage, albeit to a lesser extent, all the regions of the country if, for example, there is a common pool for health care or infrastructure development or welfare payments.

Second, in addition to how strictly we want to interpret reciprocity, there is the question of whether we should conceive of it in terms of global (or overall) mutual benefit or local (specific) mutual benefit over some aspect of the institutional structure. For quite specific transactions, it is clear that local reciprocity makes sense: as in the case of babysitting arrangements, it applies only to the specific area covered by the arrangement under consideration. However, in the case of relatively deep arrangements, covering a wide range of institutions and practices, with impacts on many different aspects of people's lives, reciprocity requires mutual advantage considered overall, not in each specific dimension. We would still consider a society as characterized by institutionalized reciprocity if one element contributed natural gas and oil and another region had deep natural harbours and a third contributed a strong manufacturing base, and so on. The key question for this understanding of 'reciprocity' is whether all regions are willing to contribute for the overall benefit, where benefit is conceived across different domains of the relationship.[39]

Many political orders could be described as characterized by institutionalized reciprocity, even if not all parts of it make a net contribution. Let us take as examples two secessionist scenarios in which the principle of reciprocity can be appealed to, and analyse the duties that are thereby generated. In the first scenario, a country contains two regions: region A is rich in a specific natural resource, and is also wealthier than region B. However, it uses some of the money generated by the natural resource to support B's plans for economic development, as well as to transfer some money to the poor of B. Now, suppose that B, which was formerly resource poor, becomes resource rich due to technological changes, which makes the uranium found under the ground suddenly valuable, whereas the dirty coal of region A is no longer the energy of choice. Changes in extraction and preferred energy sources have altered the market situation and thus altered how we value these resources. It would seem that the past support of B by A makes it incumbent on B to support A when the table is turned. For example, there may be extensive gas riches off the shore of Newfoundland, which, under the terms of the Canadian federation (in which resources lie within the jurisdiction of provinces) will benefit Newfoundland primarily. Since Newfoundland has been a beneficiary of extensive redistribution by the rest of Canada since joining in 1949, we would expect Newfoundland, if it found itself newly rich, to share its wealth with the other (now relatively poorer) parts of the federation. It would be morally problematic for Newfoundland to now attempt to secede from Canada and so gain full control of the resource wealth, without any form of compensation. The argument here doesn't categorically rule out B becoming an independent state, but it does suggest that if B becomes self-determining, it has to take account of the obligations incurred, both in terms of debt repayment of a formal kind and more informal kinds of indebtedness.

This understanding of the duties created by the principle of reciprocity can also be applied to the second, seemingly opposite example deployed by Joseph Heath, in the context of the possible secession of Quebec from Canada. He points out that, under the current terms of the federation, Alberta subsidizes Quebec, through the equalization program (designed to ensure equal services across the country), to the tune of $3000 per annum per Albertan.[40] He argues that it is preposterous to expect that Alberta is morally bound to continue this subvention or this level of subvention once Quebec has left the political project. The intuition behind this is that secession was their choice: the transfers were clearly based on membership in a common political project, based on the moral notion of reciprocity, and that it would be unreasonable to expect these transfers to continue when the recipient unit voluntarily leaves. On this view, willingness (and not actual contribution) is morally salient. It explains the differential treatment of units: we would not expect Quebec to be a net recipient of Canada's subsidy using a reciprocity argument in a post-secessionist arrangement, precisely because they are no longer willing contributors to the common political project. However, the aspiring secessionist unit has duties towards the unit that they have left even after separation if they have benefitted from previous reciprocal arrangements.

Reciprocity may also inform our obligations of support depending on the decision-making structure of the pre-secessionist state and the way in which decisions are allocated. Let us suppose, unlike in the case above, that a particular province is resource rich, but that decisions about natural resources are not an exclusive concern of provinces. Jurisdictional authority over natural resources is in the hands of the federal government and, according to the division of powers in the state, the region has very little say over natural resources in its geographical area, either because it is a unitary system or because it is a federal system where jurisdictional authority over natural resources is held by the federal government (as in the United States and unlike Canada). Now, let us suppose that decisions about non-renewable resources, which are concentrated in a particular region, P, are made by the state, comprising regions P, Q, R, for the common good of all parts of the country. In this context, a decision is made to exploit this resource at full capacity, and use the revenue, not only to meet distributive justice obligations in the state as a whole, but to invest in infrastructure throughout the state. This may of course differentially impact different regions of a state; let's assume that the investments have the effect of primarily advantaging R (an area without the resource in question). In that scenario, it would seem to be a violation of reciprocity for R, after a considerable period of time benefitting from this arrangement, to then attempt to secede without any kind of obligation to the remainder state, or to the region where the resources were located. The implications of this case are similar to that of Newfoundland seceding with rich offshore gas deposits, which it intended to use for its future sole benefit. Since political associations are cross-temporal associations, mutual benefit, I'm arguing, has to be conceived of as operating over time, and in terms of willingness to share fairly the gains of cooperation, not the actual sharing and actual benefit. On this understanding, what matters to our assessment of whether the institution is characterized by reciprocity is whether they reflect the principle of mutual benefit in the long run.

In cases where there is secession of a rich unit that has enjoyed institutional and financial support of other parts of the country in the past, unilateral secession would violate that principle of reciprocity. The principle of reciprocity does not necessarily mean that self-determination, or indeed secession, is rendered impossible, but that self-determination has to be pursued in way that is consistent with its duties to the remainder state, duties that are derived precisely from the previously shared institutional context.

In many cases, secession occurs in part because prior unjust or unfair practices have alienated the secessionist group, and the reciprocity principle never characterized the previous arrangement. In that case, the results of this argument mirror the results of just-cause theories of secession, where groups have a remedial right to secede from a political unit only if they have just cause (the state engaged in injustice). Since reciprocity did not characterize the previous (institutional) arrangement, there are no corresponding duties of reciprocity. This applies to the case of the Iraq's Kurds, who, I'm arguing, have no obligations to share the resources in a continuing, ongoing basis with Sunnis, in the context of secession. This mirrors the result of Buchanan's remedial rights theory, since the regime was, in addition to being non-neutral and unfair, also seriously unjust. Indeed, one might expect, as an empirical matter, that regimes of the latter type are likely to fail the reciprocity test.

Of course, if Kurds and Arabs were to succeed in building a new federal Iraq, based on the equality of people, some fair dispensation with respect to natural resources would have to be worked out, as well as some mechanism for permitting local forms of autonomy and autonomy at the centre. However, if the state collapses, and the Kurds separate, any duties that the Kurds have will be ones consistent with the more minimalist baseline for global justice and the common humanity of everyone in the world.

This view of the matter—where the duties are based on previous reciprocity—has the advantage of explaining our reluctance to permit rich regions to secede, or regions to secede immediately after the tables are turned. While explaining our reluctance, this argument does not actually prohibit these people from seceding—for that would negate their self-determination. It does, however, identify the kinds of duties that have to be met even in the context of secession. This has the effect of addressing Pogge's concern with the possible unjust motivations underlying secession: if these duties were generally recognized and enforced (by a generalized recognition regime,[41] say), it would ensure that these types of motives could not be at the root of the political mobilization surrounding secession. It would reduce the perverse incentives surrounding secession, while at the same time treating both rich and poor regions equally in terms of our assumptions about their motives in aspiring to the different forms of collective self-determination. Finally, the duty-creating reciprocity argument discussed above explains the asymmetrical nature of reciprocity in the context of secession, where the secessionist unit is not entitled to further contributions, but might expect to have some duties to contribute if this is required by reciprocity.

Notes

1. Ivor Jennings, *The Approach to Self-Government* (Cambridge: Cambridge University Press, 1956).
2. Robert Dahl, *Democracy and Its Critics* (New Haven: Yale University Press, 1989), 207, quoted in Miller, 'Democracy's Domain', 207.
3. Arash Abizadeh, 'On the Demos and its Kin: Nationalism, Democracy, and the Boundary Problem', *American Political Science Review*, vol. 106, no. 4 (2012), 862–882.
4. See Abizadeh, 'Democratic Theory and Border Coercion'. This argument makes sense as a response to Michael Blake's attempt to distinguish the domestic realm from the global realm in terms of the coercion of the state, and the resulting need to legitimate that coercion.
5. See, however, David Miller's argument that the concept of coercion has to be linked with the conditions for individual autonomy, and that the mere restriction of options does not necessarily show that people's autonomy is jeopardized; David Miller, 'Why Immigration Controls Are Not Coercive: A Reply to Arash Abizadeh', *Political Theory*, vol. 38, no. 1 (2010), 111–120.
6. There is also the possibility that Abizadeh might switch here to a hypothetical consent view: boundaries are legitimate if they *would* be accepted by a global democratic body. If that's the case, though, the weight of the argument shifts to the substantive justice or interests that would need to be guaranteed for hypothetical consent to work. It doesn't seem a particularly democratic form of argument, if democracy is associated with the institutional arrangements for securing consent or affirmation.
7. This point is made in my 'The Territorial Dimension of Self-Determination', in Margaret Moore, ed., *National Self-Determination and Secession*, 134–157 (Oxford: Oxford University Press, 1998).
8. In 1999 Serbs were prepared to fight for control over Kosovo, whereas, eight years previously, they had accepted the secession of the much more prosperous or objectively desirable territory of Slovenia (which did not have the same kind of emotional or national resonance for Serbs). The revered status of Kosovo in Serbian nationalist mythology has nothing to do with current occupancy patterns—even before the 1999 NATO intervention, Kosovo was over 90 percent ethnic Albanian.

9. Symbolic claims of the kind discussed here may also give grounds for preventing another group coming to occupy the land where they have not previously done so. This is a weaker argument, and should be overridden by claims of necessity by another group. By claims of 'necessity', I mean claims that a group might make that they are deprived, and that to address their deprivation they need additional land, resources, or territory. This doesn't apply directly to land already occupied—there the necessity argument takes a different form, as I argue in chapter 8.

10. Kolers writes:

> Empirical plenitude is a high degree of internal and external diversity. This property is both objective and relative. It is observer-relative, or more precisely, ethnogeographically relative. In order to see a place as internally diverse one must presuppose an ethnogeography that recognizes a multiplicity of kinds of things there. In order to see it as externally diverse (distinct from other places) one must presuppose an ethnogeography that recognizes some difference between the things there and those in a contiguous territory, or between the arrangements of things in each. This ethnogeographic relativism of plenitude is crucial to achieving rootedness in the right way—that is, cultural sensitivity without simply lowering the bar. (Kolers, *Land, Conflict, and Justice*, 115)

11. For an excellent analysis of this case, and proposals for a way forward, which we now realize were prescient, see McGarry and O'Leary, *Explaining Northern Ireland*.

12. There are areas of greater and lesser Protestant and Catholic populations. County Antrim, for example, is largely Protestant; South Tyrone is largely Catholic; but these would still not give us viable territorial entities, and there would remain the problem that the populations of the two largest cities—Belfast and Londonderry/Derry contain sizeable numbers from both communities.

13. Brendan O'Leary, 'The Nature of the British–Irish Agreement', *New Left Review*, no. 233 (January–February 1999), 66–96.

14. Lijphart initially referred to the need for a comprehensive grand coalition, but it is not necessary that power-sharing take this form. See Brendan O'Leary, 'Debating Consociational Politics: Normative and Explanatory Arguments', in Sid Noel ed., *From Power Sharing to Democracy: Post-Conflict Institutions in Ethnically Divided Societies*, 3–43 (Montreal and Kingston, McGill-Queen's University Press, 2005).

15. Proportionality is ambiguous between population proportionality and community proportionality. Most consociationalists adopt a middle ground between the two, but the emphasis on 'each community' as a building block means that smaller communities are protected to a greater level than their share of the population would warrant. In many cases—e.g., Northern Ireland—where the d'Hondt rule for executive power-sharing is conceived as a power-sharing device, the two coincide. See Brendan O'Leary, Bernard Grofman, and Jørgen Elklit, 'Divisor Methods for Sequential Portfolio Allocation in Multi-Party Executive Bodies: Evidence from Northern Ireland and Denmark', *American Journal of Political Science*, vol. 49, no.1 (2005), 198–211.

16. Consociational principles, as they applied to the Netherlands, were non-territorial in form. I am assuming that consociationalism is a set of general principles, rather than a precise 'map'. This is consistent with Lijphart's claim that consociational principles were invented by Dutch politicians in 1917, and by their counterparts in Lebanon (1943), Austria (1945), Malaysia (1955), Colombia (1958), India (in the 1960s), and South Africa (1993–94) later in the century; Arend Lijphart, *Electoral Systems and Party Systems: A Study of Twenty-Seven Democracies, 1945–1990* (Oxford: Oxford University Press, 1994), viii.

17. Nationalists can also appeal to similar ideas. See David Miller, 'Debatable Lands', *International Theory*, vol. 6, no. 1 (2014), 104–121.

18. Note that the dispute in Kashmir echoes the more philosophical argument explored earlier in chapter 5, where I discuss the view a state has territorial rights if and only if it is a just (or legitimate) state. Note here that this standard of justice is indeterminate in the following way: it's unclear whether the standards apply to the state of India as a whole, and

to Kashmir specifically, since one might think that perhaps the Indian state itself is sufficiently just or democratic to claim authority, but that there are deficiencies in the Indian state's relations with Kashmir in particular. Even more interestingly, if this is the view that we adopt, it's just not clear that either the prince or the British had territorial rights to pass along to India in the first place. That is to say, if the appropriate standard for holding territorial rights is the standard of justice, even understood in a relatively relaxed way, then, if we apply this view retrospectively, most political entities cannot be thought of as entitled to their territory in the first place, and certainly the authority of the prince of Jammu and Kashmir and the British as the paramount sovereign authority to transfer sovereign authority is brought into question.

19. In recounting this history, I have been helped by reading Neera Chandhoke, Contested Secessions: Rights, Self-Determination, Democracy, and Kashmir (New Delhi: Oxford University Press, 2012); Sumantra Bose, Kashmir: Roots of Conflict, Paths to Peace (Cambridge, MA: Harvard University Press, 2003); and Bose, Contested Lands: Israel–Palestine, Kashmir, Bosnia, Cyprus and Sri Lanka (Cambridge MA: Harvard University Press, 2007).

20. The usual problem with referendums is that there has to be a decision made in the first place about the geographical space in which the referendum ought to be held. In addition, there is the problem of timing: if the referendum is not successful, do we keep trying? This was ridiculed in Canada as giving rise to the 'neverendum'. And once it's successful, do we hold referenda to go back?

21. Miller, 'Debatable Lands', 104–121.

22. The American support for the federal principle is clear. See John McGarry, 'Canadian Lessons for Iraq', in Brendan O'Leary, John McGarry, and Khaled Salih, eds, The Future of Kurdistan in Iraq, 92–115 (Philadelphia: University of Pennsylvania Press, 2005), 92.

23. The Kurdistan Regional Government has declared its intention to hold another referendum on independence in 2014. The results of that referendum, if it is held, will be important to the argument of this section.

24. Peter Galbraith, 'Kurdistan in a Federal Iraq', in Brendan O'Leary, John McGarry, and Khaled Salih, eds, The Future of Kurdistan in Iraq, 268–291 (Philadelphia: University of Pennsylvania Press, 2005), 281.

25. Further support for Galbraith's contention is provided by the events surrounding the January 2005 elections in the Kurdish region of Iraq, when hundreds of Kurds sympathetic to Kurdish independence held an informal referendum on independence. With no advance warning, members of the Kurdish Referendum Movement erected tents outside official polling stations and asked those emerging from the ballot booths to vote in a referendum on independence. According to a spokesperson for this movement, 1,998,061 people participated in the referendum, and only 20,251 voted for remaining in Iraq. It was claimed that there was overwhelming support for independence throughout the country, with Hewler (Arbil) and Duhok in the Sulaymani province slightly less supportive than the others; Dr. Kamal Mirawdeli, 'Voting for Independence: People of Kurdistan make their choice!', KurdishMedia.com, United Kurdish voice, 9 February 2005. According to an independent eyewitness writing for the New York Times, 'almost everyone stopped to vote in the referendum, and the tally was running around 11 to 1 in favor of independence', New York Times, 2 February, 2005.

26. The regime practiced systematic repression, torture, and rape, imprisoned political opponents and leaders of ethnic minorities. These practices have been well documented by impartial international observers, such as Human Rights Watch, and by independent journalists and NGOs; Human Rights Watch, Genocide in Iraq; The Anfal Campaign against the Kurds, http://www.hrw.org/reports/1993/iraqanfal/, New York: Middle East Watch Report, July 1993; BBC News, 'Iraqi Kurds' Story of Expulsion', 3 November 2001, http://news.bbc.co.uk/2/hi/middle_east/1614239.stm; United States Agency for International Development (USAID), 2004. 'Iraq's Legacy of Terror: Mass Graves', http://www.globalsecurity.org/intell/library/reports/2004/040317_iraq_mass_graves.pdf.

27. The basic facts are disputed. It seems that Kurds form a majority in the Kirkuk region, but have not always formed a majority in the city. There is some (albeit disputed) evidence

that Kurds were only 25 percent of the population of the city in 1949. See Ofra Bengio, 'Autonomy in Kurdistan in Historical Perspective', in Brendan O'Leary, John McGarry, and Khaled Salih, eds, *The Future of Kurdistan in Iraq*, 173–185 (Philadelphia: University of Pennsylvania Press, 2005), 181. For this particular (low) estimate, Bengio cites Cecil Edmonds, *Kurds, Turks, and Arabs* (Oxford: Oxford University Press, 1957), 435. Subsequently, the Kurds formed a much larger percentage of the population—Kurds claim that they were and are a majority—but that Kirkuk was excluded from the Kurdistan region and the Ba'athist regime subjected the city to a rigorous Arabization campaign, involving the expulsion of some Kurds and the settlement of Arabs. See Bengio, 'Autonomy in Kurdistan in Historical Perspective', 181. Turkomen are also, it is claimed (by Turkey), a significant population element in the city, but that is contested.

28. This is an important issue, since Kirkuk is an oil centre, and on some federal models, natural resources fall under the control of the region where they are located.

29. This of course depends on what view we take of control of resources, and the relationship of that to jurisdictional authority over territory, which is the subject of chapter 8.

30. It is not clear exactly what 'vanity secessions' refer to. Sometimes it seems that they are motivated by some kind of pride—the vanity of being recognized; but sometimes it seems that they are associated with economic opportunism. In either case, the idea is that the group cannot claim to have been a victim of injustice.

31. Wayne Norman assumes that we would not want to countenance secessions motivated by injustice or mere vanity, and he proposes framing the constitutional mechanisms that permit secession in a way that would discourage these sorts of claims; Wayne Norman, 'The Ethics of Secession as the Regulation of Secessionist Politics', in Margaret Moore, ed., *National Self-Determination and Secession*, 34–61 (Oxford: Oxford University Press, 1998), 55.

32. Pogge, *World Poverty and Human Rights*, 191. This forms part of an argument for the dispersal of sovereignty.

33. There is also a pragmatic reason to resist a blanket prohibition on the secession of rich units. If we think that viability is a factor in secession—because related to the state's ability to perform its functions—this is related to its relative richness. It would therefore be perverse to deny richer units the possibility of secession when they might indeed be the most viable units in a collapsing federation. The limit here of course is whether they leave a viable remainder unit.

34. Nationally mobilized Kosovar elites sought to push forward a secessionist agenda prior to the 1999 Serbian onslaught and grave violation of human rights in Kosovo. I mention this because the grievous injustices do not explain the national mobilization (though it may have contributed to it); indeed, the repression on the part of the (Serbian) state can itself be partly explained in terms of a response to what they viewed as treacherous, disloyal acts by the minority—attempts at secession.

35. There are a number of different types of special duties: contractual duties, such as duties arising out of promises, contracts, and agreements; reparative duties, duties to people one has wronged, harmed, or mistreated; duties of gratitude; and associative duties, which are duties arising from the relationship as such. See Samuel Scheffler, *Boundaries and Allegiances: Problems of Justice and Responsibility in Liberal Thought* (Oxford: Oxford University Press, 2001). Other advocates of associative duties are Ronald Dworkin, *Law's Empire* (Cambridge, MA: Harvard University Press, 1986), 195–216; and Yael Tamir, *Liberal Nationalism* (Princeton: Princeton University Press, 1993), chapter 5.

36. Of course, there are different kinds of cooperation: it can be very minimal or quite deep. In some cases, for example, in coordination problems, such as two countries agreeing on a standard metric for train tracks which go across both countries, the central duty would seem to be to keep one's promises, or to keep one's side of a coordination agreement. Cooperation to overcome coordination problems does not give rise to duties associated with reciprocity, even though the agreement is mutually beneficial. There are only (1) fairly general moral duties to work towards arrangements where coordination problems are overcome, and (2) duties connected to promise-keeping, to keep agreements that are made.

37. I do not mean to imply that taking turns is sufficient to characterize the relationship as reciprocal. The turns themselves might be unequal—if she has three children in need of care, say, and I have only one. Or we might think that the relationship is not reciprocal if I end up needing her assistance, and calling upon it far more often than she needs me. Indeed, at a certain point, we might—depending on our account of exploitation and reciprocity—think that my relation with her is fundamentally exploitative, even though she keeps agreeing to it.
38. Andrew Lister has argued that Rawls's way of thinking about justice and reciprocity is implicitly the latter: mutual benefit compared to an equal division of the net benefits of cooperation among all those willing to contribute; Andrew Lister, 'Justice as Fairness and Reciprocity', *Analyse & Kritik*, vol. 33, no. 1 (2011), 93–112.
39. There is also the question of who needs to have mutual benefit. In the literature on individual cooperation, mutual benefit applies only to those who make a net contribution. This leaves out of consideration people who are willing to make a contribution but are unable to do so, perhaps because of illness or lack of ability. Many feel that duties of reciprocity ought to extend to those who are willing to share fairly, even if for some reasons they find themselves unable to make a net contribution. To make sense of this intuition, we have to appeal to the idea that there is misrecognition or disrespect involved in failing to fulfill duties; but that there is no disrespect involved when people fail to make a net contribution because they are unable. If we accept this view, it means that reciprocity is duty-creating when it follows from or is foundational on a deeper ideal of mutual respect within a relationship.
40. Joseph Heath, 'Rawls on Global Distributive Justice: A Defence', *Canadian Journal of Philosophy*, Supplementary Volume, ed. Daniel Weinstock (Lethbridge: University of Calgary Press, 1997).
41. Buchanan argues that if a state is legitimate, it should be protected from secession; and that protection is secured by general agreement among states not to recognize entities that attempt to secede from states that satisfy the legitimacy criterion. See Allen Buchanan, 'Political Legitimacy and Democracy', *Ethics*, vol. 112, no. 4 (2002), 689–719; Buchanan, *Justice, Legitimacy, and Self-Determination*. By 'legitimate', Buchanan and Keohane appeal to a moralized conception of legitimacy, where legitimacy is the 'right to rule', both in the sense that 'institutional agents are morally justified in making rules and attempting to secure compliance with them and that people subject to those rules have moral, content-independent reasons to follow them and/or to not interfere with others' compliance with them'; Allen Buchanan and Robert Keohane, 'The Legitimacy of Global Governance Institutions', *Ethics & International Affairs*, vol. 20, no. 4 (2006), 405–443, at 411. An institution is morally justified in this way if it meets the following substantive criteria: it does not contribute to grave injustices ('minimal moral acceptability'); there is no obvious alternative that would perform better ('comparative benefit'); and it respects its own guidelines and procedures ('institutional integrity'). See Buchanan and Keohane, 'Legitimacy of Global Governance Institutions', 419ff.

7

Corrective Justice and the Wrongful Taking of Land, Territory, and Property

This chapter addresses the problem of territorial injustice. In chapter 1 and in the discussion of the occupancy principle, I used as a central example the story of Sir George Somers accompanied by his crew and prospective settlers, who landed on an uninhabited island in the north Atlantic Ocean and thereby founded the country of Bermuda. Through this simple example, I could consider the idea of legitimate occupancy without complicating it with issues relating to the treatment of previous occupants and prior injustices. This example made my argument almost embarrassingly simple because it abstracted from one of the most difficult elements of most cases of settlement and occupancy. This is that most people are settled on land which was previously occupied by another group. Members of the previous group in such cases often make claims to the same land on historical grounds. Indeed, they often argue that the current occupant, who perhaps expelled them, cannot acquire territorial rights on that land because their acquisition of the territory was unjust. This chapter deals with how we should think about expulsions from territory and what corrective justice remedies are available and when they are appropriate (or superseded).

In this chapter, I suggest that the taking of land should be theorized differently from other kinds of issues of corrective justice, not only because land is not moveable, and so cannot easily be distributed and redistributed and restored to the original occupant, but because morally significant relationships between people and place are likely to develop over time, and these affect the appropriate corrective justice remedy. Through analysing these relationships, we can identify different types of wrongs involved in the taking of land, some of which apply to individuals and some to groups.

Most theorists writing in the corrective justice tradition distinguish between three different mechanisms for correcting historical injustice: *restitution,* giving back whatever it is that has been unjustly taken; *compensation*, giving something of a certain value but not the thing itself, either because restitution is impossible or in addition to restitution to make good the loss the victim has suffered meanwhile; and *apology*, again either because restitution is not possible or because there is independent reason to acknowledge the wrong even if it is. All of these can apply when land is taken, and which remedy is appropriate depends on identifying which particular rights are violated, and the justificatory arguments for the rights.

Following from the analysis in the previous chapters, we can identify at least four sorts of potential wrongs involved when land is taken,[1] primarily through expelling people from their homes and communities, in addition to the coercion that usually accompanies such events: (1) being deprived of individual rights of residency; (2) being denied group rights of occupancy; (3) being denied collective self-determination; and (4) having individual or collective property rights violated. Although analytically distinct, all of these wrongs are likely to be perpetrated when people are expelled via ethnic cleansing or in other ways. In this chapter, I return to the justificatory argument from which these rights derive their normative force, to assess what should be done to remedy the rights violation. The justificatory arguments underlying these various rights help to specify the contours of the right, the remedies that might be appropriate, and the relevance of the passage of time in cases where one of these rights has been violated.

The argument of this chapter departs from most corrective justice accounts, which tend to focus on whether and how historic injustice should matter at all, with a rough division between those who think that correcting historic injustice matters for its own sake, as the righting of a wrong,[2] and those who think it matters as a precondition for justice or social harmony in the present.[3] This chapter does not focus on all kinds of corrective justice, just on corrective justice *with respect to land*, and even then, not all kinds of territorial injustice: it does not focus on the specific wrong of imperial control, for example, which involves territorial control *and* subjugation of one group of people by another.[4] Nevertheless, the moral wrongs involved in the taking of land are certainly worth theorizing. The practice has been ubiquitous: it is the basis of the current societies in the Americas and Australasia, and there are many recent cases of 'ethnic cleansing' and subsequent border creation, or attempted border creation (Israel/Palestine, Bosnia, Cyprus, to name a few). Moreover, although there is a substantial literature on corrective justice in such cases, most of that literature focuses on the expropriation of property. If the argument of this book is correct and people have different kinds of place-related rights, it means that this literature is unlikely to grasp the full implications of the wrong done and the full extent of what might be owed to people as a matter of corrective justice.

7.1. Corrective Justice Implications of the Moral Right of Residency or Occupancy

It is often assumed that when a right of residency or occupancy has been violated, through forcible expulsion or other means, the appropriate remedy is a right of return for the expelled person or expelled people, perhaps also including an apology for the moral wrong and compensation for loss of use for the time that the people were expelled. This section discusses the widely held view that expellees have a right to return, focusing on disagreement about how long that right of return might last and the extent to which, and the conditions under which, it might fade over time. I argue in this section that the appropriate corrective justice remedy for a violation of a right of residency or occupancy is primarily a right of return, and, like Waldron, I argue that the strength of the right to return does tend to diminish over time.[5]

Our intuitions about the right of return tend to run in two directions. On the one hand, we often think that people who are forcibly expelled from a place where they enjoyed legitimate residency or occupancy should, if that right is meaningful, be able to return there. There's an injustice not only in the forcible expulsion but also in the continued denial of their ability to return to the place where they ought to enjoy legitimate occupancy. On the other hand, we tend to think that this right of return does not continue, unextinguished, with the same force, forever. After all, North America was settled by people, mainly originally from Europe, and we don't think that these descendants of Europeans, some of whom may have been forced to leave their homes and communities because of religious persecution two or three centuries ago, now have the right to return to the parts of Europe from which their ancestors came, and that European countries are violating their rights by not permitting the descendants of those people originally expelled to return. That would be equivalent to a strong right of first occupancy, which persists so that once a group has occupied somewhere, they have rights to that place forever. The implications of such a right are very counter-intuitive. However, if we accept that the force of the right diminishes over time, we leave open the possibility of perverse incentives. We seem therefore to be on the horns of a dilemma.

To address the question of whether a right diminishes with time, we must return to the justificatory argument for rights of residency and occupancy. Instead of rehearsing the arguments advanced in chapter 3, I will proceed by noting that there is a basic division between arguments that rely on welfarist considerations, where the main point is that unjust displacement constitutes a wrong because it sets back people's welfare; and arguments that rely on autonomy considerations, where the basic idea is that unjust displacement violates people's autonomy.

It is easy to see how a thoroughgoing welfarist account could justify both a right to residency and also a time-limited right of return. The welfarist could recognize the wrong involved in expulsion, because they would ground a right to residency in the well-being of the person, and then, in arguing for the diminishing nature of the right to return, appeal to facts about welfare, such as that the displaced person had built a new life and new relationships against a background of a residence in a new place. This means that the continued possession of a right to residency in the original place, which is implied by a right to return, fades over time, because the well-being interest in that residency is no longer credible.

I argued above that a right of return that continued undiminished through time was equivalent to a right of first occupancy, which is counter-intuitive. An objective account of welfare,[6] which justifies a right to return in terms of the person's well-being, can avoid collapsing into a right of first occupancy by assuming that, over time, people adjust to their new situation and the strength of the right to return diminishes. However, it is worth noting that many expelled people will deny that they can in fact live flourishing lives with the loss of occupancy and the continuing denial of their right to return. I do not think this is a lie: I was once driven in a taxi by a Greek Cypriot who had been expelled from his home and community by the Turkish army that occupied his village thirty-five years previously and he still held the key to his old house on his key chain and he kissed it when he spoke of his old village. This suggests that if we anchor the right of return in an objective theory of well-being, it will be at odds with the felt experience of many people who claim to still experience the loss of continued denial of a right to return. It ends up being either patronizing or relying on a problematic responsibility argument, whereby people are viewed as partially responsible for their failure to get over their loss.[7] Of course, the welfarist could adopt a purely subjective account of well-being, but that has the counter-intuitive consequence that rectification will vary depending only on how the person reacts to their expropriation, rather than on the nature of the injury itself.[8]

What then of an autonomy justification for the right of occupancy and right of return? In the literature on territorial rights and occupancy, both David Lefkowitz and Anna Stilz explicitly appeal to autonomy considerations. Stilz defends what I have termed residency rights in autonomy terms: she discusses the 'centrality of territorial occupancy for an individual's personal autonomy—his ability to form and pursue a conception of the good',[9] and she elaborates that '[o]ccupancy of territory is connected to autonomy because it plays an important role in almost all of our plans . . . respect for my autonomy tells in favor of allowing me to remain [in the place where I reside], since it would be impossible to move me without damage to nearly all my life-plans'.[10] There is a similar passage in Waldron's argument in 'Superseding Historic Injustice', where he identifies possession of property or territory as indispensable to life plans and then connects this with an autonomy-based argument. He writes: 'it seems plausible to suggest that continued possession of the object might be indispensable to the possessor's autonomy and that an attack on possession is an attack on autonomy'.[11] David Lefkowitz, in perhaps the most consistent and thoroughgoing treatment of autonomy justifications for a right of residency, also argues that, 'it is respect for a person's autonomy, her formation and pursuit of a territorially grounded conception of the good that grounds or justifies that right'.[12] Lefkowitz points out that focusing on the right to reside and ignoring the continued refusal to allow the person to return to the territory represents a 'truncated account of the connection between respect for personal autonomy and individuals' rights to reside in a particular territory'.[13] For Lefkowitz, those who are unjustly displaced are asserting 'a right to the opportunity to formulate and pursue life-plans premised on current and future residence in T, a right she enjoys because she (or possibly, her forebears) once rightfully resided in T and she has not voluntarily abandoned the claim to do so again'.[14] Respect for autonomy, in Lefkowitz's account, requires the person to *waive* the right to return; anything less than this would 'give those who unjustly displaced them and who persist in their unjust denial to the displaced of rights to reside in T an unwarranted control over the displaced persons' formation and pursuit of their life-plans'.[15] Lefkowitz claims that the reason we think that current North Americans do not have a right to return to their original (forebear's) homeland is that they have abandoned that right; they have, as often happens, voluntarily relinquished that land as an object of their aims and aspirations; but when they have not relinquished the right voluntarily, they retain the right of return.[16]

Lefkowitz's autonomy account justifies a very strong right of return, but it is implausible in two ways. First, his account is not symmetrical in treating the conditions for acquiring the right and losing the right. Symmetry here is not a purely aesthetic consideration: we often think that the considerations that tell in favour of the right might also tell in favour of rights loss if the considerations do not obtain. When we think about how people acquire occupancy or residency rights, we can see that they do not acquire them immediately: Sir George Somers and his fellow seamen and prospective settlers did not acquire occupancy rights on that island, with a strong right of return, in the first minute or the first hour. They developed it over time, through their relationship to each other and to the land, such that expulsion from the land would constitute a serious injustice. It would harm them, in the sense of setting back a number of their interests, and it would also wrong them, because expulsion would fail to respect their status as moral equals who attribute particular value to that land and that community. Since these considerations (about the relationship to the people and the land) ground the right, it makes sense to think that, when these considerations no longer obtain, the justificatory argument for the right no longer holds. This does not of course mean that the injustice is 'superseded': we might think that, since the injustice occurred, something ought to be done to acknowledge this and rectify it; but that need not amount to a right of return.

Second, there is a difference between a place being a fundamental condition for the exercise of autonomy (in the case of occupancy rights) and having or not having an *opportunity* to live in a place and thereby exercise autonomy with respect to that particular choice (to return to the place where one had previously lived). In the case of people who have built their lives elsewhere, perhaps due to some long-ago expulsion, they might have aims and aspirations to return, but there is a significant difference between the denial of a fundamental condition of one's central aims and aspirations, and the denial of an opportunity to have a particular place be the central place for one's plans and projects. It's clear that the former is indeed a significant harm to one's interests, whereas the latter represents a reduction in one's opportunity sets, even if that reduction is due to an injustice. There are many opportunities that we don't have and yet we still live autonomous lives.[17]

Stilz's autonomy argument is more intuitively plausible in so far as there is a neat symmetry between the conditions that tell in favour of an occupancy right and the fading of that right over time, as the conditions no longer hold. The problem is that it's not clear that the language of choice and autonomy that she adopts is apposite. After all, many people live unreflective lives; they do not *choose* their path, nor make *choices* amongst a range of *options*. Security of place and protection of one's occupancy rights (in the sense of a liberty right to remain in a place and a right of non-dispossession) are important to autonomous and non-autonomous people alike.

As I suggested in chapter 3, there is a fundamental human interest both in general, in having a place to live, and in particular, because people have attachments to place, to other people who are located in a place, and to ways of life that presuppose that people live in a place, and this is quite apart from whether or the extent to which they play a role in promoting or facilitating personal autonomy. In order to understand the importance of place-related rights and the possibility that they may weaken over time, it might be helpful to think in terms of expectations rather than autonomy.

Although Jeremy Waldron deploys the language of autonomy in discussing corrective justice, he also advances a quite different argument—an 'expectation leads to justice' argument—which I think comes closest to capturing the basis of people's place-related rights and the reasons why these rights might change over time. The idea of legitimate expectations does not rely on a background story about the role it plays in the exercise of autonomy, but it does rely on the idea that place is important to many aspects of one's life and that people could not live well if they could not rely on some basic assumptions about security of place and the general stability of the context in which they conduct their live and relationships. Moreover, like Stilz's version of the autonomy argument, the legitimate-expectations argument notes that people do often adjust to their condition and pursue plans, projects, and relationships within a new context. But it does not ground the right in personal autonomy in any sense. Rather it suggests the fundamental role that place plays in people's lives, and recognizes that the passage of time has effects: it leads people to readjust to the state of affairs, and to come to live their lives against a new background of home and community, which can give rise to new rights, new entitlements, and can also alter what we take to be the appropriate remedy to a violation of place-related rights.

The argument of this book—particularly in chapter 3—and in the appeal to the importance of place in people's plans and lives helps to explain what it means to occupy a land legitimately.[18] In the case of uninhabited islands, such as Bermuda, the qualifier is straightforward. But as I argued in chapter 3, occupancy rights are not confined to such unblemished cases: it applies also to people who occupy land that was previously occupied by another group, if the people living on the land have themselves acquired entitlements to live there. This is analogous to the position of a person who enters a territory illegally but comes to live there for many years, develops relationships and attachments in the new land, and thereby gains some entitlements to live there. This view of irregular migrants has been pressed by many recent theorists on immigration, who have pointed out that these relationships and attachments that the illegal migrant has developed are relevant to the moral status of their claim to remain. The denial of citizenship rights to such migrants based on how they initially came to reside on the territory fails to take account of the whole picture.[19] Of course, the initial injustice or original illegal entry is not rendered irrelevant: the perpetrators have to face a higher burden than someone who came to be resident there in a legal and unproblematic way. But how one comes to live in a place is not the *only* relevant consideration for residency rights, even though it is a very important one. There are other considerations—of attachment, of the value of relationships to the land and to people living there, and the expectations to realize these into the future—which might lead the individual to gain residency rights and/or the group to acquire occupancy rights (just as it may be relevant to the irregular migrant's claim to remain and become a citizen).

7.2. Legitimate Expectations, Security of Place, and the Right of Return

I have suggested that the idea of 'legitimate expectations' is helpful in thinking about the acquisition and diminution of residency or occupancy rights and the related right of return. What does it mean to have 'legitimate expectations' and how we can view expectations as a fount of entitlements? One of the clearest arguments of this type is found in Waldron's article on 'superseding injustice', where he argues that people who settled on land and property, even land or property acquired unjustly, begin to have expectations, and these expectations give rise to claims of justice. Waldron writes:

> For better or worse, people build up structures of expectation around the resources that are actually under their control. If a person con-trols a resource over a long enough period, then she and others may organize their lives and their economic activity around the premise that that resource is 'hers,' without much regard to the distant prov-enance of her entitlement. Upsetting these expectations in the name of restitutive justice is bound to be costly and disruptive.[20]

Although Waldron's argument focuses on expectations, it's clear that not just any expectation that a person might have would give rise to justice claims, but only *legitimate* expectations, which of course raises the question of what counts as a legitimate expectation.[21]

There is some ambiguity in the idea of 'legitimate expectations'. In one sense expectations cease to be legitimate when they involve injustice: a crim-inal's expectation that he will profit from his crime is illegitimate. This is a moralized sense of the term, where what one can legitimately expect is what is consistent with the relevant norms. However, there is another use of the term 'legitimately expect', which means something like 'what it is reasonable to expect to happen', which is not explicitly normative, though it could give peo-ple claims in certain cases, especially where people who move on to land come to have these sorts of expectations that the communities that they set up and the homes that they establish would remain. Of course, developing 'legitimate expectations' of the second kind is easier when the expectations are legitimate in the first, moral sense.

Waldron's discussion of legitimate expectations is most persuasive when applied to a claim to place rather than moveable property that may have unjustly come into someone's possession. His argument dovetails nicely with the justification offered here for a moral residency or occupancy right, but does not translate well into a general argument about property. This is because place is fundamental to the expectations that people develop; it is the background against which people make decisions and develop projects as they navigate through life. Waldron emphasizes that people make choices against some background knowledge of resources available to them, and changes in these resources can harm them because they alter the conditions under which they made the choices.[22] This point implies a slightly more instrumental conception of the relationship of people to land, but he also makes the point that the larger community in which people live is the stable context for all their relationships and commitments, which enable them to feel 'at home' in the world. These relationships, and people's aims and projects, and the place to which people are attached, help to give meaning to their lives.

I have argued that, typically, after a period of time, the people or group who are deprived of their land are often able to adjust their perspective to the new situation and organize their life around the lack of territory. However, what about people who were evicted from the place where they enjoyed a moral right of occupancy and are stuck in refugee camps, unable to develop projects and make plans confident of their background context? These people still suffer the effects of the original injustice, and for long-term refugees, this limbo can persist into the second generation. For people in this category, the proper remedy is the right of return. The problem, of course, is that such rights are defeasible: in many cases there will be intra-right and inter-right conflicts. Indeed, if we assume a sufficiently long period of time, the new occupants, presumably the second generation of those who perpetrated the initial eviction, will have developed moral residency or occupancy rights of their own, so that the two groups would both be entitled to such rights. This may mean acknowledging an individual right of return for refugees who have not been able to find a secure place in which their right of residency or occupancy can be realized; or the return of some land (though perhaps not all), in the case of persons who, although they were subject to forcible removal a long time ago, have not been able to adjust to their new situation and who seek return of their land.

It might be thought that since the right of return allows those people wrongly expelled the *option* to return, even if they no longer want to exercise it, it is the superior remedy, much better than simple apology or compensation. The problem, however, is that, as I've also argued, in many cases other people and other groups are living on the land, and have themselves acquired residency or occupancy rights, and are in political control of the territory; so a return to the status quo ante is either not a viable option, or it is not an option that could be exercised without additional injustice. This does not of course mean that the injustice has been superseded, since a wrong has been done which demands to be addressed in some way, but it does mean that we need to think differently about the appropriate remedy. This is especially true in cases of multigenerational injustice, where the expelled group does not consist of people who actually experienced the expulsion, but of children of the expelled, and the present occupants did not perpetrate the injustice, but are the children of the people who did.

It also follows from the individual moral right of residency argument that settlers can over time develop rights, though the exact circumstances bear on how quickly and whether they gain residency or occupancy rights. Consider, for example, the case of Cyprus, in which there are two kinds of settlers: first there are Turkish Cypriots now living Northern Cyprus, who were displaced from their homes and communities in the south, and who came to live in the property formerly owned by Greek Cypriots; and second, there are settlers from mainland Turkey (Anatolia) who have been state-sponsored and state-encouraged to settle in Cyprus, either through the military occupation of the northern part of the island, or simply to participate in the economic and political life of the community, and to change the demographic balance there. Settlement of the first kind is normatively less problematic, because the people in question have had their initial occupancy rights violated, and their reinstatement in new communities can be viewed as an attempt to give them a context in which they can try to rebuild their lives and forge new plans and relationships. To then displace them from these homes in the interests of the first occupants would involve a double injustice to these people.

In the case of the second sort of settler, however, the situation is morally more problematic. On the one hand, the argument outlined above will over time apply to them: they have rights as individuals to live in a place, to have a secure context in which to exercise autonomy, and so on. On the other hand, settlers of this kind occupy land in clear violation of international law, and this makes their case somewhat weaker in so far as it would be difficult for them to reasonably view their occupation of these lands as forming a temporally secure backdrop to the exercise of their autonomy.[35] Their sense of insecurity of possession (possession which is not legitimate or rightful) will interfere at least in the short to medium term with the extent to which they can develop legitimate expectations of continued occupancy, which forms the backdrop to their lives.

7.3. Perverse Incentives, Current Occupants, and Benefiting from Injustice

This section addresses the problem of perverse incentives, which is implicit in the idea of moral residency or occupancy rights diminishing or strengthening over time. Waldron, too, recognizes that this is a problem with his argument, namely that it 'furnishes an incentive to anyone who is inclined to violate another's rights'.[23] I think this is a serious problem, which I discuss in two quite distinct ways. First, I consider the argument that mere benefit from an injustice does not entail any obligations of justice, including corrective justice. This principle is often appealed to in cases of interpersonal morality, but I think it's flawed in cases of group-based expulsion, where one of the principal motives is acquiring territory for the group conceived of as an intergenerational community of people. Second, I try to address the institutional mechanisms available to reduce the risk of perverse incentives.

The first issue, then, is whether mere benefit from an injustice entails any obligations of corrective justice. It is important not to confuse contribution to injustice with benefit from injustice. It is useful to reflect that most of us have benefited from the serious injustice inflicted on residents of Hiroshima.[24] Anyone who has ever had an X-ray benefits from the data set on safe dosage of radiation that was compiled as a result of that event. We do not think it is plausible that this fact alone gives us special responsibility to victims of Hiroshima. However, in many cases of forcible expulsion and settlement, there is the complicating factor that they are not of 'mere benefit' to a third party in the ordinary sense: on the contrary, many expulsions are designed, not to benefit the individual person who is participating in the expulsion, but the 'nation' or the political community, which is conceived of as an intergenerational collective. It is often precisely in order to keep the territory for the benefit of their children and grandchildren, or anyway the future generation in that 'nation' or that political community, that the perpetrators engage in a project of territorial acquisition, ethnic cleansing, and resettlement. So a simple argument based on the lack of moral culpability of the benefiting generation is likely to be insufficiently complex and also to raise the problem of perverse incentives. At the minimum, as Daniel Butt has argued, the fact that the later generation of people were the *intended beneficiaries* makes it disanalogous with the case of X-ray patients and Hiroshima.[25] If the later generation recognize that a wrong was done, and recognize also that they were the intended beneficiaries of this injustice, then it gives them an additional reason that others do not have to rectify the wrong. In cases of multigenerational injustices, where the beneficiaries were born in the contested territory, and themselves have residency or occupancy rights, it would be too great a sacrifice of their own lives to restore the status quo ante, but, at the minimum, compensation and apology are required out of respect for the moral equality of the original right-holders and to make amends for the wrong done to them.

Let me move on to a more general problem of perverse incentives. Waldron acknowledges a moral hazard in his argument, but it is one he thinks we must simply accept. I think more can be said in response to the concern about moral hazard. Specifically, there is a difference between (1) a moral hazard and (2) exploiting a moral hazard. The former is an unavoidable side-effect or consequence of the operation of otherwise just rules and practices; the latter involves intentional, unfair, and/or unjust action with the explicit view of self-interested gain, at the expense of the other party's interests. If we think that it is axiomatic of good institutional design to reduce or minimize perverse incentives, then we will certainly be concerned with the problem of moral hazard.

The argument from legitimate expectations offers a partial response to this concern. One might think that the development of expectations—legitimate expectations—is different in cases where people know that the land or territory has been taken from someone else. When European peoples first interacted with indigenous peoples, more than 500 years ago, there was no clear international prohibition on conquest or settlement, so people did have an expectation of continued residence and settlement on land previously occupied by others. However, the same cannot be said of more recent cases, such as the occupying Turkish army in Cyprus, since 1974, and the Israeli occupation of the West Bank and the Gaza since 1967. In both cases, there is no doubt that settling territory under military occupation is in clear violation of the basic norms of the international system and in contravention of repeated United Nations resolutions. Indeed, the Fourth Geneva Convention, which spells out the obligations of an occupying power with respect to its original inhabitants, makes explicit that settlements of the occupying power on this territory are illegal. Under these conditions (unlike the creation of Israel in 1948, for example, which was legitimated by the UN partition plan), settlers would likely be wary of viewing their occupations as secure, and their continued use or control of this land would not quickly form a stable background from which to exercise autonomy. There are more complex cases, like East Timor and the Baltic states when they were incorporated into the Soviet Union, where settlement (of Indonesians and Russians) occurred in the context of a shared political unit. In that case, it might be unreasonable to assume that the individual settler can analyse correctly the historical trajectory and conclude that his or her settlement is illegitimate. In part this is because there is typically propaganda in one direction from the leaders of the state that she or he trust, and few countervailing arguments. The legitimate-expectation argument here, which includes an appeal to the idea of 'what is reasonable to expect', would view the settlers in these cases as more quickly developing legitimate projects and relationships and attachments, including attachments to their new land.

I argued earlier that it is implausible that settlers in Israeli-occupied territories or Turkish settlers in Northern Cyprus could easily or quickly develop legitimate expectations around the possession of the land, when it was deeply contested, as being in violation of international law, and repeatedly subject to contestation in the international community by the Palestinians, by the Israeli public (who are themselves divided on the fate of the occupied territories), by Greek Cypriots and their allies. This suggests ways to reduce the problem of moral hazard. We should develop institutional rules and practices to prevent the creation of expectations around the continued occupation of land that has been unjustly taken. This gives us a very strong reason to develop norm-governed international institutions which condemn the practice of settlement, understood as typically involving the deliberate eviction or expulsion of a group, combined with the installation of the favoured group in their place. Of course, over time, even these settlers or their children will come to enjoy moral residency or occupancy rights, but the temporal dimension will be much longer if it's clear that the settlement is illegal in international law and deeply contested. This suggests that there is an urgent need to develop robust international norms, rules, and institutional practices which unequivocally condemn such practices when they occur and continually challenge the settler group in their occupation of the land. This will prevent groups and people from quickly or easily incorporating a settled expectation with respect to the land in their life-plans, and may be useful in mitigating the exploitation of a serious moral hazard.

7.4. Collective Right to Self-Determination

In chapter 3, I argued that there is a right to collective self-determination. I discussed briefly the right to 'self-determination of peoples' enshrined in the United Nations Charter and argued that the moral right to collective self-determination follows from the idea that political communities are valuable as spaces in which members co-create their own political project, thus realizing both relationship-dependent and relationship-independent goods. When a group is deprived of its territory, it is also deprived of the main institutional conditions or means to exercise self-government or collective self-determination. Indeed, in many cases, the expulsion of people from a place is motivated primarily by the desire not for the property or riches but to prevent the victims from exercising the right of collective self-determination, and to facilitate the exercise of that right by the group that has seized territory.

The occupancy argument discussed above suggests that a group can exercise territorial jurisdiction where the members legitimately occupy the territory, and it is clear that settlement following the forcible removal of a population enjoying occupancy rights does not constitute a 'legitimate' occupation of the territory. The occupancy argument, then, establishes a clear line between legitimate and illegitimate occupation of territory. The self-determination argument, by contrast, in which territory is a second-order good, because essential to self-government, is more contextual: although it tells us that forcible population removal aimed at the denial of self-determination is a moral wrong, it is not clear that all population movements result in the same, absolute denial of collective self-determination.[26] In the cases of the Crimean Tatars or the Volga Germans, the entire population was displaced from its 'homeland' and it was unlikely that they could identify with the collective life of the larger group in which they were scattered, since the reason for their displacement was precisely to assimilate them and to deny them a viable associational life. In the case of the Sudeten Germans, by contrast, who were forcibly removed from Sudetenland (Czechoslovakia) at the end of the Second World War and, as individuals, moved mainly to West Germany, they were able to exercise forms of collective self-determination within Germany. Their residency rights had clearly been violated, and they were no longer self-determining *as Sudeten Germans*, but they were able to adjust to, and exercise collective self-determination within, a compatible political project (Germany). The same is true of the Greek Cypriots who were forcibly expelled from Kyrenia or Famagusta: they clearly had their residency and occupancy rights violated, as well as many other rights in the course of that forcible removal. But it is not clear that this was absolutely damaging for the exercise of their *collective self-determination*: true, they could not exercise meaningful self-determination as Kyrenians or Famagustans, but that had not been their primary collective identity anyway, and they could still participate in meaningful collective autonomy as Greek Cypriots. The idea of self-government does not straightforwardly tell us where boundaries should be drawn, and this is especially so when the new self-determination project matches to some extent the identity and aims and aspirations of the members of the group, as was true of Greek Cypriots who remained within the Republic of Cyprus, which was expressive of a Greek Cypriot identity, and true too of Sudeten Germans within Germany. Let me be clear: there is no doubt that Greek Cypriots experienced the loss of territory as a loss; but the real tragedy in this redrawing was not the loss of collective self-determination per se, but the violation of the moral rights of residency that was involved in this territorial 'readjustment'—the forcible transfer of people from their communities, where they had been settled and had relationships, commitments, and projects.

In other cases, however, the loss of territory means the loss of meaningful collective self-determination, because people find it difficult to adjust to different self-determination projects, even when they are formally inclusive. Consider, for example, North American indigenous peoples, who were stripped of their land and whose self-governing regimes, which they had established prior to colonization, were destroyed. It is unsurprising that they found it difficult to view the new political project (e.g., Canada, the United States) as expressive of their self-determination, since it was built on the destruction of their previous self-determining communities; and unsurprising too that the assimilation attempts that accompanied their incorporation also failed, since it is probably psychologically very difficult to adopt the identity and broad culture of the group that has engaged in widespread theft and the destruction of your foremothers and forefathers. This is also a not untypical story, which I recount here only to indicate that a historically sensitive and contextually nuanced approach is important to determining how a group may be best able to realize its right to collective self-determination, and that we cannot assume that it will be possible in any formally inclusive political project.

What corrective justice remedies follow from the argument just advanced? I have argued that groups that were denied the right of collective self-determination and occupancy have a right to return to the land from which they were expelled and establish politically self-determining institutional structures there. But notice that the two rights work in tandem. Following directly from the analysis of the relationship between moral residency or occupancy rights and territorial rights in chapter 3, we can see that changes in circumstances (which happen over time) will impact on occupancy rights, because the relationship between the right-holder and the territory is also changed. As individual members of a group may come to lose their moral rights of residency, so the group of which they are part will lose its claim to occupancy, which is a necessary condition for its claim to be entitled to exercise territorial jurisdiction over that area. A group can be collectively self-determining only over an area that it legitimately occupies, which means two things: it cannot exercise jurisdiction over other people, simply because other people live in areas that it once had occupancy rights over; and second, it can exercise robust territorial forms of self-determination only if it enjoys legitimate occupancy over the territory. Of course, that doesn't affect whether it has a right to self-determination in the first place, only the form (territorial) that exercise of the right can take.

7.5. The Right to Property

The forcible removal of people from land that they justly occupy also typically involves a violation of their legal and moral rights to property. There are two main ways to think about property rights. On the first, social convention, view, property rights are understood as rules about possession justified by reference to some primary aim of a legitimate political order such as peace or welfare, and alterable over time to suit those ends.[27] On this view, property rights are conceived of as a cluster of rights and rules surrounding acquisition, transfer, bequest, and so on, and are the creation of a legitimate political (jurisdictional) authority. Political authority is crucial to the determination of the rules surrounding property and the precise rights that citizens enjoy. On a second, natural rights, view, rights to property are grounded in the fundamental importance of private holdings to the exercise of liberty, that is the ability of persons to engage in individual or collective projects. This implies a relatively strong view of ownership in corrective justice cases, and the role of legitimate political authorities is to uphold natural rights, including the natural right to property.[28] It is also possible to have a hybrid theory of property rights, such that property rights are primarily conceived of as legal rights, and creations of the political order, but that does not mean that we cannot apply moral ideas to the property rights that we have, especially ideas about basic rights to subsistence and the idea of desert. This is my view: I think of property rights as legal rights that are created by the legal and political order but we can draw on a pre-institutional moral theory to explain why some systems of property rights are better than others.[29]

On either metatheory of property—whether one adopts the natural rights or social convention, or political, view—the expulsion of people from their property represents a moral wrong. But the two metatheories of property rights suggest somewhat different timelines for corrective justice and possibly different remedies. If we conceive of property rights as natural rights, they are not easily extinguished. On a natural rights view, property rights persist through time, regardless of the way in which they are held or the rules established by existing political authorities. This is obviously an attractive picture for those people who have been expelled from their property and land, because it insists that property rights persist undiminished over time, and it also suggests that the appropriate corrective justice remedy is full restitution of the property to its original owner. This metatheory is problematic, however, in its application to other domains. The strong conception of natural rights to property is at odds with many of the functions of current states, which involve a strong redistributive justice dimension (e.g., taxing people's property to benefit the worst-off). Indeed, many rules in contemporary jurisdictions, which permit expropriation of property when this is necessary for the common good (e.g., to build a high-way), are inconsistent with this basic view of the relationship between legitimate jurisdictional authorities, which have territorial control, and property rights. This does not condemn the natural right view of property in itself, since the more libertarian-spirited amongst us might be happy enough with these implications, but it does suggest that the social convention view of property is the one embedded in many contemporary liberal-democratic states.

The political or conventional view of property rights offers a more flexible understanding of property rights and the corrective justice method for dealing with violations. It is important not to exaggerate this point, however. Unlike moral occupancy rights, which seem to diminish over time, one of the points of property claims is to provide stability without actual possession. As Kant noted, the point of property is to convert mere possession into a legal and moral claim, so that people do not need to be in physical possession of a piece of property to own it, but only to be in a legal relation where people reciprocally recognize each other's claims to property. This means that person X's moral right of residency cannot extinguish a legal property right (of person Y), for the simple reason that property does not require continued or constant possession. (This is complicated of course, because, in some legal systems, ownership lapses if the owner does not raise objections within a specified period to someone else's taking over the property—but this is internal to the legal system itself and consistent with the social convention view.) In the normal course of events, however, if someone steals my car, I would pretty quickly have to make some adjustments—find alternative means of transport—but we don't think that these adjustments lessen my claim to restitution of my stolen car. So—on this picture—while an individual or group may develop or lose, over time, moral rights of residency or occupancy, property rights are not wholly extinguished.

There are some difficulties, however, with the rectification of social convention view of property rights violations. First, one of the problems with a social convention view about property is that, in many cases, the new legal order will not recognize the legitimacy of the previous political order or the legitimacy of the property titles that were the creation of that order. This is a problem in cases of forcible expulsion and settlement, which typically also involve a transition from one order to another. The problem here is that the new, usurping political order might be unwilling or unable to recognize the rights of the previous order as rights. Indeed, in so far as doing so would suggest that the previous order was a legitimate rights-creating entity, the conquering, usurping, expelling, and occupying entity may have a particular reason for denying the rights created by that order.

This might be especially true when the systems of property holdings are quite different—where, for one community, property involves exclusive title and use, whereas for another society it might involve more informal rights of land tenure or use. This would make it hard to integrate the two kinds of rights into one system. This might pose particular difficulties in cases where there are different conventions surrounding what counts as a property right. The social convention approach to property rights also tends not to recognize non-state actors who claim to have traditional property rights. Even when the political order might be inclined to recognize some of these rights, there is the additional difficulty, on this view of property, of identifying the source of the right.

On the other hand, because the social convention understanding of property rights is typically grounded in arguments about the social utility of recognizing such rights, these rights are potentially weakened in the face of overriding considerations about the social utility of returning them in the present day. It's always an option, on this view, for a legitimate political order to define the property right in a limited way or in a way that suggests a particular remedy for violations or expropriations. This is either a strength or a weakness, depending on one's point of view. The conventional or political view of property rights takes a much more flexible view of a (legitimate) state's ability to arrive at different sorts of solutions to complex corrective justice property cases. It also suggests that a legitimate political entity—created, say, by a negotiated political settlement involving the political representatives of both displaced and displacing communities—would have the capacity to make appropriate decisions regarding property, including transfer of property, restitution, and compensation. This might be helpful in cases where restitution of property is not possible, in part perhaps because settlers may have developed their own rights of occupancy over time.

The obvious remedy for the loss of property, when there are no complicating considerations, is full restitution of that property, perhaps accompanied by apology and compensation for the period of time when one was excluded from use and enjoyment of the property. This parallels the remedy for loss of occupancy or residency rights, which is the right of return.

But what about cases when restitution of the property is not possible or desirable? It is necessary to think about the appropriateness of models of corrective justice that do not involve restitution of the property. Is there an additional moral loss that accompanies the loss of private property per se, which cannot be corrected through compensation (assuming that restitution is either not possible or not desirable)?

Obviously, in the case of a large land-holder or an owner of a multi-unit apartment building, property holdings are investments and the relationship between the property and the proprietor is purely instrumental, so the owner is fully compensated if he or she receives market value for the lost property.[30]

What about owner-occupiers? Is there an additional moral loss not captured either by the violation of the moral rights of residency or occupancy and the violation of private property rights, corrected by compensation? The standard answer to this question—which is developed in normal cases of compensation (when people are expropriated from property that they own in the common interest)—distinguishes as I have just done between investors and occupiers, and argues for a greater level of compensation for people dispossessed of property that they live in.[31] There are two possible reasons for this. One is that this additional sum reflects the dislocation and disruption involved in expulsion, so that it is not good enough simply to get market value, but that some additional compensation is necessary to account for the disruption which is typically felt by people who are forced to leave their homes. The other reason is that this additional value is necessary to reflect a common and well-reproduced empirical finding that people value their property, their possession, at higher rates than comparable goods that they don't own.[32] None of this challenges compensation as a remedy, though this more nuanced account suggests that there is a substantial chunk of value that people attach to their homes over and above strict market value, and this endowment effect is represented by asking whether people would be willing to swap their homes for something comparable nearby.

There is, however, a third category of people—not investors and not owner-occupiers—but people whose lives are invested in a project which is significantly bound up with the property such that it is irreplaceable and that compensation would be insufficient. Consider a case where a person's life is invested in a particular project, which gives her reasons to act, and the project involves something specific about the piece of property itself, such as that it is an ancestral home that is kept in the family name in perpetuity. For such a person, the home is not substitutable in the way that compensation models of redress suggest. Or consider a case where I have built a cabin whose market value is $20,000 and somebody destroys the cabin and offers $20,000; that fails as adequate compensation, because even if I can buy another cabin I no longer have one that I've built myself. The problem here is that rights protect generic interests, in liberty, and other things, including the fact of having projects and relationships, but they do not confer any special status on particular projects of individual people. Property rights, defended in either of the two ways outlined above, do not adequately deal with the general problem of incorporating project-dependent reasons in their theory.[33]

Property rights and the associated remedial rights that people have when their property rights are violated do not vary according to individual utility functions. However, it might be possible to design legal mechanisms and rules that would give due weight to individual cases, without also creating perverse incentives for complainants to exaggerate their loss. The idea would be to design institutional mechanisms with sufficiently complex rules to try to give effect to our moral intuitions here. This might involve empowering an impartial tribunal to decide such cases on normatively justified principled grounds—for example, in assessing relative harm, to consider the rights of settlers, who may have acquired moral occupancy rights, and the rights of former proprietors, distinguishing appropriately between investors and owner-occupiers, or to consider such additional facts as that the property was built by the person herself, who regards it as irreplaceable, or that it has been in the same family for numerous generations. Such project-dependent reasons when applied to violations of property rights are, however, likely to diminish over time, because they presuppose a close relationship between the proprietor and the property in question, and this is more attenuated the longer the property is not in the possession of the person.[34]

7.6. Conclusion

In this chapter, I argued that there are four different types of moral wrongs involved in the displacement of people from land on which they are settled, and each one relies on a different justificatory argument about the nature of the wrong, which is relevant to the appropriate corrective justice remedy. The four kinds of rights that may be violated in cases of expulsion (in addition to the coercive threats and intimidation that usually characterize such events) are: (1) the individual right to reside in a place; (2) a collective or group right to occupy the place; (3) the right to collective self-determination, in which territory is a second-order moral good, because necessary to robust forms of self-government; and (4) legal and moral rights to property. Distinguishing between these different kinds of wrongs provides the tools to apply the argument to actual cases of corrective justice.

I have argued that it is important to analyse which right or rights were violated, because the moral argument that underlies the right not only suggests the appropriate remedy, but also suggests whether the moral considerations change over time. I do not, however, argue that injustice can be wholly superseded, because rights violations are not harmful just to the interests of the victims but also represent a moral wrong, a kind of disrespect for their status as moral equals.

I also argued that the moral right of residency or occupancy is appropriately rectified by a right of return, but this right diminishes over time, in large part because the original right is grounded in the idea that place is an important background framework for people's projects, choices, and relationships, and this can change over time. In addition, new rights of occupancy develop as people become settled in a place. The collective right of self-determination, which is violated in cases of group expulsion, is dependent (at least for its territorial exercise) on the group occupying a territory. It requires, that is, that the individuals comprising the group have a prior moral right of residency, and since this right diminishes or strengthens over time (as the case may be), it affects the group's ability to occupy the territory and to exercise territorial forms of self-determination. Finally, property rights can be violated when land is taken, and these typically remain in force, relatively undiminished over time. However, the appropriate corrective justice remedy for dealing with property claims may be affected by the existence of the other two rights. Restitution of property may be feasible if the property is not lived in by another family, but in many cases, compensation is the morally appropriate remedy, because restitution would involve further injustice (violating the occupant's moral rights of occupancy).

This analysis of the different kinds of moral wrongs contributes to a less ad hoc approach to corrective justice claims. It helps us to distinguish between the rights accorded to previous residents (who have had their moral rights of residency or occupancy violated), current occupants, and property owners.

The argument developed here is an important element to any theory of territory, because it is important to address the (typical) case that people are settled on land that has previously been settled by other groups, and it's relevant too to the development of principles or rules in international law aimed at preventing forcible expulsions and occupation.

Notes

1. In this chapter, when I discuss the 'taking of land' I am referring not only to moving into land, and establishing dominance there, but also moving the current occupants out. Of course, they might be different: colonialism doesn't necessarily require expulsions. Here I am referring to the loss involved in expulsions, though I also think that losing control over territory also constitutes a loss (and it certainly involves a loss of political self-determination), but I do not complicate this discussion with that kind of case.

2. David Lyons, 'The New Indian Claims and Original Rights to Land', *Social Theory and Practice*, vol. 4, no. 3 (1977), 249–272; George Sher, 'Ancient Wrongs and Modern Rights', *Philosophy & Public Affairs*, vol. 10, no. 1 (1981), 3–17; Jeremy Waldron, 'Superseding Historic Injustice', *Ethics*, vol. 103, no. 1 (1992), 4–28; and, more recently, Nahshon Perez, 'On Compensation and Return: Can the "Continuing Injustice Argument" for Compensating for Historical Injustices Justify Compensation for Such Injustices or the Return of Property?', *Journal of Applied Philosophy*, vol. 28, no. 2 (2011), 151–168.

3. Duncan Ivison, 'Political Community and Historical Injustice', *Australasian Journal of Philosophy*, vol. 78, no. 3 (2000), 360–373. Michael Ridge, 'Giving the Dead Their Due', *Ethics*, vol. 114, no. 1 (2003), 38–59; Robert Sparrow, 'History and Collective Responsibility', *Australasian Journal of Philosophy*, vol. 78, no. 3 (2000), 346–359; Janna Thompson, *Taking Responsibility for the Past: Reparation and Historical Injustice* (Cambridge, UK: Polity, 2002). See also Renée A. Hill, 'Compensatory Justice: Over

Time and between Groups', *Journal of Political Philosophy*, vol. 10, no. 4 (2002), 392–415; A. John Simmons, *Justification and Legitimacy: Essays on Rights and Obligations* (Cambridge: Cambridge University Press, 2001); and Daniel Butt, *Rectifying International Injustice: Principles of Compensation and Restitution between Nations* (Oxford University Press, 2009).

4. I am using the term 'imperialism' to refer to a situation where one group occupies the land of another, thereby violating their territorial rights, and also subjugates them, thereby denying them the capacity to be self-determining. For discussions of the wrong of imperialism, see Lea Ypi, 'What's Wrong with Colonialism', *Philosophy & Public Affairs*, vol. 41, no. 2 (2013), 138–191; Nicolas Southwood, 'Democracy as a Modally Demanding Value', paper presented at the International Conference on Democracy, Empires, and Geopolitics, Taipei, Taiwan, 10–12 December 2011; and Wellman, *Theory of Secession*.

5. Waldron, 'Superseding Historic Injustice'.

6. Derek Parfit, *Reasons and Persons* (Oxford: Clarendon Press, 1984).

7. Daniel Butt, 'On Benefiting from Injustice', *Canadian Journal of Philosophy*, vol. 37, no. 1 (2007), 129–152.

8. Seth Lazar, 'The Nature and Disvalue of Injury', *Res Publica*, vol. 15, no. 3 (2009), 289–304, at 297. I do think that different experiences of injustices and different perspectives on them have weight. I am resisting here a fully subjective account.

9. Stilz, 'Nations, States, and Territory', 583.

10. Stilz, 'Nations, States, and Territory', 583–584.

11. Waldron, 'Superseding Historic Injustice', 19.

12. David Lefkowitz 'Autonomy, Residence and Return', *Critical Review of International Social and Political Philosophy* (forthcoming), 7.

13. Lefkowitz, 'Autonomy, Residence and Return', 11.

14. Lefkowitz, 'Autonomy, Residence and Return' 11.

15. Lefkowitz, 'Autonomy, Residence and Return', 12.

16. It is not fully clear to me how exactly a person goes about voluntarily relinquishing a right. Does it mean that the person has to explicitly forgo a right? If so, what would motivate the person to do this? Or does it mean that the person simply goes about living his or her life in a way that assumes that she doesn't live in the place from which she is expelled, in which case it is much more like my argument about the diminishing importance of land in people's lives when they do not live there or have aims and aspirations connected to the place.

17. There was a court case decided by the European Court of Human Rights on just this issue. See endnote 34 for a discussion.

18. I am grateful to David Lefkowitz for this point.

19. Joseph H. Carens, 'The Case for Amnesty: Time Erodes the State's Right to Deport', *Boston Review*, 1 May 2009: http://bostonreview.net/forum/case-amnesty-joseph-carens; Ayelet Shachar, *The Birthright Lottery: Citizenship and Global Inequality* (Cambridge, MA: Harvard University Press, 2009), 116–133, 184–190; Patti Tamara Lenard and Christine Straehle, 'Temporary Labour Migration, Global Redistribution and Democratic Justice', *Philosophy, Politics, Economics*, vol. 11, no 2 (2011), 206–233.

20. Waldron, 'Superseding Historic Injustice', 16.

21. Many expectations don't give rise to claims of justice: there are many choices that are made against a background of relatively stable rules and hence expectations, but when these change, we don't necessarily think that people have a claim of justice to the status quo ante, or to compensation. This is true for example of people investing in skills in the labour market.

22. This is similar to the standard account of the moral wrong associated with promise-breaking, where it is the breaking of expectation-inducing promises that represents a free-standing moral wrong.

23. Waldron, 'Superseding Historic Injustice', 19.

24. Norbert Anwander, 'Contributing and Benefiting: Two Grounds for Duties to the Victims of Injustice', *Ethics & International Affairs*, vol. 19, no. 1 (2005), 39–45, at 40.

25. Butt, 'On Benefiting from Injustice'.

26. This point is made by Chaim Gans, *Limits of Liberal Nationalism* (New York: Cambridge University Press, 2003), especially chapter 3; and Chaim Gans, 'Is There a Historical Right

to the Land of Israel?', *Azure*, 5762, no. 2 (winter 2007): http://www.azure.org.il/article. php?id=32. Interestingly, Gans presents an argument in terms of self-determination that is very similar to my own. He distinguishes between settlement within the 1948 borders of Israel and the occupied territories after 1967. For Gans, the settlement after 1967 is unjustified, given that the Jews have already realized their primary right to self-determination (within the original borders of the state of Israel).

27. For an authoritative treatment of this view, see Liam Murphy and Thomas Nagel, *The Myth of Ownership: Taxes and Justice* (Oxford: Oxford University Press, 2002).

28. This view is usually attributed to Locke: Locke, *Second Treatise*, bk II, chap. V, 285–302. For a more recent expression, see Robert Nozick, *Anarchy, State, and Utopia* (New York: Basic Books, 1974).

29. James Tully, *A Discourse on Property: John Locke and His Adversaries* (Cambridge: Cambridge University Press, 1980); Margaret Kohn, 'Indigenous Land and the Right to a City', unpublished manuscript. July 2013 version. For an excellent attempt to bridge the divide, see Bertram, 'Property in the Moral Life of Human Beings'.

30. There is, however, a problem in knowing what constitutes 'fair market value'. Do we assume that it's the market value prior to a settlement, when security of property is not assured and prices are therefore likely to be depressed? Or do we assume compensation at the level of market value *after* a settlement, when property titles are assured by the settlement itself?

31. For the distinction between investment property and family homes, and differential treatment of them, see the Newfoundland government's legislation on expropriation from family homes. The government also concedes that compensation of family homes may not reflect the true value to the family. See Family Homes Expropriation Act, 2010: http:// www.assembly.nl.ca/legislation/sr/statutes/f01.htm.

32. R. H. Thaler, 'Toward a Positive Theory of Consumer Choice', *Journal of Economic Behavior & Organization*, vol. 1, no. 1 (1980), 39–60. In the classic version of this experiment, Thaler presented half the class at Cornell with coffee mugs and allowed them to trade, but very little trading occurred, which researchers attributed to the endowment effect: goods that are included in one's endowment (goods that one owns) are valued more highly than comparable goods not held, so that buyers and sellers could not reach a price. This effect has also been shown to have the effect that losses (of possession) are more painful to the proprietor (than gains). See here Jochen Reb and Terry Connolly, 'Possession, Feelings of Ownership and the Endowment Effect', *Judgment and Decision Making*, vol. 2, no. 2 (2007), 107–114.

33. See here Samuel Scheffler, *Equality and Tradition: Questions of Value in Moral and Political Theory* (Oxford: Oxford University Press, 2010).

34. One of the appellants in a case regarding compensation for the loss of property in Northern Cyprus argued to the European Court of Human Rights that she had a right to a 'family home' to which she felt a strong attachment (not merely a house or monetary equivalent). The court did not reject the form of the argument, but denied her specific claim on the grounds that she did not provide evidence to support it. She had left the home at the age of two and had developed projects and relationships in other places for thirty-five years since the loss of this home. Demopoulos vs. Turkey (Eur. Ct. H. R. 1 March 2010); full document accessed at: http://hudoc.echr.coe.int.

35. This argument has the virtue of explaining why we might think there is a difference between the partition of Palestine, and its settlement, and subsequent settlements in the Occupied Territories. After 1948, there were good reasons to think that Jewish settlement was legitimate; Israel was recognized by the United Nations as a legitimate international entity, and the land was created as the result of the partition, at a time when this was regarded as a legitimate mechanism for state-creation. That is, it was done in an international context of numerous other state-created partitions (the partition of British India, partition of Ireland, and so on), so the land claimed seemed to support the legitimate object of expectations of continued occupancy.

8

Territorial Rights and Natural Resources

In this chapter, I argue that the same value of collective self-determination that generates a right of jurisdiction also generates a right to control natural resources, and I discuss the limits of that argument, focusing especially on the limits of justice.

The issue of entitlement to control over and/or benefit from natural resources is a live political issue in many parts of the world and directly relevant to our conceptions of the rights of political communities and individuals. In this chapter, I advance three arguments for why we might think that resources should be considered part of territorial right, while also exploring the limits of these arguments.

There are two distinct kinds of claim over resources. The first occurs when states or political communities claim unoccupied territory as theirs. In my discussion of the occupancy principle in chapter 3 and boundary drawing in chapter 6, I did not discuss unoccupied land. Yet there are many cases of disputes over unoccupied land: there are rival claims over unoccupied islands in the oceans, claims to the ocean bed, to the air, and in the earth deep underground. I argue in this chapter that unoccupied land is basically viewed as a resource by the rival claimants, and their respective claims should be conceived of as property claims. I argue that these kinds of cases should not be treated as *territorial* disputes but as property disputes, mainly connected to gaining benefit from resources, and I spell out the normative implications of this insight, and what it means for global institutional design.

The second kind of case is where there are natural resources—oil, fertile land, water, coal—on the land that is co-extensive with the area that the group occupies and so within the bounds of the group's jurisdictional authority (according to my conception of that domain, spelled out in chapters 3 and 6). Outsiders often make claims to these resources, pressing on a luck egalitarian idea of the resources as undeserved, and assume a conception of the world as commonly owned. I articulate a middle ground between a strong resource-rights conception, associated with current views of state sovereignty, and a cosmopolitan conception that views these groups as having no special claims to resources within their midst, indeed, thinking of them as a kind of unde-served advantage. This structure helps me to define the limits of territorial right over resources.

These two types of case have to be approached differently. The first kind of case examines territorial disputes in a narrow or familiar bilateral situation where there are a limited number of contestants arguing about territorial rights in a small part of the globe. The second kind of case examines territorial holdings, and especially rights to resources, in a multilateral context, where the central questions are the justice of the distribution of resources of the earth as a whole.[1] As Tamar Meisels has argued, in cases of bilateral conflict, there are a number of different principles—such as principles of corrective justice—that might apply. I argue that in cases of unoccupied land, the relationship between territory and resources is such that the pressing question is what jurisdictional level should govern use and access and benefit from the resource. These cases are different from cases where the land is occupied or has been occupied.

8.1. Resources, Land, and Arguments about Resources

I define the term 'natural resources' in a deliberately open way: to refer to any-thing, derived from the environment and not made by humans, that is instru-mental to satisfying human wants and needs.[2] They are part of the 'natural wealth' of the world. This is a very open definition: land, water, air, and sun-shine are resources, as well as plants, animals, and mineral ores.[3] It is largely consistent with the international law definition of resources, and with the one argued for by Chris Armstrong, except in two crucial respects, outlined below.[4]

One of the difficulties with the definition of resources is how land is con-ceived. We often use the term 'resources' to refer to the coal or minerals or plant life that are part of the natural wealth of the world, but we do not include the geographical sites where the resources are located 'as resources'. In this chap-ter, I consider resources that are distinct from the geographical location: in fact, the second half of the chapter is primarily interested in resources in this sense. However, there is a sense in which land is also a resource, because it too is instrumental to human purposes and part of the natural wealth of the world. For this reason, in section 8.2, I consider also claims to the physical location, when these are unoccupied (so the occupancy principle does not determine boundaries) and when they are valued primarily as areas from which wealth can be extracted.

Armstrong's definition of a natural resource enumerates every physical item on earth and above and below the earth as a resource, even things as yet unclaimed whose uses are as yet undiscovered, and that includes every mosquito, every dust mite, every particle of sand in the earth, as a resource, some of it not very valuable. I disagree with this conception of resources, and instead argue that resources are not natural kinds but contain an important relational element, such that something gets transformed from being part of the natural world to being a resource by being viewed instrumentally. Although natural resources have a physical character—as oil or coal or firewood or plant life—they are transformed into resources by being instrumental to people's purposes, and this relational character is part of how we individuate resources and distinguish resources from things in the physical world that are not resources. This means that what counts as a resource is historically, culturally, and individually variable. Different people will individuate resources differently: in Kolers's telling example involving a tree, if one person needs the bark and someone else the leaves and someone else the wood, then that counts as three different resources. If another person needs the whole tree, then that person considers the tree as a resource; and if he or she is in market competition with the other three, he or she will likely have to pay the combined price of all three components to get it.

Although I agree with Kolers that something can be a resource for one person, because instrumental to the satisfaction of his or her wants and needs, and not a resource for someone else, because that person does not view the object instrumentally, this does not meant the second person cannot recognize that the thing is a resource, at least for someone: they can recognize its usefulness in satisfying claims of others. Even if a group does not want to think of the Black Hills as a resource—perhaps because they view it as sacred—it does not mean that they are unable to recognize that the minerals deposited there are a resource for someone, that it is instrumental to some other person's or group's claim. They have the capacity to see things not only from their own point of view but to imaginatively place themselves in the situation of others and see that the Black Hills are a resource for someone else.[5]

We can all recognize that there are both general claims for resources, especially when the resource is useful to satisfying general human needs, like the need for food or energy or water, and special claims, which can be particular in two distinct ways: it can be a claim that there is a special relationship or attachment to a resource, and it can be a claim for a particular resource. The main challenge is to consider general and particular claims together. In this, the chapter departs from much work in the egalitarian tradition, which tends to assume that all resources are valuable in exactly the same way and that the only question is a fair distributive principle to decide on the allocation of the natural wealth of the world. Like territory itself, resources have a strong claimant-relative component. I do not offer a full theory of resources, but I agree with Kolers that a complete theory would include not only the production, but also the consumption of goods, including the production and absorption of waste (such as greenhouse gases).[6] I do not think that anything I say here precludes that fuller account, although I do not consider it directly.

There are at least three reasons why we might think that natural resources are part of 'territorial right'; however, these arguments help justify a presumption of control over resources, not the right to full benefit from natural resources.

The first argument appeals to an idea, first articulated by Locke in the context of justifying private property: when land is held in common for general use, and without authoritative rules governing that use in the common interest, there is little incentive for any particular person to invest their time and effort in developing the land to improve its productivity. Since the land is common, there is no way for an individual to ensure that she will benefit from her investment because the prospective investor cannot exclude free-riders from reaping the rewards without contributing to the labour. Moreover, it may be rational to deplete the resources, to prevent other less scrupulous people from getting there first. For Locke, Nozick, and others, the moral of the story is that, given the tragedy of the commons, exclusive ownership and control of the land (private property) is likely to make everyone, even the propertyless, better off overall.

However, there is another, not incompatible, solution to the tragedy of the commons: to establish a legitimate political order, with jurisdictional authority over natural resources (land, water, minerals in the ground, etc.) to ensure that the uses to which they are put conform to the common good. This would mean that there would be rules on the number and size of fish harvested in the lakes and rivers, or rules on the safe extraction and taxation of valuable minerals, for example, and coercive means to enforce these rules. This is not necessarily an argument for *state* sovereignty in contrast to global sovereignty, but it indicates that, until we have an authoritative (coercive) global political structure, it is necessary for the state to regulate these resources in the common good.

The second, related argument for including resource rights in territorial rights is implied by the Kantian version of the statist argument. The idea is that we need states for the sake of justice, in particular for having a clearly defined and enforced system of property rights. But a state must have rights over resources on its territory if it is to have the right to define and delimit property rights. This provides an argument for including control over resources as part of the rights that a state must have.

Both of these arguments give us a contingent reason for the regulation of natural resources at the level of the state. The logic of the Lockean tragedy of the commons argument suggests that the appropriate locus of regulation depends on the natural resource in question, and in many cases, local regulation is insufficient. For some natural resources, such as fish, a statist political structure will be insufficient, because the tragedy of the commons can re-emerge over the oceans, and lead to them being over-harvested (unless there are clear and enforced rules to limit this). However, for many natural resources, rules established by and enforced within the state are sufficient to ensure that natural resources are extracted and transferred in accordance with the common good.

The Kantian argument also does not offer any particular reason why natural resources should be in the control of the state rather than a supranational or transnational body. It applies to whatever the justice-enforcing body is, and that could be a state or it could be a global authority. In the current world order, and in the one envisioned by Kant, the state is the arbiter of property rights, and that suggests a presumption in favour of state control over resources.

I do not disagree with either of these arguments for control over resources, but the focus of the rest of the chapter is on a third argument, which establishes a more precise connection between control over natural resources and the moral value of collective self-determination. It links collective control or jurisdictional authority over resources with collective self-determination of the political community. On this argument, self-determining political communities need to have jurisdictional authority over resources, mainly because rules around the extraction and use of resources where they live impinge on many different aspects of the collective life of the community. We should expect different societies, with different cultures or different values or different projects, to favour different property regimes and to have different approaches to the treatment of land and potential resources.[7] If the people did not have control over this, they would not have significant control over the collective conditions in which they live.

Before discussing that third argument, and the cosmopolitan critique of it, I will discuss cases where that argument is not particularly relevant, because the resources in question are not within the ambit of the territorial domain of the self-determining group. These are cases of contested land that is not occupied by any particular group.

8.2. Claims to Unoccupied Areas and Resources

In chapter 2, where I discussed what I meant by the term 'territory', I argued against the idea of territory as a kind of property. In this section, I present a more nuanced view: I reject the property conception of territory as a *general* approach to territorial rights, but I also suggest that one of the reasons why that view of territory has such a powerful hold on our imagination is that the contemporary world is marked by disputes over who has jurisdictional authority over land, where the land is viewed purely instrumentally, as a kind of resource, and the different claimants are essentially making property-type claims. That view—that territorial jurisdiction is a kind of property 'owned' by the country—is particularly relevant in areas where, by definition, no people are present or occupying the territory. The current scramble for the oceans has more than a hint of the view that territory is a kind of property. It is widely attributed to the fact that there are thought to be rich mineral deposits to be exploited.

There are many different countries making claims for jurisdiction over the seabed. The Arctic is the seat of competition between Russia, Canada, the United States, and Denmark. China and South Korea are in conflict over a part of the East China Sea; China is also asserting claims to the South China Sea, as are Malaysia, Philippines, and Taiwan; Tanzania and the Seychelles are in dispute in the Indian Ocean; Japan and South Korea are in dispute over a chain of uninhabited islands and the adjacent seabed. Canada is in dispute with France over Saint-Pierre and Miquelon, tiny islands less than 25 kilometres from Newfoundland, which are part of France, and which front on a continental shelf thought to be rich with oil deposits. Britain, France, Ireland, and Spain have all made claims in the Celtic Sea; and Britain and Argentina are rivals in the South Atlantic. This profusion of claims, counterclaims, and conflict is fuelled by the belief that the ocean bed is rich in resources, and that territorial rights will enable the country that is granted jurisdictional authority over the offshore ocean to gain control of these. Disputes over islands are closely connected to disputes over the seabed, since securing authority over an island usually means gaining the resources in the adjacent seabed.

The parallels with property are not difficult to see. The area in question is not really land that anyone lives on and so cannot be viewed as central to the people's collective self-determination. If we assume that these territorial disputes over the ocean are primarily about who gets to benefit from them as resources, then that raises the question of the appropriate jurisdictional unit to establish and enforce property rules (and rights to tax the extracted resources). In what follows, I maintain the analytical distinction between territory and property to suggest that these should be reconceived as cases of disputed property, and that what is therefore needed is to ascertain the appropriate level of jurisdiction to regulate them.

8.2.1. Territorial Claims in Coastal Waters

Territorial claims in coastal waters should be subject to a careful contextual assessment of precisely the situation of the group, and their claim, and the extent to which it might be bound up with collective self-determination. Consider the claims of people who live in coastal communities, who argue that authority over (some part of) the ocean is central to gaining collective control over their existence. Their argument is that there are important self-determination issues connected to control of the oceans. This claim should not be dismissed.

There are many cases of fishing communities who make their living in symbiotic relationship to the sea; whose lives are bound up with the weather and the tides, and the life cycle of the various fish that serve as the backbone of their economy and the reason why the villages exist. Countries have claimed that this interest ought to give them jurisdictional authority beyond their borders, to regulate access to fish that live near the coastline. This argument was repeatedly made by successive Newfoundland governments to the Canadian federal government: they argued that the government should unilaterally extend their jurisdiction from the original six nautical mile limit to twelve miles and then to 200 miles. This was in order to regulate foreign trawlers fishing in the Grand Banks off the coast of Newfoundland, equipped with advanced electronic navigation systems, radars, and sonars, which enabled them to track the fish. These arguments were rehearsed (and opposed) by different countries, with small variations, at the United Nations Conferences on the Law of the Sea (UNCLOS I in 1958 and UNCLOS II in 1960), where minute steps were agreed on to try to deal with this problem.[8] During this period there was no restriction on the number of fish caught, and the small inland fishing boats, typical of the Newfoundland fishery, could not compete with the large technologically sophisticated fishing trawlers of the Soviet Union, Spain, and Japan. The only international restriction on fishing during this period was on the size of net mesh, but this was insufficient and insufficiently policed. Not only was the original six-mile limit insufficient, but so was a larger, but geologically arbitrary limit. Since fish swim, it was pointless (from the perspective of regulating and conserving the fishery) to control a six- or ten-mile limit beyond the shore. Even the 200-mile limit was not fully effective, since the Grand Banks, where the fish live and reproduce, do not follow a linear line of 200 miles, sometimes protruding beyond the 200 miles. Clearly, then, in this situation, a multilateral agreement or international governance agency aimed at regulating all aspects of the commercial fishery, from all countries, would have been desirable. Indeed, for a long time, and certainly at the two failed UNCLOS conferences, both the United Kingdom and Canada supported the creation of an international agency to regulate fishing. Failing agreement on that, control of a larger swathe of the area beyond the coast by the adjacent and affected country at an earlier point would have been better than the relatively laissez-faire approach to fish stocks that was adopted. By the time the moratorium on cod fishing was declared in Canada in 1992, and the rules were in place, the predictable ecological disaster had happened: all the fish were gone, and 35,000 fishers and plant workers from over 400 fishing communities in Newfoundland were unemployed and their way of life destroyed.[9]

These two factors (about ways of life relative to coastal communities and geological formations) are now incorporated in the 1987 UN Convention on the Law of the Sea, where they serve as reasons for conferring territorial jurisdiction on one state rather than another. Scientific evidence is brought to bear on whether that part of the ocean being claimed represents a geological extension of the land mass, and social science evidence about community reliance on the sea is also pertinent. Primarily, however, the convention specifies rules designed to resolve disputes which are agreed on in advance of a full analysis of the seabed itself, so each country may hope to benefit from such a rule.

Obviously for a resource like fish, which require a healthy ocean in which to live and reproduce, the most appropriate level of jurisdiction is international: ideally, we (the world community) should create an effective multilateral body to govern the entire water body. This is because dividing up fish resources between states is suboptimal: the tragedy of the commons can re-emerge over the oceans, and lead to the over-harvesting of fish generally (unless there are clear and enforced rules to limit this). It is, however, not always easy to create such an international governance agency or to get multilateral agreement. This was true of regulation of the cod fishery. In that case, control of the Grand Banks by the relevant interested state would have been preferable: local fishermen whose lives were bound up with the cod fishery were also the ones most concerned to maintain its long-term sustainability.

8.2.2. Territorial Claims to the Seabed and Uninhabited Islands

Beyond the coastal areas, things look very different. It is hard to think of territorial claims in the High Arctic or the seabed far from the coast or uninhabited islands in the claimed territorial waters as connected to a strong interest in self-determination on the part of the political community. In general, apart from the coastal areas discussed above, territorial claims over the oceans are not connected to self-determination: the contending states view the oceans and especially the seabed instrumentally, as a kind of property, and the key reason why countries contend for jurisdictional authority is that they seek to benefit from exploitation of resources deep in the ocean or on the seabed.

If that analysis is right, then, the key question is what is the appropriate level at which the rules of property—the rules of acquisition, transfer and bequest—should be applied; and that depends on the resource in question and how best to regulate its use in the common interest. I've argued above that disputes over the ocean should be regulated by a (yet to be created) international governance authority: this would recognize that the seabed and the ocean generally are not the locus of any group's self-determination, but that the process of extracting wealth from the ocean or regulating over-fishing and pollution should, ideally, be placed under the auspices of a jurisdictional body larger than the state, for the benefit of all. Unfortunately, however, it is very difficult to get agreement on this and so another possible, although second-best, solution is to agree on principles to assign which current jurisdictional authority-holder (which state) should have the capacity to regulate which kind of property claim.

This is the strategy adopted in the 1982 UN Convention on the Law of the Sea, which specified that all countries that had ratified the convention before May 1999 had ten years to claim any extension of the continental shelf beyond the normal 200 miles.[10] Any other countries wanting to make a claim had ten years from the date on which they ratified the treaty in which to do so, which meant that, in the Arctic, Denmark, which ratified the treaty in 2004, had until 2014; Canada's deadline was 2013, and the United States, which has not yet ratified the treaty, has no deadline. The claims are all decided by the Commission on the Limits of the Continental Shelf, and then further referred to either the International Court of Justice in The Hague or to a special tribunal.[11] The basis of the decision is specified in the convention: all claims will be settled on a scientific basis, through analysis of the geological formation of the continental shelf and subsidiary principles about the depth of the ocean.

The same logic applies to the numerous claims for uninhabited islands dotted throughout the world's seas and oceans, which often involve multiple claims and counterclaims. Most of these are basically uninhabited—although in many cases there are military garrisons or a military or coast guard presence maintained by the claimant state(s).[12] In all these cases, there are no legitimate self-determination issues: the islands are viewed as either extensions of national power (because they have strategic importance) or are sources of wealth. But none of them are central to self-determination. There are no authoritative claims that any country can make for one of these unoccupied islands; in this context of multiple claims and counterclaims, the appropriate solution is to construct international governance agencies to act as stewards for these islands in the common interests of everyone. Although this is the correct normative position on such disputes, it is not likely to be implemented in the near future. It does however help us to think more clearly when we distinguish these sorts of territorial disputes from the ones more intimately connected to community self-determination in section 8.3.

This analysis is relevant for one of the most interesting and potentially explosive territorial disputes between two major countries in East Asia; the dispute between China, Taiwan, and Japan over the Senkaku/Diaoyu islands, which are uninhabited islands in the South China Sea, almost exactly equidistant from the southwestern tip of Japan and Taiwan.[13] Both Japan and China have arguments to bolster their claims: Japan annexed the islands, which were unoccupied, following the Sino-Japanese War in 1895, and Japanese sovereignty was largely unchallenged until relatively recently, when oil was discovered offshore. China, however, claims that uninhabited does not mean unoccupied in the relevant sense, and they point out that Chinese documents going back to the seventeenth century have been found which clearly place the islands within the Chinese territorial maritime boundary. Since the islands were not occupied in the relevant sense discussed in this book, neither represents a compelling argument.

From 1945 to 1972, the islands were under US authority and the Americans transferred an administrative right to Japan, but not a right of sovereignty, thus leaving the territorial status of the islands unclear. In 2012, the Japanese government purchased three of the islands from a private property owner, the Kurihara family, whose property holding on the islands stems from the American administrative period, explicitly to bolster its claims to sovereignty. It is, however, doubtful that this strengthens its moral claim at all. First, the legitimacy of the property right itself depends on agreement that the property is recognized by a prior legitimate authority, and that is precisely the question. Moreover, territory and property, as I've argued above, are distinct: the purchase of property does not affect the territorial status of the country in which the property is purchased. There are many Americans who own property in Canada, and Saudis who own property in London, but this does not affect the territorial rights of either Canada or the United Kingdom. Many people are of course confused about this issue, as vestiges of the earlier property view of territory still remain. Since there are no relevant self-determination issues, this dispute should be viewed as primarily an extended property dispute, where each side views these islands as a source of potential national wealth and national aggrandizement. And the appropriate way to deal with such a dispute is to erect or establish a clear impartial jurisdictional authority, capable of regulating property claims in accordance with the common good. This suggests the need for an international agency to administer these and similar islands.

8.2.3. Territorial Claims to Airspace and the Subterranean Depths of the Earth

States also make other claims for control over resources in the air and in the subterranean depths of the earth. On the issue of resources in the earth, I argue in section 8.3 that there are legitimate self-determination issues surrounding much resource exploitation on land that the group occupies, and I discuss how we should balance the community's interests in self-determination with the rights of people living outside the borders. What, though, should we think of claims to control the subterranean depths of the earth?

Suppose there were some valuable mineral or transformative chemical in the molten rock beneath the earth's crust and there were ways to extract these resources without affecting life on the surface of the planet. This is, as yet, science fiction, but in such a case it would be hard to imagine that there are genuine self-determination issues here. Since there are no strong claimant-relative interests in the depths of the earth that are not also generalizable to other claimants, we should view it as if it were unowned or not conclusively claimed. The claimants are viewing the earth primarily as property, as instrumentally valuable to wealth creation. It follows from this that human activity with respect to it should be regulated in the common interest; that any attempt to extract resources from the depths of the earth or to deposit pollution inside it should be subject to rules established in the mutual interests of all, ideally also by an international or multilateral agency with coercive capacity.

What about the regulation of the air above the earth's surface? Can this be defended in terms of the self-determination of the political community? There is a legitimate interest that political communities have in regulating airspace, because this is essential to military defence. If we think that political communities have a right to defend themselves against aggression, which is implied by the idea that they have territorial rights in the first place, then they have a right to control entry and exit in their airspace. As an extension of this interest, political communities are thought to have a right to regulate air travel over their territory. In the current world order, this extends to air traffic control, which is also parcelled out on a territorial basis according to agreed rules. The tax levied on planes going over airspace is an important source of revenue, especially for countries strategically located on a number of important air traffic routes. This though does not show that there is a strong self-determination interest in regulating air traffic. However, there is a partial self-determination reason for control over airspace to be held by each state—since the same instruments that regulate air traffic in the air traffic control towers also identify hostile attackers. For this reason, it makes sense for states to maintain control over their airspace, as long as control is exercised in accordance with general agreements on such matters, and are coordinated with other states which also regulate air traffic.

The atmosphere could also be a source of wealth, if the molecules in the atmosphere could be extracted and sold. Is there a territorial right to elements in the atmosphere directly above the landmass associated with a political community? It is hard to see that there is a self-determination interest in such control if—a big 'if'—the extraction could take place in a way that does not affect the political community itself. But this would need to be regulated: we would not want to take the multinational corporations' word for it that it was not detrimental in any way.

Any discussion of property regulation would be incomplete if we discussed only the production of goods, not their consumption, nor the by-products of their production; and there is now a very rich normative literature on the unfair burdens attached to the production of greenhouse gases, which spew out into the atmosphere to the detriment of many people beyond the border. This is a large issue, which I do not have the space to deal with adequately here, except to note that the logic that applied to regulation of property interests in the oceans also applies in this case. There is no reason why control over the extraction of resources in the air, or the dumping of pollution into the air, should be regulated at the level of the state, since the air, like the oceans, is shared. However, as with the oceans, it might be the case that countries cannot agree to create such an institution: in that case, agreement on principles to regulate these activities (combined with some enforcement methods) is an alternative way to balance interests.

8.3. Territories that Are Occupied by People and Claims to Natural Resources within Those Territories

In the section above I have considered land that is unoccupied and suggested that in some cases, such as control of coastal waters and some control over airspace, there may be good self-determination arguments for control of that resource by political communities, but that in many cases we have a duty to create transnational or multinational institutions with jurisdictional authority to regulate these areas and these resources in the common interest.

In this section of the chapter, I consider a more fundamental challenge: this is where outsiders, people not members of the self-determining community, make claims to resources within the territory of the community. Their arguments often rest on a version of luck egalitarianism, and the strongly held intuition that physical proximity to a resource amounts to undeserved good (or bad) luck. In some ways this kind of argument pitches the self-determination argument against distributive-equality arguments.

We often have deep but conflicting intuitions about such cases. In places like Brazil, for example, there is a direct conflict between the claims of the urban poor, who argue that their poverty should be addressed through, among other things, exploitation of the natural resources of the Amazon, and the claims of Amazonian indigenous people, who are living on huge swathes of the Amazonian jungle, who claim an interest in collective self-determination, and, for cultural reasons, tend to resist attempts to exploit these resources. In many cases, we are sympathetic to both kinds of claim and it is important to assess them in relation to one another and ascertain the limits of each of these arguments.

The statist view about such things, as I suggested in chapter 1, is that whatever justifies the state justifies its territory as an indispensable part of state sovereignty and all aspects of state sovereignty, or territorial right, including control over natural resources and over the flow of goods and people across borders. In chapter 1, I rejected this view, arguing that we need to examine the justificatory argument behind rights to territory to determine whether, or the extent to which, they justified control over these other elements of territorial rights. An alternative view, considered here, is the view of cosmopolitans, who argue that state control over natural resources is a form of undeserved advantage to the state and its citizens. This suggests that state sovereignty and control over resources should be completely disaggregated.

I argue in the remainder of this chapter that the strong statist argument for control over resources and the strong cosmopolitan view of resources as a form of undeserved advantage are wrong in different ways. The strong statist position is wrong in assuming that the state's jurisdictional authority extends to all aspects of resources. At best, the idea of collective self-determination offers a limited and defeasible right to *control* the rules governing the acquisition, transfer, and use of natural resources but does not justify a right to the full stream of benefit from the resource. The strong cosmopolitan position fails to take seriously the relationship between collective self-determination and control over natural resources. I argue instead that collective self-determination should be given priority regarding control of resources, but I also justify the global redistribution of wealth from rich countries, in order to support the right to subsistence of others.[14]

What is the relationship between control over natural resources and collective self-determination? In section 8.1 I suggested reasons for thinking that natural resources have to be regulated in relation to some jurisdictional authority, but asked why should that authority be constituted at the level of the political community? In many cases—where people are not occupying the land and exercising self-determination over the collective conditions of their lives—there is no reason; indeed, regulation might be more effective at another level. In areas that are occupied, however, I argue that control over natural resources, while not *entailed* in the exercise of jurisdictional authority, is justified in the same way as that authority, in terms of the value inherent in collective self-determination.

Collective control, in the form of jurisdictional authority over resources, is an important dimension of collective self-determination, particularly the cultural dimension of different rules regarding land. More concretely, we can imagine a group of self-determining people who, for various (cultural, ideological, religious) reasons eschew private property, as the Maoris did for example. We might expect that such a group would make a rule that property is not individually held but collectively controlled, and therefore forbid its alienation. The rules that they make as self-determining people establish the terms of ownership. It is hard to see how a people could exercise important control over the collective conditions of their existence *unless* they have the capacity to make such rules. The connection between collective self-determination and control over resources is also brought out in the example I briefly mentioned early: that of the Lakota Sioux, who have resisted strip mining in the Black Hills because, for them, the hills are sacred.[15] If they were without this sort of control, they would be unable to make decisions about what happens to the land that they live on, the rivers that they drink from and swim in, the wetlands close to the river that they enjoy and/or hunt in, and unable to live in accordance with their religious beliefs. For the Lakota Sioux, any significant form of collective self-determination would have to involve making rules regarding use of the Black Hills. It is not simply a question of the fair distribution of existing resources on the assumption that the resources will be used and that some minimum level of resources is necessary to exercise effective self-determination. Rather, the exercise of collective self-determination might involve eschewing development of a particular piece of land, perhaps because it is fragile wetlands and development of the resource would be ecologically damaging, or because the land itself is viewed as sacred territory.

This gives us good reasons to think that control over natural resources is an important part of collective self-determination. If people lack this kind of control, then, to that extent, they lack robust forms of collective self-determination (although they might still be self-determining in other ways). Of course, this doesn't tell us that control has to be embedded in the state, rather than at some lower or (possibly) higher level. Moreover, although control over resources is crucial for self-determination, it does not follow that the state, or self-determining entity, is entitled to a full stream of benefit from the exploitation of the resource. This then is not a strong entailment relationship (such that control over natural resources is necessarily *entailed* in the idea of collective self-determination), but the weaker claim that meaningful self-determination will involve decisions about the rules surrounding the acquisition, transfer, and use of natural resources. These are important dimensions of collective life, and if a people lacks this capacity, it is, to that extent, limited in the powers of self-determination it has. However, it does not follow that the group is entitled to exclusive benefit from the resource.

8.3.1. Global Luck Egalitarianism with Respect to Natural Resources

Once we allow that significant collective self-determination typically involves control over natural resources, we run up against the problem of how land or territory is to be fairly divided. Specifically, luck egalitarians will not be satisfied by the argument made thus far, and will point out that it seems unjust if one group's land is large, fertile, and resource-rich, while another group's land is meager, barren, and resource-poor. Even if we concede that the mere fact that natural resources are differentially distributed does not automatically mean that resource-endowed countries are wealthy and resource-poor countries are poor—indeed, it may be the case that the opposite is often true, as the literature on the 'resource curse' suggests[16]—it would seem prima facie better to have control over a territory rich in resources than one poor in resources. This is because we might expect secondary benefits from control over natural resources, such as the power to tax the resources, or employment or other related benefits yielded by proximity to important resources. If this is so, it seems problematic from a justice perspective if group A controls a territory rich in many kinds of resources, while group B exercises their self-determination, such as it is, over a small, resource-less, landlocked desert.

A significant strand in the global justice literature appeals to this fairness intuition, and so extends luck egalitarianism from the domestic sphere, where it requires that people are compensated for undeserved bad luck, to the global sphere, where birth in relatively rich or poor states also seems to be a matter of good (or bad) fortune.[17] Distributive justice involves redistribution with a view to mitigating (or sometimes equalizing) the effects of these undeserved advantages. One of the most plausible luck egalitarian arguments in the global justice literature refers to the arbitrary distribution of natural resources amongst countries. Charles Beitz develops an argument for thinking that the distribution of natural resources amongst countries is analogous to the arbitrary distribution of talents among people. He writes that, 'the fact that someone happens to be located advantageously with respect to natural resources does not provide a reason why he or she should be entitled to exclude others from the benefits that might be derived from them.'[18] Therefore, the parties to the international original position, from which principles of international justice are derived, would think that the resources (or the benefits derived from them) should be subject to a resource redistribution principle.[19]

Thomas Pogge makes this claim about the arbitrary distribution of natural resources in support of his case for the global resource dividend. He proposes a tax on natural resources, designed to transfer substantial but not staggering amounts of money from well-off states to poorer ones through a small charge on certain limited natural resources. In line with his ecumenical strategy in arguing for various reforms, he puts forward a number of distinct but not necessarily compatible arguments for such a tax. The global resources dividend proposal is not particularly problematic, if it is conceived of as a mechanism to combat global poverty,[20] but his argument for it relies on a controversial argument against jurisdictional control over natural resources.

Pogge argues that the rich world 'harms' the poor by conferring on it a 'resource privilege', whereby governments have jurisdictional authority over natural resources. He describes rich countries as complicit in harm to the poor because they negotiate with poorer countries (or, more accurately, the governments of poorer countries) about their resources. Pogge cites two Yale economists, Ricky Lam and Leonard Wantchekon, who detected an empirical relationship between the possession of rich natural resources and poverty (and mediated through the tendency to military dictatorship).[21] According to this thesis, affluent countries are thereby implicated in a cycle where the possession of resources generates various negative effects on poor (but resource-rich) countries, especially military coups and dictatorships and corruption. This cycle is caused by the fact that resource riches engender strong motives to seize political power: possession of the resource then generates income to help rulers maintain power (it enables them to buy support and fund the police and military). Rich countries are implicated in this 'harm' because they assume that all governments have the 'territorial right' to make decisions about the use and transfer of resources in their territory—and thus they help to fuel the cycle.

Implicit in Pogge's argument is the assumption that there is a responsibility on the part of all parties to an agreement about natural resources to ensure that no one is improperly excluded from the benefit of natural resources. But what it means to be wrongly excluded can be interpreted in two different ways. On the first reading, the people who live on the land and are governed by the state are wrongfully excluded. Their interests are not taken into account; the government of the corrupt, dictatorial, but resource-rich state enters into an agreement with a multinational oil company, with the expertise to drill for, refine, and transport oil, and the citizens of the country are excluded both from the decision-making process and from the agreement-generated benefits. It is not difficult to understand and agree with this argument, since government is standardly thought to be aimed at tracking the interests of the governed, and indeed to be fundamentally authorized by the governed, so the citizens, on this account, are improperly excluded. In addition to the government of the state in question, rich multinational companies, and the countries that fail to regulate them, are complicit in this injustice. This is fairly uncontested, on at least the standard theories of state legitimacy, which posit some kind of pre-existing entitlement on the part of citizens to have a government authorized by them and operating in their interests. This interpretation of Pogge's argument does not undermine the idea of control over natural resources necessary to collective self-determination; it simply suggests that the right to control natural resources should apply to legitimate governments, not illegitimate kleptocratic ones, and the current international order does not do enough to distinguish between legitimate and illegitimate regimes.[22]

The second interpretation is that the global poor in general are improperly excluded from the benefit of global natural resources. This is a much more contentious claim, and rests on different foundational concerns than the first interpretation. The resources-leads-to-corruption dynamic details the ways in which the citizens of country A are not benefiting from the resources of A, and thereby suggests that the citizens of the country in which the resources are located are wrongfully excluded. However, in justifying the global resources dividend proposal, Pogge suggests that the citizens of many different countries all over the world are improperly excluded from benefiting from the resources in the world. He writes: 'this payment they [rich countries] must make [the global resource dividend] is called a dividend because it is based on the idea that the global poor own an inalienable stake in all limited natural resources.'[23] He also says that it should be conceived of as compensation: 'The better-off enjoy significant advantages in the use of a single, natural resource base from whose benefits the worse-off are largely, and without compensation, excluded',[24] and in this section, it seems that the better-off and worse-off are conceived of as the global well-off and the global poor. For this argument to work, we must assume that the world's poor have some basic (pre-institutional) entitlement to the world's natural resources, although the exact nature of this entitlement is unclear.

There are two problems, however, with the global justice version of Pogge's argument, and by extension the luck egalitarian position with respect to resources that it suggested. Both problems stem from a failure to take into account the different, morally important ways in which specific people are attached to natural resources, and their corresponding rights. The first counterclaim, which is extensively discussed by David Miller, points out that natural resources do not just fall like *manna* from heaven. The transformation of naturally occurring things into resources which have use-value involves activities that require social contexts or human labour, in which not all human beings participate equally.[25] In many cases, the resource's value is mediated through social and technological contexts which make it difficult to describe the value as inhering independently in the resource. This raises a problem for luck egalitarians because it questions their central assumption that resources are a matter of pure luck, unconnected to social choices and human responsibility.[26] Persuasively, Miller points out the difficulty of calculating the unimproved value of land, when much of the value of land stems from its proximity to other places of human creation—proximity to cafés, restaurants, theatres, shopping, and so on. Even in less problematic cases, such as oil, diamonds, copper, and other such items, minerals have to be discovered, mined, often extracted from contaminated elements, and so on—all of which relate the resource to specific people in particular ways.[27] Even if we don't have a crude Lockean labour theory of value, it would seem that people who produce or transform a resource, or whose immediate environment is spoiled by resource extraction, may have some claim on it, or at least an increased claim vis-à-vis someone thousands of kilometres away who has never even seen the resource or doesn't know how to use it.

Secondly, the global luck egalitarian assumes that land is a natural resource, and so instrumental to the satisfaction of human wants and needs. Indeed, at the beginning of this chapter, I noted that it is definitional of the term 'resources' that it is instrumental in just this way. The connection between land and collective self-determination is also instrumental: in this world of territorially defined states, a group can be self-determining, have meaningful forms of self-determination, only if that group also has land. However, it would be a mistake to think that the only relationship between land and the people is an instrumental one, where the land is viewed, potentially, as a geographical domain in which self-determination is exercised, as a source of wealth, as material to be worked or exploited, or otherwise transformed into economic use-value. This instrumental conception is not how all people view the land on which they live, as I argued at some length in chapter 3, in support of both an individual residency right and a group occupancy right. Consider the Lakota Sioux's refusal to sell or accept any financial compensation for mining in the

Black Hills, when they view the Black Hills as sacred and want the mining stopped. The same is true of Maori land in New Zealand, which cannot be sold now, precisely because the Maori people stopped the practice when they realized what selling the land actually meant.[28] This was also relevant to a large open copper mine in Bougainville, Papua New Guinea, which was resisted by local peoples—who were ethnically and linguistically akin to Solomon Islanders, but who were governed within Papua New Guinea—in large part because the transformation of the land that the mine involved was incompatible with their way of life. Nomadic peoples, too, seek to use the land to sustain their way of life, and this involves opposing attempts to extract resources from the land, which involve building and transportation networks.[29] And this non-instrumental view is held not only by marginalized (indigenous and/or nomadic) peoples. Even in modern, industrialized societies, the use to which land is put, and the relationship of land to resource extraction, is, and should be, a hotly contested issue. The instrumental conception is not necessarily the right one, or the dominant one, when we are considering whether to allow strip mining in a wetlands area or oil drilling in the fragile High Arctic, or whether an old cemetery should be ploughed over to make room for a shopping complex. There are other values here which bear on the kind of society the collectively self-determining group wants to create.

These examples also highlight the non-neutral assumptions implicit in the global egalitarian literature, which assumes what is precisely in question, namely that land is of purely instrumental value, that it is a stock of resources from which value can be derived and distributed equally to all people in the world. Indeed, the non-instrumental conception is not confined to small, nomadic, or traditional societies: it is extremely widespread, because it is implicit in all particularized territorial claims. If someone has a claim to *this* particular river, rather than to a drinking, swimming, energy resource in general, they must value the river for more than just instrumental reasons, because otherwise they would be willing to accept some other river. Disagreement about whether land is just a resource is a different source of conflict from rival historical claims, because the first represents a disagreement about whether a resource should be developed at all, whereas in the second everyone may agree on developing resources, but they each may have an attachment to the same particular set of resources. Nevertheless, the attachment to the particular land can be explained only by appealing to non-instrumental (e.g., symbolic or cultural attachment) values. Even in cases where the people have a partially instrumental conception of land, in the sense that, unlike the Lakota Sioux, they do intend to make use of the land or water, to fish or farm or mine, they do not view the land in purely instrumental terms, so that the world's land can be dispensed in straightforwardly just or equal 'packages'. Many national minorities and indigenous groups claim entitlement to particular pieces of land for reasons quite specific to their historical relationship to the land.

8.3.2. Land, Resources, and Subsistence

While the global justice theorists' focus on the instrumental and arbitrary character of land and other 'resources' is misguided, there is a very plausible insight contained within it, namely that resources are important to subsistence, and subsistence is a basic right of everyone.[30] On this view, the entitlement in question is a more general one: it is to a basic right to subsistence or a basic right to the necessary conditions for a decent life, and access to resources is justified as part of this.[31] This formulation is suggested by Locke in his account of the relationship of human beings to the resources of the world, where he argues that all people have a basic right to subsistence ('Men, being once born, have a right to their Preservation, and consequently to Meat and Drink, and such other things, as Nature affords for their Subsistence').[32] However, just as is the case with people who have rights in land that is commonly held, and who can therefore use the common land for their own subsistence, they do not have rights to control what other people do with it in the pursuit of their subsistence.[33] It is not, therefore, an equal voice or equal jurisdictional control conception.

This account of the link between resources and the right to subsistence is attenuated in the sense that the right to a minimum can be met in a variety of ways. Indeed, it makes more sense to think directly about the redistribution of wealth, rather than in terms of any direct redistribution of the fruits of natural resources or imposition of a tax on natural resources.

As I argued in section 8.3 above, the focus on resources is based on a misguided luck egalitarian view of resources as directly instrumental to the satisfaction of people's needs; but it is wealth, or income, that is directly instrumental to the satisfaction of people's needs, and that can be directly applied to ensure that people's basic rights to subsistence are met. The basic right to what is necessary to a decent life can be met through a variety of institutional mechanisms, and while this could take the form of a tax on marketable resources, it could also be discharged more directly in terms of a tax on a country's wealth. Once we abandon the luck egalitarian focus on resources, we can think more directly about the best ways to meet this obligation globally. A direct mechanism to redistribute wealth has a certain degree of plausibility. After all, does Mexico have an obligation to redistribute its wealth that Taiwan or South Korea do not have (assuming they are equally wealthy), because it has more natural resources? Should a tax be organized on the resources of the Democratic Republic of Congo that doesn't apply to countries like Singapore (except insofar as Singaporeans are potential consumers of the resources that originate in the Congo)?

This of course means that countries with rich natural resources that decide not to use them may not owe much to the poorer countries of the world. However, we are comfortable with the analogous argument, applied to individuals. If an individual decides not to use his or her intelligence to become a doctor and make lots of money, but works at a low-paying job instead, that person doesn't pay a lot in taxes, even if he or she has copious natural talents. This means of course that those countries that do develop their resources will have to share. But if everyone knows this, then every country can make that decision.

The entitlement of everyone to a basic minimum or a basic right to subsistence is a limitation on the exercise of collective self-determination, and implies that collective self-determination is legitimate only if it is consistent with the basic subsistence rights of everyone. The term 'consistent with' can be used in a number of different ways, some more stringent than others. Here, the term 'consistent with' does not mean that the basic subsistence rights of everyone must already be met, but rather, the weaker claims that: (1) political communities in which people are collectively self-determining are themselves necessary for people to secure their basic rights; (2) the subsistence rights of others can be met without violating collective self-determination; and (3) collective self-determination is not the reason why these rights aren't met. Fairer global rules regarding trade and development, as well as substantial redistribution from the wealthy to the poorer parts of the world are justified and, I believe, sufficient to meet subsistence rights. However, in line with the argument advanced in the first part of this chapter, this redistribution cannot be aimed at *equalizing* wealth, since full equality would destroy incentives to properly care for resources in the first place. As is suggested above, the rules surrounding resources are not only important for people to achieve control over the conditions of their existence, but are an important element in the solution to the 'tragedy of the commons'. Moreover, the distinction drawn above between the right to control resources and the right to the full stream of benefit from resources, which is not central to self-determination, suggests that there need be no tension between self-determination and the subsistence rights of the global poor.

This happy scenario of course assumes that many peoples will decide to use the natural goods over which they have jurisdictional authority and thereby create wealth, which can be subject to redistribution. But it ignores the vexed question of whether political communities have obligations of justice to cultivate resources when doing so could help meet the basic needs of the global poor. This problem emerges in relation to groups that, in order to be collectively self-determining in an effective way, claim rights over a territory, which involves the right to set the terms under which natural resources are used in the first place, and then decides not to use its natural resource. If the basic needs of people outside a state can be met only if states give up some control over their 'resources', are they required to do so? Is it so important for the Bedouins or the Lakota Sioux or the Bougainvillians to maintain their traditional way of life that that they should be permitted to do so *even if* this meant that the basic needs of everyone could not be met? If we have a strong sense of people's entitlement to having their basic needs met, then the failure to cultivate resources to the fullest seems like an expensive taste that no theory of justice should countenance.

This is a serious challenge because throughout this chapter, I have rejected the view that the Bougainvillians or the Lakota Sioux are merely pursuing an expensive cultural 'taste'. I have argued the opposite: that control over resources is necessary to meaningful self-determination, which is itself of significant moral value. There is, however, the theoretical possibility that failure to exploit potential resources (resources in the eyes of some) jeopardizes subsistence rights. I do not think it is obvious that subsistence rights should automatically trump the right to collective self-determination. Although people's lives are more important than their capacity to be fully collectively self-determining, Jeremy Waldron has helpfully pointed out that when rights conflict, we do not necessarily look at which right is morally most important, but also at how direct the relationship is between the fundamental interest in question (the interest that the right is supposed to protect) and the policy.[34] Here, I can only express scepticism that mining the Black Hills or tapping the oil from the Bedouin lands is directly necessary to meet subsistence rights, and that there are no other alternatives. This suggests that there is a presumption against violating people's right to self-determination as a first method of recourse to ensure the subsistence rights of all.

One can imagine cases, however, where the priority is reversed, and where access to a particular natural resource is absolutely necessary to meet people's basic subsistence rights. Consider, for example, a serious illness, leading in many cases to death, which is caused by the bite of a particular kind of mosquito, but which can be cured by a drug which requires access to a mineral, which is found in land X, far away from the mosquito-infested area. The people living on X decide not to mine this mineral. On my account, people living on X (Xers) do have an interest in collective self-determination and this does give them a presumptive right to make this sort of decision. However, this interest in self-determination over the resource in this case is outweighed by the interests of people living in the mosquito-infested area, who are falling ill from an easily preventable disease. The interests in self-determination are not absolute, but require a careful assessment, especially weighing exactly how necessary the mineral or resource is to the prevention or treatment of the disease (is it the *only* cure?) and whether collective self-determination indeed requires the decision not to exploit it. At best, then, the argument here indicates a presumption in favour of control over resources, grounded in the interests in collective self-determination, but this would be defeasible when strong and essential interests of others were at stake.

8.4. Conclusion

This chapter has advanced a number of distinct but related arguments, all of which are aimed at challenging the robust view of territorial rights frequently advanced by states on their own behalf. In line with the argument of chapter 2, that the correct conception of territory is the jurisdictional authority view, where territorial rights are viewed as the geographical domain in which the people exercise jurisdictional authority over their lives, I have suggested that claims to vast tracts of the ocean bed, or uninhabited islands or unpopulated lands in the Arctic and Antarctic region, should be viewed as claims to resources, not territory. In all these cases, states like to make maximal claims, so that they can exploit their resources, much like property holders seek to benefit from their individual property holdings. In many of these cases there are no strong self-determination arguments that justify the states' claims over these areas, except that these activities need regulated at some level—and that the locus of that regulation in part depended on the resource in question and the level at which the 'tragedy of the commons' problems could be effectively solved.

This chapter also defended the idea of rights to control natural resources within the territory of the political community as implicit in meaningful forms of collective self-determination. Since collective self-determination implies a 'people' conceived of in non-statist terms, it is possible that the people exercise self-determination at substate level, as I implied in chapter 6, and this obviously includes indigenous communities within the overarching state. To return to the Amazonian indigenous communities, their claim to allow the Amazonian jungle to remain untouched, its resources unexploited, relies on a prior idea of these communities as enjoying rightful occupancy, which includes some control over the collective conditions of their lives, and non-exclusive forms of jurisdiction.

This chapter argued too that global luck egalitarianism as applied to natural resources fails to consider the various particularist attachments that people have. The luck egalitarian account of natural resources was criticized as being insensitive to the various morally important ways in which people are related to land, and to the expressive value of land for peoples and communities, which is not captured in the instrumental view of territory as a source of natural resources and as a domain in which self-determination can occur. The urban poor in São Paolo, who appeal to the basic unfairness of the distribution of resources, are relying on their urgent need, but are not sensitive to the relationship that the indigenous communities have to the area in which they live and which they claim is important for their self-determination.

I also argued that self-determination, and implicitly jurisdictional authority over resources, must take a form consistent with the right to subsistence of everyone. To address this, I distinguished between jurisdictional authority over resources and the right to the full stream of benefit from the exploitation of resources; only the first is central to collective self-determination. Even the right to control resources is a defeasible right when significant interests of others living outside the self-determining community are at stake. I did not offer a full theory of commensurability of value, but suggested a way of approaching moral judgments in these kinds of cases, relying not merely on the importance of the interest in question, but how closely tied the right (to the resources) is to the fundamental interests of the self-determining community.

Notes

1. Meisels, *Territorial Rights*, 139–140.
2. This is consistent with the conventional view of a resource advanced by Chris Armstrong, 'Justice and Attachment to Natural Resources', *Journal of Political Philosophy*, vol. 22, no. 1 (2014), 48–65, at 48, note 1.
3. This is not a purely subjectivist account of a resource. I also believe, though I do not argue for it here, that it is improper to treat some things as resources. I accept the view that human babies and organs should not be commodified like a resource. The attitudinal component of my account applies only to those things that we are not under a general duty not to treat as a resource.
4. Armstrong writes: 'I assume, for the purposes of this paper, the conventional definition of natural resources under international law, which depicts them as non-human-made goods taken from the "natural wealth" of the world. As such they are distinct from man-made products but also from the geographical sites from which they can be taken'; Armstrong, 'Justice and Attachment to Natural Resources', 48, note 1. My account is distinct from Armstrong because (1) I have an intentional element similar to Kolers in distinguishing the physical world from resources, and (2) I think that the geographical sites can be a resource.
5. Avery Kolers seems to resist this implication. For him, it seems that the Lakota Sioux just don't consider it a resource, and their view is decisive if they are the appropriate territorial right-holding agent.
6. Avery Kolers, 'Territory, Environment, and Global Distributive Justice', paper given at the American Political Science Association meeting, Toronto, Ontario, 2–5 September 2009, 9.
7. The second argument—about collective self-determination—not only has implications for control over natural resources, but for regime type. It seems to require some institutional mechanisms to ensure that the political order is democratically organized and accountable.

If we endorse the second argument about collective self-determination, it seems we are also committed to promoting the conditions for the realization of self-determination, and these might well include internal self-determination. This is because the argument will fail if there are no mechanisms of vertical accountability between the political elite, which has control over resources, and the people in whose name the elite governs. Without these mechanisms in place, the resources could be used simply for the benefit of the political elite, and this would violate people's collective self-determination, the very argument on which the control of resources rests.

8. George A. Rose, *Cod: The Ecological History of the North Atlantic Fishery* (St John's, NL: Breakwater, 2007), 390.

9. Gien Lan, 'Land and Sea Connect: The East Coast Fishery Closure, Unemployment and Health', *Canadian Journal of Public Health*, vol. 91, no. 3 (2000), 121–124; Rose, *Cod*, 390.

10. The extension of the continental shelf could not, however, be more than 350 miles from land, and it could be no more than 100 miles from the point at which the ocean was 2.5 km deep. See 'The Scramble for the Seabed', *The Economist*, 14 May 2009, 29–30, at 29.

11. *Economist*, 'Scramble for the Seabed'.

12. The Liacourt Rocks, disputed by Japan and South Korea, are volcanic rocks, inhabited by many bird and plant species. There have been, since 1991, two South Korean permanent residents, sent to the rocks to bolster Korean claims; and there is now a considerable coast-guard and lighthouse staff presence that is maintained by Korea. In the Spratly Islands, too, there are no indigenous inhabitants, but there are several military garrisons maintained by claimant states. The legitimacy of these is dependent on the legitimacy of the claim in the first place, and in this book I consider these as basically uninhabited, where the legitimacy of the occupancy is open to question.

13. Joyman Lee, 'Senkaku/Diaoyu: Islands of Conflict, *History Today*, vol. 61, no. 5, 2011, http://www.historytoday.com/joyman-lee/senkakudiaoyu-islands-conflict.

14. This paper bears some similarities to Chris Armstrong, 'National Self-Determination, Global Equality and Moral Arbitrariness', *Journal of Political Philosophy*, vol. 18, no. 3 (2010), 313–334. Like Armstrong, I argue that self-determination arguments and global egalitarianism should not be viewed in oppositional terms. However, the argument of my paper differs from his, because Armstrong does not examine the link between self-determination and resources.

15. This example was initially deployed by Jeff Spinner-Halev, for slightly different purposes; Jeff Spinner-Halev, 'From Historical to Enduring Injustice', *Political Theory*, vol. 35, no. 5 (2007), 574–592.

16. Ricky Lam and Leonard Wantchekon, 'Political Dutch Disease', NYU Working Paper (2003), http://www.nyu.edu/gsas/dept/politics/faculty/wantchekon/research/lr-04-lo.pdf; Leonard Wantchekon, 'Why Do Resource Dependent Countries Have Authoritarian Governments?', *Journal of African Finance and Economic Development*, vol. 5, no. 2 (2002), 57–77; Leif Wenar, 'Property Rights and the Resource Curse', *Philosophy & Public Affairs*, vol. 36, no. 1 (2008), 2–32.

17. Caney appeals to a moral arbitrariness objection that bears strong resemblance to the luck egalitarian distinction between choices and circumstances. In support of his favoured egalitarian principle of justice (a global equality of opportunity principle), Caney writes: 'If one thinks, as egalitarian liberals do, that it is unjust if persons fare worse because of their class or ethnic identity one should surely also think that it is unjust if persons fare worse because of their nationality. The logic underpinning equality of opportunity entails that it should be globalized'; Simon Caney, *Justice Beyond Borders: A Global Political Theory* (Oxford: Oxford University Press, 2005), 123.

18. Beitz, *Political Theory and International Relations*, 138.

19. Beitz, *Political Theory and International Relations*, 138.

20. One argument that is suggested by Pogge but not fully developed is that such a tax would be relatively easy to collect and administer because it would be levied on a defined set of items, rather than by states directly on individual wealthy citizens of their countries. Pogge also expresses concern that the global resources dividend should be based on resources whose extraction is easy to monitor, so that the costs of overall collection are low. He also

suggests that it should be levied on resources that are harmful for environmental reasons, such as crude oil; and make sure that it is on resources that would not greatly impact the price of goods that are needed to satisfy basic needs; Pogge, *World Poverty and Human Rights*, 206.

21. Pogge, *World Poverty and Human Rights*, 163.
22. For a good discussion of proposed global reforms based on this understanding of state legitimacy, see Buchanan, *Justice, Legitimacy, and Self-Determination*.
23. Thomas Pogge, 'Eradicating Systemic Poverty: Brief for a Global Resources Dividend', in Thom Brooks, ed., *The Global Justice Reader* (Oxford: Blackwell, 2008), 439.
24. Pogge, 'Eradicating Systemic Poverty', 443.
25. Miller's argument is targeted at Hillel Steiner's left luck egalitarianism. Hillel Steiner is able to acknowledge the role of unequal labour on land in his luck egalitarian theory, which argues that people are vested with two fundamental rights: the first is the familiar, libertarian self-ownership right; the second is a right to an equal share of the value of global natural resources. He clarifies that redistribution applies only to unimproved land, which of course leads Miller to complain that it is very difficult to disentangle the original natural value from the value which is connected to human creation. See Steiner, 'Territorial Justice'; and 'Sharing Mother Nature's Gifts: A Reply to Quong and Miller', a paper given to the *Justice and Territory* conference, Dublin, 2010 (a longer version is in *Journal of Political Philosophy*, vol. 19, no. 1 [2011], 110–123). Steiner is able to take into account, at least at the theoretical level, unequal labour on land, but does not address the issue of unequal attachment. He also adopts a purely instrumental view with respect to land and other things.
26. Miller, *National Responsibility and Global Justice*.
27. I agree with Miller's criticism of global luck egalitarianism as applied to resources, which focuses on the various ways in which people interact with land, and with resources, and on how these choices and activities give rise to responsibility and to desert. However, my argument is distinct from this in two ways. First, the emphasis that I've placed on self-determination is more foundational than his responsibility argument, since it's a presupposition of his argument that we must think that the communities in question ought to be self-determining, that is, the kind of entity that is capable of making choices and bearing responsibilities. Second, Miller's emphasis simply on responsibility seems to be an attempt to run a version of the luck egalitarian view at the global level. Luck egalitarianism relies on a distinction between choices and circumstances, and argues that people should be held responsible for their choices, but should not be held responsible for unchosen disadvantage. Miller simply applies the same logic at the collective level. Just as individuals shouldn't externalize the costs of their (self-determined) individual choices, so too nations shouldn't externalize the costs of their (self-determined) collective choices. The problem with this is that it doesn't defeat luck egalitarianism at the individual level, but leaves us with two levels of responsibility: if we hold nations responsible for the costs of their collective choices, the inevitable result is that some individuals within the nation will suffer unchosen disadvantages (e.g., individuals who were outvoted in the collective decision, future generations, etc.).
28. See here Spinner-Halev, 'From Historical to Enduring Injustice'.
29. Kolers, *Land, Conflict and Justice*, 53–54.
30. For a compelling defence of a basic right to subsistence, see Henry Shue, *Basic Rights: Subsistence, Affluence, and U.S. Foreign Policy*, 2nd edn (Princeton: Princeton University Press, 1996).
31. I understand the basic right to subsistence as a sufficientarian right, but I do not mean to imply that it is minimalist. I think that the idea is not bare subsistence, but a decent life, where that is variable in different societies.
32. Locke, *Second Treatise*, bk II, chap. V, 285–302.
33. This point is made in Mathias Risse, 'How Does the Global Order Harm the Poor?', *Philosophy & Public Affairs*, vol. 33, no. 4 (2005), 360.
34. Waldron, 'Rights in Conflict'.

9

Territorial Rights and Rights to Control Borders and Immigration

In this chapter, I consider whether the argument advanced in chapter 3, which justifies a people in exercising jurisdictional authority over territory, can be extended to justify the people in exercising control over the flow of persons and goods over borders. Control over borders, and especially immigration, is often thought to be a standard entitlement of states, and is a territorial right since it applies whenever people seek to enter the geographical domain (territory) of the state, whether or not they try to become a member of the particular community.

Throughout this book, I have assumed that the appropriate way to think about justification for institutions is not whether a particular right or rule or principle can be justified to each affected person taken alone: rather, just as with private property rights, the justification is at the level of the *system* of plural territories and of connected territorial rights. I do not aim to show therefore that the political community's interest in excluding individual A could outweigh that individual's interest in being permitted into the country. That would be very hard to show, because prospective migrants often have a significant interest in being admitted, and it is doubtful that there is a significant countervailing interest that the community could have to exclude that particular individual from settling in the state. The burden of proof suggested in the idea that we should justify territorial rights to each affected individual rests however on a fallacy of composition. It infers that something is true of the whole from the fact that that thing is true of some part of the whole, or even every part of the whole. But this is not true. We know this from zero-sum games, like athletic races, where the fact that someone would win if she ran faster does not mean that everyone would win if everyone ran faster. In the case of regulation of borders, letting in a single prospective migrant who seeks to live peaceably in the community will certainly not have a deleterious effect on the self-determination of the political community. However, it does not follow that having millions of migrants entering one's political community will have no effect on the self-determination of the community. The structure of the problem with respect to migration explains why the issue is so troubling and so contentious: we are all capable of adopting and reasoning from both perspectives. It also explains the well-known fact that in many political communities voters are in favour of the political order exercising significant control over immigration, but when confronted with individual cases of people who seek to migrate to a political community for perfectly good reasons, people are also likely to think that that person should be permitted to stay. In this chapter I argue that states do have a pro tanto, qualified right to exclude immigrants, grounded in the self-determination of political communities argument which I advanced earlier to justify jurisdictional authority over territory.

One of the challenges facing a theory such as mine, which begins from the idea that people are attached to a place, and that as a group they have a legitimate interest in maintaining control over that place as a place of a certain kind (a point which I argued for in chapter 3) is that it seems to run up against two kinds of criticisms: one is an empirical objection to the claim that this is indeed a fundamental interest that people generally have, and the second is a normative objection, which I consider in two versions. The normative objections to control over borders are both versions of the claim that preventing people from entering a state (immigration control) is a violation of people's basic rights, though there are different views about which basic rights are violated.

The empirical criticism is quite simple. In chapter 3, I provided evidence that individuals and groups are attached to place: they feel wronged when they are forcibly removed from a place, and the magnitude of the wrong does not seem to be fully captured by the process of coercion that typically accompanies such events. There is ample evidence that individuals and groups have place-related attachments, and I argued that they have rights of non-dispossession, as well as interests in controlling the character and kind of physical space in which they live, as part of control over the collective conditions of their lives. Against this, it is important to acknowledge that, in addition to people having attachments to homes and communities and relationships, both to each other and to place, humans also move, quite frequently, and establish new relationships, and become settled in new homes and communities. Indeed, one of the reasons why the issue of immigration is a hotly contested topic in the contemporary world is precisely because people are not rooted like trees. Many people seek to move, particularly from poorer countries to richer ones, where there are better opportunities, and it is likely that even more people would move if we lived in a world of relatively open borders. While there is evidence that humans have an interest in stability and place, as I emphasized in chapter 3, there's also clear empirical evidence that humans have an interest in being able to migrate, and we need to place these two kinds of interests into relation with one another. We need to balance the legitimate interest in having and maintaining relationships with people and attachments to place, and the legitimate interest in being able to move, including across borders. This chapter does not treat the two as contradictory: the fact that humans have attachments to people and place but in many cases seek to move and can change their attachments and relationships does not falsify the previous argument. Rather, both ideas have to be incorporated into a more complete, nuanced normative theory of rights over territory. The right to exercise control over borders has to be limited by the legitimate interests underlying individuals' aspirations to move across space and see and live in new places. The structure of the argument below is to justify the right and then explore the limits of the right.

This brings me to the normative critique of immigration controls. Cosmopolitans have been at the forefront of questioning robust theories or assumptions of state sovereignty in general, and state control of immigration in particular, arguing either: (1) that state control over immigration constitutes illegitimate coercion against people who are not authors of the rules to which they are subject, an argument advanced most prominently by Abizadeh, which I examined in chapter 6;[1] or (2) that it violates the rights of foreigners, either (2a) their right to free movement,[2] or (2b) their distributive justice rights (or both).[3] These arguments are, however, not usually framed in terms of the overall theory of territory. This chapter examines the extent to which the justificatory argument for rights over territory elaborated in this book can justify rights to control borders, and particularly the right to control human migration across borders, as well as the limits of such rights.

In order to approach the question of whether there is a right to exclude people *as individuals* from settling land that is legitimately occupied, it might be helpful to frame the problem in the terms of my original example. Imagine that some time after the arrival of Sir George Somers on the island of Bermuda, a Spanish ship arrives and its passengers also seek to settle there. In the discussion in chapter 6, I imagined that the Spanish were attempting to settle as a community either on the exact location of the English settlement, thereby violating the latter's rights of residency and occupancy, or on the opposite side of the island. The question that we are now confronting is a little different. What if the occupants of the Spanish ship do not seek to settle as a community on the same location on which the English have already settled—so it is not a colonization project—but seek to be admitted as individuals into the community that the English settlers, led by Sir George Somers, have already created? Do they have rights of access? Do the English have the right to exclude them from their settlement project? And if they do, what would justify that exclusion? The question I am concerned with is this: are there any grounds on which the

English settlers could justifiably deny would-be immigrants the opportunity to join their community?

In line with the question above, I disaggregate the broader question of 'control over borders or movement into the territory' into distinct phenomena: immigration (where immigrants are understood as individuals who seek to reside in the territory while abiding by the established legal system there, and who may even intend to eventually incorporate as a member of the relevant political community), which is different from colonization (which involves the settlement of a group of people as a group, where they reproduce their culture on territory already occupied), and different again from other forms of 'movement across borders', to travel, to see religious sites, to study, and so on. This chapter is focused mainly on issues of immigration. I argue that a political community (Sir George Somers and the English settlers) do have grounds connected to realizing the goods embodied in collective self-determination, although not all political communities are entitled to full control of borders. This chapter begins (section 9.1) by reviewing very briefly the positions taken on the political community's right to exclude by the extant theories of territory, before advancing my own. I then extend my argument of the relationship-dependent and relationship-independent goods that political communities realize to claim that that there is a right to control immigration (section 9.2). It's not clear that this is really a separate territorial right, rather than an extension of jurisdictional authority within the territory, but, in any case, the reasons that justify people, conceived of as a collective agent, having jurisdictional authority over territory also justify control over borders. I then consider the question of whether this particular territorial right may constitute a violation of justice, the conditions under which it does, and how this limits state claims to control borders (section 9.3).

9.1. Different Approaches to Territorial Rights and the Right to Exclude

Before I begin, it is useful to recall how the other theories of rights over territory would approach the question of rights over borders. The property account of territory, associated with Locke and some contemporary libertarians, can justify excluding people from the territory. If we think of territory as similar to property we have little difficulty arguing that there is a capacity to control borders. Many libertarians support open borders, as an extension of freedom of association: the idea here is that the right to private property includes the right to associate with whomever one likes on one's property. However, the view of territory that many of them hold—according to which 'the territorial claims of states are justified by *and derived from* the territorial claims of individuals'[4]—tends to view the domain of the state as an amalgam of individual property holdings. If state territory is an amalgam of land that is privately owned by individuals, and property owners are free to do with their property what they please, then individuals are free to enter the territory of another if they obtain permission.[5] This raises the question of the burden of proof presupposed in the idea of permission of property owners, which in turn bears on the precise relationship between property rights and freedom of movement and association. Suppose individual A seeks to gain access to B's property, exercising his right to freedom of movement and also association (with B), with whom he has permission to visit. Does he just need B's permission? What about C and D, whose property surrounds B? Does he need their permission too? Are C and D entitled to withdraw permission, or is it incumbent on them to respect A's rights of freedom of movement and association and give permission, in which case the property right that they enjoy is limited by other rights? The answer to this question is directly relevant to the burden of proof necessary to get a closed border round an area. To get a closed border round an area, do you need to have unanimous agreement of every property owner in that area? Or do you need the unanimous agreement of every property owner to permit the person to *enter* the area, as is suggested by the freedom of association argument? Steiner, who is the most prominent proponent of this version of libertarianism, does not address this issue,[6] but says only that the decision is located at the level of individual property owners (but not which ones). He writes: 'all land titles would be private ones and an unwelcome foreigner would *ipso facto* be no more welcome than an unwelcome fellow resident'.[7]

In contrast to Steiner, Locke and contemporary Lockeans such as A. John Simmons argue that the right (to control entry and exit on property) is transferred to the political authority, and a majority could vote to close a border. When property owners create a state through freely incorporating their property, Locke and contemporary Lockeans argue that individual agents have to agree to decision rules about the governance of the land so created. It is not clear from the individualist Lockean picture what exactly the decision rule would be, though the argument is consistent with democratic principles. This means that the parties to the agreement, the people who freely joined together to create a political community, have a right to decide for themselves what policy to adopt with respect to immigration. The view is consistent with an open-door policy with respect to immigration—just as it also permits massive migration from one privately owned piece of land to another. However, it also permits completely closed societies with no immigration. On this account, it seems that the English settlers are permitted to allow the prospective Spanish immigrants to settle in Bermuda, on their area of jurisdiction, but they are also entirely within their rights to refuse permission.

What about Kantian arguments for territorial right and their implications for the right to exclude prospective immigrants? As I argued in chapter 5, Kant's argument explains the need for the state, but does not explain all aspects of state authority that we normally associate with rights to territory. Specifically, with respect to the movement of people and goods over territory, it seems to follow from Kant's position that the state can legitimately prevent people from travelling to a territory only when this would threaten the lawful order itself. This is because jurisdictional authority is necessary to make property rights conform to the supreme law of morality, which explains why jurisdictional rights are important, but it is not clear that this extends to the right to prevent people from entering the territory of the state. The state would be justified in restricting entry if prospective migrants threatened the creation or maintenance of lawful order. In support of this interpretation, Kant, in his essay 'Perpetual Peace', outlines the right of a stranger or visitor to access and reside in a territory, 'as long as he behaves in a peaceable manner in the place he happens to be in'.[8] This seems to suggest a right to reside on the territory and not be treated with hostility.[9] This right enjoyed by individuals suggests a duty on the part of states to permit people to freely enter their territory, and thereby suggests that immigration policies, designed to prevent some people from entering state territory, for a range of diverse public policy reasons are unjustified.

Although the structure of the Kantian argument suggests that free movement can be inhibited only if it is threatening to justice, this is not an entitlement as we would normally understand it, since Kant also seemed to think that the judgment should be left to the host and that they were entitled to turn the visitor away as long as this did not lead to their [the visitor's] deaths. This suggests discretionary control—and we know that states exercise control over borders for reasons other than simply defending the state from destruction—but it is not clear what the argument for this is.

Kant also argued against a right of *settlement*, which he seems to have understood as a collective endeavour by a group of people to reproduce their culture and political society on land already occupied and governed. It's not fully clear why he assumed that settlement on land constitutes a violation of rights and freedoms of people already living there: the fact that he permits movement but not settlement suggests that he assumed that humans have some kind of right of residency and right to control the area in which they resided.[10] On the other hand, Kant distinguished the right of peaceable abode from the behaviour of many so-called civilized countries which settled and occupied territories, and oppressed the native population.[11] This runs together a number of separate problems, such as the unequal treatment of the original inhabitants and the conquest of the territory, but I am assuming that he regarded both as problems, which raises the question: what (in his argument) justifies thinking that settlement itself is a violation of rights of the original inhabitants?

Despite his plausible distinction between movement and settlement, and the related suggestion of some kind of right of residency and right to control place, it is difficult to see how the structure of the Kantian argument in terms of realizing the conditions of Right can explain why particular collective entities would have particular reasons, internal to their associational life, for designing policies in certain ways rather than other ways or for limiting membership. It is difficult to see how, on a justice perspective, we could justify any restriction on borders unless it was damaging to justice itself.[12]

What about cultural nationalist theories? The main proponent of cultural nationalism—David Miller—has written on both territory and immigration, but has not discussed the two together in a definitive statement of how he relates them to each other.[13] It is nonetheless possible to reconstruct how they are connected. The rights to jurisdictional authority that cultural nations have— to preserve their culture, way of life, and the value that they have invested in land—could be extended to explain why such groups are entitled to control the flow of migrants, viz., to preserve continuity of culture, to preserve the value in land, and the way of life of the particular cultural community. This argument would still uphold some rights for prospective migrants—refugee rights, for example—but the cultural nationalist explanation of territorial rights would seem to apply straightforwardly to justify the idea that nations have rights to control borders.

9.2. Peoples, Relationships, and the Right to Exclude

Let us return to Sir George Somers and the occupants of the ship that ran aground in Bermuda. Recall that in chapter 3, the moral rights of residency and occupancy involved examining the relationship between people and land. Rights of jurisdiction, held by a people, involved an analysis of the relationship between the people who are either in or are aspiring to a political relationship. I imagined in chapter 3 that at some point after Sir George Somers, crew, and prospective colonists found themselves stranded on the island, they reconciled themselves to their situation: they worked together to build houses and common public spaces and build a life there. They were involved not only with securing goods for their survival, but in a relationship with one another. We supposed that that relationship was valuable: it involved both relationship-independent goods and relationship-dependent goods. They had a relationship-independent interest in being governed in a non-arbitrary way, by a political order that respected their human rights and treated them fairly, and in living somewhere. And there are also goods that are special to the relationship itself. In many of our relationships—think here of intimate relationships or close friendships—goods can be realized only by particular others, and cannot be met satisfactorily by assigning a substitute. In my example, we imagined that, through this experience of shipwreck and survival and building a community, the crewmen, prospective settlers, and Sir George Somers himself came to love their island home and became attached to it, naming the distinctive plants, coves, and estuaries, caring for the beach and hills. Moreover, the people on the island developed a valuable community relationship which involved enduring interactions that were orientated towards the other participants in the relationship.[14] The people in that relationship aspired to be engaged in a political project with other members of the settlement: they developed an identity as participants in a political project that involved governing themselves according to rules and procedures that they worked out among themselves, on land to which they were attached; and they worked towards sustaining that relationship through their projects, aims, and collective institutions. On my view this group constituted a collective agent in so far as the members of the group shared a collective identity, and their actions and goals can be explained only through recognizing this social identity. In this political relationship, they participated in and benefited from these relationship goods; and the main good was a relationship-dependent one: that of creating a common life together, producing or maintaining institutions and practices that help to shape the collective circumstances of their existence, including their relationship to the land.

In chapter 3 I also outlined the interest that people have in ensuring some stability and security over the place that they live in. I argued there that people have an interest in ensuring that the place where they live retains a certain character; that they live their lives against the relatively stable background of a secure institutional structure and environmental context, for within this they can make plans, pursue goals, and have relationships. People have an interest in ensuring that, both individually and collectively, they have control over their lives, over the place that they live, and over the collective character of their community. I explored the way in which this right can justify anti-gentrification policies and tenancy rights in market societies. However, it's also clearly applicable to the right to control borders, since people can also ensure control over place by controlling the movements of people into and out of these places. This does not of course show that people are entitled to do anything they please to give effect to their control over places—for example, they cannot violate human rights in the process—but it does suggest that we can at least acknowledge that Sir George Somers and his community have a legitimate concern to prevent unwanted changes in their environment, changes that they are not in control of and which unsettle the secure pursuit of their lives and relationships.

Against this background of individual and community interest in control over place, and the relationship-dependent and -independent goods that they can realize, it is evident why people, mobilized into political communities, might seek control over borders, and specifically control over who can join the political community and settle on the territory. Jurisdictional authority is a mechanism by which members of political communities implement and maintain their own conception of how they want to organize their society, and so is a necessary condition for exercising the right of self-determination. It is not a right to defend justice as a universal ideal: rather, moral value is located in each particular state or in each particular collective self-determination project.

Rules about entry and exit can be straightforwardly understood as an extension of jurisdictional authority. This is often obscured from view because people tend to think of jurisdictional authority as involving the state and its citizens, and immigration rules typically apply to people seeking entry (non-members).[15] In fact, however, rules about entry and exit are just one sort of rule that co-members of the political community make to govern their relations within a territory. To see this, imagine that a potential immigrant manages to get to a territory and then the jurisdictional authority says that they can only stay on the territory if they have a visa of a certain type. Under one description of this, you could say, as Simmons does, that it is a direct right against aliens.[16] However, I want to claim that it should be seen, not as something distinct from the exercise of jurisdictional authority, but flowing from it. It's true that the rules often apply before the immigrant actually arrives, but this way of exercising jurisdictional authority over territory is easily explained: it is more efficient to check that the visa is of the right type, that the person has the proper kinds of permission *before* they enter the territory, than to wait until they are actually on the territory, and so subject to removal. Control over immigration clearly involves exercising authority over citizens as well, who may be legally prohibiting from hiring people who have entered the country without proper documentation, and so on. Thinking about immigration simply as a right against outsiders obscures from view the way in which rules about migration and immigration are a direct exercise of jurisdictional authority, applied across a geographical domain (a territory).

There are good reasons why a collectively self-determining group, which has significant forms of control over the conditions of their existence, would seek to have control over who and how many enter their community. There are both relationship-independent and relationship-dependent reasons connected to this self-determination project, which impacts on the question of the right to exclude. First, let us consider the relationship-independent reasons. Control over many aspects of one's collective life—education policies, health care policies and services, and so on—are impacted by issues connected to demographic balance, between rural and urban communities, for example, the rate and flow of migrants, and the kinds of migrants that one accepts. At some level, then, it would be difficult for political communities to make collective choices without some capacity to make choices over this vital component of many different policies. Indeed, it is hard to see how a political community could exercise significant control over the collective conditions of their existence if they lacked this kind of control.[17] If members of the group collectively lack this power, they also lack the ability to exercise robust forms of self-determination.

There are also relationship-dependent reasons which suggest a right to exclude. In many cases, it is an important part of the relationship that it is with particular people, with the people who are identified (by themselves and by others) as members of a certain collective or community. This is true of indigenous peoples, for example, who seek to be collectively self-governing as indigenous peoples, or of particular nations (institutionalized in states) or minority national communities who aspire to and often have various forms of substate autonomy. They have a shared identity, a shared 'we' as people who seek to be collectively self-determining over their common life, and to do so in a particular place. This would be undermined if they did not have the capacity to determine the membership of the political community as well as the terms of their relationship with each other and their relationship to the land that they live on.

At this point it is important to reflect on how exactly the different kinds of relationship reasons bear on the right to exclude. Relationship-independent reasons are connected to legitimate democratic policy goals, and how immigration policies connect to these goals. The idea here is that a self-determining political entity needs to exercise control over immigration as an aspect of control over other dimensions of collective life in general. Control over entry is strongly connected to the pursuit of different kinds of collective goals, such as the balance that a community might wish to strike between urban and rural interests, to the demographic pressure on education and health services, and the kind of labour market that the state might want to encourage and gaps that it might want to correct. This connection between relationship-independent reasons and the exercise of self-determination (which connects to jurisdictional authority over a number of domains) is relatively uncontroversial.

Reasons of the second kind—about *who* can be included in the relationship—bear on the claim that self-determination includes a right to determine what 'the self' is, by which I mean the composition of the polity.

This is more controversial. As I mentioned in the introductory chapter, political theory has focused on the relationship between the state and citizens and their respective rights and duties, but has hardly discussed at all how the physical (territorial) borders or the borders between citizens and non-citizens are drawn. This lacuna in political theorizing is connected, I think, to a worry that there may be no principled basis to draw these borders (a view which this book takes issue with) and the related worry that entitlement to decide (discretion over) the composition of the polity itself will open the door to objectionable racist immigration policies.

I will consider this second point, because I think it underlies the reluctance by political theorists to offer any account of membership and border justifications. I take the central challenge to my account here is that it could justify very illiberal, indeed racist immigration policies, such as the White Australia policy, and I agree that this would be a very unwelcome (counterintuitive) result.

I deny that this is an implication of my argument. It is tempting to think that every agency, every institution, has to be designed precisely to realize justice. But this is almost certainly false. There are many, diverse reasons to create a whole range of institutions—tribunals to enforce patents, institutions designed to reduce greenhouse gas emissions, institutions designed to regulate currency transactions, or global trade organizations. Many of them are not primarily orientated towards improving the justice of our world. They may be justified because they help to create greater efficiencies, or facilitate more trade, or ensure a cleaner world, or provide incentives for innovation. They may be designed with quite different policy goals in mind, or a different policy end (than justice), although they also have justice effects which have to be considered. Although this is an obvious point, normative theorists are very focused on justice—many seem to assume that every institution, every policy, every rule is justified primarily from that angle. It's clear, however, that we live under a complex network of institutions and rules, justified or created for different reasons, although of course they can also be assessed in part by justice criteria. In this chapter, I've argued that an important moral value that underlies territorial rights is the value of collective self-determination. This doesn't mean that we pay no attention to justice considerations: we should ensure that the institutions and policies that we enact are designed to fulfil the end that justifies those institutions and to do so in a way that doesn't violate human rights and pays attention to the unfair distribution of benefits and burdens that are so created.

It is not hard to show that there is a serious problem with policies aimed at selecting individuals on a racial or ethnic basis. One of the most basic principles of a just political order is that people should receive equal treatment by the state. Laws should apply to everyone equally, without regard to their race or ethnicity or gender. This idea of equality before the law is a basic principle of a just political order, and it would be violated by an immigration policy that explicitly discriminated on these grounds. This applies to immigration policies just as much as to other policies, if you accept my earlier argument that immigration policy should be seen as an extension of, not separable from, the exercise of jurisdictional authority. The principles that inform immigration procedures should also inform other kinds of government procedures. Immigration can exclude some and include others as long as the procedures by which they do this are fair and non-discriminatory, just as publicly funded educational institutions can admit some and exclude others, as long as the process is fair and the criteria are publicly justifiable and transparent. Indeed, I can think of no publicly admissible reason to use racist criteria in designing an important policy—unlike, for example, linguistic criteria or work skills, which might impact differentially on different prospective migrant groups.[18]

Even if one doesn't accept my earlier point that immigration policies are a simple extension of jurisdictional authority, one might think that a basic principle of non-discrimination is essential to treating people inside the political community as equals. Here the issue is not that racist immigration rules violate the basic rights of prospective migrants, as in the argument above, but that, insofar as most polities are heterogeneous, and include many different kinds of peoples and ways of life in their midst, a discriminatory immigration policy would have the effect of relegating a portion of their citizenry to second-class status. It would be symbolic of their marginalized status within the political community. This second reason applies even if we are unpersuaded by the first argument (though I think the first argument is right).

That said, it's important to consider whether some restrictions on immigration or encouragement of specific flows of immigrants on cultural grounds could be justified. I think that they can, in a very narrow band of cases, all connected to their effect on collective self-determination. I've argued in this book that people have, in addition to their individual identities, collective identities, and that it is important that these group-based identities are also appropriately recognized, so that people are not dominated as members of particular collective groups. Although I do not have space to argue for it fully here, we can think of the right of self-determination, conferred on different similarly situated peoples, as helping to ensure that the international order is structured in such a way that it supports the conditions of (inter-peoples) non-domination.[19] As Philip Pettit has argued in another context, a people can be subject to domination, as is the slave to the master, even if the aggressive power or master does not actually interfere with the actions of the dominated. It inheres in the structure of relations, and especially the all-present threat of interference that affects the choices and actions of dominated agents.[20] The institutional mechanisms—the legal and moral international rights—by which a people realizes collective self-determination gives it protection from the threat of interference, and thereby ensures that inter-people relations are on a footing of non-domination, rather than structured by domination and subordination. This is relevant because the collective self-determination of peoples can be undermined, not only by other collective agents interfering in a group's actions, but in certain instances by the exercise of individual rights. This phenomenon is well understood in relation to property rights, where the right to alienate property on indigenous lands contributes to the destruction of indigenous communities and their assimilation into white society. But other individual rights, too, can be destructive of collective agency, especially when the balance between groups is altered, making possible the rule of one group over another. In this kind of context, where the group is vulnerable to inter-group domination, it may be justified to distinguish between migrants based on their group identities: this is so when there is a danger that a high level of migration from a particular (demographically dominant) group threatens to undermine the associational life of the smaller (host) group. Tibetans may be justifiably concerned about large-scale migration of Han Chinese into their country, even if the migration were not at the behest of the Chinese state, and indigenous people in the Americas in the late nineteenth century were rightly concerned about the ways in which inward migration of non-indigenous people could undermine their capacity to form and maintain their own political societies. Even though each individual migrant might be moving for perfectly good, justifiable reasons, the net effect of large-scale migration of individuals who are also members of a group that is potentially dominant may be to undermine the capacity of the minority group to govern its collective life. This is what happened to Manitoba, which was majority indigenous (Metis and First Nations) when it joined Canada in 1870; without control of inward migration, the indigenous people were increasingly marginalized in the society (as well pushed by 'numbered treaties' to increasingly small areas of land).[21] All this is to say that it is not just the deliberate settlement of one group in areas occupied by others that can lead to the destruction of the associational life of smaller people: large-scale migration of individuals who happen to be members of a dominant group can lead to the destruction of a (typically, smaller) community's capacity to determine the context in which they live and control the land that they occupy, if they independently arrive in large numbers.

Although most political theorists have not discussed borders (between land, between people) in anything like the detail that is warranted, there is a tradition of argument, drawing on associative duties, of which mine is one, which potentially bears on issues of immigration. The basic idea behind an associative-duties argument is that some duties (associative duties) arise through people being related to one another in certain ways, and from certain features of the relationship. In this literature, very little is said about how the people in question came to be in that relationship with each other. In the global-justice literature, for example, one of the justifications for thinking that we owe differential obligations to people domestically and globally is based on the idea that, while each person is equally important from a moral point of view, with some people we are in relations that carry with them stronger duties, and this can justify differential treatment of different people. The upshot of this argument is that we owe all human beings simply as such humanitarian duties, which can be defined minimally or in more demanding terms, but that compatriots are entitled to equal treatment. The special associative obligations connected to equality are based on arguments about what is special to the political community. These egalitarian associative obligations are triggered when individuals are subject to a comprehensive network of coercive laws (Blake, Nagel) or institutionalized reciprocity (Sangiovanni).[22] The standard version of this associative-duties argument seems to justify the view that not only does the political community not under a duty to admit the prospective migrant, but that the egalitarian duties that apply distinctively among co-citizens could ground sufficient reasons to limit immigration (e.g., in order to control the labour-market effects of low-skilled immigration). Indeed, one might argue that these reasons, while in some sense relationship-relative, are not only acceptable to those within the relevant relationship, but to all persons who can recognize the value in the relationship from an impersonal standpoint.[23]

Let me, though, focus on the idea that we are not required to enter into particular social relations with others, even if that might benefit them or create some kind of good. This has often been noted in relation to freedom of association arguments, where Wellman in particular has pointed out that, in the absence of an existing relationship, people cannot ordinarily be required to be in relationships with other people, in order to confer benefits or rights on them.[24] We do not generally suppose that individual A is entitled to be able to enter into a social relation with any one he or she wants. Suppose it could be shown that intimate relationships are good for people's health and happiness. Nevertheless we would not want to require people to enter into relationships with other (perhaps needy) people, simply because it would be good for that needy person, or perhaps just desired by that person. Relationships are mutual and particularistic in the sense that they are orientated towards specific persons. Many are not chosen—the voluntarist picture is wrong—but it is nevertheless true that relationships in general can be foisted on people in only quite limited sets of conditions.[25]

What are these conditions? We often find that we are in a relationship with a person through no act of will particularly—family relationships are of this kind—and this may give rise to particular kinds of obligations. We may also find that our family obligations expand due to the choices, projects, and behaviour of people that we are already related to, but which are not chosen by us. In my family, for example, I am expected to buy birthday presents for my nieces and nephews. This is not exactly a moral duty—though there is a kind of reciprocal basis for this rule—but it is definitely a social expectation. I may find that the number of nieces and nephews that I have to buy for has increased, due to the decisions of my brothers and sisters and their various partners. I had no choice in the creation of nieces and nephews, but I can determine as a kind of fact of the matter that I am in an extended family relationship with a new person (my new niece) and that I may have associative obligations as a result. The same is true in political communities, which are intergenerational communities of people who are united together with a shared sense of identity. The individual members of the group change as new babies are brought into being and people die. In such cases, there are good reasons for extending both occupancy rights and political rights to the children of legitimate occupants, as I suggested in chapter 3. We do not, in that sort of case, have a choice in the composition of members that we are related to through our group identity, or politically. But in cases where someone is neither related to me, nor appropriately related to people who are related to me (the niece and new citizen example) the situation is quite different. Their desire to be in a relationship with me is simply not determinative. Even a strong and reasonable desire to be in a relationship with me does not give you a claim to enter into a relationship with me if I do not wish to be in a relationship with you.

Is it a puzzling disanalogy that we treat infants born to citizens as citizens, as legitimate occupants, and so accept the unchosen obligations that result from this, but that we do not do the same for migrants, who seek to come to the territory? Some might think that the differential treatment of babies and potential migrants needs further explanation. I have provided the basis of this explanation in my focus on relationship interests in chapter 3, which gives us reason for thinking that children of occupants, who are in an appropriate kind of relationship to legitimate occupants, should have this status extended to them. The same is not true of prospective migrants, whose claim is not rooted in any kind of existing relationship but on the desire and/or aspiration to be in a relationship. Further, if we are to have any control over the social conditions of our existence, and the obligations that we have as a result of these complex social interactions, we have to have some control over which people we are related to and how. Indeed, we may even think that the fact that it is permissible to exercise control in the one case (migrants) but not in the other (infants) may make the exercise of some control in the migrant case, where it is permissible (which I'll consider below), even more imperative.

9.3. Objections Considered

Even if the account of territory outlined above offers a coherent account of the moral value of territory and its relation to self-determination, and even if we accept the view advanced above in which control over immigration is straightforwardly an extension of the political community's jurisdictional authority, there would still be a problem if immigration controls were thought, in their essence, to violate basic human rights or constitute a serious injustice. In the sections that follow, I consider criticisms that take this form: the first is that restrictions on immigration violate the moral rights of people to free movement; in the second part, I examine the criticism of borders that focuses on its global distributive-justice implications.

9.3.1. Free Movement

One of the central criticisms of restrictions on immigration is that they violate the moral rights of people to freedom of movement. This argument is often put forward by libertarians (although interestingly it is in tension with one strand of the libertarian position, namely, their conception of territory as property, which I discussed above) but is also advanced by egalitarian liberals, too. Joseph Carens, for example, has argued that, 'at the level of principle, a commitment to freedom and equality as fundamental moral values would require states to have open borders'.[26] He defends this claim on two grounds: the first is that freedom of movement, 'the right to go where you want . . . is an important human freedom',[27] which he sometimes describes as a basic right; and the second is in terms of the requirements of egalitarian global distributive justice. Although Carens is careful to note that the idea of 'freedom of movement as a basic human right' does not involve, for him, an absolutist position, and therefore that this human right has to be balanced by other considerations and limitations, it nevertheless counts as a morally weighty consideration when it is placed in the balance against other factors or goods.

Before I begin, I think that one problem with this objection to immigration controls grounded in a right to freedom of movement is that it fails to distinguish clearly between freedom of 'movement' and freedom of 'settlement'. Much of the plausibility and weightiness of this argument is derived from the visual and psychological connotations of 'movement', because it implies a very intrusive regulation in physical movement. And indeed, some types of migration controls do place burdensome and unreasonable restrictions on autonomous movement for purposes that do not entail long-term settlement. But the type of movement that is really at issue in arguments about control over borders is the movement associated with labour and resettlement, although of course there are also quite reasonable restrictions on people likely to commit crimes or engage in terrorist activity. It's easy to agree that movement is a basic human right and that there should be a high burden of justification for constraining a person's ability to travel, to go to a certain place at a certain time, and even more generally his or her decision to live in a particular location within a particular broad community, which is why restrictions on movement within the same country are so unconscionable. If, for example, there was an island not far away from Bermuda, on which another community had settled—say, the Spanish ship had eventually landed on it—we might think that to realize the good of freedom of movement, people from one island should be able to go on hikes, visit, and generally move around in the other island. Settlement, however, is quite different, for it is directly and obviously related to self-determination in a way that 'human movement' generally is not. The most obvious contemporary example is Palestine, where the settlement of Jewish families might increase the social welfare and autonomy of those specific families but it clearly interferes with the Palestinian's self-determination. Refusing the right of Christians or Jews to religious pilgrimage in Jerusalem (if, for example, there was an intrusive Palestinian jurisdiction over these sites) would be an unreasonable restriction on autonomous movement.

To return to the idea of freedom of movement (which is not conflated with settlement), it is important to consider what that right involves and what are its limits. On my argument, people have legitimate interests in their preserving their relationships both with each other and with land, and in ensuring some background continuity against which they make decisions and plan their lives, and that this may justify control over inward migration. Control is a restriction on liberty; all restrictions on liberty require justification, in the sense that there ought to be good policy reasons to justify it, but, I will argue, not all restrictions count as a violation of a basic human right to free movement.

Most arguments about freedom of movement are grounded in a more fundamental right to personal autonomy more generally, but the maximalist interpretation of the right to freedom of movement rests, I argue below, on a misunderstanding of the nature of autonomy. As Taylor has argued, autonomy cannot be cashed out in quantitative terms, so that each individual interference in human action counts as a denial of liberty.[28] Driving down a street in London, England, or in New York involves many individual interferences in liberty in the form of red traffic lights, but this doesn't mean that this person is less free than someone driving down a relatively empty street in Ceaușescu's Romania or Gaddafi's Libya. We don't think of liberty or autonomy in quantitative terms, but as involving very important liberties that are designed to protect those individual interests that are sufficiently important that they warrant holding others under a duty.[29] The ideal of autonomy, on which the right to freedom of movement is based, assumes that people are self-choosing, self-creating beings, and are entitled to make decisions over the shape of their own lives in important areas. This requires not simply the possession of the basic capacity for choice, but a range of options, or a range of valuable options, from which to choose. However, it does not require maximal scope for choice or maximal options. It is sufficient for the realization of the basic or underlying value of autonomy that there are a sufficient number of acceptable choices from which the individual chooses.[30]

The problem with appealing to the right to cross borders as a simple extension of the basic human right to free movement is that it seems to require the adoption of a maximal view of the right to freedom of movement. While it is surely the case that people who are denied the right to free movement—they are strapped into chains—are denied a basic liberty right, it is less clear that this argument works with every restriction on options or on movements. The reason for this is that the right to freedom of movement, like most autonomy-based rights, are most plausibly described in sufficientarian terms, rather than given a maximalist interpretation. Suppose the individual is not strapped in chains, but simply locked in a prison cell, or a bedroom. Does that violate his or her freedom of movement? It would seem so: the person's movements are too restrictive, too confining to be consistent with the exercise of autonomy. The ideal of autonomous agency, which is at the root of the right to freedom of movement, requires a certain scope of free movement, or free action, but this sufficientarian understanding of the scope for freedom of movement does not view every and all limitation on free movement *as a violation of the right*. Government policies, practices, and regulations involve all kinds of restrictions on human actions, including prohibitions on where people can go and regulations regarding how they can act. On the sufficientarian account of the right to free movement, defended here, each person is entitled, as a matter of human rights, to a sufficient degree of freedom of movement. This would mean that restrictions—that is, reduced options to one's free movements—might need to be justified by reference to justified policy goals—the state ought still to justify its actions and to justify restrictions on people's choices—but they are not a violation of the basic right, as long as they are beyond what is sufficient to protect autonomous agency.

Of course, it may be the case that even a sufficientarian understanding of the right to free movement requires that one be able to cross (at least some) borders, but that would require additional arguments and is not plausible in the standard case of an individual living and residing in a country that is reasonably large and inclusive of many options, from which he or she can build an autonomous life. This is nevertheless an important point, because it suggests that the self-determination projects of very small communities cannot be made consistent with respect for free movement (even on the sufficientarian account). To see the problem, it is important to distinguish between the right of entry and the right of exit. Most people would say that no state, however large, has the right to prevent people from exiting. This is relatively uncontroversial (and is not derived from a sufficientarian account of the right to freedom of movement, but from the kind of relationship that ought to obtain between co-citizens). However, if we have a world divided up between different states, and different political communities, each exercising control over borders, it could be the case that there are people inside a small state, who, although formally free to leave, can't gain entrance to anywhere else. That is a problem, since I think that the territorial ordering of the world is justifiable only if basic rights are protected (and that means that they are possible to exercise). This problem could be solved if larger states were required to allow entrance to people in smaller states who otherwise would not have sufficient freedom of movement or adequate options, or it might mean that a state that is so small that it cannot on its own satisfy the (sufficientarian) understanding of the right of free movement ought not to have full territorial rights. It can legitimately exercise control over its collective life only if it enters into political relations with another state, which ensures that the right (to freedom of movement) is satisfied. On this argument, then, it's not true that every existing state has a right to control its borders: this is justified only in cases where the political community is sufficiently large and the members of it have a sufficient range of options that we can conclude that there is an adequate amount of movement and scope for autonomy within it. In cases of individuals who are members of other, smaller political communities, they may meet the sufficientarian threshold only if the political community has entered into reciprocal agreements with other communities, such that this (sufficientarian understanding of freedom of movement) is satisfied. It is morally incumbent on both these smaller communities to claim self-determination only within a larger state or an economic zone like the European Union, which permits freedom of movement within the zone, and on larger communities to make the necessary arrangements so that the rights of these individuals are respected by the border control arrangement.

The above argument about freedom of movement also provides an additional explanation of why neighbourhoods, where people have occupancy rights, cannot normally control exit (for that would violate the autonomy of the people)[31] and can only control entry if that is agreed to in the context of a larger community (existing states) that permits free movement and travel.

The sufficientarian account of freedom of movement and adequate options can also explain the difference between restrictions on border control within the state and between states. The regulation of goods and people across borders is important if political communities are to enjoy robust forms of collective self-determination, and we do not typically associate substate entities with these kinds of stronger self-determination. This is why we do not typically have passport controls within countries, to regulate people's movements. The type of internal passports we often associate with apartheid South Africa or communist Russia are forms of internal surveillance and control, part of a package of mechanisms designed to control the population. They are not associated with the idea of strong, democratically authorized collective self-determination. We might think differently of internal controls, however, if the entity exercising those controls did have strong decentralized self-determination below the level of a state. If Tibet was able to exercise self-determination within a larger China, and this involved regulation of internal (within China) inward migration, we would regard it differently than similar forms of control exercised by the state, in the interests of enhancing its power.

The sufficientarian understanding of the right to freedom of movement is different from Carens's view, which, on this issue, is much closer to libertarianism, because he requires every restriction to be balanced and justified against the fundamental human right (to free movement). Although Carens points out, as a caveat, that rights aren't absolute, the weighting metaphor that Carens invokes is misleading. Although, of course, all restrictions ought to be justified and balanced (otherwise the state is engaged in wholly arbitrary actions), not all restrictions violate the right to free movement and the onus of justification is much different. On the view presented here, many rights, including the right to free movement, are sufficientarian in nature, and there is a significant role for the state in providing a framework in which the protection of basic autonomy is guaranteed, as long as that framework permits significant autonomous action and an adequate range of choices. Carens's weighting metaphor, with arguments for restrictions on the one hand and the violation of a fundamental right to free movement on the other, is quite different from the sufficientarian understanding of the right, which suggests that restrictions on liberty of course have to be justified in the sense that there must be reasons to restrict one's liberty, but that not all restrictions constitute a violation of a right to free movement, and that the weight of justification is much reduced.

9.3.2. Distributive (In)justice

There is, however, another, pressing cosmopolitan criticism of border controls from a justice direction, namely, that they consolidate inequalities and so are inimical to global justice and they violate people's basic rights to subsistence or to live a decent life. This criticism, I will argue below, has some teeth, and I will discuss its plausibility and limitations.

In his argument for open borders, Joe Carens does not rely solely on the argument considered above, that restrictive borders violate a right to free movement. He also argues that it would be 'only in a world of open borders that we could meet the requirements of global distributive justice with respect to both opportunities and outcomes'.[32] The idea here is that many people in the world live inadequate lives—they are impoverished, under-nourished, and have few opportunities. We do not need to suppose that the affluent world *caused* their poverty and lack of opportunity. Nevertheless, these people may still complain that a world divided up between territorially organized political units, which prevent people from crossing borders and improving their situation, is morally illegitimate. It consolidates inequality or deprivation, because it prevents them from taking courses of action which could remedy this situation. This is a criticism, not of particular immigration restrictions, but of the territorial ordering of the world into political communities with discretionary power over entry.[33]

Note that here the claim cannot simply be that there is no right because the consequences of acting on the right are bad, that is to say, that self-determination over territory is unhelpful to us if our aim is to address inequality. If political communities are entitled to make decisions about their collective life, to exercise jurisdictional authority, of which this is part, then it seems that political communities have this entitlement—this territorial right—regardless to some extent of whether the exercise of the right would result in suboptimal consequences. Rather, the claim here must be that the exercise of territorial right itself violates the moral rights of people.

A stronger version of the argument would say that people have a right to a decent life, and included among these are subsistence rights. This means that, while territorial rights or immigration policies do not need to be designed to optimize welfare, or to equalize welfare, or to promote equality, it is a source of serious moral concern if they jeopardize people's basic rights. There are of course different understandings of people's basic rights, but here I will follow Henry Shue in arguing that people have basic or fundamental rights to life, liberty, security, and subsistence.[34] On Shue's view, in addition to basic rights to liberty and to security, there is a basic right to subsistence. This is because people cannot fully enjoy any right if they lack the minimal essentials for an active and healthy human life.

Above, I argued that territorial rights are justified in terms of people realizing relationship-dependent and relationship-independent goods, most of them connected to making decisions to govern their collective life together. Control over immigration or borders generally is then justified as an extension of jurisdictional authority and (like jurisdictional authority) in terms of the moral value of collective self-determination. The question now confronting us is whether the rules concerning membership in the community itself and terms of entry, which are justified as part of the exercise of jurisdictional authority, are, indeed, consistent with the basic rights of all.

What does it mean for collective self-determination (over immigration) to be justified if it is consistent with the basic rights of everyone?

A first important point to emphasize is that the exercise of collective self-determination is not necessarily inimical to basic subsistence rights. Indeed, establishing an effective jurisdictional authority is important in ensuring that people can achieve their basic rights to subsistence, because through establishing rules of justice people regulate their lives together, which makes it possible for them to live better. They establish property and taxation regimes which are important for improving their economic well-being, both individually and collectively, and, especially, they develop processes and institutions to solve collective problems.

Second, concern for basic rights justifies the obligations that different political communities have to refugees. If people's lives and liberties are threatened, they are entitled to a safe haven. This is a quite different issue from the question with which this chapter was primarily concerned: now we are imagining that a Spanish ship arrives on the island, the people in desperate straits, their ship run aground, and the sailors are seeking refuge on the island. That is a different kind of case, and there is a requirement of justice and humanity to give refuge to such people, and Sir George Somers and the people who live in that community have an obligation to give them safe haven and possibly subsequently incorporate them fully in the political community. The idea that states have an obligation to accept refugees until it is safe for them to return to their originating country is now enshrined in the UNHCR *Convention and Protocol Relating to the Status of Refugees* (1951), which outlines the obligations of states with respect to refugees. Even if the interest that political communities have in collective self-determination means that they are not required to accept individual people seeking to improve their lot, they must still accept refugees. Since it is likely that countries adjacent to oppressive regimes do more than other countries to meet this obligation, other countries should strive to fulfil that duty too, by bearing some of the costs and by accepting their fair share of refugees.

Related to this discussion of refugees is a question that has recently arisen about the merits of extending the category of 'refugee' to include people fleeing as a result of territory loss, which in turn is the result of human-induced global climate change. In international law, the category of refugee applies to people who are 'being persecuted for reasons of race, religion, nationality, membership of a particular social group or political opinion'.[35] Recently, there have been a number of works in political theory which argue that the category of 'refugee' should be extended to people who live on territory that is disappearing as a result of climate change.[36] This raises the question: what does my theory of territory have to say about such people?

It arises here in my discussion of immigration (although it could have been put in chapter 7 on corrective justice) because there is a growing literature connected to territorial rights and climate change, which advocate that the category of 'refugee' be extended to include people who are fleeing from climate disasters, focusing especially on cases where rising sea levels cause the total submersion of the whole territory inhabited by these people. I am ambivalent about this proposal, as I explain below, though I do think that such people have claims for automatic entry into societies or land that are in a position to help.

About the specific proposal, it is worth noting that, while there are many areas of the world that are now affected and will undoubtedly be affected in the future by global climate change, extending the refugee definition to include people fleeing from rising water (in addition to fleeing from persecution) will not track most people who are affected by climate change. People along the coasts of India or the estuaries of Bangladesh can flee inland. They will become internally displaced people, not refugees. It will affect only those people fleeing because their whole country will disappear. According to the 2013 Report of the Intergovernmental Panel on Climate Change, this is expected to happen to Kirabati, Tuvalu, Maldives, and the Federated States of Micronesia. This is devastating for those people, but they are not a significant population group in comparison to the people indirectly affected by climate change or who we expect will be internally displaced.[37] Moreover, beyond the most obvious cases, such as submerged islands, it's very difficult to distinguish the drivers of economic migration from climate change more generally. Most economic migrants—to be discussed below—migrate for a number of reasons, both negative ones, connected to the inadequacies of their current place, and positive ones, such as the expectations that they have about how they will fare in a different country. Amongst the negative reasons, which typically motivate economic migrants, are things that could be connected to human-induced global climate change. I am thinking here about such things as the soaring price of food, increased desertification, drought, and disappointments in agricultural output as a result of changed ecosystems. All of these are potentially partial drivers of economic migration, and it is not clear how exactly we can distinguish ordinary economic migration from climate change–induced migration, since climate change will probably play a partial role in explaining why people are motivated to move. I think that the main motive for extending refugee status to people living on an island about to be submerged is that most of us feel that these people should have the kind of automatic right of entry into another land or territory that we accord to refugees, since they will die if their country is submerged.[38] I agree that they should have automatic entry, but I think that this is motivated by a natural duty of rescue. Inhabitants of submerged islands are absolutely entitled to be rescued from their plight, and those of us in a position to help have a duty to rescue them. It may be that it is useful to pursue this goal through an existing legal category like 'refugees', but the moral motive is simply urgent rescue and that justifies the same kind of automatic entry that applies to refugees. Finally, it is worth remembering that the loss that these people will have suffered if their island is submerged cannot be corrected in any meaningful way through refugee status or some kind of parallel individual 'right to rescue' status. These people will have lost not only their homes, but their island, the place that they grew up in, are attached to, where their family is buried, and so on. They will also, if they are dispersed, lose the capacity to be politically self-determining as a group and so on. Being accepted as individuals into another place is better than being submerged, but it does not come close to addressing their loss. If there were unused territory elsewhere in the world, there would be an argument for giving them that, since it would not involve unjustly displacing someone else, even though it could not replace the island that they grew up in. But the unused territory that exists in the world is usually uninhabited for a reason: the frozen Arctic and Antarctica, deserts and mountains, are all relatively unpopulated, but giving them territory there may well be a recipe for permanent marginalization. So—this is a tragic case where the loss that these people experience cannot be corrected or addressed in any meaningful way.[39] Of relevance here, though, is that whatever immigration policy we adopt, it ought to ensure that it institutionalizes some kind of duty to rescue or right to be rescued, which addresses the dire situation of people, like those in islands about to be submerged.

Let me turn now to the situation of economic migrants. I have argued that border controls are pro tanto justified, but that concern about basic rights and subsistence rights suggests that immigration controls should be organized in ways and accompanied by policies that address serious deprivation in those parts of the world which we typically think of as 'migrant-sending societies'.

Although there is some debate about the precise consequences of restrictive immigration, or the reverse—more permissive immigration—I think it is very likely that restrictive immigration policies have a deleterious effect on the achievement of basic subsistence rights of people in poorer parts of the world. This is so for two reasons, which are in some tension with one another. The first is that selective immigration policies adopted in the West lead people in the sending societies to be worse off than they would otherwise be. There is some empirical evidence of the devastating effects of the brain drain on sending countries. Consider the following: three-quarters of Ghanaian doctors who graduated between 1985 and 1994 left the country within the ten years following graduation.[40] There are more Malawian doctors in the city of Manchester, United Kingdom, than in the whole of Malawi, which is a country ravaged by AIDS and facing an acute physician shortage.[41] In many parts of Africa, there is a serious nursing shortage, mainly because the vast majority of trained nurses have left for the developed West.[42] This is not simply a shortage in a key area. The exit of the educated middle class—people with social capital—for richer regions of the world is devastating for the country as a whole, because these are precisely the class of people who elsewhere have been crucial to economic development. The richest and best educated are also less likely (than poorer or less educated migrants) to send remittances back to their country of origin. This might seem to be an argument against permissive immigration and to raise doubts about the inequality-reducing effects attached to open borders. I think that it would be a mistake to interpret it in this way.[43] The current policies of countries like Canada, the United Kingdom, and Australia *target* well-educated people with much needed skills. We cannot extrapolate from the effects of this scheme to an institutional arrangement that more closely resembles an 'open border' regime. In fact, I attribute these negative effects to restrictive immigration (restricted to people who are desirable to the host society), and doubt that these effects would be felt in an immigration regime that was truly welcoming of 'huddled masses'.

In addition to creating labour market gaps and distortions in the sending society, and draining the country of the best-educated, most desirable people, restrictive immigration consolidates inequality by preventing many individuals from seeking to improve their individual lives through migration to more economically advantaged parts of the globe. In their authoritative study of the effects of immigration policies based on a points system, McHale and Kapur conclude by arguing that an immigration policy that permitted a large number of temporary work visas to poorer individuals would be helpful to global development and to providing a greater number of opportunities to live a decent life for larger numbers of the global poor. We do not need to endorse their conclusions: not all policies need to be aimed precisely at addressing global poverty—as long as the points system is aimed at other, legitimate public policy goals—but it does mean that states should design their immigration policies in such a way as to avoid these consequences.

In other words, we should accept the state's right to control entry for reasons connected to the self-determination of the political communities, but only if these are accompanied by measures that are aimed at addressing the concern for the basic rights of the people who are either excluded or left behind. Some of the effects of the 'brain drain' could be mitigated by compensation to the sending country, which, after all, invested its resources in the education and training of workers who they then lose to richer parts of the world. (Alternatively, the sending society could try to prevent these people from leaving, or the host societies could close down the programme. However, I am assuming that these programmes are potentially justifiable: they are opportunity-enhancing for the individual migrants, and useful for the host society, so compensation to the sending society seems a more optimal result.[44])

The claims of individual prospective migrants who seek to escape their insecure economic situation through migration but are denied entry do not need to be addressed through open or relatively open borders. Obviously, there are some people who are so deprived, so needy, that there is a basic duty of rescue and this may involve crossing borders. That is relatively unproblematic. More troubling are people whose lives are fraught with insecurity, who lack the economic security to pursue decent lives, and their claims could be addressed in a world with no mobility restrictions. What should be done in this case? Here the answer is that migration is one mechanism to address global poverty. It's undoubtedly true that many richer countries could have and should have a more permissive migration policy for these types of migrants. But it's wrong to think that this ought to be the full answer, in part because it would be much better if people didn't have to move to get their basic rights addressed. Redistribution of wealth and global development assistance are also means to address basic economic rights. If a society admits fewer immigrants, it should undertake a larger share of responsibility (relative to its wealth) to ensure that subsistence rights are met through other means. As Robert Goodin has argued, 'if rich countries do not want to let foreigners in, then the very least they must do is send much more money to compensate them for being kept out'.[45] Although I have not employed the language of compensation and do not think that economic assistance should be necessarily directed at the individual prospective migrants (rather than the class of people who are in danger of having their basic rights not met), the policy prescription of redistribution from rich countries to poorer, migrant-producing countries is essentially the same.

In conclusion, people have a right to establish their own rules to be collectively self-governing, and this involves control over immigration. This must be consistent with the basic rights of people everywhere to subsistence. In many cases, this can be achieved in a number of ways, including higher levels of immigration from poorer to richer regions, but also through mechanisms of global distributive justice. We need not suppose that that has to be confined to income redistribution; it may include reform of the international order to enact fairer trade rules, including ending subsidized agriculture in the rich countries, taxing international financial transactions and directing the proceeds to meeting basic needs, and other kinds of development assistance aimed at directly benefiting the poor. There is no blueprint for how we ought to be meeting the obligations imposed by a general right to subsistence, but I've argued that we do not need to assume that open borders are a direct corollary of that argument. Indeed, I've argued that the interest that a political community has in collective self-determination confers on it a prima facie right to control the terms of entry. However, the exercise of territorial right must be made consistent with the basic subsistence rights of everyone, and this means that they should take measures to ensure that the material needs of people in poorer places are met.

9.4. Conclusion

Although this chapter has focused on immigration—which is a hotly contested issue in its own right—it has abstracted from many of the issues that are the focus of debate amongst people interested in the ethics of migration. It has mainly considered the relationship of my account of the nature and justification of territorial right to the specific right to control borders. In pursuing this line of inquiry, I have not focused much on the kind of people who seek to migrate, and the reasons that they have. I have concentrated on the standard case of people who seek to migrate from one country, often poor, to another, richer one, usually for good reasons, such as to pursue a better life and have greater opportunities. The main focus of this chapter has been to consider the ways in which the right to control borders is connected to the self-determination of the people in the political community: to their connection to place, and to each other, and the relationship-dependent and -independent reasons that they have to exercise such control.

I have argued that these interests generate a qualified and pro tanto right to control borders, including the power to exclude potential migrants. It is a qualified right because it has to be pursued in ways consistent with basic human rights. In line with this, I have argued that not all political communities can exercise the most robust forms of self-determination, associated with border control, because some states are too small to provide an adequate level of freedom of movement on their own, and cannot guarantee that other societies will let their members in and so cannot ensure that those individuals have a sufficient range of freedom of movement. I have also argued that border controls are unhelpful to people seeking to improve their lot and may be a reason why it is difficult for people to meet their basic needs. Since this is so, richer political communities have obligations to ensure that the basic entitlements of people to live a decent life are met. However, this cannot be a direct argument for open borders, since there are a number of ways in which rich people might assist poorer people in meeting basic subsistence rights, such as fairer global rules around trade, resources, and development assistance. It does though suggest that if we are to exercise control over borders in ways consistent with human rights we need to do much more than we currently do to address the lot of the global poor.

Notes

1. See Abizadeh, 'Democratic Theory and Border Coercion'. In a paper developed in large part in opposition to Michael Blake's attempt to distinguish domestic justice from global justice through the idea that state coercion raises particular legitimacy issues, Abizadeh argues that immigration controls represent coercion against prospective migrants. See, however, Miller's argument that the concept of coercion has to be linked with the conditions for individual autonomy, and that the mere restriction of options does not necessarily show that people's autonomy is jeopardized. Miller, 'Why Immigration Controls are not Coercive'.
2. Gillian Brock, *Global Justice: A Cosmopolitan Account* (Oxford: Oxford University Press, 2009); Joseph H. Carens, *The Ethics of Immigration* (Oxford: Oxford University Press, 2013), 236–245.
3. Carens, *Ethics of Immigration*, 233–236; Loren Lomasky and Fernando R. Tesón, eds. Forthcoming. *A Classical Liberal Theory of Global Justice*.
4. Hillel Steiner, 'Libertarianism and the Transnational Migration of People', in Brian Barry and Robert Goodin, eds, *Free Movement: Ethical Issues in the Transnational Migration of Peoples and of Money*, 87–94 (University Park: Penn State Press, 1992), 92, emphasis in original.
5. Of course not all libertarians view territory as property. There are some libertarians and near libertarians, such as David Schmidtz and Christopher Morris, who accept a jurisdiction–property distinction. See the excellent book by Christopher Morris, *An Essay on the Modern State* (Cambridge: Cambridge University Press, 1998); David Schmidtz, 'Justifying the State', *Ethics*, vol. 101, no. 1 (1990), 89–102; David Schmidtz, 'The Institution of Property', *Social Philosophy and Policy*, vol. 11, no. 2 (1994), 42–62.
6. As I argued in chapter 2, this form of Lockean libertarianism essentially eliminates the possibility of legitimate territorial jurisdiction as we understand it, so a harsher critic might complain that it is unclear what kind of guidance they could give us in criticizing existing practices of state control over immigration.
7. Steiner, 'Libertarianism and the Transnational migration of People', 91.
8. Kant, 'Perpetual Peace', 106.
9. Kant, 'Perpetual Peace', 105. He terms this the 'cosmopolitan right of universal hospitality'.
10. For a sophisticated treatment of Kant's views relevant to immigration, see Sarah Fine and Andrea Sangiovanni, 'Immigration', in Darrel Moellendorf and Heather Widdows, eds, *The Routledge Handbook of Global Ethics*, XX–XX (London: Routledge, 2014).
11. Kant, 'Perpetual Peace', 106.
12. It is hard to see how the justice-based perspective associated with Kant could incorporate what I think are the two main motives underlying policies with respect to borders: these are that the policies should be consonant with the general terms of the associational life of the community and that the power to make these decisions is one which is central to

the idea of people being collectively self-governing. People within relationships get to decide the terms of the relationship, both the terms on which it is conducted and who it is among (and this is true even when the relationship is institutionally defined). One possible way round this problem is to describe justice in a sufficiently capacious way that it includes democracy as constitutive of justice, and then we could give moral significance to the exercise of jurisdictional authority (including authority over justice) as a constituent element of justice. This is roughly the structure of Ryan Pevnick's argument in *Immigration and the Constraints of Justice: Between Open Borders and Absolute Sovereignty* (Cambridge: Cambridge University Press, 2011), where he folds democratic rights into justice.

13. Chapter 8 of Miller's *National Responsibility and Global Justice* is intriguingly entitled 'Immigration and Territorial Rights'. It sets out his account of immigration and the main issues but it pre-dates most of his work on territory and territorial rights.

14. See Seglow, *Defending Associative Duties*, chapter 2.

15. See here Abizadeh's opening premise in 'Democratic Theory and Border Coercion', 37–38.

16. Simmons, 'On the Territorial Rights of States', 300.

17. Anna Stilz has objected to a tight connection between jurisdictional authority and immigration rules and policies. She has argued that we can't imply control over immigration from the territorial right of jurisdiction, and she cites as evidence for the lack of entailment cases where states have some jurisdictional authority but where the authority does not extend to control of immigration (Ontario has no immigration controls against Quebec, for example). Annie Stilz, 'The Exclusion Project', paper given to the American Political Science Association meeting, Toronto, Ontario, 2–5 September 2009. However, as it stands, this point confuses the level of authority with the particular power. In all federal systems, power can be divided in different ways—so that the federal government might have control over currency, foreign policy, and defence, but perhaps not over education and health (as is the case in Canada). However, this doesn't mean that there's no relationship between jurisdictional authority and the power in question, only that jurisdictional authority is divided and multi-tiered. Second, Stilz's example fails to distinguish jurisdictional authority from the decision to exercise the power. Just because a country, or unit, chooses not to exercise its power, its authority, doesn't mean that it doesn't have it, just as the fact that China doesn't monitor its food (properly or at all) doesn't mean that it shouldn't, or doesn't have the power. I am indebted to Tristan Rogers for this example.

18. Caleb Yong, *Justice, Legitimacy and Movement across Borders*, PhD diss., Oxford University, 2014; Caleb Yong, 'Selecting Immigrants', unpublished manuscript, 2014.

19. See here Iris Marion Young, 'Self-Determination as Non-Domination: Ideas Applied to Israel/Palestine', *Ethnicities*, vol. 5 no. 2 (2005), 139–159; and Iris Marion Young, *Global Challenges: War, Self Determination and Responsibility for Justice* (Cambridge, UK: Polity).

20. As Pettit argued, domination exists when the relationship between two agents is such that one agent is subject to arbitrary interference, or to the constant threat of arbitrary interference, by another agent. Philip Pettit, *Republicanism: A Theory of Freedom and Government* (Oxford: Oxford University Press, 1997).

21. For background on the Canadian case, I have been aided by Ian McKay, 'The Liberal Order Framework: A Prospectus for a Reconnaissance of Canadian History', *Canadian Historical Review*, vol. 81, no. 4 (2000), 617–645; Michel Ducharme and Jean-François Constant, *Liberalism and Hegemony: Debating the Canadian Liberal Revolution* (Toronto: University of Toronto Press, 2009); Andrew Smith, 'Toryism, Classical Liberalism, and Capitalism: The Politics of Taxation and the Struggle for Canadian Confederation' *Canadian Historical Review*, vol. 89, no. 1 (2008), 1–25; and Janet Ajzensat, *The Canadian Founding: John Locke and Parliament* (Montreal: McGill-Queen's University Press, 2007).

22. Michael Blake, 'Distributive Justice, State Coercion, and Autonomy', *Philosophy & Public Affairs*, vol. 30, no. 3 (2001), 257–296; Thomas Nagel, 'The Problem of Global Justice', *Philosophy & Public Affairs*, vol. 33, no. 2 (2005), 113–147; and Andrea Sangiovanni, 'Global Justice, Reciprocity, and the State', *Philosophy & Public Affairs*, vol. 35, no. 1 (2007), 3–39.

23. I am grateful to Caleb Yong for this point.

24. Christopher Heath Wellman, 'Immigration and Freedom of Association', *Ethics*, vol. 119, no.1 (2008), 109–141. See also Christopher Heath Wellman and Phillip Cole, *Debating the Ethics of Immigration: Is There a Right to Exclude?* (Oxford: Oxford University Press, 2011).
25. This is compatible with the view that all individuals need to be members of *some* system of social and political cooperation to meet their basic needs. There is a good moral reason to ensure that all persons have access to membership in some (minimally just) system of social and political cooperation. But this is compatible with the claim that we do not have to enter into this relationship with particular others simply according to their choice.
26. Joseph H. Carens, 'Open Borders and the Claims of Community', paper given at the American Political Science Association meeting, Toronto, Ontario, 2–5 September 2009; also see Carens, *Ethics of Immigration*, 327.
27. Carens, *Ethics of Immigration*, 227.
28. Charles Taylor, 'What's Wrong with Negative Liberty', in *Philosophical Papers*, vol. 2, *Philosophy and the Human Sciences*, 211–229 (Cambridge: Cambridge University Press, 1985).
29. Joseph Raz, *The Morality of Freedom* (Oxford: Oxford University Press, 1986).
30. This point is made by David Miller, 'Immigration: The Case for Limits', in Andrew I. Cohen and Christopher H. Wellman, eds, *Contemporary Debates in Applied Ethics*, 193–206 (London: Wiley-Blackwell, 2005). There he considers three arguments that purport to justify unlimited migration, the first of which is for a general right to freedom of movement and claims that this must include the freedom to move into, and take up residence in, states other than one's own. This Miller denies because he claims that the physical extent of that right is limited—that liberal societies in general offer their members sufficient freedom of movement to protect the interest in freedom of movement. For views of autonomy consistent with the sufficientarian account of freedom of movement, see Blake, 'Distributive Justice, State Coercion, and Autonomy'; Gerald Dworkin, 'Is More Choice better than less?' *Midwest Studies in Philosophy*, vol. 7 (1982), 47–61; Thomas Scanlon, 'The Significance of Choice', in Sterling M. McMurrin, ed., *The Tanner Lectures on Human Values*, vol. 8, 149–216 (Cambridge: Cambridge University Press, 2011).
31. I write 'additional' because it is simply a standard liberal view that exit should not be restricted. However, since the argument I gave in my discussion of the occupancy principle—about the desirability of control of the context in which people live together—could be applied to both entry and exit, it is worth clarifying the reasons why control over exit is not being considered.
32. Carens, 'Open Borders and the Claims of Community', 10. He makes the same point, somewhat less succinctly, in Carens, *Ethics of Immigration*, 234.
33. For a stark, possibly hyperbolic statement of this kind, consider Putnam's claim about the importance of remittances (and technology transfer). Putnam writes: 'So powerful is this effect that despite "brain drain" costs, increasing annual northward immigration by only three percentage points might produce net benefits greater than meeting all our national targets for development assistance *plus* cancelling all Third World debt *plus* abolishing all barriers to Third World trade'; Robert D. Putnam, 'E Pluribus Unum: Diversity and Community in the Twenty-First Century: The 2006 Johan Skytte Prize Lecture', *Scandinavian Political Studies*, vol. 30, no. 2 (2007), 137–174, at 141.
34. Technically, Shue does not refer to 'human rights' but to a moral minimum conception, defined as, 'the least that every person can demand and the least that every person, every government and every corporation must be made to do'; Shue, *Basic Rights*, 19.
35. A 'refugee' is defined as a person who, 'owing to well-founded fear of being persecuted for reasons of race, religion, nationality, membership of a particular social group or political opinion, is outside the country of his nationality and is unable or, owing to such fear, is unwilling to avail himself of the protection of that country; or who, not having a nationality and being outside the country of his former habitual residence as a result of such events, is unable or, owing to such fear, is unwilling to return to it'; UNHCR, *Convention and Protocol Relating to the Status of Refugees* (1951), art. 1a: http://www.unhcr.org/3b66c2aa10.html.

36. Gianfranco Pellegrino, 'Climate Refugees: A Case for Protection', in Marcello Di Paola and Gianfranco Pellegrino, eds, *Canned Heat: Ethics and Politics of Global Climate Change*, 193–209 (London: Routledge, 2014); Mathias Risse, 'The Right to Relocation: Disappearing Island Nations and Common Ownership of the Earth', *Ethics & International Affairs*, vol. 23, no. 3 (2009), 281–300; and Avery Kolers, 'Floating Provisos and Sinking Islands', *Journal of Applied Philosophy*, vol. 29, no. 4 (2012), 333–343.
37. IPCC. 'Summary for Policymakers', in Thomas F. Stocker et al., eds, *Climate Change 2013: The Physical Science Basis. Contribution of Working Group I to the Fifth Assessment Report of the Intergovernmental Panel on Climate Change* (Cambridge: Cambridge University Press, 2013); Cleo Paskal, *Global Warring: How Environmental, Economic and Political Crises Will Redraw the World Map* (New York and London: Palgrave Macmillan, 2010); and Alexander Gillespie, 'Small Island States in the Face of Climatic Change: The End of the Line in International Environmental Responsibility', *UCLA Journal of Environmental Law and Policy*, vol. 22, no. 1 (2009), 107–129.
38. Risse, 'Right to Relocation', 281–282.
39. This is, though, a good reason why human-induced climate change needs to be addressed more effectively now—but that is a different book.
40. Devesh Kapur and John McHale, 'Should a Cosmopolitan Worry about the "Brain Drain"?', *Ethics & International Affairs*, vol. 20, no. 3 (2006), 305–320, at 307.
41. Kapur and McHale, 'Should a Cosmopolitan Worry?', 307.
42. Kapur and McHale, 'Should a Cosmopolitan Worry?', 308.
43. This is a mistake I think in Anna Stilz's thought-provoking paper on immigration. Stilz argues that permissive immigration may be bad for the world's worst off: she points out that women with dependents, the aged, and the ill would be less mobile, and less likely to migrate to a new country, and she draws on empirical evidence about the brain drain to show the likely effects in sending societies. However, I think she makes the mistake of incorrectly extrapolating from current data about immigration effects (on sending societies) to their effects under a much different sets of institutional arrangements; Stilz, 'Exclusion Project'.
44. An objection could be raised that compensation wouldn't help the country that is missing nurses and doctors, but I think this is not true. Compensation that is aimed at providing clinics and paying health care staff competitive rates (competitive with the lure of employment abroad) would help stem the tide.
45. Robert E. Goodin, 'If People were Money . . .', in Brian Barry and Robert E. Goodin, eds, *Free Movement: Ethical Issues in the Transnational Migration of Peoples and of Money*, 6–22 (University Park: Penn State Press, 1992), 9.

10

The Right to Territorial Integrity and the Legitimacy of the Use of Force

This chapter discusses one of the most significant practical entailments of the theory of territory defended in this book. This book—and particularly chapters 3, 6, 7, and 8—advanced arguments addressing the question: how should territorial claims be adjudicated? In this chapter, I consider cases where the principles advanced here have not been complied with. The question that is raised in this case is: under what circumstances can *force* be used to put things right? I argue in this chapter that not every territorial injustice justifies the use of force, but some do.

I approach this issue by considering the idea of *territorial integrity*. The principle of territorial integrity—or the right to territorial integrity that is possessed by states (or, on legitimate-state theory, by legitimate states)—has been invoked in three kinds of cases: to prohibit unilateral secession; to prohibit border changes, and to prohibit the use of force by one state to acquire the territory of another state, which is defined as an act of aggression.

The chapter proceeds by discussing in very general terms the legitimate use of force as this applies to territorial rights and to self-determination, drawing mainly on standard arguments in just-war theory. I discuss how my theory justifies the defensive rights of states, and then the implications for more controversial cases which pertain to the legitimacy of force being used where the territorial integrity of a state is attacked or needs to be defended. I show that the collectivist (but non-statist) argument that I've developed for thinking about territorial rights leads to a revisionist account of the legitimate use of force in cases where the territorial integrity of the state is at stake. These revisions flow from two aspects of my argument. First, on my theory, the right to territory is held by a collective entity, the people, which may or may not be co-extensive with the state; this yields a more fluid and variegated approach to territory than we find in the literature on international law or international relations. Second, the moral value that underlies this right is the self-determination of political communities, which sets my approach apart from the individualism of most theorizing about war.

I begin this chapter by examining the standard case, which is the right of the state to defend itself, and particularly to defend its territory. I link defensive rights with the self-determination of political communities, while trying to avoid the statist assumption that the territorial integrity of the state is a good in itself. I suggest that, even in this standard case, the argument developed here yields different and illuminating results. I then move to other cases which raise the issue of how we understand the role of territorial integrity in the international community of states, and the use of force either to defend or breach it. I consider more contentious cases, asking and answering the questions of what my theory says about: (1) military force used to regain territory or territorial rights, and I discuss in this context the German remilitarization of the Rhineland in 1936; (2) annexing territory that contains a majority of people who identify with your state, such as the Russian Federation's recent annexation of Crimea; (3) force used by secessionists to break up an existing territorial state, as in the Eritrean war of independence; (4) force used by a majority against the secessionists, such as that used by the Ukrainian government to combat separatists in the Crimea or the Eastern Ukraine; (5) outside intervention in a state that arguably contains two or more disparate communities, resulting in break-up of the state, for example the Kurdish area in the north of Iraq. I spell out how my self-determination argument for the territorial rights of peoples would deal with each of these cases.

I have dealt with some related issues already, particularly in the chapters on secession and border change (chapter 6) and on corrective justice as it applies to stolen land and the right of return (chapter 7). However, the focus of this chapter is somewhat different, because it raises the more specific issue of the legitimate use of force.

10.1. Just Cause in War

In this section, I develop an account of the justified use of force that agrees with many of the central contentions of just-war theory, and especially the requirement that a necessary condition for fighting a just war is that the war must be fought with a just cause. Unless there is a just cause, the resort to military force is wrong. Of course, even if the war is fought with just cause, it may fail other requirements of justice: it may be fought in an unjust way, for example by failing to respect the fundamental distinction between combatants and non-combatants or by involving a disproportionate response to a particular event. The focus of most work in just-war theory until quite recently has been on the question of what counts as a just cause.[1] A long line of theorists stretching from Grotius to Fabre and McMahan agree that for a state to have a just cause to use force, a serious wrong must have been committed, or (on some accounts) is about to be committed, to which the use of force is a response.

What counts as a serious wrong that might justify the use of force? Jeff McMahan, who has developed an influential contemporary account of just war, identifies two substantive independent just causes of war: resisting aggression and preventing major humanitarian crimes perpetrated by a government against its citizens. Other possible reasons—forcibly disarming an aggressor, deterring future aggression, and preventing lesser humanitarian crimes—do not, for McMahan, count as just causes, but do contribute to war's justification and are deployed when considering whether a war is proportionate.[2] There is no territorial element in this justification of just war, other than the assumption that the territorial boundaries of another state should be breached only in defence of one's territory or to prevent a humanitarian crisis. There is no discussion of the relationship between territory and people who are not already institutionally organized in a state, and little attention is devoted to the possibility of the legitimate use of force in contexts that do not count as war between conventional actors (state armies).

I agree with many of these central claims: that self-defence against wrongful attack is justified; that war should be pursued only as a last resort; that the act of war must satisfy the proportionality and discrimination requirements (meaning that it should not involve a disproportionate response to a particular event and that reasonable care should be taken to minimize harm, especially to non-combatants). In what follows, I apply this account of justified use of force to see what is implied when territorial integrity is at issue; and, following Allen Buchanan, I focus not simply on an objective justification of the morality of war, but on the appropriate rules, policies, and practices surrounding war.[3] I aim therefore to provide normative criteria to assess the rules, policies, and practices that we take to be directly action-guiding for leaders, for combatants, and for ordinary people in assessing the legitimacy of the use of force.

10.2. The Standard Case: Defensive War

The current international order is characterized by a clear prohibition on aggressive warfare that links aggression with the violation of the territorial integrity of the state. The United Nations Charter specifies that all members should 'refrain in their international relations from the threat or use of force against the territorial integrity or political independence of any state'.[4] This article rules out in principle military means as an instrument of state policy. At the same time the UN Charter, article 51, permits rights to national defence: 'Nothing in the present Charter shall impair the inherent right of individual or collective self-defence if an armed attack occurs against a member of the United Nations', although with the caveat that the exercise of this right should be delayed 'until the Security Council has taken measures necessary to maintain international peace and security'. If a foreign state threatens the political sovereignty or territorial integrity of a state through armed invasion, the state that is being attacked has a right in international law to defend itself.

It is not only international law that endorses the state's right to defend itself. This view is widely held, pacifists excepted. In spite of this near consensus on a right of self-defence (in war), it is difficult for individualist liberals to defend this intuition. Historically, the state's right of self-defence was justified by analogy with, or as an extension of, the right of individual self-defence. Prominent thinkers writing on just war have concurred: Michael Walzer argues that the right of a polity to go to war in its own defence is 'the collective form' of the right enjoyed by individual members to defend themselves against violations of their rights to life and liberty.[5] It is relatively unproblematic to understand that individual persons have a right to defend themselves from aggression: that, in the face of attack, they have a right to defend themselves through violent means. If we think of the defensive rights of the attacked state as an amalgam of the defensive personal rights of individuals living within the attacked state, then an attack by one sovereign state on another state is at the same time an attack on the rights—lives and liberties—of individual persons living within the threatened state. This way of conceiving of defensive warfare views war primarily as a relation between individuals. It conceives of defensive war, Rodin emphasizes, as 'an application, *en masse*, of the familiar right of individuals to protect themselves and others from unjust lethal attack'.[6]

This view has a number of advantages, but the principal one is that it is consonant with much individualist and rights-based contemporary political philosophy, and straightforwardly roots defensive war in the value of the lives of individual persons. It identifies the problem with aggressive war in the fact that it threatens the personal lives of many people in the state that is attacked. On this view, defensive war is justified by appeal to the familiar idea of individual rights.

Alternatively, we could say—somewhat more mysteriously—that defensive rights in war are not an amalgam of many individual defensive rights but they are *analogous* with them: just as someone can respond to an armed attack against her person with force, including lethal force, if that is proportionate to the threat involved, so can the people, viewed collectively, as members of the state.

Recently, however, we have been given good reasons to question the relationship between defensive rights in war and the self-defence rights of the individual. In his persuasive book, David Rodin has considered at length the view that defensive rights to war are reducible to individual self-defence or analogous with it, and found them wanting. First, Rodin argues that the liberties enjoyed by soldiers of a defending state go beyond what is justified in terms of a personal right of self-defence. Specifically, soldiers fighting a defensive war are permitted to use violence against soldiers even when they pose no imminent threat, and this condition does not obtain in cases of personal defensive rights.[7] In particular, individuals are not justified in using lethal force to defend their backyard against trespassers (who violate their property rights) but an attack on any part of the territory of the state constitutes an act of aggression which can be met by lethal force.

Second, the requirement of necessity in the personal case generates a requirement for threatened persons to retreat if it is possible to avoid harm. However, if this is used as an analogy for the case of national self-defence, it would give rise to a general duty to appease aggression and this is not how the right of national defence is normally understood.

Third, and related to the above point, Rodin discusses what he calls 'the argument from bloodless invasion', where an aggressor attacks a piece of land, which leads to no loss of life, as long as the defending country does not invoke its right to defend. This is meant to show that the end of 'defending the lives of citizens is not a necessary condition of national-defense'. As Rodin writes: 'The right of national-defense is effective in international law in the face of attacks against a state's "territorial integrity or political independence", but this condition is both logically and factually independent of the question of whether the lives of individual citizens within the state are threatened.'[8] I believe this provides decisive grounds for rejecting the individualist account of the state's right to defend itself against attack.

At the heart of the argument of this book is the idea that there are good reasons why political decisions should be made by the community through its institutions, and that this involves political communities making decisions, negotiating their collective lives, within their territory, without external coercive intervention. I do not regard the right of self-defence as a separate territorial right, which is how I considered the right to control immigration (chapter 9) or the right to control resources (chapter 8). Rather, I take it that, if the argument that I've advanced in this book goes through—that people, through their political institutions, have rights to exercise jurisdictional authority and control resources and immigration over their territory, within the limits of justice—then they have a right to defend themselves in the exercise of these rights. The right of defence is a second-order right, and it is held by political communities and justified in terms of the moral value of these communities.

In this book, I linked the value of political communities with the self-determination of peoples, and this implies an account of the just international order, which is concerned with the structural relations of power in the international order and the capacity of people within this system to be collectively self-governing. On my view, defensive rights in war are justified because they are necessary to defend this system of collectively self-determining political communities, which embody the good of collective self-determination. The justification that I've offered for a right of national defence, rooted in institutional morality, can explain why attack on territory alone, where no one is killed, is problematic: if we do not permit defence against purely political aggression, then *all peoples are vulnerable.* If we are not permitted to fight back against aggression, then all peoples are at risk of having their collective self-determination undermined, and we will live in an institutional order characterized by relations of domination and subordination. My argument, which justifies killing even when the threat is only against territory, is not an argument typically deployed in interpersonal morality, but it makes sense when we adopt the lens of institutional morality. While it is not usually the case that we can infringe people's rights for the greater good in interpersonal morality, it does make sense to design institutions that realize fundamental moral values and to try to do so in ways that minimize perverse effects. In my view, then, defence against attack on territory, even if the aggression is purely political, is justified as a lesser evil.

This raises three general questions (or worries) that could be asked of my account. (1) Does this account mean that there is no right of national defence when the state does not represent a people? (2) Does it mean that there is no right of national defence when the state encompasses several peoples? (3) What does this account imply with respect to people who are seeking to secure their self-determination against a state?

To address the first two concerns (the third will be addressed at length in section 10.3.3), there are two reasons why we should be extremely cautious about licensing foreign aggression against *any* state, both of which rest on the desirability of precautionary principles in institutional design. The first is that it is sometimes difficult to ascertain whether a particular state does or does not have a political community (whether it represents one itself or whether there is a 'people' trapped in the state, longing for self-determination), and difficult also for outsiders (or even insiders!) to be certain about the extent or depth of motivation for self-determination, or whether liberation movements do in fact represent the desires and aspirations of the people that they claim to represent, or whether their preferred picture is supported only by some of the relevant population.[9]

Second, even if we suspect that the state does *not* represent a political community, that no one identifies with the state, but that it is viewed as an agent of control rather than self-determination, it does not follow that outside states should be permitted to attack it with impunity. There should be a high bar of justification for armed intervention, especially to achieve, or aid others in achieving, a purely political goal, because intervention involves the predictable killing, not only of soldiers on both sides but of civilians too, even when they are not targeted. A general prohibition on foreign aggression is a very good institutional rule, aimed at limiting military action. Moreover, and perhaps decisively for a consequentialist understanding of these rules, a too permissive rule about intervention may enable unjust states to use 'liberation' as a pretext for establishing their own forms of control within the territory of the state, and thereby deny internal forms of self-determination. More will be said about such cases below (particularly in section 10.3.5).

10.3. More Complicated Cases than Simple Defence against Aggression

In the standard case of a state defending itself on territory that it legitimately occupies, my conclusions and those of the principal theorists in the just-war tradition agree; but we disagree on the argument that justifies the right of self-defence. Indeed, I claimed above that my argument offers a better explanation of the right of self-defence than can be provided by individualist arguments. However, the justification that I've offered for self-defence rights has different implications (from the standard argument for defensive rights) in a number of contested cases, all connected to the fact that, on my argument, the fundamental holder of territorial rights—and thereby the right to defend these rights—is the people, not the state.

In this section, I consider the implications of my account in five cases that are either relatively recent or contemporary. These are all cases which bear on the justified use of force to defend or breach the territorial integrity of states, and three of the examples (Crimea and Ukraine, Eritrea and Ethiopia, Kurdistan and Iraq) bear on the third worry—what the account implies for people who seek to secure self-determination against the state.

10.3.1. Military Force to Regain Territory and/or Territorial Rights that Were Previously Held

First let us consider the legitimacy of using military force in cases where the political community once had jurisdictional control over an area, and other associated territorial rights, and uses force to regain them.

In order to address this issue, it is necessary to specify in more detail the normatively relevant context, including which territorial rights have been violated, and how this interacts with the complex principles generally accepted in just-war theory. One kind of case that falls under this rubric is where rights of residency or occupancy have been violated. Here I am thinking about cases where the loss of territorial rights came about by the wholesale expulsion of large numbers of people in the political community in the area in question. I've argued earlier in the book that individuals have rights of residency and groups have rights of occupancy, and that they also have a right to return to the area if they have been expelled or have had to flee to avoid fighting. The use of force to regain these rights, and enforce a right of return, is justified (represents a just cause), because it is in response to a serious wrong.

I also argued in chapters 3 and 7 that the rights of residency and occupancy are temporally limited. Rights that are grounded in considerations of people's place-related attachments and projects develop over time, which in turn suggests that the strength of the right will fade over time as people are no longer resident in the area and learn to make choices and develop relationships and attachments in a new context. Because time affects both the right of residency and the right of return, it can affect the justice of the cause and will have bearing on other considerations too, such as the proportionality principle, which asks us to ensure that the violence and suffering caused by war is proportionate to the good realized. The proportionality requirement will be harder to realize over time, since the person's interest in residency or occupancy and the good achieved will diminish over time. In cases of recent expulsion, then, it is relatively unproblematic to justify military force to ensure that individuals and people's rights of return are respected. Indeed, if it is soon after the expulsion itself, it may not be the beginning of the war, but a continuation of it.

What about a case where the people remain in the area and individual and group rights of residency and occupancy are respected, but the people are not permitted to be politically self-determining as a group? I described the right to be self-determining over a particular area as a kind of territorial right. I consider this kind of case in section 10.3.3.

What about a case where the group remains in residency or occupancy of the territory, with some rights of local jurisdiction, but past behaviour has been used as a justification to strip the political community of some of its territorial rights? This is the case of Germans in the Rhineland prior to 1937: according to the terms of the Locarno Treaties and Treaty of Versailles, the area west of the Rhine River and a small strip to the east (which together are known as the Rhineland) could not have any German military presence. The makers of the Treaty of Versailles included this stipulation to insure against further German aggression. Their argument was that prior aggressive war can lead to a state having forfeited some rights that we normally associate with rightful control over territory, such as the right to exclude foreign troops from its territory. At this point, let us set aside the question of whether the terms of the Versailles Treaty constituted 'victor's justice'—an unjustly punitive response to the act of aggression committed by Germany in the First World War.[10] The question at issue is whether, independently of Germany's having ratified the Locarno and Versailles treaties, it is possible for a state, through its bad behaviour, to lose its right to exclude military personnel from its territory. The answer to this question bears on the question of whether the German reoccupation of the Rhineland on 7 March 1936, in violation of these two treaties, could be justified.

There is no doubt that the Rhineland was historically, imaginatively, and relationally within the German heartland. This was not disputed, even at the time. As Lord Lothian (in)famously said in a British parliamentary debate shortly after Germany sent troops into the area: Germany was doing no more than walking into its own backyard. However, the question we are asking is not simply: who has territorial rights there? It is the more complex question: what justifies the use of force in this case?

I have erected an argument for territorial rights in terms of self-determination, and the right to defend those rights through military force. This does not however justify a political community doing anything it pleases in the name of self-determination. First, there is a particularly high bar to the use of coercive force, since it involves killing combatants and (predictably) non-combatants. Second, since the argument applies generally to all peoples in the exercise of their self-determination, it implies duties to uphold the system of self-determining states, each exercising jurisdiction over its specific domain and location. It justifies, that is, a system of self-determining entities, committed to maintaining peace, respecting basic human rights, and ensuring that everyone can be a member of a system of political cooperation, grounded in relations of reciprocity and community. The same argument—in terms of the self-determination of territorially distinct political communities—that justifies exclusive jurisdiction also grounds the rules of non-aggression and respect for other peoples' self-determination. It seems reasonable therefore that a country could, through bad behaviour, lose the right to defend itself; lose its right to station troops on its own territory, precisely because other peoples, other territorial right-holders, rightly worry that this is a first step towards aggression and a threat to the system of peace that they have established.[11] In principle, then, the argument that I've developed could certainly accept that past action, and the evidence that it provides about future aggressive attacks, can justify demilitarization of an area. It is doubtful whether it could justify *permanent* demilitarization, which seems disproportionate and punitive, especially because, if the concern about future aggression is based on past aggressive acts, these concerns should diminish over time, whose passing may lead to peaceful and reciprocal cooperation. However, temporary demilitarized status seems justifiable.

The Nazi remilitarization of the Rhineland also failed the requirement of last resort. Even if the Nazi government was not reconciled to its status, they had good reasons to think that at some point in the future it would be possible to change it. The British foreign secretary, Sir Anthony Eden, stated in February 1936 that the British government sought an agreement on an air pact that would outlaw bombing, and that Britain would consider revising the Versailles and Locarno agreements in directions that Germany wanted, including revisiting the demilitarized status of the Rhineland, if, in return, Germany would agree to such a pact. But no substantive negotiations took place: less than a month after this communication, Germany sent its troops into the Rhineland. With nineteen infantry battalions and a small amount of air cover, the German army crossed the border into the Rhineland area.

The German occupation also violated the requirement of proportionality. This may seem an odd statement, since the remilitarization itself did not produce violence (although it may have set the stage for later violence). But since this was a major violation of a treaty, it had the potential to start another war. That it did not was due mainly to French psychological unwillingness, not lack of military readiness: indeed, the French were in a relatively strong position to enforce the terms of the treaties against the Germans. The Nazi regime, which initiated the crisis, knew that it risked war, and this was merely to achieve, on the best reading, a popular public policy aim.

In short, while my theory does recognize that the territorial rights over that region ultimately resided with the German people, the specific rights in question (right to defend the territory, rights to exclude foreign troops from the territory) could be forfeited by a violation of the laws of international society, which themselves are justified by their role in securing a world of peaceful, self-determining entities.

10.3.2. Annexation of Territory that Contains a Majority of People who Identify with Your State

Since, on my theory, the state holds territorial right on behalf of the people, and the people are defined without recourse to existing political boundaries, the two may not coincide. One such case is the annexation of territory that contains a majority of people who identify with the annexing state. Annexation is usually thought to be a violation of the territorial integrity of the state and, in international law, it represents an act of aggression that threatens the peace and security of the world.

But should we view this kind of case in these statist terms? After all, if the state is merely the vehicle for the people's self-determination, and there are relationships and attachments that bind the people together, then shouldn't we respect these sentiments and relationships and organize our institutions in such a way that they recognize these aspirations for self-determination and this shared collective identity?

There are conflicting views about how we should interpret this kind of annexation and the normative weight that we should give to the fact that many people residing on the territory want to be part of the neighbouring state. If they welcome the sovereignty of the other state, in what sense is the other state annexing it? The claim about illegal annexation suggests that the territory properly 'belongs' to the previous state, but that is exactly what is in question once we no longer hold the view that the relationship between the state and territory is one of ownership but instead should in some way incorporate the aspirations and identities of the people living on the territory.

In order to consider the complex issues raised, I will discuss the case of the Russian annexation of the Crimea in 2014. Some background is in order. The Crimean peninsula was annexed initially to the Russian Empire in 1783, and was part of Russia, and then the Russian part of the Soviet Union (the RSFSR) until 1954, when it was transferred to the Ukrainian Soviet Socialist Republic, and it remained part of Ukraine when the Soviet Union fell apart. The population comprises a narrow Russian majority (60 percent) and significant Ukrainian (24 percent) and Tatar (indigenous; 10 percent) populations. From a detached perspective,[12] considering only the plural identities and relationships within the peninsula, it seems that it would have been equally acceptable for Crimea to be (1) an autonomous region within Ukraine, with significant protections and autonomy for its Russian and Tatar populations (as well as cross-border links to Russia), or (2) an autonomous region within Russia, with significant protections and autonomy for its Ukrainian and Tatar populations (as well as cross-border links to the Ukraine). Moreover, Ukraine had been, since independence, an extremely fragile state, both enormously corrupt and incompetent, as well as marked by serious division—between its largely Catholic, Ukrainian-speaking, and pro-Western west and its Orthodox, Russian-speaking, and pro-Russian east—with every election result since independence following this basic division. If, at independence, there was support for remaining within Ukraine, it masked deep divisions on how the different groups within Ukraine saw the future of an independent Ukraine, whether as a country friendly with Russia, and part of a kind of Slavic alliance, or a country that looked towards Europe and the West.

In 2014, following a constitutional crisis in Ukraine in which the pro-Russian government led by the president, Viktor Yanukovych, was

deposed—not through constitutional means, though with ample moral justification[13]—the interim government took a number of steps which were hostile
to the Russians of Crimea (and eastern Ukraine): for example, the Ukrainian
parliament voted to revoke the official status of the Russian language (though
the new interim president refused to sign it into law), and it also indicated a
desire that Ukraine move closer to the West. Pro-Russian forces responded by
taking control of the Crimean peninsula. Armed men occupied the Crimean
parliament; the parliament called for a referendum on joining Russia, which,
by an overwhelming margin (96.77 percent, though with many Ukrainians
and Tatars abstaining), voted in favour of jointing Russia. The Ukrainian parliament claimed that Crimea was an illegally occupied territory. The United
Nations General Assembly (but not the Security Council, for obvious reasons)
passed a resolution that declared the occupation of the Crimean peninsula illegal. On 21 March 2014 Russian president Putin signed a treaty with the parliament of Crimea, formally incorporating Crimea into Russia.[14]

People are likely to respond in different ways to this case. On the one hand,
some will think that the constitutional direction of a country, and indeed what
country the territory should be part of, should be decided by the people living there. This is assumed in the Canadian constitutional landscape, where
it is accepted that the future of Quebec should be decided by the Québécois,
though the terms of that divergent future would have to be negotiated with
the rest of Canada. Similarly, in the United Kingdom, it was accepted that
Scotland's constitutional status should be decided by people living on the territory of Scotland. Against this, many in the West invoked international law
to condemn the violation of Ukraine's territorial integrity—and these voices
included the United States, which had in the previous ten years repeatedly
violated different aspects of international law.[15] These contradictory impulses
raise the question: why shouldn't the Crimean people be able to decide their
own political and constitutional future, just as the Scots or the Québécois are
entitled to do? Isn't the reference to international law unprincipled, in the sense
that it is invoked when the government in question likes what it requires, but
ignored when it doesn't? We need to move beyond the invocation of abstract
principles like 'protect the territorial integrity of the Ukraine' or 'the people
should decide' and attend to why we might be inclined to support the principle that Scotland should decide its future, but be nervous about the process in
Crimea.

The argument of this book suggests that the future of the Crimean peninsula should rest with the people living in Crimea, although, as I emphasized
in chapter 6, in many such cases, the best solution would involve autonomy,
links with the other community, power-sharing, and other more imaginative
arrangements, designed to reflect the plural identities and relationships in the

region, which are not reflected by a dichotomous pro-Russian or pro-Ukrainian sovereignty. If we think that Crimea is internally diverse, with different internal communities and identities, there are two possible autonomy-based solutions, within Russia and within Ukraine.[16] If they are equally good, there is no case for military force to initiate change. Suppose though that inclusion in Russia is preferable (say, that's what the majority of Crimeans prefer), but the status quo is effective autonomy (non-exclusive jurisdiction) within Ukraine, the protection of language rights, and substantial links between Crimea and Russia to give institutional recognition to this relationship. In that case, while in some sense Crimea should decide, and should be permitted to decide, Russia would not be justified in using force to bring about that outcome (because there is already an adequate degree of self-determination). As it turned out, however, the Ukraine government was both corrupt and incompetent, and was not offering the Russian-speaking population in Crimea substantial protections of their identity, and, it was feared, was jeopardizing its links to Russia.

10.3.3. Armed Force Used by Secessionists to Break up an Existing Territorial State

In this section, I consider whether secessionists are justified in using armed force to break up an existing state. This is an important issue: violence is regularly used by secessionists to realize their ends, as occurred in the United Kingdom when the Irish Republic seceded; and in many other, more recent cases, such as the Kurds of Turkey and Iraq, Tamils of Sri Lanka, Moros of the Philippines, and the South Sudanese in Sudan. To consider this kind of case—which is typically called 'secession' if one is hostile and 'national liberation' if one is not—I will consider how the argument developed thus far applies to cases like Eritrea, which fought a protracted war in order to secede from Ethiopia.

Italy, the former colonial power, occupied Eritrea from 1859 until 1941, at which point British forces defeated Italy in Eritrea, and Eritrea was governed by the British as an occupying power and then in a trustee relationship under the auspices of the United Nations from 1949. The trusteeship relationship was understood as temporary, and different external powers had different views about who should ultimately 'get' Eritrea. The Russians argued that it should be returned to Italy (which they expected might turn communist); Ethiopia thought it should be joined to it; Arab countries argued for an independent state, which would be majority Muslim; and the Americans sided with Ethiopia to federate Eritrea with Ethiopia, in order to reward Ethiopia for its support during the war. As for the Eritreans themselves, the representatives, organized into the Independence Bloc of Eritrean Parties, repeatedly argued

that a referendum should be held to settle the question of Eritrean sovereignty.[17] In the end, Great Power interests held sway. As the American ambassador to the United Nations, John Foster Dulles, remarked, 'From the point of
view of justice, the opinions of the Eritrean people must receive consideration.
Nevertheless, the strategic interest of the United States in the Red Sea basin
and the considerations of security and world peace make it necessary that the
country ... be linked with our ally Ethiopia'.[18] In 1952 Eritrea was assigned by
the UN to Ethiopia, with no consultation with the Eritrean people and little
regard for their aims, aspirations, and distinctiveness.

In 1962 Ethiopia abolished the federal arrangement and extended the
Ethiopian empire across the country, in the process unilaterally revok-
ing Eritrean autonomy. The Eritrean People's Liberation Army was formed,
with support largely from Muslim and low-lying areas but gradually gaining
support across the country (and amongst Christians). What followed was a
thirty-year civil war, which involved death, destruction, and numerous atroci-
ties. In addition to the civil war, there were intra-Eritrean fighting amongst different liberation groups. In 1992 the armed liberation movement, the Eritrean
Peoples' Liberation Front (EPLF), captured the capital of Eritrea, Asmara, and
established a provisional government. This led the United Nations, with agreement from Ethiopia, to set a date for a referendum on Eritrean independence.
The proposal to secede was overwhelmingly supported by voters in all parts of
the country.

Was the Eritrean armed struggle justified? On the theory advanced here, the
Eritreans constituted a people who sought to be collectively self-determining
on their own territory. They met the conditions for peoplehood: they had a
shared identity, history, aspirations for collective self-determination, and were
in legitimate occupancy of land on which to be territorially self-governing.
Their rights of self-determination were being denied by being incorporated
into a state with which they did not identify and with whom they lacked
a pre-existing relationship structured by extensive cooperative practices.
Important powers in the international community, and Ethiopia itself, were to
blame too for failing to consider the aspirations and identities of the Eritrean
people when they drew borders and assigned them to a particular political
configuration without consulting them.

It is important, though, in considering the legitimacy of the use of force,
to distinguish between adequate self-determination and full or maximal self-
determination. The use of force has to meet a high bar of justification, and
the good achieved has to be significant in order to meet the proportionality
requirement (to justify the killing that inevitably follows). It's very difficult
to make proportionality calculations, so the usual solution is simply to insist
that war can be justified to resist aggression and to address the most egregious

human rights violations, such as genocide and ethnic cleansing, but not otherwise. Applying this standard, Eritrea was entitled to political self-determination, but had it been granted a significant degree of autonomy within Ethiopia, then the civil war would not have been justified despite the Eritreans' wish for an independent state. There is an additional good to be realized by opting for maximal autonomy, and exclusive jurisdiction, in contrast to non-exclusive jurisdiction over a territory in a federal (and power-sharing) arrangement. However, since sufficient autonomy was available to Eritrea, this additional good could not outweigh the terrible consequences that followed from initiating war. But once the autonomy provisions originally granted to Eritrea had been overridden, and Eritrea was absorbed into the Ethiopian empire, the calculation changed.

10.3.4. Military Force to Keep Countries Together: Ethiopia and Ukraine

In this section, I consider force used by a majority against secessionists, such as the Ukrainian government or the Ethiopian government, to combat separatists in the Crimea or Eritrea, respectively.

It follows from what I've argued so far that, if a 'people' is justified in using force to secure its right to self-determination, other people have a duty to refrain from interfering in the exercise of that right. This of course would remove the need of secessionists to exercise their right through force. I implied that Ethiopia should have respected the Eritrean aspiration for exclusive jurisdiction, should not have dismantled the federal system that allowed the Eritreans to exercise some self-determination over their own affairs, and should not have resisted with military force the subsequent Eritrean quest for self-determination. Ethiopia, I argued, is under a moral duty to facilitate Eritrean self-determination, just as Eritreans are morally required to respect Ethiopian self-determination on their own territory. It is incumbent on both sides to be willing to negotiate the central issues and the process by which this self-determination could be achieved.

Is Ukraine justified in using military force to deal with secessionists in Crimea or the Russian-speaking part of eastern Ukraine?[19] One important question is whether the secessionist group constitutes a 'people' in the relevant sense argued in chapter 3, and so is entitled to seek self-determination. Here we can distinguish between the claims of the Crimeans and of Russian-speakers in the eastern Ukraine. As I suggested in section 10.3.2, there is a long history of political relationships between Crimeans of all ethnic groups, and between Crimeans and both Russians and Ukrainians. This suggests that Crimeans were entitled to some form of autonomy status within that defined territory (the Crimean peninsula)—with forms of power-sharing, constitutional guarantees of their status, and links with people in the other communities—and that Ukraine was morally required to respect this, to ensure that these links and relationships were preserved, or to negotiate other links with them in the event that they sought to pursue their self-determination within Russia.

The situation of people in eastern Ukraine is less clear, and more problematic, in part because the conflict there is potentially more destabilizing: there is no clearly defined border in the eastern Ukraine, so there is an incentive for armed men (would-be secessionists) to create a border through political violence and ethnic cleansing, as happened in Bosnia in 1992–95. This is relevant to calculations about proportionality. At a less pragmatic, more normative level, it is doubtful whether the Russian speakers have a claim to be 'a people', with rights of self-determination. Unlike in Crimea, which has institutionalized self-government, and a long history of political relationships, there is no sustained identity and mobilization on the part of the Russian speakers in this part of the Ukraine, which suggests that they do not meet the criterion of being a people. For example, the 11 May 2014 referenda held in two towns in eastern Ukraine, Donetsk and Luhansk, do not provide empirical evidence to support the kind of strongly shared persistent aspirations to collective self-determination which marks 'peoplehood'. They were seriously procedurally flawed.[20] It was unclear how they defined the relevant domain to run the referenda. The referenda themselves were hastily organized, with no electoral rolls, no electoral commission, no independent observers, no voting lists; there were many reports of multiple voting, polling station irregularities, and a great deal of confusion about what voters were asked to endorse (some thought 'self-rule' implied more local governance and local forms of autonomy, some thought that this would lead to union with Russia).[21] If the residents of this area do not constitute a people entitled to exclusive jurisdiction, then the government in Kiev is not under a duty to respect their claims for maximal collective self-determination and so is morally entitled to use force in response. They are entitled to use force only as a last resort, by which I mean after pursuing compromises aimed at constitutional protection for the Russian speakers' language and identity and offering them non-exclusive jurisdictional control over local matters of concern to them.

10.3.5. Outside Intervention in Cases where Rights to Collective Self-Determination Are at Stake

If people have rights—individual human rights, individual rights of residency, group rights of occupancy, rights of collective self-determination, and other rights—the question arises: what should we do when these rights are violated by the state that is supposed to uphold them?[22] Is the use of force against other countries justified in order to protect rights?

This question arises in general form for all theorists of the morality of war. The standard justification for force in just-war theory accepts that its use may be necessary when the state is egregiously violating the most fundamental human rights. What these are, and how many people's rights have to be violated to justify external armed intervention, is a very contentious question. The specific question which I will pose and attempt to answer concerns the obligations of outsiders when rights of collective self-determination are violated. What does the argument of this book imply for outside intervention in a state that arguably contains two or more disparate communities, resulting in the break-up of the state, for example the invasion of Iraq, supposing it had been motivated by support for the Kurds?

To approach an answer to this question, it is worth reflecting on the kind of justification for force implicit in most relevant normative theories and my account of territorial rights. First, let's consider third-party duties with respect to failed states. On my argument, people can fail to have their rights respected, not only by living in a state that violates them but by living in a state that cannot protect them. I've argued that this is a problem, and that if a people aspire to be collectively self-determining on territory that they legitimately occupy, other peoples have duties to help them create and maintain propitious conditions for their own self-determination, to develop their institutional capacity, and perhaps improve the technological and communication links that are central to effective governance. There is a third party duty to assist people living in failed states to have an effective vehicle for their own self-determination. This can give rise to a duty of intervention, but it is extremely constrained. It is limited both temporally and in its goals: it should be for only the minimum amount of time needed to ensure a more effective governing agency, and with the aim only of ensuring that there is a vehicle, an institutional structure, by which the people can organize their own self-determination.

Most just-war theories, and mine is no exception, agree that there is a strong case for third-party intervention in cases of egregious rights-violation; but that intervention ought to be exceptional and of minimal duration.[23] The requirement that the rights violations have to be serious or egregious or 'shock the conscience of mankind' follows from the fact that military force involves killing. It is difficult to make calculations of proportionality—of when the good achieved by military force will outweigh the coercion and loss of life that flows from war—so the appropriate rule is to argue that the rights violations have to be serious and egregious, such as an act of aggression or ethnic cleansing and genocide. Analogously, while failure to respect political self-determination

rights is indeed a source of injustice, it is not of the magnitude that would justify coercive intervention to secure them.

Reluctance to justify external intervention is also undergirded by a liberal worry that the state is not only a source of good, but of evil too, and this
holds true for intervening states as well as those intervened in. When intervening states put their own soldiers' lives at risk, and bear costs that they do
not need to, we are rightly worried that they are motivated not by concern for
the humanity and suffering of the subject population—although some participants will indeed be moved by this—but by more dubious, more sinister
motives. This is especially so when the intervention itself proceeds without
being authorized by appropriate internationally legitimate agencies.[24] This latter source of concern—the worry about motives of those who are prepared to
respond and incur costs to discharge an imperfect duty—could be addressed
by creating an international institution tasked with the job of legitimating and
coordinating intervention, though this is not without problems (since members of the 'appropriate bodies' typically invoke vetoes to protect themselves
in abusing their own citizens).[25]

The comments above reflect not simply a normative worry about the appropriate stance to take to intervention, but a prudential worry, too. If I'm right
that people value their own collective autonomy, their own institutions that
enable them to enjoy collective self-government, then we should expect external intervention to be particularly burdensome for the intervening state and
less likely to be successful than organic change by members of the political
community on whose behalf the intervention is taking place. This may be
because the motives of the external interveners are regarded with suspicion
(sometimes rightly so) or it may be because they are not in the best position to
effect change or understand the complexities of the society. An intervention
can be justified to secure peace or promote human rights only if there is a very
good probability that it will be successful. Moreover, there is no cookie-cutter
plan of the right or just ordering of a society, no top-down way in which each
community should order its policies and practices, and this means that intervention, while sometimes justified and necessary, should certainly be seen as
a last resort, and undertaken only in cases of serious humanitarian emergency
in a time- and goal-limited way.

There are some cases where realizing the good of collective self-determination ought to play a role in justifying war. Although military intervention by
third parties to assist in the achievement of self-determination aims is not an
independent just cause, because not able to outweigh the risks and burdens
attached to committing to war, it may be a conditional just cause, which can
be weighed in the calculations of benefits and burdens when intervention is
also justified on other grounds. To see how that would work, consider the

1990–91 Gulf War. The coalition, led by the United States and authorized by the United Nations, agreed to a ceasefire after restoring Kuwaiti sovereignty, but it stopped short both of deposing the Iraqi leader and of creating an environment in which the Kurdish people in the north of the country, who almost certainly represent a 'people' under my definition, could enjoy robust and internationally recognized rights of collective self-determination. This was almost certainly a mistake. Promoting Kurdish autonomy would have been a good which helped to justify the war in its proportionality dimension; it would have had the effect of deterring other states, who perhaps harbour distinct political communities within their own borders, from committing acts of aggression against them. And it was, at the point that the ceasefire was agreed to, quite achievable without significant further loss of life.

10.4. Conclusion

In this chapter, I've considered the implications of my argument for the right to use force. I've argued that it provides a distinctive and superior account of defensive rights in war, and that it can be applied to other cases where the territorial integrity of states is either threatened or is being defended. I have argued that this account is consistent with what we intuitively feel is right in a number of cases. In part this is because many of the concerns that we might have about the implications of this argument are addressed when we consider the moral requirements that generally attach to the use of force. In part it is because the argument proceeds at the level of institutional morality, about the defence of institutional practices and principles, and so situates the rules or practices or rights within an overall system that is meant to address concerns about perverse consequences. And in part it is because we think that states matter to the extent that they give institutional expression to political communities, and the argument of this book builds on that basic intuition.

To some extent, the argument presented here not only justifies the defensive rights of states but also national liberation rights. This is neither a recipe for disaster, nor is it incoherent. Just as a people ought to be able to defend their existing rights to collective self-determination (national defensive rights) so they ought to be able to secure their collective self-determination through the use of force, if that is necessary and meets the conditions widely accepted in the just-war tradition concerning proportionality, not targeting non-combatants and so on, for the justified use of force. The same argument that justifies national defensive rights also justifies national liberation rights, as long as the group meets the relevant criteria of 'peoplehood'. This is a plausible position: there is a significant moral difference between external aggression and internal uprisings or rebellions or secessionist movements. The former cannot be countenanced and so is rightly protected by national defensive right; but the latter could be legitimate, if it is genuinely in defence of a political community and meets the burden of justification for the use of force. This means that a state's right to territorial integrity, upheld in international law, and often thought to be part of the defensive right, in fact defends the state only against external aggressors who seek to dismember it, but it does not apply to the people who live in the state, who may be seeking to create their own institutional structure to defend their political community. This matches our intuitions: we rightly think that there is something seriously wrong with a state or regime that kills its own people to defend itself, but the same does not apply when the state (or agents of the state—i.e., soldiers) kill(s) foreign aggressors.

One might complain that the account developed in this chapter contains an incoherent asymmetry. I've argued that an independent country can use force to repel an annexer (this applies even if the annexer promises that it will grant autonomy to the annexed region once the takeover is complete), but a region that has sufficient autonomy ought not to use force to achieve maximal autonomy. What can explain this asymmetrical treatment? The basic idea is that the use of force must cross a significant bar: if an aggressor attacks a country, but promises that (autonomy) rights will be respected in the post-conflict scenario, individuals in the attacked country will rightly doubt the veracity of that promise, given that the aggressor has already violated the basic norms of the international order. The argument that I developed in section 10.2 above, where I discussed defensive rights, applies here: if we do not permit the attacked country to defend itself, all political communities live in a state of insecurity with respect to their territorial entitlements. By contrast, in the case of a people who enjoy significant but non-exclusive jurisdiction, the logic is different: they can pursue political avenues, lobby, pressure, and vote for arrangements that give them the exclusive jurisdiction to which they are entitled, but the good that they would achieve is not sufficient to justify the death and destruction that inevitably follows from war.

Notes

1. The account of just cause plays a complex role in arguments, because it bears on other conditions that are also relevant to assessing the justice of military force. For example, the 'right intention' condition requires that those who use force are motivated by a desire for just cause; the 'proportionality' condition permits war only if the harm is not out of proportion to the goods achieved, and the goods are limited to those defined in the just cause condition; and the 'last resort' condition permits war only if there is no better (less destructive) way of achieving the goods, and, again, the relevant goods are defined in the specification of relevant just cause; Thomas Hurka, 'Liability and Just Cause', *Ethics & International Affairs*, vol. 21, no. 2 (2007): 199–218.

2. Hurka, 'Liability and Just Cause', 199–204.
3. Allen Buchanan, 'A Richer Jus ad Bellum', unpublished manuscript.
4. United Nations Charter, art. 2, para. 4.
5. Michael Walzer, *Just and Unjust Wars: A Moral Argument with Historical Illustrations* (New York: Basic Books, 1977), 54.
6. Rodin, *War and Self-Defense*, 127.
7. Rodin, *War and Self-Defense*, 127–128.
8. Rodin, *War and Self-Defense*, 131, 132.
9. This does not mean that there can be no evidence brought to bear on this question: sometimes the fact that state X does not represent a single, or shared, political community is evident in the results of democratic elections (where some people have voted for minority nationalist parties—'nationalist' here in the sense that the parties mobilize people to achieve collective self-determination for some other nation beyond the one embodied in the state) or in persistent, and supported, extra-political mobilization on behalf of such a group. When these apply, we might be able to say that the state lacks a political community.
10. See Cécile Fabre, *Cosmopolitan Peace* (Oxford: Oxford University Press, forthcoming), chapter 7 on 'Punishment for Crimes of War'.
11. I am grateful to Allen Buchanan for a very helpful conversation on this example.
12. By the term 'detached', I mean: without considering either what state Crimea was part of or the result of the 2014 referendum there.
13. In the protests preceding the crisis, Yanukovych's government had ordered that live rounds should be fired at unarmed protesters. However, that does not fully address the question of the constitutional legality of his removal from office. The interim prime minister Yatsenyk did not follow the impeachment process as specified by the Constitution of Ukraine. This process involves formally charging the president with a crime, a review of the charge by the Constitutional Court of Ukraine, and a three-quarters majority vote in favour of impeachment in the Ukrainian parliament (the Rada).
14. BBC News, 'Ukraine: Putin Signs Crimean Annexation', 21 March 2014, www.bb.cco.uk/news/world-europe-26686949.
15. The use of force in both Afghanistan and Iraq was in violation of article 2, paragraph 4, of the Charter of the United Nations, which is the provision of the charter that prohibits the use of force against the territorial integrity or political independence of another sovereign state. Neither invasion was authorized by the United Nations.
16. As I argued in chapter 6, referenda are of limited usefulness as a tool for determining political identities, relationships, and aspirations. First, they are insufficiently dynamic: they deliver a verdict about what people want which doesn't take into account the reaction of the other side to the set of preferences voted for. For example, a voter might vote for joining country X but not want to join the country under any conditions or at any costs. He or she may, that is, have a preference for independence, but would not prefer it if she knew the costs that attach to it. Second, people often vote strategically, in order to strengthen the hands of their preferred side. Third, in many cases referenda offer limited choices. The Crimean referendum offered only two choices, Ukraine or Russia, when there should have been a third choice on offer: significant autonomy, minority protections, Russian-language protection guaranteed, negotiations on links with Russia. (To some extent, this is because of the complications that arise in a three-choice question.) The two questions being put to the vote were:

    1. Are you in favour of the Autonomous Republic of Crimea reuniting with Russia as a constituent part of the Russian Federation?
    2. Are you in favour of restoring the Constitution of the Republic of Crimea of 1992 and of Crimea's status as part of Ukraine? From BBC News, 'Is Crimea's Referendum Legal?', 13 March 2014, http://www.bbc.co.uk/news/world-europe-26546133.

17. David Birmingham, *The Decolonization of Africa* (London: Taylor and Francis, 1995), 32–36.
18. Chetena Hallemariam, Sjaak Krooon, and Joel Walters, 'Multilingualism and Nation-Building: Language and Education in Eritrea', *Journal of Multilingual and Multicultural Development*, vol. 20, no. 6 (1999), 475–493, at 478.

19. Even if we think that the Russian annexation is unjust, it's not clear that Ukraine is justified in responding with military force, with predictable loss of life, unless there is a reasonable prospect of success. This is extremely doubtful against Russia's very large and better-equipped army; Kieran Oberman, 'The Crimean Crisis: Justified Secession, Russian Aggression or Both?', *Just World Institute*, 5 March 2014, http://blogs.sps.ed.ac.uk/jwi/2014/03/05/the-crimean-crisis-justified-secession-russian-aggression-or-both.

20. Mark Tran, 'Ukraine: Referendum on "Self-Rule" in Eastern Regions Begins', *The Guardian*, 11 May 2014, http://www.theguardian.com/world/2014/may/11/ukraine-referendum-for-self-rule-in-eastern-regions-begins-live-updates.

21. Tran, 'Ukraine: Referendum on "Self-Rule" in Eastern Regions Begins'.

22. Note that this problem can't be dealt with simply by weakening the power or authority of the state. If, as I've argued, states should have the power to fulfil the task of creating and maintaining rules and practices that govern people's lives, they necessarily also have the capacity to do so in ways that fail to respect the human rights of people who are so governed. This is a familiar problem, a version of which was discussed long ago, in a dialogue between Socrates and Thrasymachus in Plato's *Republic*.

23. Since the bulk of this section is focused on Iraq and the Kurds, it may be appropriate here to clarify that there is little doubt that the Iraqi regime of Saddam Hussein practised systematic repression, torture, and rape, and imprisoned political opponents and leaders of ethnic minorities. These practices have been well documented by impartial international observers, such as Human Rights Watch, and by independent journalists and NGOs. In the 1988 Anfal campaign alone, in which the Saddam regime gassed the Kurds in more than forty villages, approximately 182,000 people were killed, and more were blinded and maimed; Human Rights Watch, *Genocide in Iraq: The Anfal Campaign against the Kurds*. New York: Middle East Watch Report, July 1993; BBC News, 'Iraqi Kurds' Story of Expulsion', 3 November 2001, http://news.bbc.co.uk/2/hi/middle_east/1614239.stm; USAID, 'Iraq's Legacy of Terror: Mass Graves'.

24. In this case—where the duty is imperfect and only some states are prepared to act on it—we have good reason to question the motives of the intervening state. A more typical problem is that, in many cases, there just isn't sufficient motive to intervene. This was true in Rwanda in 1994 and Congo between 2011 and 2013. See Sudarsan Raghavan, 2013. 'In Volatile Congo, a New U.N. Force with Teeth', 3 November 2013, www.genocidewatch.org/drofcongo.html.

25. The world in which we currently live is very far from world government and some coordination of responses in the face of the egregious violations of human rights would be an improvement over the current (statist) status quo. International agencies, though, are also problematic: collective autonomy could be imperilled if a single agency, or single state, in the name of securing order, justice, and good government, were enabled easily to expand their own territorial rights. The very worry about state power and tyranny that makes us think that intervention is sometimes a good should also make us worry about licensing intervention as a common practice in our current world order.

11

Conclusion

There are currently more than seven billion people on Earth, and it is esti-mated that there will be more than nine billion by 2050. Many of these people will expect a middle-class lifestyle: we will need more houses, more cars (or other method of transport), more clothes, more food, varied holiday destina-tions, and so on. Yet, there is no more land; indeed, there is *less* land, as global warming is predicted to increase the volume of water in the oceans and flood low-lying areas and islands. It is reasonable to expect that there will be increas-ing conflict, over land, over territory, over resources. This pressure will not just generate a one-off dispute but conflict that is likely to continue in the future, as people who are displaced feel that an injustice has been done, and people who settle and control an area develop new attachments to the place and to people in that place.

It might be thought that if this prediction of increased conflict is correct we need a new way of dealing with territory. Some might think that in an age of predicted scarcity we should view the world as held in common, and that territorially distinct political communities will be an outmoded way of organ-izing life on this planet. If, however, we take seriously the fact that people have attachments to place and to others that presuppose a particular place, the com-munal solution may not be a good solution at all. At worst, it might lead to land grabs and resource grabs by the most powerful; at best, it could be a fair but suboptimal redistribution of resources, which is achieved at the expense of people's commitments, relations, and attachments, and especially their place-related attachments. It is difficult to see how the view that the world is held in common can take seriously individual and group attachment to land, and how it could be rendered consistent with significant forms of control over the collective life that people share with one another.

Moreover, as pressure grows on food production, it's going to be very hard to resist market forces, and keep land as forest, for example, or as wilderness. I think the only chance is local control by people who care about the territory they live on and see it as more than just an economic resource. This has been an important theme of this book: the importance of respecting both the particularity of land and the self-determination of peoples.

I believe we can do better than either the current ad hoc treatment of territory or the common-ownership view: we can develop principles that respect individual and group place-related attachments, and aspirations for collective self-determination, whilst articulating limits to their aspirations for control over land and resources, limits that are governed by respect for people's rights, including subsistence rights.

I began this book by lamenting the lack of a theory of territory. My main goal when I began writing it was to address this lacuna, by advancing a theory that justifies rights over territory, both against those who think that territorial rights cannot be justified and those who think they can, but who offer a different theory. In this book, I defended the idea of territory and territorial rights in terms of political self-determination and I have argued throughout that this provides an intuitively plausible explanation of the relationship between territory, the state, and people, and that it justifies (within limits) those elements that we normally associate with territorial rights: rights of jurisdiction, rights over resources, rights to control borders, and so on. The main goal was theoretical: to systematize our thinking about territory and offer a normative theory that made sense of the various elements that we think are important in a theory of territory.

But as I've suggested throughout this book, this is not a purely theoretical exercise: it is of pressing practical importance that we develop a systematic theory of territory. In order to resolve territorial disputes—disputes over resources, disputes over boundaries, disputes over the oceans, and disputes rooted in historical injustices—in a principled way, without appeal to ad hoc reasoning about each particular issue, we need a coherent account of the relations between people, land, and the governing authority. There are, as I've emphasized throughout this book, already a number of important conflicts facing us, about which we have insufficient, or contradictory, normative guidance: not only over unoccupied islands, the ocean, the seabed, the frozen Arctic, but boundary conflicts between states (or communities within states), secessionist conflicts, and irredentist conflicts. There are contradictory impulses about justified armed intervention, and there is continued pressure on borders for control over land and resources generally, from prospective migrants and from the desperate poor, who see the exploitation of resources as critical to escape their poverty.

It is in part because we haven't yet considered in a systematic way the normative significance of territory, nor related territory to other principles and goods that we think are important, that these disputes fester. Parties on all sides appeal to what they think are good normative arguments. Without a consensus on the principles that should regulate these disputes, all sides believe that their position is justified, which makes resolution all the more difficult.

It is my hope for this book that it will spark a dialogue which brings territory to the centre of political theory. And this is important not only philosophically—so that we can bring together arguments concerning authority over persons with arguments for authority over territory—but also in order to develop coherent principles to govern our international order as we enter what I think is a potentially more dangerous, more conflict-ridden period. If we achieve agreement, even of an overlapping-consensus kind, on these rules or principles, we would have the basis for a stable rule-governed international order, which would be a significant improvement over the status quo. Even better, however, is a justificatory argument for these rules and principles which is rooted in a philosophical understanding of the normative basis of territory and other normatively important aspects of the international order.

BIBLIOGRAPHY

Books, Journals

Abizadeh, Arash. 2002. 'Does Liberal Democracy Presuppose a Cultural Nation? Four Arguments', *American Political Science Review*, vol. 96, no. 3, 495–510.

Abizadeh, Arash. 2008. 'Democratic Theory and Border Coercion: No Right to Unilaterally Control Your Own Border', *Political Theory*, vol. 36, no. 1, 37–65.

Abizadeh, Arash. 2012. 'On the Demos and Its Kin: Nationalism, Democracy, and the Boundary Problem', *American Political Science Review*, vol. 106, no. 4, 862–882.

Ajzensat, Janet. 2007. *The Canadian Founding: John Locke and Parliament.* Montreal: McGill-Queen's University Press.

Akenson, Donald Harman. 1991. *God's Peoples: Covenant and Land in South Africa, Israel, and Ulster.* Montreal and Kingston: McGill-Queen's University Press.

Anstis, Sebastian C. St. J., and Mark W. Zacher. 2010. 'The Normative Bases of the Global Territorial Order', *Diplomacy and Statecraft*, vol. 21, no. 2, 306–323.

Anwander, Norbert. 2005. 'Contributing and Benefiting: Two Grounds for Duties to the Victims of Injustice', *Ethics & International Affairs*, vol. 19, no. 1, 39–45.

Armstrong, Chris. 2010. 'National Self-Determination, Global Equality and Moral Arbitrariness', *Journal of Political Philosophy*, vol. 18, no. 3, 313–334.

Armstrong, Chris. 2013. 'Resources, Rights and Global Justice: A Response to Kolers', *Political Studies*, vol. 62, no. 1, 216–222.

Armstrong, Chris. 2014. 'Justice and Attachment to Natural Resources', *Journal of Political Philosophy*, vol. 22, 48–65.

Arneil, Barbara. 1996. *John Locke and America: The Defence of English Colonialism.* Oxford: Oxford University Press.

Arneson, Richard. 1982. 'The Principle of Fairness and Free-Rider Problems', *Ethics*, vol. 92, no. 4, 616–633.

Bachvarova, Mira. 2011. *Non-Domination and the Accommodation of Minority Social Practice*, PhD diss., Queen's University, Canada.

Baldwin, Thomas. 1992. 'The Territorial State', in Hyman Gross and Ross Harrison, eds, *Jurisprudence: Cambridge Essays*, 207–230. Oxford: Clarendon Press.

Banai, Ayelet. 2014. 'The Territorial Rights of Legitimate States: A Pluralist Interpretation', *International Theory*, vol. 6, no. 1, 140–157.

Beitz, Charles. 1979. *Political Theory and International Relations.* Princeton: Princeton University Press.

Benedek, Emily. 1992. *The Wind Won't Know Me: A History of the Navajo-Hopi Land Dispute.* New York: Alfred A. Knopf.

Bengio, Ofra. 2005. 'Autonomy in Kurdistan in Historical Perspective', in Brendan O'Leary, John McGarry, and Khaled Salih, eds, *The Future of Kurdistan in Iraq*, 173–185. Philadelphia: University of Pennsylvania Press.

Bennett, Christopher. 1995. *Yugoslavia's Bloody Collapse: Causes, Course and Consequences*. New York: New York University Press.

Bertram, Christopher. 2013. 'Property in the Moral Life of Human Beings', *Social Philosophy & Policy*, vol. 30, nos. 1–2, 404–424.

Birmingham, David. 1995. *The Decolonization of Africa*. London: Taylor and Francis.

Blake, Michael. 2001. 'Distributive Justice, State Coercion, and Autonomy', *Philosophy & Public Affairs*, vol. 30, no. 3, 257–296.

Blake, Michael, and Mathias Risse. 2007. 'Migration, Territoriality and Culture', KSG Working Paper No. RWP07–009 (February): http://papers.ssrn.com/sol3/papers.cfm?abstract_id=963130.

Blake, Michael, and Mathias Risse. 2009. 'Immigration and Original Ownership of the Earth', *Notre Dame Journal of Law, Ethics, and Public Policy*, vol. 23, no. 1 (special issue on immigration), 133–167.

Borrows, Jon. 1997. 'Living between Water and Rocks: First Nations, Environmental Planning and Democracy', *University of Toronto Law Journal*, vol. 47, 417–468.

Bose, Sumantra. 2003. *Kashmir: Roots of Conflict, Paths to Peace*. Cambridge, MA: Harvard University Press.

Bose, Sumantra. 2007. *Contested Lands: Israel–Palestine, Kashmir, Bosnia, Cyprus and Sri Lanka*. Cambridge, MA: Harvard University Press.

Brice-Bennett, Carol. 1994. *Dispossessed: The Eviction of Inuit from Hebron, Labrador*. [RCAP commissioned paper]. Ottawa, ON: Minister of Supply and Services.

Brock, Gillian. 2009. *Global Justice: A Cosmopolitan Account*. Oxford: Oxford University Press.

Buchanan, Allen. 1991. *Secession: The Morality of Political Divorce from Fort Sumter to Lithuania and Quebec*. Boulder: Westview.

Buchanan, Allen. 1997. 'Theories of Secession', *Philosophy & Public Affairs*, vol. 26, no. 1, 3–61.

Buchanan, Allen. 2002. 'Political Legitimacy and Democracy', *Ethics*, vol. 112, no. 4, 689–719.

Buchanan, Allen. 2003. 'The Making and Unmaking of Boundaries: What Liberalism Has to Say', in Allen Buchanan and Margaret Moore, eds, *States, Nations, and Borders: The Ethics of Making Boundaries*, 231–261. Cambridge: Cambridge University Press.

Buchanan, Allen. 2004. *Justice, Legitimacy, and Self-Determination: Moral Foundations for International Law*. Oxford: Oxford University Press.

Buchanan, Allen. 2005. 'Are Human Rights Parochial?', paper given to the Political Philosophy Group, Queen's University, Kingston, Ontario, October 2005; *Philosophy & Public Affairs* (forthcoming).

Buchanan, Allen. 'A Richer Jus ad Bellum', unpublished manuscript.

Buchanan, Allen, and Robert Keohane. 2006. 'The Legitimacy of Global Governance Institutions', *Ethics & International Affairs*, vol. 20, no. 4, 405–443.

Buckinx, Barbara. 2011. *Reducing Domination in Global Politics*. PhD diss., Princeton University.

Butt, Daniel. 2007. 'On Benefiting from Injustice", *Canadian Journal of Philosophy*, vol. 37, no. 1, 129–152.

Butt, Daniel. 2009. *Rectifying International Injustice: Principles of Compensation and Restitution between Nations*. Oxford: Oxford University Press.

Calimont, Donald, and Dennis William Magill. 1974. *Africville: The Life and Death of a Canadian Black Community*. Toronto: McClelland and Stewart.

Caney, Simon. 2005. *Justice Beyond Borders. A Global Political Theory*. Oxford: Oxford University Press.

Carens, Joseph H. 1987. 'Aliens and Citizens: The Case for Open Borders', *Review of Politics*, vol. 49, no. 2, 251–273.

Carens, Joseph H. 2009a. 'Open Borders and the Claims of Community', paper given at the American Political Science Association meeting, Toronto, Ontario, 2–5 September 2009.

Carens, Joseph H. 2009b. 'The Case for Amnesty: Time Erodes the States's Right to Deport', *Boston Review*, 1 May 2009: http://bostonreview.net/forum/case-amnesty-joseph-carens.

Carens, Joseph H. 2013. *The Ethics of Immigration*. Oxford: Oxford University Press.

Catala, Amandine. 2013. 'Remedial Theories of Secession and Territorial Justification', *Journal of Social Philosophy*, vol. 44, no. 1, 74–94.

Chandhoke, Neera. 2012. *Contested Secessions: Rights, Self-Determination, Democracy, and Kashmir.* New Delhi: Oxford University Press.

Christiano, Thomas. 2006. 'A Democratic Theory of Territory and Some Puzzles about Global Democracy', *Journal of Social Philosophy*, vol. 37, no. 1, 81–107.

Cohen, G. A. 1983. 'The Structure of Proletarian Unfreedom', *Philosophy & Public Affairs*, vol. 12, no. 1, 3–33.

Cohen, G. A. 1997. 'Where the Action Is: On the Site of Distributive Justice', *Philosophy & Public Affairs*, vol. 26, no. 1, 3–30.

Connor, Walker. 1994. *Ethnonationalism: The Quest for Understanding.* Princeton: Princeton University Press.

Conquest, Robert. 1970. *The Nation Killers: The Soviet Deportation of Nationalities.* London: Macmillan.

Copp, David. 2006. 'On the Agency of Certain Collective Entities', *Midwest Studies in Philosophy*, vol. 30, 194–221.

Daes, E.-I. A. 2004. 'Indigenous Peoples' Permanent Sovereignty over Natural Resources', Final report of the Special Rapporteur to the UN Sub-Commission on the Promotion and Protection of Human Rights. UN Doc. E/CN.41/Sub.2/2004/30. http://www1. umn.edu/humanrts/demo/IndigenousSovereigntyNaturalResources_Daes.pdf.

Dagger, Richard. 1997. *Civic Virtues: Rights, Citizenship, and Republican Liberalism.* New York: Oxford University Press.

Dagger, Richard. 2000. 'Membership, Fair Play, and Political Obligation', *Political Studies*, vol. 48, no. 1, 104–117.

Dahl, Robert. *Democracy and Its Critics.* New Haven: Yale University Press, 1989.

Darrell, Owen. H. (1997) 2005. *Sir George Somers Links Bermuda with Lyme Regis.* Hamilton, Bermuda: O. H. Darrell.

Ducharme, Michel, and Jean-François Constant. 2009. *Liberalism and Hegemony: Debating the Canadian Liberal Revolution.* Toronto: University of Toronto Press.

Dworkin, Gerald. 1982. 'Is More Choice Better than Less?' *Midwest Studies in Philosophy*, vol. 7, 47–61.

Dworkin, Ronald. 1984. 'Rights as Trumps', in Jeremy Waldron, ed., *Theories of Rights*, 153–167. Oxford: Clarendon Press.

Dworkin, Ronald. 1986. *Law's Empire.* Cambridge, MA: Harvard University Press.

Dworkin, Ronald. 2000. *Sovereign Virtue: The Theory and Practice of Equality.* Cambridge, MA: Harvard University Press.

Edmonds, Cecil. 1957. *Kurds, Turks and Arabs.* Oxford: Oxford University Press.

Edmundson, William. 1998. *Three Anarchical Fallacies.* Cambridge: Cambridge University Press.

Elazar, Daniel. 1994. *Federalism and the Way to Peace.* Kingston, ON: Queen's University Institute of Intergovernmental Affairs.

Elden, Stuart. 2009. *Terror and Territory: The Spatial Extent of Sovereignty.* Minneapolis: University of Minnesota Press.

Elden, Stuart. 2010. 'From Territorium to Territory', talk presented at the Munk Centre, University of Toronto, March 2010.

Emerson, Rupert. 1971. 'Self-Determination', *American Journal of International Law*, vol. 65, no. 3, 459–465.

Emerton, Patrick, and Toby Handfield. 2014. 'Understanding the Political Defensive Privilege', in Cécile Fabre and Seth Lazar, eds, *The Morality of Defensive War*, 40–66. Oxford: Oxford University Press.

Eriksen, Thomas Hylland. 1993. *Ethnicity and Nationalism: Anthropological Perspectives.* London: Pluto.

Fabre, Cécile. 2012. *Cosmopolitan War.* Oxford: Oxford University Press.

Fabre, Cécile. 2014. 'Cosmopolitanism and Wars of Self-Defense', in Cécile Fabre and Seth Lazar, eds, *The Morality of Defensive War*, 90–114. Oxford: Oxford University Press.

Fabre, Cécile. Forthcoming. *Cosmopolitan Peace.* Oxford: Oxford University Press.

Feinberg, Joel. 1970. 'The Nature and Value of Rights', *Journal of Value Inquiry*, vol. 4, no. 4, 243–260.

Fine, Sarah. 2013. 'The Ethics of Immigration: Self-Determination and the Right to Exclude', *Philosophy Compass*, vol. 8, no. 3, 254–268.

Fine, Sarah, and Andrea Sangiovanni. 2014. 'Immigration', in Darrel Moellendorf and Heather Widdows, eds, *The Routledge Handbook of Global Ethics*, XX–XX. London: Routledge.

Flikschuh, Katrin. 2010. 'Kant's Sovereignty Dilemma: A Contemporary Analysis', *Journal of Political Philosophy*, vol. 18, no. 4, 469–493.

Galbraith, Peter. 2005. 'Kurdistan in a Federal Iraq', in Brendan O'Leary, John McGarry, and Khaled Salih, eds, *The Future of Kurdistan in Iraq*, 268–281. Philadelphia: University of Pennsylvania Press.

Gans, Chaim. 2003. *The Limits of Nationalism*. New York: Cambridge University Press.

Gans, Chaim. 2007. 'Is There a Historical Right to the Land of Israel?', *Azure*, vol. 5762, no. 2 (winter): http://www.azure.org.il/article.php?id=32.

Gilabert, Pablo, and Holly Lawford-Smith. 2012. 'Political Feasibility: A Conceptual Exploration', *Political Studies*, vol. 60, no. 4, 809–825.

Gilbert, Margaret. 1989. *On Social Facts*. Princeton: Princeton University Press.

Gilbert, Margaret. 2006. *A Theory of Political Obligation: Membership, Commitment, and the Bonds of Society*. Oxford: Clarendon Press.

Gillespie, Alexander. 2009. 'Small Island States in the Face of Climatic Change: The End of the Line in International Environmental Responsibility', *UCLA Journal of Environmental Law and Policy*, vol. 22, no. 1, 107–129.

Goodin, Robert E. 1992. 'If People were Money . . . ', in Brian Barry and Robert E. Goodin, eds, *Free Movement: Ethical Issues in the Transnational Migration of Peoples and of Money*, 6–22. University Park: Penn State Press.

Goodin, Robert E. 2007. 'Enfranchising All Affected Interests, and Its Alternatives', *Philosophy & Public Affairs*, vol. 35, no. 1, 40–68.

Graff, James A. 1994. 'Human Rights, Peoples, and Self-Determination', in Judith Baker, ed., *Group Rights*, 186–215. Toronto: University of Toronto Press.

Grotius, Hugo. 2007. *The Rights of War and Peace, Including the Law of Nature and of Nations*. New York: Cosimo Classics. (Originally published in 1625.)

Hallemariam, Chetena, Sjaak Kroon, and Joel Walters. 1999. 'Multilingualism and Nation-Building: Language and Education in Eritrea', *Journal of Multilingual and Multicultural Development*, vol. 20, no. 6, 475–493.

Harris, Rosemary. 1972. *Prejudice and Tolerance in Ulster*. Manchester: Manchester University Press.

Hayward, Tim. 2005. 'Thomas Pogge's Global Resources Dividend: A Critique and an Alternative', *Journal of Moral Philosophy*, vol. 2, no. 3, 317–332.

Heath, Joseph. 1997. 'Rawls on Global Distributive Justice: A Defence', *Canadian Journal of Philosophy*, Supplementary Volume, ed. Daniel Weinstock. Lethbridge: University of Calgary Press.

Heath, Joseph. 2014. *Morality, Competition, and the Firm*. Oxford: Oxford University Press.

Hendrix, Burke. 2008. *Ownership, Authority, and Self-Determination*. University Park: Pennsylvania State University Press.

Hibbert, Christopher. 1982. *The French Revolution*. London: Penguin.

Hildebrand, Klaus. 1973. *The Foreign Policy of the Third Reich*. London: Batsford.

Hill, Renée A. 2002. 'Compensatory Justice: Over Time and between Groups', *Journal of Political Philosophy*, vol. 10, no. 4, 392–415.

Hindriks, Frank. 2008. 'The Freedom of Collective Agents', *Journal of Political Philosophy*, vol. 16, no. 2, 165–183.

Hobbes, Thomas. 1968. *Leviathan*, edited, with an introduction, by C. B. Macpherson. Harmondsworth: Penguin. (Originally published in 1651.)

Hohfeld, Wesley Newcomb. 1978. *Fundamental Legal Conceptions as Applied in Judicial Reasoning*, ed. Arthur Corbin. Westport, CT: Greenwood. (Originally published in 1920.)

Holder, Cindy. 2004. 'Self-Determination as a Basic Human Right: The Draft UN Declaration on the Rights of Indigenous Peoples', in Avigail Eisenberg and Jeff Spinner-Halev, eds, *Minorities within Minorities: Equality, Rights and Diversity*, 294–316. Cambridge: Cambridge University Press.

Horowitz, Donald L. 1985. *Ethnic Groups in Conflict*. Berkeley: University of California Press.

Horton, John. 1992. *Political Obligation*. London: Macmillan.

Hume, David. 1978. *A Treatise of Human Nature*, edited by L. A. Selby-Bigge and P. H. Nidditch. Oxford: Clarendon Press. (Originally published in 1739.)

Hurka, Thomas. 2005. 'Proportionality in the Morality of War', *Philosophy & Public Affairs*, vol. 33, no. 1, 34–66.

Hurka, Thomas. 2007. 'Liability and Just Cause', *Ethics & International Affairs*, vol. 21, no. 2, 199–218.

Ignatieff, Michael. 1995. 'Nationalism and the Narcissism of Minor Differences', *Queen's Quarterly*, vol. 102, no. 1, 13–25.

Intergovernmental Panel on Climate Change (IPCC). 2013. 'Summary for Policymakers', in Thomas F. Stocker et al., eds, *Climate Change 2013: The Physical Science Basis. Contribution of Working Group I to the Fifth Assessment Report of the Intergovernmental Panel on Climate Change*. Cambridge: Cambridge University Press.

Ivison, Duncan. 2000. 'Political Community and Historical Injustice', *Australasian Journal of Philosophy*, vol. 78, no. 3, 360–373.

Jaggar, Alison M. 2000. 'Feminist Ethics', in Hugh LaFollette, ed., *The Blackwell Guide to Ethical Theory*, 348–374. Oxford: Blackwell.

James, Aaron. 2012. *Fairness in Practice: A Social Contract for the Global Economy*. New York: Oxford University Press.

Jennings, Ivor. 1956. *The Approach to Self-Government*. Cambridge: Cambridge University Press.

Jones, Colin. 2002. *The Great Nation: France from Louis XV to Napoleon*. New York: Columbia University Press.

Jourdan, Silvester. 1610. *Discovery of the Barmudas, otherwise called the Isle of Divels by Sir Thomas Gates, Sir George Sommers and Captayne Newpont, with divers others*. London: John Windet. Early English Books Online.

Kagan, Shelly. 1991. *The Limits of Morality*. Oxford: Oxford University Press.

Kant, Immanuel. 1970. *Kant's Political Writings*. Edited by H. S. Reiss. Cambridge: Cambridge University Press.

Kapur, Devesh, and John McHale. 2006. 'Should a Cosmopolitan Worry about the "Brain Drain"?' *Ethics & International Affairs*, vol. 20, no. 3, 305–320.

Kershaw, Ian. 2000. *The Nazi Dictatorship: Perspectives of Interpretation*. London: Arnold.

Klosko, George. 2004. *The Principle of Fairness and Political Obligation*, 2nd edition. Lanham, MD: Rowman and Littlefield.

Kofman, Daniel. 2007. 'The Normative Limits to the Dispersal of Territorial Sovereignty', *The Monist*, vol. 90, no. 1, 67–87.

Kohn, Margaret. 2013. 'What is Wrong with Gentrification?' *Urban Research and Practice*, vol. 6, no. 3, 297–310.

Kohn, Margaret. 'Indigenous Land and the Right to a City', unpublished manuscript. July 2013.

Kolers, Avery. 2009a. *Land, Conflict, and Justice: A Political Theory of Territory*. Cambridge: Cambridge University Press.

Kolers, Avery. 2009b. 'Territory, Environment, and Global Distributive Justice', paper given at the American Political Science Association meeting, Toronto, Ontario, 2–5 September 2009.

Kolers, Avery. 2012a. 'Floating Provisos and Sinking Islands', *Journal of Applied Philosophy*, vol. 29, no. 4, 333–343.

Kolers, Avery. 2012b. 'Justice, Territory and Natural Resources', *Political Studies*, vol. 60, no. 2, 269–286.

Kumar, Rahul. 2003. 'Who Can Be Wronged?', *Philosophy & Public Affairs*, vol. 31, no. 2, 99–118.

Kymlicka, Will. 1995. *Multicultural Citizenship*. Oxford: Oxford University Press.

Laborde, Cécile. 2010. 'Republicanism and Global Justice: A Sketch', *European Journal of Political Theory*, vol. 9, no. 1, 48–69.

Lægard, Sune. 2010. 'What is the Right to Exclude Immigrants?', *Res Publica*, vol. 16, no. 3, 245–262.

Lægard, Sune. 2013. 'Territorial Rights, Political Association, and Immigration', *Journal of Moral Philosophy*, vol. 10, no. 5, 645–670.

Lam, Ricky, and Leonard Wantchekon. 2003. 'Political Dutch Disease', NYU Working Paper. http://www.nyu.edu/gsas/dept/politics/faculty/wantchekon/research/dutch.pdf.

Lan, Gien. 2000. 'Land and Sea Connect: The East Coast Fishery Closure, Unemployment and Health', *Canadian Journal of Public Health*, vol. 91, no. 2, 121–124.

Lazar, Seth. 2008. 'Corrective Justice and the Possibility of Rectification', *Ethical Theory and Moral Practice*, vol. 11, no. 4, 355–368.

Lazar, Seth. 2009. 'The Nature and Disvalue of Injury', *Res Publica*, vol. 15, no. 3, 289–304.

Lazar, Seth. 2010a. 'Endings and Aftermath in the Ethics of War', CSSJ Working Papers Series, SJ016 (November).

Lazar, Seth. 2010b. 'The Responsibility Dilemma for *Killing in War*: A Review Essay', *Philosophy & Public Affairs*, vol. 38, no. 2, 180–213.

Lazar, Seth. 2014. 'National Defence, Self-Defence, and the Problem of Political Aggression', in Cécile Fabre and Seth Lazar, eds, *The Morality of Defensive War*, 11–39. Oxford: Oxford University Press.

Lefkowitz, David. 2004. 'Legitimate Political Authority and the Duty of Those Subject to It: A Critique of Edmundson', *Law and Philosophy*, vol. 23, no. 4, 399–435.

Lefkowitz, David. Forthcoming. 'Autonomy, Residence and Return', *Critical Review of International Social and Political Philosophy*.

Lenard, Patti Tamara, and Christine Straehle. 2012. 'Temporary Labour Migration, Global Redistribution, and Democratic Justice', *Philosophy, Politics, Economics*, vol. 11, no. 2, 206–233.

Levy, Jacob T. 2004. 'National Minorities without Nationalism', in Alain Dieckhoff, ed., *The Politics of Belonging: Nationalism, Liberalism, and Pluralism*, 155–173. Lanham, MD: Lexington.

Lijphart, Arend. 1994. *Electoral Systems and Party Systems: A Study of Twenty-Seven Democracies, 1945–1990*. Oxford: Oxford University Press.

Lijphart, Arend. 2004. 'Constitutional Design for Divided Societies', *Journal of Democracy*, vol. 15, no. 2, 96–109.

Lipsey, Richard G., and Kelvin Lancaster. 1956. 'The General Theory of Second Best' *Review of Economic Studies*, vol. 24, no. 1, 11–32.

List, Christian, and Philip Pettit. 2011. *Group Agency: The Possibility, Design, and Status of Corporate Agents*. Oxford: Oxford University Press.

Lister, Andrew. 2011. 'Justice as Fairness and Reciprocity', *Analyse & Kritik*, vol. 33, no. 1, 93–112.

Locke, John. 1988. 'The Second Treatise of Government', in Peter Laslett, ed., *Two Treatises of Government*. Cambridge: Cambridge University Press. (Originally published in 1689.)

Lomasky, Loren, and Fernando R. Tesón, eds. Forthcoming. *A Classical Liberal Theory of Global Justice*.

Lovett, Frank. 2010. *A General Theory of Justice and Domination*. Oxford: Oxford University Press.

Luban, David. 1980. 'Just War and Human Rights', *Philosophy & Public Affairs*, vol. 9, no. 2, 160–181.

Lugones, Maria. 2000. 'Multiculturalism and Publicity', *Hypatia*, vol. 15, no. 3, 175–181.

Lyons, David. 1977. 'The New Indian Claims and Original Rights to Land', *Social Theory and Practice*, vol. 4, no. 3, 249–272.

Malcolm, Noel. 1994. *Bosnia: A Short History*. New York: New York University Press.

Margalit, Avishai, and Joseph Raz. 1990. 'National Self-Determination', *Journal of Philosophy*, vol. 87, no. 9, 439–461.

May, Larry. 2005. *Crimes against Humanity*. Cambridge: Cambridge University Press.

McGarry, John. 2005. 'Canadian Lessons for Iraq', in Brendan O'Leary, John McGarry, and Khaled Salih, eds, *The Future of Kurdistan in Iraq*, 92–115. Philadelphia: University of Pennsylvania Press.

McGarry, John, and Niophytos Loizides. 2014. 'Ukraine Needs Federalism and Power-Sharing', *Open Democracy Review*, 22 May. http://www.opendemocracy.net/od-russia/john-mcgarry-neophytos-loizides/ukraine-needs-federalism-and-powersharing.

McGarry, John, and Brendan O'Leary. 1995. *Explaining Northern Ireland*. Oxford: Blackwell.

McKay, Ian. 2000. 'The Liberal Order Framework: A Prospectus for a Reconnaissance of Canadian History', *Canadian Historical Review*, vol. 81, no. 4, 617–645.

McMahan, Jeff. 2009. *Killing in War*. Oxford: Oxford University Press.

McMahan, Jeff. 2014. 'What Rights May Be Defended by Means of War?', in Cécile Fabre and Seth Lazar, eds, *The Morality of Defensive War*, 115–156. Oxford: Oxford University Press.

Meisels, Tamar. 2003a. 'Can Corrective Justice Ground Claims to Territory?', *Journal of Political Philosophy*, vol. 11, no. 1, 65–88.

Meisels, Tamar. 2003b. 'Liberal Nationalism and Territorial Rights', *Journal of Applied Philosophy*, vol. 20, no. 1, 31–43.

Meisels, Tamar. 2009. *Territorial Rights*, 2nd edition. Dordrecht: Springer.

Miller, David. 1995. *On Nationality*. Oxford: Oxford University Press.

Miller, David. 1998. 'Secession and the Principle of Nationality', in Margaret Moore, ed., *National Self-Determination and Secession*, 62–78. Oxford: Oxford University Press.

Miller, David. 2005. 'Immigration: The Case for Limits', in Andrew I. Cohen and Christopher H. Wellman, eds, *Contemporary Debates in Applied Ethics*, 193–206. London: Wiley-Blackwell.

Miller, David. 2007. *National Responsibility and Global Justice*. Oxford: Oxford University Press.

Miller, David. 2008. 'Review of Margaret Gilbert's *A Theory of Political Obligation*', *Philosophical Quarterly*, vol. 58, no. 233, 755–757.

Miller, David. 2009. 'Democracy's Domain', *Philosophy & Public Affairs*, vol. 37, no. 3, 201–228.

Miller, David. 2010. 'Why Immigration Controls Are Not Coercive: A Reply to Arash Abizadeh', *Political Theory*, vol. 38, no. 1, 111–120.

Miller, David. 2011. 'Property and Territory: Locke, Kant, and Steiner', *Journal of Political Philosophy*, vol. 19, no. 1, 90–109.

Miller, David. 2012. 'Territorial Rights: Concept and Justification', *Political Studies*, vol. 60, no. 2, 252–268.

Miller, David. 2014. 'Debatable Lands', *International Theory*, vol. 6, no. 1, 104–121.

Miller, David, and Sohail H. Hahmi, eds. 2001. *Boundaries and Justice: Diverse Ethical Perspectives*. Princeton and Oxford: Princeton University Press.

Moellendorf, Darrel. 2009. *Global Inequality Matters*. Basingstoke: Palgrave Macmillan.

Mojzes, Paul. 1995. *Yugoslavian Inferno*. New York: Continuum.

Moore, Margaret. 1998. 'The Territorial Dimension of Self-Determination', in Margaret Moore, ed., *National Self-Determination and Secession*, 134–157. Oxford: Oxford University Press.

Moore, Margaret. 2001. *Ethics of Nationalism*. Oxford: Oxford University Press.

Moore, Margaret. 2014. 'Collective Self-Determination, Institutions of Justice, and Wars of National Defence', in Cécile Fabre and Seth Lazar, eds, *The Morality of Defensive War*, 185–202. Oxford: Oxford University Press.

Morris, Christopher. 1998. *An Essay on the Modern State*. Cambridge: Cambridge University Press.

Murphy, Liam B. 1998. 'Institutions and the Demands of Justice', *Philosophy & Public Affairs*, vol. 27, no. 4, 251–291.

Murphy, Liam, and Thomas Nagel. 2002. *The Myth of Ownership: Taxes and Justice*. Oxford: Oxford University Press.

Nagel, Thomas. 1975. 'Rawls on Justice', in Norman Daniels, ed., *Reading Rawls: Critical Studies on Rawls' 'A Theory of Justice'*, 1–16. New York: Basic Books.

Nagel, Thomas. 2005. 'The Problem of Global Justice', *Philosophy & Public Affairs*, vol. 33, no. 2, 113–147.

Narayan, Uma. 1998. 'Essence of Culture and a Sense of History: A Feminist Critique of Cultural Essentialism', *Hypatia*, vol. 13, no. 1, 86–103.

Näsström, Sofia. 2011. 'The Challenge of the All-Affected Principle', *Political Studies* vol. 59, no. 1, 116–134.

Nine, Cara. 2008. 'A Lockean Theory of Territory', *Political Studies*, vol. 56, no. 1, 148–165.

Nine, Cara. 2010. 'Ecological Refugees, States Borders, and the Lockean Proviso', *Journal of Applied Philosophy*, vol. 27, no. 4, 359–375.

Nine, Cara. 2012. *Global Justice and Territory*. Oxford: Oxford University Press.

Norman, Wayne. 1998. 'The Ethics of Secession as the Regulation of Secessionist Politics', in Margaret Moore, ed., *National Self-Determination and Secession*, 34–61. Oxford: Oxford University Press.

Norman, Wayne. 2006. *Negotiating Nationalism*. Oxford: Oxford University Press.

Nozick, Robert. 1974. *Anarchy, State, and Utopia*. New York: Basic Books.

O'Leary, Brendan. 1999. 'The Nature of the British–Irish Agreement', *New Left Review*, no. 233 (January–February), 66–96.

O'Leary, Brendan. 2005. 'Debating Consociational Politics: Normative and Explanatory Arguments', in Sid Noel ed., *From Power Sharing to Democracy: Post-Conflict Institutions in Ethnically Divided Societies*, 3–43. Montreal and Kingston: McGill-Queen's University Press.

O'Leary, Brendan, Bernard Grofman, and Jørgen Elklit. 2005. 'Divisor Methods for Sequential Portfolio Allocation in Multi-Party Executive Bodies: Evidence from Northern Ireland and Denmark', *American Journal of Political Science*, vol. 49, no. 1, 198–211.

Papastergiardis, Nikos. 2000. *The Turbulence of Migration: Globalization, Deterritorialization and Hybridity*. Cambridge, UK: Polity.

Parekh, Bhikhu. 2002. *Rethinking Multiculturalism: Cultural Diversity and Political Theory*. Cambridge, MA: Harvard University Press.

Parfit, Derek. 1984. *Reasons and Persons*. Oxford: Clarendon Press.

Paskal, Cleo. 2010. *Global Warring: How Environmental, Economic and Political Crises Will Redraw the World Map*. New York and London: Palgrave Macmillan.

Patten, Alan. 2011. 'Rethinking Culture: The Social Lineage Account', *American Political Science Review*, vol. 105, no. 4, 735–749.

Patten, Alan. 2014. *Equal Recognition: The Moral Foundations of Minority Rights*. Princeton: Princeton University Press.

Pellegrino, Gianfranco. 2014. 'Climate Refugees: A Case for Protection', in Marcello Di Paola and Gianfranco Pellegrino, eds, *Canned Heat: Ethics and Politics of Global Climate Change*, 193–209. London: Routledge.

Perez, Nahshon. 2011. 'On Compensation and Return: Can the "Continuing Injustice Argument" for Compensating for Historical Injustices Justify Compensation for Such Injustices or the Return of Property?', *Journal of Applied Philosophy*, vol. 28, no. 2, 151–168.

Pettit, Philip. 1997. *Republicanism: A Theory of Freedom and Government*. Oxford: Oxford University Press.

Pettit, Philip. 2007. 'Responsibility Incorporated', *Ethics*, vol. 117, no. 2, 171–201.

Pevnick, Ryan. 2011. *Immigration and the Constraints of Justice: Between Open Borders and Absolute Sovereignty*. Cambridge: Cambridge University Press.

Philpott, Daniel. 2014. 'Sovereignty', *Stanford Encyclopedia of Philosophy* online: http://plato.stanford.edu/entries/sovereignty/.

Pogge, Thomas. 2002. *World Poverty and Human Rights*. Cambridge, UK: Polity.

Pogge, Thomas. 2008. 'Eradicating Systemic Poverty: Brief for a Global Resources Dividend', in Thom Brooks, ed., *The Global Justice Reader*, 439–453. Oxford: Blackwell.

Putnam, Robert D. 2007. 'E Pluribus Unum: Diversity and Community in the Twenty-First Century: The 2006 Johan Skytte Prize Lecture', *Scandinavian Political Studies*, vol. 30, no. 2, 137–174.

Rawls, John. 1971. *A Theory of Justice*. Cambridge, MA: Harvard University Press.

Rawls, John. 1999. *The Law of Peoples*. Cambridge, MA: Harvard University Press.

Raz, Joseph. 1984. 'Rights-Based Moralities', in Jeremy Waldron, ed., *Theories of Rights*, 182–200. Oxford: Oxford University Press.

Raz, Joseph. 1986. *The Morality of Freedom*. Oxford: Oxford University Press.

Raz, Joseph. 1988. 'Autonomy, Toleration, and the Harm Principle', in Susan Mendus, ed., *Justifying Toleration: Conceptual and Historical Perspectives*, 155–175. Cambridge: Cambridge University Press.

RCAP. 1996. *Report of the Royal Commission on Aboriginal People*, vol. 1, *Looking Forward, Looking Back*. Ottawa, ON: Minister of Supply and Services.

Reb, Jochen, and Terry Connolly. 2007. 'Possession, Feelings of Ownership and the Endowment Effect', *Judgment and Decision Making*, vol. 2, no. 2, 107–114.

Reinikainen, Jouni. 'The Expiration of the Right to Territorial Restitution', unpublished manuscript.

Rickless, Samuel C. 2011. 'The Moral Status of Enabling Harm', *Pacific Philosophical Quarterly*, vol. 92, no. 1, 66–86.

Ridge, Michael. 2003. 'Giving the Dead Their Due', *Ethics*, vol. 114, no. 1, 38–59.

Ripstein, Arthur. 2009. *Force and Freedom: Kant's Legal and Political Philosophy*. Cambridge, MA: Harvard University Press.

Risse, Mathias. 2005. 'How Does the Global Order Harm the Poor?', *Philosophy & Public Affairs*, vol. 33, no. 4, 349–376.

Risse, Mathias. 2008. 'On the Morality of Immigration', *Ethics & International Affairs*, vol. 22, no. 1, 25–33.

Risse, Mathias. 2009a. 'The Right to Relocation: Disappearing Island Nations and Common Ownership of the Earth', *Ethics & International Affairs*, vol. 23, no. 3, 281–300.

Risse, Mathias. 2009b. 'Common Ownership of the Earth as a Non-Parochial Standpoint: A Contingent Derivation of Human Rights', *European Journal of Philosophy*, vol. 17, no. 2, 277–304.

Risse, Mathias. 2012. *On Global Justice*. Princeton: Princeton University Press.

Royal Commission on Aboriginal Peoples (RCAP). 1994. *The High Arctic Relocation: A Report on the 1953–55 Relocation*. Ottawa: Supply and Services.

Rodin, David. 2002. *War and Self-Defense*. Oxford: Clarendon Press.

Rose, George A. 2007. *Cod: The Ecological History of the North Atlantic Fishery*. St John's, NL: Breakwater.

Rose, Richard. 1971. *Governing without Consensus: An Irish Perspective*. London: Faber.

Sangiovanni, Andrea. 2007. 'Global Justice, Reciprocity, and the State', *Philosophy & Public Affairs*, vol. 35, no. 1, 3–39.

Scanlon, Thomas. 2011. 'The Significance of Choice', in Sterling M. McMurrin, ed., *The Tanner Lectures on Human Values*, vol. 8, 149–216. Cambridge: Cambridge University Press.

Scheffler, Samuel. 2001. *Boundaries and Allegiances: Problems of Justice and Responsibility in Liberal Thought*. Oxford: Oxford University Press.

Scheffler, Samuel. 2010. *Equality and Tradition: Questions of Value in Moral and Political Theory*. Oxford: Oxford University Press.

Schmidtz, David. 1990. 'Justifying the State', *Ethics*, vol. 101, no. 1, 89–102.

Schmidtz, David. 1994. 'The Institution of Property', *Social Philosophy and Policy*, vol. 11, no. 2, 42–62.

Scott, James C. 1990. *Domination and the Arts of Resistance: Hidden Transcripts*. New Haven: Yale University Press.

Scott, James C. 1998. *Seeing Like a State: How Certain Schemes to Improve the Human Condition Have Failed*. New Haven: Yale University Press.

Searle, John. 1998. 'Social Ontology and the Philosophy of Society', *Analyse & Kritik*, vol. 20, no. 2, 143–158.

Seglow, Jonathan. 2013. *Defending Associative Duties*. New York: Routledge.

Shachar, Ayelet. 2009. *The Birthright Lottery: Citizenship and Global Inequality*. Cambridge, MA: Harvard University Press.

Sher, George. 1981. 'Ancient Wrongs and Modern Rights', *Philosophy & Public Affairs*, vol. 10, no. 1, 3–17.

Shue, Henry. 1996. *Basic Rights: Subsistence, Affluence, and U.S. Foreign Policy*, 2nd edition. Princeton: Princeton University Press.

Sidgwick, Henry. 2005. *The Elements of Politics*, 3rd edition. London: Elibron Classics.

Simmons, A. John. 2001. *Justification and Legitimacy: Essays on Rights and Obligations*. Cambridge: Cambridge University Press.

Simmons, A. John. 1992. *The Lockean Theory of Rights*. Princeton: Princeton University Press.

Simmons, A. John. 1995. 'Historical Rights and Fair Shares', *Law and Philosophy*, vol. 14, no. 2, 149–184.

Simmons, A. John. 2003. 'On the Territorial Rights of States', in Ernest Sosa and Enrique
    Villanueva, eds, *Social, Political and Legal Philosophy: Philosophical Issues*, vol. 11,
    300–326. Malden, MA, and Oxford: Blackwell.
Singer, Peter. 1972. 'Famine, Affluence, and Morality', *Philosophy & Public Affairs*, vol. 1,
    no. 3, 229–243.
Smith, Andrew. 2008. 'Toryism, Classical Liberalism, and Capitalism: The Politics of Taxation
    and the Struggle for Canadian Confederation', *Canadian Historical Review*, vol. 89, no. 1,
    1–25.
Southwood, Nicholas. 2011. 'Democracy as a Modally Demanding Value', paper given at the
    International Conference on Democracy, Empires, and Geopolitics, Taipei, Taiwan,
    10–12 December 2011.
Sparrow, Robert. 2000. 'History and Collective Responsibility', *Australasian Journal of
    Philosophy*, vol. 78, no. 3, 346–359.
Spinner-Halev, Jeff. 2007. 'From Historical to Enduring Injustice', *Political Theory*, vol. 35,
    no. 5, 574–597.
Spinner-Halev, Jeff. 2012. *Enduring Injustice*. Cambridge: Cambridge University Press.
Steiner, Hillel. 1992. 'Libertarianism and the Transnational Migration of People', in Brian
    Barry and Robert Goodin, eds, *Free Movement: Ethical Issues in the Transnational
    Migration of Peoples and of Money*, 87–94. University Park: Penn State Press.
Steiner, Hillel. 1996. 'Territorial Justice', in Simon Caney, David George, and Peter Jones, eds,
    National Rights, International Obligations, 139–168. Boulder, CO: Westview.
Steiner, Hillel. 2008. 'May Lockean Doghnuts Have Holes? The Geometry of Territorial
    Jurisdiction: A Response to Nine', *Political Studies*, vol. 56, no. 4, 949–956.
Steiner, Hillel. 2011a. 'Sharing Mother Nature's Gifts: A Reply to Quong and Miller', *Journal of
    Political Philosophy*, vol. 19, no. 1, 110–123.
Steiner, Hillel. 2011b. 'The Global Fund: A Reply to Casal', *Journal of Moral Philosophy*, vol. 8,
    no. 3, 328–334.
Stilz, Anna. 2009a. 'Why Do States Have Territorial Rights?' *International Theory*, vol. 1,
    no. 2, 185–213.
Stilz, Anna. 2009b. 'The Exclusion Project', paper given at the American Political Science
    Association meeting, Toronto, Ontario, 2–5 September 2009.
Stilz, Anna. 2011a. 'Nations, States, and Territory', *Ethics*, vol. 121, no. 3, 572–601.
Stilz, Anna. 2011b. 'Collective Responsibility and the State', *Journal of Political Philosophy*,
    vol. 19, no. 2, 190–208.
Sumner, L. W. 1987. *The Moral Foundation of Rights*. Oxford: Clarendon Press.
Tamir, Yael. 1993. *Liberal Nationalism*. Princeton: Princeton University Press.
Tan, Kok-Chor. 2004. *Justice without Borders: Cosmopolitanism, Nationalism and Patriotism*.
    Cambridge: Cambridge University Press.
Taylor, Charles. 1985. 'What's Wrong with Negative Liberty', in *Philosophical Papers*,
    vol. 2, *Philosophy and the Human Sciences*, 211–229. Cambridge: Cambridge University
    Press.
Thaler, R. H. 1980. 'Toward a Positive Theory of Consumer Choice', *Journal of Economic
    Behavior & Organization*, vol. 1, no. 1, 39–60.
Thompson, Janna. 2002. *Taking Responsibility for the Past: Reparations and Historical Injustice*.
    Cambridge, UK: Polity.
Tomlinson, John. 1999. *Globalization and Culture*. Chicago: University of Chicago Press.
Tuck, Richard. 1999. *The Rights of War and Peace: Political Thought and the International Order
    from Grotius to Kant*. Oxford: Oxford University Press.
Tully, James. 1980. *A Discourse on Property: John Locke and His Adversaries*.
    Cambridge: Cambridge University Press.
Raimo Tuomela. 2005. 'We-Intentions Revisited', *Philosophical Studies*, vol. 125, no. 3,
    327–269.
Tuomela, Raimo, and Kaarlo Miller. 1988. 'We-Intentions', *Philosophical Studies*, vol. 53,
    no. 3, 367–389.
van der Vossen, Bas. 2014. 'Locke on Territorial Rights', *Political Studies* [early view, 8 January].

van Middlelaar, Luuk. 2013. *The Passage to Europe: How a Continent Became a Union*. New Haven: Yale University Press. (Originally published in Dutch in 2009.)

Waldron, Jeremy, ed. 1984. *Theories of Rights*. Oxford: Clarendon Press.

Waldron, Jeremy. 1988. *The Right to Private Property*. Oxford: Clarendon Press.

Waldron, Jeremy. 1989. 'Rights in Conflict', *Ethics*, vol. 99, no. 3, 503–519.

Waldron, Jeremy. 1992. 'Superseding Historic Injustice', *Ethics*, vol. 103, no. 1, 4–28.

Waldron, Jeremy. 1993. 'Special Ties and Natural Duties', *Philosophy & Public Affairs*, vol. 22, no. 1, 3–30.

Waldron, Jeremy. 1995. 'Moments of Carelessness and Massive Loss', in David Owen, ed., *Philosophical Foundations of Tort Law*, 387–407. Oxford: Oxford University Press.

Waldron, Jeremy. 2002. 'Redressing Historic Injustice', *University of Toronto Law Journal*, vol. 52, no. 1, 135–160.

Waldron, Jeremy. 2004. 'Settlement, Return, and the Supersession Thesis', *Theoretical Inquiries in Law*, vol. 5, no. 2, 237–268.

Waldron, Jeremy. 2009. 'Proximity as the Basis of Political Community', paper presented at the Workshop on Theories of Territory, King's College, London, 21 February 2009.

Walzer, Michael. 1977. *Just and Unjust Wars: A Moral Argument with Historical Illustrations*. New York: Basic Books.

Walzer, Michael. 1980. 'The Moral Standing of States: A Response to Four Critics', *Philosophy & Public Affairs*, vol. 9, no. 3, 210–229.

Walzer, Michael. 1983. *Spheres of Justice: A Defense of Pluralism and Equality*. New York: Basic Books.

Wantchekon, Leonard. 2002. 'Why Do Resource Dependent Countries Have Authoritarian Governments?', *Journal of African Finance and Economic Development*, vol. 5, no. 2, 57–77.

Watner, Carl. 2010. 'The Territorial Assumption: Rationale for Conquest', *Journal of Libertarian Studies*, vol. 22, 247–260.

Wellman, Carl. 1985. *A Theory of Rights: Persons under Laws, Institutions, and Morals*. Totowa, NJ: Rowman and Allanheld.

Wellman, Christopher Heath. 2005. *A Theory of Secession: The Case for Political Self-Determination*. Cambridge: Cambridge University Press.

Wellman, Christopher Heath. 2008. 'Immigration and Freedom of Association', *Ethics*, vol. 119, no. 1, 109–141.

Wellman, Christopher Heath, and Phillip Cole. 2011. *Debating the Ethics of Immigration: Is There a Right to Exclude?* Oxford: Oxford University Press.

Wenar, Leif. 2008. 'Property Rights and the Resource Curse', *Philosophy & Public Affairs*, vol. 36, no. 1, 2–32.

Wilson, Paul. 1982. *Black Death, White Hands*. Sydney: George Allen and Unwin.

Winthrop, Robert. 1869. *The Life and Letters of John Winthrop, Governor of the Massachusetts-Bay Company at their Emigration to New England, 1630*. Boston: Little, Brown.

Yong, Caleb. 2014. *Justice, Legitimacy and Movement across Borders*. DPhil diss., Oxford University.

Yong, Caleb. 2014. 'Selecting Immigrants', unpublished manuscript.

Young, Iris Marion. 1990. *Justice and the Politics of Difference*. Princeton: Princeton University Press.

Young, Iris Marion. 2005. 'Self-Determination as Non-Domination: Ideas Applied to Israel/Palestine', *Ethnicities*, vol. 5, no. 2, 139–159.

Young, Iris Marion. 2007. *Global Challenges: War, Self Determination and Responsibility for Justice*. Cambridge, UK: Polity.

Ypi, Lea. 2008. 'Sovereignty, Cosmopolitanism and the Ethics of European Foreign Policy', *European Journal of Political Theory*, vol. 7, no. 3, 349–364.

Ypi, Lea. 2012. 'A Permissive Theory of Territorial Rights', *European Journal of Philosophy*, vol. 22, no. 2, 288–312.

Ypi, Lea. 2013. 'Territorial Rights and Exclusion', *Philosophy Compass*, vol. 8, no. 3, 241–253.

Ypi, Lea. 2013. 'What's Wrong with Colonialism', *Philosophy & Public Affairs*, vol. 41, no. 2, 138–191.

Newspapers, Magazines, Internet Resources

Alpert, Lukas I. 2014. '5 Reasons Putin Gives for Annexing Crimea', *Wall Street Journal*, 18 March. http://blogs.wsj.com/five-things/2014/03/18/5-reasons-vladimir-putin-gave-for-annexing-crimea/.

BBC News. 2001. 'Iraqi Kurds' Story of Expulsion', 3 November. http://news.bbc.co.uk/2/hi/middle_east/1614239.stm.

BBC News. 'Is Crimea's Referendum Legal?', 13 March 2014. http://www.bbc.co.uk/news/world-europe-26546133.

BBC News. 2014. 'Ukraine: Putin Signs Crimean Annexation', 21 March. www.bbc.co.uk/news/world-europe-26686949.

'Broken homes and Broken Hearts', https://www.youtube.com/watch?v=_gSrNH5_nk0.

CBC News. 2010. 'Halifax Apologizes for Razing Africville', 24 February. http://www.cbc.ca/news/canada/nova-scotia/halifax-apologizes-for-razing-africville-1.894944.

Demopoulos vs. Turkey. 2010. (Eur. Ct. H. R. 365, 1 March 2010). Full document accessed at http://www.asil.org/ilib100318.cfm.

Dershowitz, Alan M. 2002. 'The Case for Torture Warrants'. http://www.alandershowitz.com/publications/docs/torturewarrants.html.

Dorling, Danny. 2014. 'Overseas Property Buyers Are Not the Problem: Landlord Subsidies Are', *The Guardian*, 10 February.

The Economist. 2000. 'China's Uighurs: A Train of Concern', 12 February.

The Economist. 2009. 'The Scramble for the Seabed', 14 May.

The Economist. 2013. 'History Wars in North-East Asia', 18 August.

The Economist. 2013. 'China and Japan: Relations on the Rocks', 25 August.

Human Rights Watch. 1993. *Genocide in Iraq: The Anfal Campaign against the Kurds*. New York: Middle East Watch Report, July. http://www.hrw.org/reports/1993/iraqanfal/

Kelly, Michael B. 2014. 'Ukraine Torn between East and West', *Business Insider*, 3 March. http://www.businessinsider.com/heres-one-economic-reason-russias-invasion-of-crimea-pulls-in-europe-2014-3.

Lee, Joyman. 2011. 'Senkaku/Diaoyu: Islands of Conflict', *History Today*, vol. 61, no. 5. http://www.historytoday.com/joyman-lee/senkakudiaoyu-islands-conflict.

Oberman, Kieran. 2014. 'The Crimean Crisis: Justified Secession, Russian Aggression or Both?', *Just World Institute*, 5 March. http://blogs.sps.ed.ac.uk/jwi/2014/03/05/the-crimean-crisis-justified-secession-russian-aggression-or-both.

Raghavan, Sudarsan. 2013. 'In Volatile Congo, a New U.N. Force with Teeth', *Genocide Watch*, 3 November. http://www.genocidewatch.org/drofcongo.html.

Tran, Mark. 2014. 'Ukraine: Referendum on "Self-Rule" in Eastern Regions Begins', *The Guardian*, 11 May. http://www.theguardian.com/world/2014/may/11/ukraine-referendum-for-self-rule-in-eastern-regions-begins-live-updates.

United Nations High Commissioner for Refugees (UNHCR). 1951. *Convention and Protocol Relating to the Status of Refugees*. http://www.unhcr.org/3b66c2aa10.html.

United States Agency for International Development (USAID). 2004. 'Iraq's Legacy of Terror: Mass Graves'. http://www.globalsecurity.org/intell/library/reports/2004/040317_iraq_mass_graves.pdf.

INDEX

CPSIA information can be obtained
at www.ICGtesting.com
Printed in the USA
BVHW032303120219
540116BV00002B/65/P

9 780190 845797